French Catholic Missionaries and the Politics of Imperialism in Vietnam, 1857-1914

A DOCUMENTARY SURVEY

Patrick J.N. Tuck

LIVERPOOL UNIVERSITY PRESS

FOR

MY PARENTS

Liverpool Historical Studies, no. 1
General Editor: P.E.H. Hair

Published in Great Britain, 1987,
by the Liverpool University Press,
Senate House, P.O. Box 147, Liverpool L69 3BX,
on behalf of the Department of History, University of Liverpool.

British Library Cataloguing in Publication Data are available.

ISBN 0 85323 136 2

CONTENTS

ABBREVIATIONS

A.P.F.	Annales de la Propagation de la Foi
A.S.M.E.	Archives de la Société des Missions Etrangères
A.N.S.O.M	Archives Nationales (Section Outre-Mer)
A.O.M	(Dépôt des) Archives d'Outre-Mer
B.S.O.A.S	Bulletin of the School of Oriental Studies
B.S.E.I.	Bulletin de la Société des Etudes Indochinoises
B.A.V.H.	Bulletin des Amis du Vieux Hué
M.R.E	Ministère des Relations Extérieures (Quai d'Orsay)
S.H.L.	Service Historique de la Marine
S.M.E.	Société des Missions Etrangères

PREFACE

This book of documents is not intended to survey the whole field of missionary activity in Vietnam for the period which it covers. It deals only with relations between French colonial government and the French Société des Missions Etrangères - the sole French missionary order operating in the region. Its general object is to acquaint undergraduate historians with some of the problems of collating and interpreting historical evidence through study of related samples of primary documentation. It is designed to present a selection of evidence rather than to draw conclusions. A brief commentary before each section of the documentation establishes major changes in the historical situation, and a chapter of biographical notes at the end details the careers of significant individuals. The background of particular documents can be established from secondary works and other collections of texts cited in the bibliographies attached to each section. For the English-speaking student the documents are presented in translation in order to reduce the burden of reading material in French. But some knowledge of French is plainly essential if this collection is to be related effectively to the body of relevant research and documentation already in print.

The source limitations of this collection need to be noted for they have confined its scope. The compilation reflects dealings between and within higher French administration and the French missionary hierarchy. It contains few documents generated by French regional administration in Vietnam, and none at all from the archives of individual vicariates of the Société des Missions Etrangères. Nor does it contain much material derived from Spanish missionary or Vietnamese administrative sources. This is regrettable since conditions varied considerably between vicariates, and such differences will only be faintly perceptible from this collection. The local records of the Apostolic vicariates may no longer even exist; and the archives of French and Vietnamese provincial administrations, kept in the National Archives of Vietnam, were not available to me. While regrettable, these have not been wholly disabling restrictions since the materials presented from Government-General, Colonial Ministry and Paris missionary records cover most aspects of relations between government and the mission relevant to the main themes of this book. It has been possible, moreover, to compensate a little in other ways for the unavailability of provincial, Vietnamese, and Spanish missionary records. The major French government sources at Aix-en-Provence - the archives of the Colonial Undersecretariat (later Ministry), and of the central administration of

Indochina - contain a random scattering of provincial materials. These are insufficient for a thorough synthesis, but on some issues they offer enough for constructive speculation. Although records relating to the Spanish Dominican vicariates of Central and East Tonkin - now kept in Manila - were not consulted, letters from their Spanish Dominican bishops published in the Annales de la Propagation de la Foi were used. The greatest limitation has been the paucity of documentation available to me from Vietnamese court and administrative sources. I have however, been able to provide samples, if not a regular flow, of Vietnamese petitions and edicts translated, probably rather loosely, by missionaries and colonial officials. These have been taken either from published contemporary works or from enclosures in French official correspondance. The terminology of the French translations of these Vietnamese documents often betrays the partisan perspectives of the translators, and I have tried to convey these nuances of bias in the English. But plainly, English translations of possibly inaccurate and partisan French translations have to be treated with great caution.

Much of the material presented here has not been published before, especially for the latter part of the period. But some material from government and mission sources relating to the 1860s and 1870s has appeared in print in three important collections which deal with missionary questions: Georges Taboulet's formidable but highly partisan La Geste Française en Indochine (Paris, 2 vols. 1955); E. Vo Duc Hanh's detailed but more balanced La Place du Catholicisme dans les relations entre la France et le Viet-Nam de 1851 à 1870, (3 vols. Leyden 1969); and N-D. Lê's exuberant but disorganised Les Missions-Etrangères et la pénétration française au Vietnam (Paris, 1975). Each of these works has important limitations. While Taboulet appears to have had access not only to the central archives of the Société des Missions Etrangères but also to the archives of the Indochina vicariates, missionary activities form only a subsidiary theme of his second volume (1858-1914) in which little missionary material is cited. Vo Duc Hanh's work suffers from a contrasting deficiency. Though it is an exceptionally thorough and detailed exposure of missionary relations with the French and Vietnamese authorities during a brief but crucial period (1851-1870), it contains no documentation from S.M.E. records posterior to 1859. Lê's book, though covering the same subject across a longer chronological period (c.1850-c.1882), suffers from a complete absence of primary documentation from missionary sources.

The present work supplies some of the shortcomings, whatever its other limitations. For I have had access to enough missionary material to make possible the pursuit of the major themes of this collection through to 1914.

ACKNOWLEDGEMENTS

I wish to record my thanks to the late R.P. Jean Vérinaud, Archivist of the Missions-Etrangères de Paris, not only for his kind permission to publish documents from the mission's records, but also for giving me so many profitable and enjoyable hours of his company discussing the history of the mission in Vietnam. He was a man of wry humour and surreptitious generosity, and his death is a great loss. I shall miss him grievously.

I should also like to express my gratitude to the directors and staff of the many French official archives visited in the course of preparing the present book. I thank them for giving me access to the materials in their care and for their courteous and unstinting help in locating particular items. I received particular help from Mlle M.A. Ménier and Mme Pouliquen of the Archives Nationales (Section Outre-Mer), and from M.J. Maurel of the Dépôt des Archives d'Outre-Mer at Aix-en-Provence, and I am glad to acknowledge my debt to them. My thanks are also due to the director and staff of the Archives of the Quai d'Orsay, and of the Service Historique de la Marine for similar assistance. I am grateful too, to Nguyen Ngoc Tri, curator of the Vietnamese section of the British Museum, and to Professor Hoang Xuan Han for help with illustrative material. I would also like to express my gratitude to the British Academy and to the Department of History, University of Liverpool, for the generous grants which have made it possible for this book to be published; and to Dr Michael de Cossart for his kindness in devoting time and expert attention to the many technical and editorial problems arising from its production. Finally, I take pleasure in expressing my particular thanks to Professor Nguyen The Anh of the C.N.R.S., Paris for reading and criticising the preliminary version of this book. Needless to say, responsibility for all its imperfections is mine alone.

NOTE ON TOPONYMS

'Cochinchina'

Variations in French use of the term 'Cochinchina' are likely to cause confusion. Before the late 1860s Europeans conventionally referred to all Vietnam south of Tonkin as 'Cochinchina'. The Vietnamese term 'Annam', which came to be much employed by French political authorities for the central provinces of Vietnam, was not used at all by the mission in naming its vicariates for jurisdictional purposes during the nineteenth century.

The vicariates of 'Cochinchina' and 'Tonkin' were both founded in 1659. 'Cochinchina' was divided in 1844 and further subdivided in 1850 to form three vicariates in all. By the start of the period covered in this book, the vicariate of 'North' Cochinchina (cr. 1850) consisted of all central Annam, including Hue, from the lower half of Quang Binh down to the northern frontier of Quang Nam. From 1850 the vicariate of 'East' Cochinchina consisted of southern Annam (below Hue) from Quang Nam down to the northern borders of Baria and Bien Hoa. From Baria and Bien Hoa southwards the vicariate of 'West' Cochinchina (cr.1844) consisted of what the French navy tended to refer to as 'la basse Cochinchine', comprising most of the provinces of what became the French colony of Cochinchina in the 1860s. When the vicariate of Cambodia was formed in 1850, however, the Vietnamese-controlled provinces of Hatien, Rach Gia and Bac Lieu were included in its canonical jurisdiction. These were territories of mainly Khmer settlement, and were conventionally included in the French definition of 'basse Cochinchine'.

'Tonkin'

As for the term 'Tonkin', the jurisdictional designations employed by the missions were equally haphazard. Since 1678, when East Tonkin was first transferred from the French Société des Missions Etrangères (S.M.E.) to the Spanish Dominican mission, the ecclesiastical frontier between 'East' and 'West' Tonkin was established along the course of the Red River up to Son Tay and then along the Clear River as far as Kwangsi. When new vicariates of 'South' and 'Central' Tonkin were hived off from 'East' and 'West' Tonkin in 1846 and 1848 respectively, their positions approximated only vaguely to the points of the compass and to political geography. The vicariate of 'South' Tonkin, created from the S.M.E. vicariate of West Tonkin, was not situated within the political frontiers of Tonkin at all: it was located wholly within what the Vietnamese, and later the French, referred to as 'Annam', and ran southwards from Thanh Hoa to the middle of Quang Binh. The Spanish Dominican vicariate of 'Central' Tonkin, created from the Spanish vicariate of East Tonkin in 1848, was not situated in the interior of Tonkin, as its name seems to imply: it was a small coastal enclave in the Red river delta. Finally, when the S.M.E. vicariate of 'Maritime' Tonkin was created from the upper portion of the vicariate of South Tonkin in 1901, it too consisted almost wholly of two provinces of northern Annam - Thanh Hoa and Nghe An. However the bishop's seat at Phat Diem lay in an enclave across the border, just inside Tonkin.

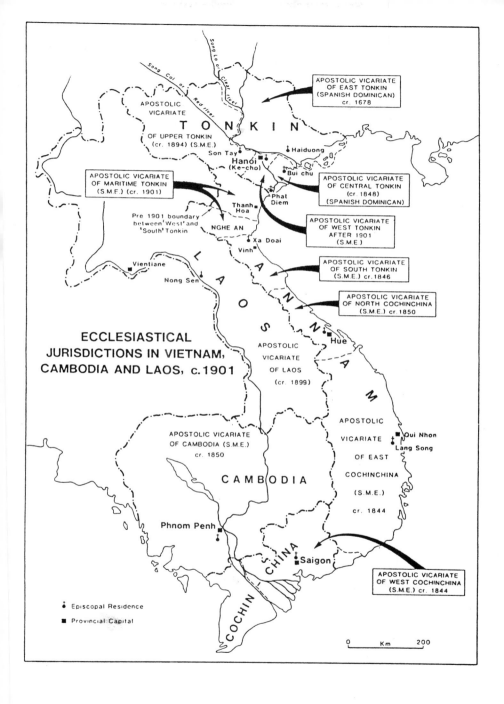

ECCLESIASTICAL JURISDICTIONS IN VIETNAM, CAMBODIA AND LAOS, c.1901

Song Lo or Clear River

Song Col or Red River

APOSTOLIC VICARIATE OF EAST TONKIN (SPANISH DOMINICAN) cr. 1678

APOSTOLIC VICARIATE

T O N K I N

OF UPPER TONKIN (cr. 1894) (S.M.E.)

Son Tay

Haiduong

Hanoi (Ke-cho)

Bui chu

APOSTOLIC VICARIATE OF MARITIME TONKIN (S.M.E.) (cr. 1901)

APOSTOLIC VICARIATE OF CENTRAL TONKIN (cr. 1848) (SPANISH DOMINICAN)

Phat Diem

Thanh Hoa

Pre 1901 boundary between 'West' and 'South' Tonkin

NGHE AN

APOSTOLIC VICARIATE OF WEST TONKIN AFTER 1901 (S.M.E.)

Xa Doai

Vinh

APOSTOLIC VICARIATE OF SOUTH TONKIN (S.M.E.) cr.1846

Vientiane

L A O S

Nong Sen

A N N A M

APOSTOLIC VICARIATE OF NORTH COCHINCHINA (S.M.E.) cr.1850

Hue

ECCLESIASTICAL JURISDICTIONS IN VIETNAM, CAMBODIA AND LAOS, c.1901

APOSTOLIC VICARIATE OF LAOS (cr. 1899)

APOSTOLIC VICARIATE OF CAMBODIA (S.M.E.) cr. 1850

C A M B O D I A

APOSTOLIC VICARIATE OF EAST COCHINCHINA (S.M.E.) cr. 1844

Qui Nhon

Lang Song

Phnom Penh

COCHIN CHINA

Saigon

APOSTOLIC VICARIATE OF WEST COCHINCHINA (S.M.E.) cr. 1844

COCHIN

◆ Episcopal Residence

■ Provincial Capital

0   Km   200

9

Vietnamese tactics of conciliation: Emperor Tu Duc invites Christians to live peaceably under his jurisdiction, July 1864. **(Doc. 16)**

(3) Chasseloup-Laubat's arguments against Captain Aubaret's draft treaty of retrocession, 4 November 1864. **(Doc. 17)**

(4) Popular reactions in Annam to the French conquest of western Cochinchina in June 1867. Impressions of Bishop Sohier, 28 December 1867. **(Doc. 18)**

(5) Popular repercussions in Tonkin: report of Bishop Theurel, 18 February 1868. **(Doc. 19)**

(6) Further Franco-Vietnamese treaty negotiations: the religious question. Prefect Ba Tuong's report on the the draft clause concerning religious toleration, 29 January 1868. **(Doc. 20)**

(7) French perceptions of the divergence between Tu Duc and the scholar class on tactics for dealing with Christians: Note by Admiral de la Grandière, April 1870. **(Doc. 21)**

II

MISSIONARIES AND GOVERNMENT IN FRENCH COCHINCHINA UNDER THE ADMIRALS, 1859-1879.

A   Missionary adjustment to the new order, 1859 - 1870 (pp. 81-7)

(1) Captain Aubaret, Admiral Bonard's political adviser, suggests leaving missionaries to operate completely independently. c.1862-3. **(Doc. 22)**

(2) French missionary views on the impact of French invasion upon the Cochinchina mission. **(Docs 23-27)**

(3) Frictions between French missionaries and colonial government in Cochinchina, 1860-1868. **(Docs 28-32)**

B   Material support for the mission (pp. 88-97)

(1) Chasseloup-Laubat's decision not to establish a concordatory clergy, 18 November 1864. **(Doc. 33)**

(2) Official funding for missionary work. Report by Admiral-Governor Dupré, 1 February 1873. **(Doc. 34)**

(3) The colonial government's objections to the growth of the French mission's property in Cochinchina. Report by Admiral-Governor Krantz, 8 September 1875. **(Doc. 35)**

(4) The West Cochinchina vicariate's account of its income and resources: Bishop Colombert's report, 23 July 1875. **(Doc. 36)**

(5) Arrangements for regularising the French mission's property rights in Cochinchina, 1875-7. **(Docs 37-39)**

11

12

(3) Extract from the report to the Chamber of Deputies of the commission for the treaty of 15 March 1874. **(Doc. 85)**

(4) Speeches in the Chamber of Deputies' debate on the ratification of the 1874 treaty. **(Doc. 86)**

C   The aftermath of the Garnier affair and the operation of the treaty of 1874. (pp.175-93)

(1) Vietnamese scholars organise attacks on Christian villages in Tonkin and north Annam, 1873-4. **(Docs 87-8)**

(2) A petition from the mandarins to the Emperor Tu Duc deploring the terms of the proposed Franco-Vietnamese treaty, February 1874. **(Doc. 89)**

(3) Petition by the scholars to the Emperor Tu Duc, Feb.- March 1874. **(Doc. 90)**

(4) Resident Rheinart (Hanoi) deplores Christian provocations, 29 March 1874. **(Doc. 91)**

(5) A missionary account of the scholars' methods of mobilisation against Christians, 21 June 1874. **(Doc. 92)**

(6) Resident Rheinart's account of Vietnamese attacks on Christians at Nghe An from 1873-1876. **(Doc. 93)**

(7) Difficulties of the Vietnamese court in arranging indemnities for Christians. **(Doc. 94)**

(8) The Emperor Tu Duc's admonition to Christians, 28 October 1875. **(Doc. 95)**

(9) The Vietnamese court's reluctance to implement parts of clause 9 of the treaty, 30 October 1875 **(Doc. 96)**

(10) Captain Philastre (Hue) warns that excessive indemnity claims by Christians will prolong social reprisals, 7 March 1877. **(Doc. 97)**

(11) Consul Turc (Haiphong) compares behaviour of the French Catholic mission in Tonkin unfavourably with that of the Spanish, 1 April 1876. **(Doc. 98)**

(12) The Emperor Tu Duc's edict against interference by missionaries and bishops in trials involving Christians, 1876. **(Doc. 99)**

(13) Consul Turc (Haiphong) supports episcopal interference in trials involving Christians, 10 November 1877. **(Doc. 100)**

(14) Admiral Duperré deplores episcopal interference in trials of Christians, 1876-1877. **(Doc. 101)**

(15) Admiral Lafont condemns missionary demands for administrative autonomy for Christian villages in Annam-Tonkin, 26 January 1878. **(Doc. 102)**

(16) Consul de Kergaradec complains at an infringement of clause 9, 1 May 1879. **(Doc. 103)**

(17) The captain of the Duchaffaut explains the local social and political effects of the formation of Christian 'corporations' in Khanh Hoa (East Cochinchina), 8 June 1878. **(Doc. 104)**

(18) Bishop Colombert (Saigon) considers that the treaty of 1874 has protected freedom of worship effectively, 26 January 1883. **(Doc. 105)**

IV

THE TONKIN WAR AND THE CAN VUONG RESISTANCE, 1883–1886.

A **The French mission and the war in Tonkin, 1883–1885.** (pp. 194-204)

(1) Commander Rivière shuns missionary help in delta clearance operations, November 1882. **(Doc. 106)**

(2) Commissioner-General Harmand and the Convention of August, 1883. A missionary view of Harmand, and Harmand's views on the prospective utility of the missions in northern Annam. **(Docs 107–8)**

(3) The Patenôtre treaty of 6 June, 1884. Article 13 guarantees freedom of worship. **(Doc. 109)**

(4) Bishop Puginier warns of Ton That Thuyet's preparations for moving the court to Cam Lo, 6 November 1884. **(Doc. 110)**

B **The Can Vuong movement and the postwar massacre of Christians, 1885–6.** (pp. 205-25)

(1) Bishop Puginier warns General de Courcy of the Hue court's preparations for resistance, 7 July 1885. **(Doc. 111)**

(2) Puginier denounces the Regent Nguyen Van Tuong for complicity in organising resistance to French rule. **(Doc. 112)**

(3) Royal decree, issued by Regent Ton That Thuyet, ordering the massacre of Christians. Undated: after July, 1885. **(Doc. 113)**

(4) Massacres in Annam: a missionary's view, September 1885. **(Doc. 114)**

(5) Bishop Colombert opposes the despatch of arms to Christians at Qui Nhon, 1886. **(Doc. 115)**

(6) Bishop Puginier's analysis of an insurrectional proclamation by Ton That Thuyet, September 1886. **(Doc. 116)**

(7) Resident-General Paul Bert's attitude to the mission and to recent massacres, 1886. **(Docs 117–8)**

(8) Missionary attitudes to French protectoral policy in Tonkin and

Annam. **(Doc. 119)**

(9) Bishop Puginier on the scholar elite. **(Doc. 120)**

(10) A French official complaint at Christian resistence to Vietnamese authority in Annam, 1886. **(Doc. 121)**

(11) Resident-General Paul Bert's circular of advice to Residents on the treatment of Christian grievances, 1886. **(Doc. 122)**

V

THE FRENCH MISSION AND THE CONSOLIDATION OF THE FRENCH IMPERIAL FRONTIER IN SOUTH-EAST ASIA, 1881-1904.

A **French frontier problems in the Mekong valley, 1881-1885.** (pp. 226-235)

(1) Bishop Vey of Siam complains that the French consul is undermining the social authority of local missionaries. **(Doc. 123)**

(2) The French mission in Siam a political embarassment to the French consulate, 1882. **(Doc. 124)**

(3) Consul Harmand prevaricates over issuing passports for missionary work in Siamese Laos, 1883. **(Doc. 125)**

(4) Opinion of Bishop Bourdon of Upper Burma on the appointment of a French consul. **(Doc. 126)**

(5) Jules Ferry's general policy for Upper Burma fom 1883. **(Docs 127-8)**

(6) Bishop Bourdon hopes for a British annexation of Upper Burma. **(Doc. 129)**

(7) Bishop Bourdon's opinion of the French consulate, and Consul Haas' view of the Bishop's role. 1885. **(Docs 130-1)**

(8) Bishop Simon (Mandalay) describes the transformation of the mission's situation in Upper Burma after British annexation, 1889. **(Doc. 132)**

B **The French mission and Siam, 1886-1904.** (pp. 236-247)

(1) Bishop Puginier encourages French pursuit of Vietnam's claims to Siamese territories on the Upper Mekong. **(Doc. 133)**

(2) The Mayrena affair, 1888-90. **(Docs 134-138)**

(3) Bishop Vey (Bangkok) and the Siam crisis of 1893. **(Docs 139-40)**

(4) The Quai d'Orsay refuses Bishop Vey's request to obtain more treaty privileges from Siam for the mission, 1893. **(Docs 141-2)**

VI

THE MISSION UNDER POLITICAL ATTACK IN FRENCH INDOCHINA, 1891-1914.

A **The growth of anticlericalism in French Indochina, 1891-1899.** (pp. 248-54)

(1) Bishop Colombert (West Cochinchina) finds Governor-General de Lanessan unexpectedly helpful towards the mission, January 1893. **(Doc. 143)**

(2) Lanessan tries to restrain Bishop Gendreau (West Tonkin) from defending the mission in the press against anticlerical polemics, July 1893. **(Doc. 144)**

(3) Bishop Gendreau's reply to Lanessan, July 1893. **(Doc. 145)**

(4) Bishop Depierre (West Cochinchina) appeals to the Cochinchina Justice department for protection from anticlerical attacks in the colony's press, June 1897. **(Doc. 146)**

(5) Bishop Depierre voices his objections personally to the editor of Le Mékong. **(Doc. 147)**

(6) Camille Pâris abuses the mission for its part in the Mayrena affair. **(Doc. 148)**

B **The triumph of Radical republicanism in France and the legislative onslaught on clerical interests.** (pp. 255-63)

(1) Text of the Law on Associations, 1 July 1901. **(Doc. 149)**

(2) The aims of the Law concerning Religious Teaching (1904) in its application to Indochina. **(Doc. 150)**

(3) Speeches on the Leygues amendment to the Law on Secondary School Teaching, March 1904. **(Doc. 151)**

C **Freemasons and the polemic against the missions in Indochina, 1905-1907.** (pp. 264-273)

(1) Camille Pâris renews his attacks, 1905. **(Docs 152-3)**

(2) Father Guerlach's ripostes. **(Docs 154-5)**

(3) Missionaries accused of involvement in slavery, 1907. **(Doc. 156)**

(4) Lanessan accuses the missions of covert opposition to French rule, 1907. **(Doc. 157)**

(5) Masonic petitions for the application of recent anticlerical legislation to Indochina, 1907. **(Docs 158-9)**

D   The debate within the Indochina administration on the application of the laws of 1901, 1904 and 1905 against the missions. (1905-1907) (pp. 274-84)

(1) Comments by senior officials on the legislation of 1901:

   (a) Resident-Superior Fourès of Tonkin opposes the application of the Law of 1 July, 1901 on political and financial grounds, 13 March 1905. **(Doc. 160)**

   (b) Resident-Superior Moulié of Annam considers the law of 1901 to be unworkable in Annam and advises against alienating a pro-French influence, 18 March 1905. **(Doc. 161)**

   (c) Acting Governor-General Broni summarises the views of the majority of senior officials, 19 September 1905. **(Doc. 162)**

(2) Comments by senior officials in 1906-7 on the legislation of 1905.

   (a) Governor-General Beau reports that the law of 1905 is inapplicable to Indochina, 29 January 1906. **(Doc. 163)**

   (b) Acting Resident-Superior Lévecque of Annam recommends reducing the political influence of the missions, but leaving their property rights intact, 31 August 1906. **(Doc. 164)**

   (c) Acting Resident Groleau of Tonkin warns of the danger of inciting Vietnamese Christian reaction by dispossessing the missions, 20 October 1906. **(Doc. 165)**

   (d) Acting Governor-General Broni suggests adapting the law of 1901 to achieve some of the effects of the (inapplicable) Law of Separation of 1905 in Indochina, 12 December 1906. **(Doc. 166)**

   (e) Governor-General Beau recommends the application of clauses 6 and 11 of the Law of 1901 to Indochina. **(Doc. 167)**

(3) Bishop Mossard and the 'Lois spoliatrices', 1906. **(Doc. 168)**

(4) The reason given to the Dislère commission for the Quai d'Orsay's refusal in 1907 to negotiate with Spain as a preliminary to applying the Law of 1901 to Annam-Tonkin. **(Doc. 169)**

E.   **Governor-General Klobukowski and the prewar crisis in Indochina: the mission suspected of sedition, 1908-1910.** (pp. 285-96)

(1) The effects of the Russo-Japanese war on Vietnamese nationalism. Acting Governor-General Bonhoure's report, July 1908. **(Doc. 170)**

(2) The French mission accused of planning a political press campaign, July-August 1908. **(Docs 171-2)**

INTRODUCTION

THE FRENCH STATE AND FRENCH MISSIONARY ENTERPRISE IN ASIA FROM THE SEVENTEENTH TO THE MID NINETEENTH CENTURIES.

Royal chartered companies and French missions in Asia under the Ancien Régime.

From the establishment of French mercantilism in the early seventeenth century until the collapse of the Compagnie perpetuelle des Indes in the middle years of the eighteenth, French missionary interests in Asia received steady - and sometimes energetic - support from the commercial, naval and diplomatic agencies of the French crown. The French monarchy and its ministers, instrumental in designing, funding and promoting the long succession of chartered companies which came to trade from Senegal to the coast of China, shared the aims of Catholic missionary proselytism and showed a consistent commitment to their promotion. In this the French crown was encouraged by the Papacy, which regarded French missionary and commercial enterprise as a more vigorous force for promoting christianisation in Asia than the declining trading empire of Portugal. The vitality of French commitment to missionising was shown by the foundation in 1644 of the Société des Missions Etrangères, a major new order devoted to asiatic proselytism. By the 1660s the Papacy had begun to modify the Portuguese canonical monopoly over the asiatic missions by creating new vicariates for French missionaries to direct.

Supported by the French monarchy and encouraged by the Papacy, French missions tended to develop in close cooperation with French mercantile establishments. Their mutual assistance took a variety of forms. The regulations of some of the early French chartered companies specified responsibility for supporting and promoting christianisation. Missionaries took part in official embassies to asiatic rulers from whom trade and proselytising privileges were sought. Missionaries operating beyond the range of the companies' trading networks occasionally negotiated permission from asiatic monarchs to set up company trading settlements. Administrators of company settlements regularly borrowed trading capital from local French missions. And on occasions the Crown was persuaded to supply troops and naval support for combined mercantile and missionary ventures, such as the attempt to oust Protestant Dutch and British influence from Siam in the 1680s. Within the bounds of financial and political practicability, the French monarchy, through its chartered companies, treated French commercial and missionary interests as an integrated complex of responsibilities in Asia.

But in the latter part of the eighteenth century, state involvement in French commercial and missionary enterprise in Asia dwindled. The decline in state support was gradual and irregular. The disasters of the Anglo-French wars of the 1750s and 1760s in India damaged the credit of the last and most successful of the Crown's chartered companies, the Compagnie perpetuelle des Indes. The company's finances became implicated in the Crown's debt crisis, and it was finally wound up in 1769. With the company's demise the crown abandoned its direct financial interest in Asian trade. As a result the French trading effort lost its main investment input and shrunk to a series of marginal private operations. The French Crown by no means abandoned its political or religious responsibilities. It continued to deploy the royal navy against British shipping in the Indian ocean at times of continental war. It also lent occasional diplomatic support to missionary enterprises: in one notably late instance, Louis XVI endorsed a treaty drafted in 1787 by Pigneau de Béhaine, Bishop of Adran, pledging military and financial support to install Prince Nguyen Anh on the throne of Vietnam. But in most respects the general impetus of state encouragement for missionary work was already slackening off when the onset of the French revolution in 1789 marked a sharp break in metropolitan support for the missions.

The decline of missionary enterprise in Asia during the French Revolution and under the Napoleonic Empire, 1789–1815.

With the fall of the monarchy in 1792 the missionary orders were deprived not only of state protection, but of other forms of assistance from France, particularly the aristocratic and ecclesiastical patronage on which French missions traditionally depended for funding and promoting recruitment. Starved of resources and personnel - and even, in many instances, formally abolished as clerical bodies in France - French missions had contracted to a shadow of their former establishments by the beginning of the nineteenth century. After the revolution and during the Napoleonic empire, if missions and state agencies cooperated, they tended to pursue parallel but dissimilar objectives more often than shared aims.

Although Napoleon aspired to revive and reshape the French role in Asia, the decline of French trade and missionising in Asia was not reversed by the achievements of his transitory empire. From 1797 Napoleon sought to oust the British from India and to strengthen French power in the Indian Ocean and the Southeast Asian archipelago. The success of such an enterprise offered the prospect of reviving substantial state assistance to French missionaries as informal and widely dispersed agents of French political influence. Napoleon's project began promisingly with his successful invasion of Egypt, but the undertaking foundered with the destruction of the French fleet by Nelson off the Nile in 1798. Napoleon did not lose all hope of finding alternative means to oust the British from Asia, but his continuing effort to overthrow British dominion produced the reverse effect of his intentions: they encouraged the further contraction of French naval and commercial power. By 1815 French influence in Asia had subsided abruptly as a result of naval defeats in the region. The loss of Mauritius deprived the French of their only sizeable harbour in the Indian Ocean and confined them to the island of Bourbon, and to their scattered settlements in India - principally Pondicherry, Chandernagore, Mahé and Karikal. Meantime French trade in Asia had failed to expand spontaneously under the Empire, even though the constraints of chartered company monopoly had been removed over thirty years before. From French Indian ocean and coastal dependencies, private entrepreneurs with little capital backing continued to operate a marginal trade with China through the Southeast Asian archipelago. Although French missionaries and traders were occasionally able to serve eachothers' interests, official agencies in the region offered little support or endorsement for missionary objectives.

The revival of French missionary enterprise in Asia after 1815.

After the fall of Napoleon, missionary activity revived before any other form of French enterprise in Asia, commercial or political. The regeneration of the missionary orders began from France, where the Bourbon Restoration in 1815 saw not only the resuscitation of clerical political influence, but the development of a groundswell of popular religious reaction against the radicalism of the revolutionary and napoleonic regimes. The effects of these changes were slow to reach the missions in Asia, for the reanimation of the central institutions of the major missionary orders took time. The Lazarists and the Société des Missions Etrangères were reauthorised between 1816 and 1820, but the famous seminary of the Missions Etrangères in the rue du Bac was not reopened until 1823. A more significant stimulus to missionary revival was the foundation at Lyons in 1822 of a powerful new fundraising organ, the Congrégation de la Propagation de la Foi. This religious body became the central financial institution of the whole Catholic missionary movement in France. By 1839 annual donations to the Propagation de la Foi had reached almost 2 million frs The success of its efforts was the clearest symptom of growing public support for the missions and marked the real beginning of the missionary resurgence.

The vital financial effects of its fundraising did not become fully visible until the 1830s, when French missionary activity in the Far East began to grow massively. The Lazarists, the Marists, the Congrégation de la Mission, the French branch of the Jesuit order, and above all the Société des Missions Etrangères, received substantial contributions to extend their existing missions and open up new territories. In 1839 Pope Gregory XVI formally acknowledged the primacy of French missionary enterprise in the Far East by persuading the court of Lisbon to abandon the Padroado, Portugal's claim to monopoly over appointments to the older episcopal sees in Asia. Most of these were now transferred to French missionaries. A further fourteen new vicariates or apostolic prefectures were created and assigned either to French priests of the Lazarist and Jesuit orders, or to the Missions Etrangères during the 1830s and 1840s.

The Société des Missions Etrangères took the lion's share of the new creations, adding substantially to its traditional responsibilities in mainland Southeast Asia. Here, vicariates already under the control of the Missions Etrangères were split and multiplied. Except for East Tonkin, which remained with Spanish Dominicans based on the Spanish Philippines, all vicariates in Vietnam were confirmed to the Missions Etrangères. The vicariate of Cochinchina (which then included Annam and Cambodia), was partitioned into two vicariates in 1844, and further subdivided to form a third in 1850. In 1846 West Tonkin was divided and a new vicariate of South Tonkin established. Further afield, a new vicariate in Malaya was created from the division of the vicariate of Siam in 1841. Finally, other new vicariates in Japan, Manchuria, Tibet and Burma (Ava and Pegu) were created between 1831 and 1856. These too, along with four vicariates in South China, were given to the Missions Etrangères. Despite the enormous geographical extension of its responsibilities - which still included a see in India allocated in 1776 and subdivided once in 1845, and again in 1850 - the main focus of the Missions Etrangères' responsibilities remained Vietnam. Here the number of converts claimed - 3-400,000 - far outran those of all other Catholic missions in Asia, except for the Spanish Philippines.

The French state and French missionary expansion in Asia, 1815 to 1840.

Until the 1840s, French missionary expansion in Asia relied very little on state support. The restored Bourbons certainly showed favour to the missionary orders by reauthorising them. But little was done through state action to protect and promote missionary activities in the Far East. Without continental allies, and anxious to avoid collision with Britain's interests in Asia, Restoration governments declined to pursue a general revival of French naval power and diplomatic influence in the Far East. In consequence the state simply lacked the agencies to give more than occasional local assistance.

The religious reaction in France had hardly begun to benefit the missions when the main line of the Bourbon dynasty gave way to the Orleanist branch in the revolution of 1830. The Restoration régime had at least been favourably disposed to the missionary cause; its Orleanist successor was not. Confronted by a conservative Catholic hierarchy which was packed with Restoration appointments and opposed to the principles of the revolution of 1830, Louis Philippe's cabinets adopted an anticlerical stance. Despite a brief and belated attempt at flirtation with nascent liberal Catholicism, the Orleanist monarchy maintained an anticlerical posture until its demise in the revolution of 1848. Consequently missionaries coming out to Asia in ever greater numbers after 1830 could scarcely expect official state support.

Yet, paradoxically, French missionaries in the Far East were to receive far more official help from the anti-clerical Orleanist regime than from the pro-clerical governments of the Restoration. For the later cabinets of Louis Philippe revived French commitment to expansion in East Asia; and in the course of establishing new agencies for extending French influence, they acknowledged responsibility for protecting missionaries - not as a religious obligation, but as a national duty.

The revival of French forward policy in East Asia, 1840-1848.

The premiership of Guizot (1840-1848) marked the beginning of a coordinated policy of promoting French trade through the opening up of a new arc of French naval power and diplomatic leverage across East Asia from the Indian Ocean to China and the South Pacific. The renewal of French intervention in East Asia was not the product of initiatives or pressures from local secular interests in the region, which were still minimal; it was essentially a function of state policy, and an attempt to provide for future commercial needs. Guizot was especially envious of British and U.S. commercial expansion in Asia and the Americas, and tried to emulate it. French commerce seemed disinclined to expand spontaneously into East Asia, and Guizot sought to encourage it through government action. Guizot was uninterested in the acquisition of substantial territories, and shied away from the international complications and local commitments entailed in largescale colonisation. He was exclusively preoccupied with the extension of French commercial growth. France's international position was still weak, and any development of French interests in East Asia was to some extent dependent on British tolerance. So instead of territorial acquisition Guizot planned an imperialism of informal influence, promoting the expansion of French commercial networks in Asia through the medium of commercial treaties backed by naval coercion. To protect the future growth of French commerce he adopted the strategy of developing isolated naval stations as 'points d'appui', or naval strongpoints adjoining major maritime trade routes.

The French navy, accustomed to a certain independence in gathering geographical and scientific intelligence, had already pointed the way. Since the early 1800s occasional naval expeditions had been commissioned to explore and chart the Pacific. Here, somewhat at random and without prior authorisation, French naval officers had annexed the Marquesas in 1841 and forced a protectoral treaty on Tahiti in 1842. Approached for restrospective sanction, Guizot had accepted the possible utility of these islands for French Pacific whaling interests. But he aspired to a more coherent strategy. New commercial opportunities were opening up in China, where British success in the Opium war of 1839-42 had recently eliminated major restrictions on British trade with the Celestial empire. The possibility of developing a lucrative French trade with China exerted a powerful attraction. Guizot was persuaded to authorise the search for a naval base closer to China's sealanes, similar to the new British acquisition of Hong Kong. When the Chinese themselves showed signs of welcoming French influence as a means of counterbalancing British political pressure, Guizot was presented with a favourable opportunity for diplomatic intervention.

The French establish a permanent diplomatic and naval presence on the China coast, 1844-1848.

Chinese receptiveness to French overtures encouraged Guizot to pursue a commercial convention modelled on the British treaty of Nangking (1842). In briefing the French plenipotentiary, de Lagrené, Guizot showed no particular interest in obtaining privileges for the French missions in China. His essential concern was with trade. But French mercantile and financial interests were not currently pressing to enter the China market; and there was only one French commercial house operating on the China coast in this period. In the circumstances French missionaries rather than French traders became the first beneficiaries of Guizot's China initiative.

In the Franco-Chinese negotiations leading to the treaty of Whampoa (1846), missionaries, acting as interpreters, persuaded Guizot's envoy, de Lagrené, to obtain an edict of religious toleration, the first such proclamation ever to be extracted from the Chinese. The scale of the

French missionary presence, the urgency of their requests for protection, and French diplomatic success in obtaining the new edict of toleration, all encouraged Lagrené and his successors to make missionaries themselves a medium of French diplomatic influence. Lagrené led the way in establishing a French monopoly of responsibility for all Catholic interests in China, a diplomatic role which eventually came to be acknowledged by the Papacy as the French 'protectorate' of Catholic missions.

Meantime, as France's only diplomatic agency in the whole of East Asia, the French legation in Canton concerned itself with the security of missionaries throughout the region, from Japan and Korea to Vietnam and Siam. In this wider duty it was supported by a roving French naval force which was now to become virtually a permanent presence. Once installed as official agencies on the China coast, French diplomats and naval personnel formed an epicentre of French policymaking. They came to play mutually reciprocating roles in support of missionary interests throughout coastal East Asia, exerting a local gravitational pull which influenced the ultimate direction and pattern of French political commitments in the region.

The attention of French naval personnel was particularly drawn to Vietnam in the early 1840s. By reason of the geographical location of Vietnam as a territorial appendix to South China, the advantages of finding a foothold there - possibly at Tourane or Poulo Condore - had already entered the navy's calculations. Guizot continued to fight shy of mainland footholds which might result in extensive local political involvement. But the attention of French naval officers and diplomats was persistantly engaged throughout the 1840s by a series of particularly fervent appeals from French missionaries in Vietnam demanding protection from persecution. Missionary complaints not only outlasted the demise of Guizot's ministry; they were to continue with increasing intensity into the 1850s. It was the issue of missionary persecution - and French naval responses to it - which did most to determine the eventual French invasion of Vietnam.

Further reading

On the French East India Company in the eighteenth century

H. Weber, **La compagnie française des Indes.** (Paris, 1904)
W.H. Dalgleish, **The Company of the Indies in the Days of Dupleix.** (Easton, Chemical Publishing Co., 1933)

On missions

J.B. Piolet (ed.), **Les missions catholiques françaises au XIXe. siècle.** 2 vols. (Paris, A.Colin, 1903).

Georges Taboulet, **La geste française en Indochine.** (Paris, Maisonneuve, 1955.)

O. Werner, **Katholischer Missions-Atlas.** (Freiburg-im-Breisgau, Herder, 1884).

A. Launay, **Atlas des missions de la Société des Missions-Etrangères.** (Lille, 1890)

On the revival of French interest in Asia in the early nineteenth century.

H. Cordier, **La France et l'Angleterre en Indo-chine et en Chine sous le Premier Empire.** (Leiden, 1903)

J.F. Cady, **The Roots of French Imperialism in Eastern Asia.** 2nd. edn. (Cornell, 1967).

J. Laffey, 'Les racines de l'impérialisme française en Extrême-Orient à propos des thèses de J.-F.Cady', **Revue d'Histoire Moderne et Contemporaine,** XVI (1969), pp. 282-299.

D. Johnson, **Guizot: Aspects of French History 1787-1874.** (London, Routledge and Kegan Paul, 1963).

Alistair Lamb, **The Mandarin Road to Old Hue.** (London, Archon, 1970)

FRENCH INTERVENTION IN VIETNAM.

I A   Vietnamese persecutions

The persecution of Christianity in Vietnam was never motivated by purely metaphysical issues. Vietnamese religious tradition was unusually eclectic and broadly tolerant of other beliefs. The universal cult was ancestor-worship, which combined easily with an animist tradition of belief in the presiding spirits of villages and towns. A further dimension of religious observance was the moral search for the means to harmonise human activity with the will of Heaven. Practitioners of Confucianism adhered to an ethical system which emphasised the responsibilities of the individual towards his family and village, and towards constituted political authority. Overall, Vietnamese religious tradition was absorbant and syncretic, allowing for the pursuit of many paths to the Truth. In contrast with this, the exclusive spiritual claims of Christianity merely seemed irrational and eccentric to the Vietnamese.

However, missionary strategies of conversion were exceptionally intrusive. The social and political effects of their proselytism could be highly disruptive. It was this which aroused popular as well as elite hostility. In order to attract and keep the convert to the Catholic faith, missionaries frequently needed to rupture the bonds which held him to his community and which compelled his obedience to constituted authority. The missionaries of the Société des Missions Etrangères and the Spanish Dominicans poured scorn on the cosmographical tradition - the religion of Heaven and Earth - which provided justification for political obedience to imperial sovereignty and its delegates. They discouraged financial contribution to the village cult of tutelary spirits. They encouraged the convert to evade his obligation to support the worship of his family's ancestors, or contribute to the upkeep of the family tombs. By breaking such communal ties Christian missionaries offered a social, and ultimately a political, challenge to Vietnamese society far more palpable than the abstract propositions of theological discourse. By officials and peasants alike Christianity was characterised as an essentially antisocial, subversive cult.

The French Catholic missions under Emperor Gia Long, (1801-1820),

Missions and their Christian proselytes had been intermittantly persecuted from the earliest years of their apostolate in the seventeenth century. By the end of the eigtheenth century and in the wake of the Tay Son rebellion they had come to enjoy a period of exceptional favour owing to the assistance they had given to instal the head of the Nguyen dynasty as sovereign of a reconstituted and newly unified Vietnamese empire. The role of Bishop Pigneau de Béhaine in assembling a military and naval force of mercenaries in support of Prince Nguyen Anh had been particularly crucial in winning royal political protection for the the missions during of the latter's reign as the Emperor Gia Long. In acknowledging his political debt to Christian missionaries, Gia Long had also used them, along with French personnel appointed to the mandarinate, as a medium of tentative contact with the West.

But in favouring and utilising Christian missionaries Gia Long took a calculated political risk. Christian heterodoxy reflected some discredit on a newly established monarchy anxious to reinforce its legitimacy with landowning and bureaucratic elites still mistrustful of Nguyen rule. Missionaries were also actively encouraging the involvement of French commercial and political interests in Vietnam, hoping for their support in the spread of Christianisation. Here too, Gia Long showed some awareness of the danger of encouraging an excess of western intrusion. By the time of his death the growth of the threat from the West and the spreading unpopularity of Christianity were seen as related issues by an anti-western, anti-Christian faction at court with which Gia Long's·successor, Minh Mang, was closely associated.

Persecution of missionaries under Emperors Minh Mang (1820–41) and Thieu Tri (1841–1847).

Minh Mang's attitude to the West and to the question of Christianity were of a piece with his general strategy for consolidating dynastic control. His predecessor had employed mainly tactical, short-term measures to reinforce his personal power - abolishing court offices which mitigated his authority, building up his army, moving his capital to Hue in central Vietnam, and buying off and polarising the political claims of his two leading generals through palatine appointments in the North and South respectively. Minh Mang, however, pursued long-term measures of structural consolidation. The keynote of change in his reign was adherence to classical orthodoxy. It is plain that Minh Mang's objective was to express the authority of the dynasty in the purest classical language of Chinese political and cosmographical theory. This did not augur well for the Catholic missions. Minh Mang reinforced both the legitimacy and the administrative power of the Nguyen monarchy by recreating the Chinese bureaucratic model in its most idealised form. He installed the classic bureaucratic apparatus of the six boards, a censorate and imperial secretariats based on pre-Manchu Chinese precedents. The palatine jurisdictions of Gia Long's generals were phased out and replaced by a structure of administration which strengthened metropolitan control over 31 newly created provinces. Here the hierarchy of senior appointments also matched the pattern of Chinese provincial administration. For his reformed mandarinate Minh Mang adopted the standard Chinese system of recruitment by merit, imposed hierarchical distinctions in dress, and instituted payment by salary. The Chinese character system of the K'ang-hsi dictionary was proclaimed to be the language of administration; and recruitment of officials was by examination in the Chinese classics.

While creating a system which strengthened imperial control over an enlarged bureaucratic elite, Minh Mang showed himself responsive not only to the views of the officials of the mandarinate, but also to opinion within the larger body of scholar-literati from which the administration recruited its personnel. The Chinese bureaucratic model incorporated a tradition of petitioning the throne on important issues, and the plethora of memorials from scholars and mandarins against Christianity transmitted to the throne in the 1820s, 1830s and 1840s reflect both the nature of elite hostility to missionary proselytism and some enthusiasm for the standards of orthodoxy being maintained by the dynasty. Inevitably the process of legitimising the restored Nguyen dynasty by an emphasis on orthodoxy entailed the fall from favour of the socially heterodox, politically subversive cult of Christianity.

Nevertheless, proscription of Christians did not follow immediately on Minh Mang's succession in 1820. Minh Mang, like Gia Long, was wary of offering provocation to foreign powers by victimising their nationals. Moreover he was reluctant to challenge the power of the main protector of Christians in Vietnam, Le Van Duyet, last of Gia Long's leading generals, who as governor of Cochinchina enjoyed virtually autonomous power over the south until his death in 1832. Hence the emperor initially responded to anti-Christian petitions of the early 1820s **(Doc. 1)** with a decree of 1826 summoning all missionaries to live in enforced residence at the capital, Hue. However, the scale of missionary proselytism was by now giving cause for intense unease: there are estimated to have been over 300,000 Christians scattered throughout Vietnam, with major concentrations in the weakly held viceroyalty of Tonkin. Moreover Christian involvement in the major insurrections of the reign (1826-8, 1833-5) associated them with dissidence. Christians in Tonkin were known to be particularly closely aligned to the political cause of the Lê pretenders to the imperial throne. In 1830 a decree was passed proscribing Christianity and ordering the arrest of all priests and the destruction of churches. After the proven implication of Christians in the rebellion of Duyet's adopted son, Le Van Khoi, in Cochinchina (July 1833) Minh Mang sanctioned more active persecution in 1836, followed by executions and further edicts of expulsion in the later 1830s, rising to a peak of intensity with the execution of eleven Vietnamese priests in 1840. Only fear of foreign intervention after the British assault on Canton in the Opium war (1840-41) appears to have brought these persecutions to a temporary halt. The suspension of persecution was maintained by Minh Mang's successor, the Emperor Thieu Tri (1841-47) until the closing months of his own reign.

The French navy provokes Vietnamese reprisals against Christians: the first Tourane attack, 1847.

A squadron of six vessels under the command of Captain Cécille had been sent out with Lagrené's diplomatic mission in 1844: it had been given the specific task of searching for a <u>point d'appui</u> in East Asia. Guizot wanted to obtain a naval station in East Asia that would free the French from dependence on British, Spanish or Portuguese held ports. Tourane (Da Nang) on the coast of central Vietnam had been considered as a possibility: the port had been promised to the French under the terms of the Franco-Vietnamese treaty of 1787; but this agreement was unratified and inoperative. Tourane, however, remained an attractive proposition to the French navy. It occupied a central position on the Vietnamese coast, within easy reach of the South China ports. Tourane bay offered a good anchorage and commanded access inland to the Vietnamese capital of Hue. In 1839 a French corvette commander, Lt Fourichon, had proposed Tourane for consideration as a suitable naval base. This suggestion was ignored by the naval ministry, but it was renewed in July 1843 by Ratti-Menton, a French consular envoy to China. Guizot, however, was keen to avoid the risk of political entanglements with the Vietnamese. He declared against Tourane and in favour of a remoter spot, Basilan island in the Sulu archipelago. But Basilan island proved to be unavailable, for although the French had managed to arrange financial terms with the Sultan of Sulu for its purchase, the Spanish claimed Basilan as a dependency of the Phillipines and had blocked the transaction. The French were still casting about for an alternative base when French missionaries in Vietnam, appealing for naval intervention and diplomatic assistance, redirected French official attention back to Tourane.

There was a precedent for successful French naval intervention on behalf of missionaries in Vietnam. Even before the arrival of Captain Cécille's squadron in 1844, a Captain Favin-Levêque had entered the port of Tourane in October 1842 and succeeded in persuading Emperor Thieu Tri's officials to release five imprisoned French missionaries. This transaction had been peaceable. But the French squadron under Captain Cécille needed little prompting to mount displays of force. Cécille had been authorised by Guizot to offer assistance to missionaries, provided that this could be done without compromising the French flag. During the ensuing decade, naval interventions on behalf of the missionaries in Vietnam became insistant, and finally violent.

In June 1845 a Captain Fornier-Duplan was sent to demand the release of Mgr Lefebvre, bishop of Isauropolis and Vicar Apostolic of Lower Cochinchina, from imprisonment at Hue. He succeeded in arranging the bishop's despatch to Singapore. Mgr Lefebvre, however, returned immediately to Saigon, where he was again recaptured. Again he was rescued, this time through mediation by the captain of a British vessel, but again he returned to Saigon. Finally, in April 1847 a French frigate, La Gloire and a corvette, La Victorieuse were despatched to to demand the release of the bishop - who was already at large again - and to ask for freedom for Christian worship. The consequences of this visit were disastrous. It resulted in a French naval bombardment of Tourane, when five Vietnamese ships were sunk and numbers of Vietnamese sailors killed before the French force disengaged and departed. Accounts of the conflict, otherwise widely divergent, agree in describing the unwillingness of the French commander, Captain Lapierre, to observe the ordinary formalities of communication with the Vietnamese court. Lapierre's high-handedness had provoked the Vietnamese to prepare naval countermeasures which Lapierre interpreted as a threat to massacre the French force. This he later gave as his reason for initiating the bombardment.

The predicament of French missionaries in Vietnam merely grew worse as a result of this naval assault. To the Vietnamese, the character of French actions appeared arrogant and violent, but above all indecisive. Lapierre's naval action was neither followed up nor explained away. As a result, and contrary to its purpose, the intervention provoked reprisals. Emperor Thieu Tri, who had begun to show signs of willingness to compromise with French requirements on the religious question, withdrew into a position of complete intransigence. He issued a series of four anti-Christian edicts in rapid succession. Although he died within months of the French attack, his posture of defiance set a precedent for his successor, Emperor Tu Duc, to follow. Tu Duc continued to express outrage at the Tourane attack; but he had a further motive for embarking on a persecution of some vigour. The sympathy shown by Christians for the claims of his elder brother, Prince Hong Bao, to the succession particularly irked him. The insecurity of

Tu Duc' succession right and his comparative youth and dependence on advisors influenced the proclamation in 1851 **(Doc. 2)** and 1855 of the most draconian decrees against Christians yet to emerge. Despite their severity of tone, these decrees were only patchily implemented by provincial officials. Apart from expulsions and imprisonments, they resulted in the execution of only two French priests and approximately ten Vietnamese Christians between 1853 and 1856. Only after the second French bombardment of the Tourane forts in 1856 - the overture to the French expeditionary assault of 1858 - did the scale of the enforcement of persecutory decrees suddenly increase. This signified the start of a syndrome which was to become familiar over the next three decades: the phenomenon of popular attacks on Christians accompanying each phase of French political intervention or advance.

Further reading.

On Vietnamese perspectives

R.B. Smith, **Vietnam and the West.** (London, Heinemann, 1968).
A.B. Woodside, **Vietnam and the China Model: a comparative study** of **Vietnamese and Chinese government in the first half of the nineteenth century.** (Cambridge, Mass. 1971).
R.B. Smith, 'Politics and Society in Vietnam during the early Nguyen period', **Journal of the Royal Asiatic Society,** 1974, pp. 153-169.
Bui Quang-Tung, 'La succession de Thieu-Tri', **Bulletin de la Société des Etudes Indochinoises,** n.s. XLII, 1-2, (1967).
L. Cadière, **Croyances et pratiques religieuses des vietnamiens.** (Paris, 1958).
Vo Duc Hanh, **La place du catholicisme dans les relations entre la France et le Vietnam.** (3 vols. Leiden, 1969).

On French initiatives in the 1840s and early 1850s.

(In addition to Taboulet vol.I, Cady, Johnson and Lamb, cited on p. 28)

Capt. M. Cécille, 'Cochinchine et Tonkin. Extrait d'un rapport de M. Cécille, Commandant...en station des mers de Chine'. **Annales maritimes et coloniales,** LXXXVII, (1844), pp. 750-80.

1. Petition from the Scholars, presented to the Emperor **Minh Mang** by the chief mandarin of the Judiciary. Hue, August 1826.

This religion is false and contrary to true doctrine. It seduces the people and abuses their simplicity. It uses fear of torture and hell to frighten the weak, and delight in the pleasures of heaven to attract others. It has reached the point of publishing a special calendar. It even has its own courts for judging matters.... Since this religion entered the kingdom thousands of people have come to profess it in all provinces. Those who are imbued with this doctrine are animated with a zeal which drives them out of their senses and makes them run hither and thither like madmen.

The devotees of this religion do not venerate the spirit of clarity; they do not perform ancestor worship.... They multiply day by day. They continually build new churches.... That is why we raise our eyes to His Majesty and beg him to correct these abuses. (L.E. Louvet, La Cochinchine religieuse. (2 vols, Paris, 1885), vol. 2, pp. 504-5)

2. The Emperor **Tu Duc**: Edict against Christianity. 30 March 1851.

Royal Ordinance.

The doctrine of Jesus comes from the Europeans: it forbids ancestor and spirit worship. To mislead men and bemuse its adepts it talks of Heaven and holy water. Its propagators, well knowing that the law of the kingdom cannot tolerate such an evil doctrine, present to the people an image of a tortured Jesus, their master, to seduce the ignorant and make them confront death without repentance. What a deplorable illusion! What a strange obsession!

In the reign of King[1] Minh Mang this senseless cult was severely prohibited by several decrees: every time a Christian refused to abandon it he was very rigorously, promptly and remorselessly punished. From the time of Thieu Tri many orders were given to renew prohibition of this perverse doctrine. Except for the aged and infirm, no refractory Christian was ever granted exception.

That is why our venerable predecessors have always acted with consummate care, rigour and prudence to eliminate its inherently evil principles. By the faithful observance of ritual and by the study of music and a respectable style of clothing they have attained a high level of culture. The basis of our own civilisation is proper behaviour;   but it would soon be degraded if the doctrine of these men with hearts of savages and the habits of animals were to be put into practice.

When the heart is corrupt and not promptly reformed, proper religious feeling is stifled within it.   Correcting bad habits and spreading enlightenment is therefore of great benefit for the morality of future generations.

We, Tu Duc, faithful to our age-old way, which is to listen and observe in all our acts, our judgements, our orders, to attend closely to what is seemly, to study with care what is apt and relevant, have charged our officials to submit a report on the subject of a petition addressed to us by our Privy Council on the need to proscribe the evil religion of Jesus.   Here is the advice which our officials give:

That the priests from Europe should be thrown into our rivers or into the depths of the sea for the glory of the true Religion.   Annamese priests, whether they agree to trample on the cross or not, shall be cut in half so that all may know the severity of the Law.

We have examined these proposals and find them in conformity with true reason.   Our mandarins have been ordered to put them into effect, but in secret and without proclamation.   And so, if European priests infiltrate furtively into our kingdom to circulate through our provinces, in order to mislead and beguile the hearts of our people, whoever denounces them or delivers them up to our officials will receive, first, eight taels of silver, and then half the belongings of those who are protecting these guilty men: the other half goes to the Treasury.

As for their protectors, great or small, it matters not for how short or long a time they have been succouring a European, they too shall each be cut in half and cast into the deeps, except for children under the age of reason, who shall be sent far away.   Those who were absent and had no knowledge of priests being lodged in their homes will be exempted from prosecution.   (Translation by Mgr Retord, <u>Annales de la Propagation de la Foi</u>, 1852, XXIV, p. 11 ff.)

(1). Even though Vietnamese emperors (or <u>vuong</u>) claimed the same moral role and spiritual attributes as Chinese emperors, the French habitually referred to them as 'kings'.

APPEALS, CONSULTATIONS AND DECISIONS.

The arrival in power of Louis Napoleon and the development of the missionary question in East Asia.

The breach between the Catholic hierarchy and the state which had lasted since 1830 was ended by the swing towards reaction which followed the upheavals of May and June in the revolution of 1848. The arrival in power of Louis Napoleon Bonaparte as first President of the Second Republic marked the beginning of a close conjuncture between the Church and the conservative new régime. Catholic bishops had openly supported Louis Napoleon's candidature for the presidency; and in return, they had been promised a broad programme of concessions to the Catholic interest.

Following the coup of 1851 which established the Second Empire, clerical support for Louis Napoleon - now Napoleon III - became even stronger, and was to last until his intervention against Papal interests during the Italian war with Austria in 1859.

Napoleon III's rapprochement with the Catholic church encouraged the more vocal expression of missionary needs, and explains the relative ease with which missionary complaints were now transmitted to the highest levels of government. Even so, there is no simple correlation between missionary pressure and state action. The pro-clerical tendency of the Bonapartist regime in the 1850s does not in itself explain Napoleon III's willingness to intervene in favour of missionaries in Vietnam. The operation of state policy in East Asia was as closely related to Napoleon's conception of his own dynastic - and France's secular - interests as to his concern to retain clerical support. If Napoleon III's proclaimed wish to safeguard missionary interests provided the occasion for French intervention in Vietnam, it does not explain the ultimate purposes of his policy.

Missionary pressure for French intervention in Vietnam, 1850-1856.

In the early years of the Second Republic, government interest in East Asia had palled to apathy. The withdrawal of the Legation in China had even been considered as a possible economy measure in 1849. Yet in 1850-1 missionary complaints both from China and Vietnam had multiplied. Particularly strong protests from the Legation in China and from the Seminary of the Missions Etrangères followed the publication of Emperor Tu Duc's draconian decrees of 1851 against Christians. In mid 1852, eight bishops of Far Eastern vicariates submitted a memorial to Napoleon III pointing out that the lack of official French response to the persecution of missionaries throughout East Asia - particularly in

Korea, China and Vietnam - was giving an impression of French national weakness. They demanded the despatch of a further naval force to boost French prestige. In August and September 1852 the French minister in China, Comte de Bourboulon, sent more detailed despatches, drafted in cooperation with Fr Libois of the Missions Etrangères, demanding intervention on an unprecedented scale. Citing news of the recent executions of Frs Bonnard and Schoeffler in Vietnam, Bourboulon proposed an expedition to demand a treaty of commerce and to impose religious toleration upon the Vietnamese. He suggested that Tourane should be retained as a guarantee of Vietnamese observance of such a treaty.

At first the Ministry of Marine and the Quai d'Orsay gave a favourable response to these proposals, and made preparations to implement them. But on further reflection the navy found too many competing demands on its resources to give effect to the project. Then the Taiping conquest of South-central China early in 1853 abruptly altered the priority of French concerns in the region, shifting attention away from Vietnam to the Chinese coastal ports - particularly Shanghai - where French missionary and commercial communities had found themselves beleaguered by Taiping rebels. Of far greater significance in delaying French intervention in Vietnam was the deepening Near Eastern crisis which led, in 1854, to the Crimean war. This conflict diverted virtually all available naval and military resources, paralysing any possibility of French naval action against Vietnam for a further two years.

The Montigny mission, 1856-7.

The local predicament of missionaries in Vietnam was still one of pressing urgency, however. Unable to resolve it by force during the Crimean campaign, the French next resorted to an unarmed diplomatic mission to Hue in the hope of negotiating a solution.

Charles de Montigny, Vice-consul at Shanghai, already deputed to negotiate a commercial treaty with Siam on the model of a recent British agreement, was ordered to extend his diplomatic mission to Vietnam. He was instructed to press the Vietnamese 'in a steady and insistant way' for a treaty of religious tolerance and commerce. But Montigny's arrival in Vietnam was long delayed: after concluding the agreement with Siam, he diverted to Kampot in pursuit of an ephemeral opportunity for a similar agreement with Cambodia. In the interval a French naval officer was sent to Tourane to prepare the way for Montigny's negotiations with the court of Hue. In mid September 1856 Captain Lelieur of the <u>Catinat</u>, attempting to present formal notification of Montigny's mission, found himself ostracised by Vietnamese officials at the port. Frustrated at his inability to deliver a copy of Montigny's intended demands, Lelieur exceeded his instructions and bombarded Tourane. He then disembarked a force to spike the sixty-six guns of the Vietnamese batteries covering the bay. Temporarily shaken by this assault, the Vietnamese court, in its dealings with Lelieur's successor, Captain Collier of the _Capricieuse_, authorised the formal acceptance of the French proposal to negotiate. The Vietnamese governor of Quang Nam, replying in early November 1856 on behalf of the court, agreed to negotiate an agreement 'in conformity with Vietnamese laws'. But by the time of Montigny's final arrival at the end of January 1857 the war party at the Hue court had achieved a reversal of this policy; and when Montigny finally met the Vietnamese delegation in February 1857, he was presented with a draft treaty which referred in belittling terms to Napoleon III and offered nothing of what the French were known to want. After two weeks of fruitless wrangling Montigny broke off negotiations and withdrew from Tourane, leaving behind a draft proposal which stipulated, _inter alia_, that Catholicism should be accepted as 'one of the state religions' of Vietnam. The advocates of resistance at the Hue court appeared to be vindicated, for Montigny's tame withdrawal seemed to confirm their impression of French impotence. As a well-known Vietnamese poem later expressed it: 'The French barked like dogs but ran away like goats.'

Napoleon III contemplates an expedition: January–November 1857.

The final decision to despatch an expedition to Vietnam was taken personally by Napoleon III against the wishes of most of his ministers following a series of specific appeals from representatives of the missionary interest. The Empress Eugénie, closely linked to the clerical lobby at court and particularly sympathetic to the missionary cause, is commonly credited with having influenced the decision. It is possible that her role was to facilitate access to the emperor by missionaries and their diplomatic and naval supporters.

In January 1857 Abbé Huc, a Lazarist missionary, wrote directly to Napoleon III to persuade him of the desirability of an expedition to annex Vietnam. Huc, though never having visited Vietnam, was acting as a spokesman for Fr Libois, the Procurator of the Missions Etrangères at Hong Kong, with whom he was on close terms. Libois, for his part, had long pressed the French legation at Canton to promote awareness in ministerial circles of missionary difficulties in Vietnam. In his note to the Emperor **(Doc. 3)** Abbé Huc particularly stressed the material benefits of a French occupation, as well as urging the necessity of giving protection to missionaries. As a direct result of Huc's appeal, Napoleon III set up a small commission in April 1857 under Baron

Brenier, a senior official of the Quai d'Orsay, to investigate Huc's proposal for an expedition. The composition of the Brenier Commission was weighted heavily in favour of a positive recommendation: it contained two naval officers, Admiral Fourichon and Captain Jaurès, who had both served on the China station and who actively supported intervention; and Brenier himself also appears to have favoured this course. In May 1857 the commission recommended the imposition of a French protectorate over Vietnam **(Docs 4, 5)**. Among the witnesses interviewed by the commission were three missionaries - Abbé Huc, Fr Chamaison and Mgr Pellerin, bishop of Biblos and Vicar Apostolic of North Cochinchin - all of whom represented the material advantages of establishing a political footing in Vietnam in the most favourable possible light. Bishop Pellerin took a leading role, along with Abbé Huc, in mobilising French intervention. After tendering evidence to the Commission, Pellerin organised a publicity campaign in favour of an expedition through the medium of the formidable Vueillot brothers, who ran L'Univers, the most combative organ of the clerical press. Interviewed twice by Napoleon - in late June and at the end of August - Pellerin himself preached to packed congregations in Notre Dame cathedral and at the Eglise St Laurent on the plight of the Vietnam missions.

The generally unfavourable reaction of Napoleon III's ministers to the Brenier commission's recommendations emphasises how personal this decision was to Napoleon III himself. The Foreign Minister, Walewski, though not initially in favour of intervention, deferred to Napoleon's views. When presenting the Brenier report to a hostile a cabinet for consideration in the emperor's absence in mid-July 1857, Walewski concealed till the end of the discussion the fact that the decision had, in principle, already been taken. Only when the ministers realised that they had been tricked into offering frank opinions in contradiction to the Emperor's views did they offer their hasty assent to an expedition **(Doc. 6)**.

Napoleon III was not primarily actuated by a desire to secure protection for missionaries on their own account. The missionary question raised the broader issue of sustaining French prestige in the East. Moreover, the material and strategic advantages - as well as the cost and scope - of intervention seem to have been carefully calculated. After the July decision Napoleon III hesitated for a further four months over how to proceed. Neither the scale of the expedition, nor its exact terms of reference were finally decided until 21 November 1857. This was largely because its diplomatic implications and logistical problems were closely related to a major crisis which was currently developing in China.

The international situation in 1857.

One traditional obstacle to French intervention in Vietnam had been the fear of encountering British disapproval. A sense of rivalry with the British had certainly stimulated the recent extension of French naval and diplomatic interests in East Asia, but the French remained wary of appearing to offer a direct challenge to British concerns. With the onset of the Crimean war in 1854 Napoleon had moved France into an alignment with Britain closer than any attempted by his predecessors since the Restoration. But despite Anglo-French alliance in the Near East, the two powers remained competitors in the Far East, and here it remained important to avoid any occasion for collision. Napoleon's decision to send an expedition to Vietnam entailed this risk. It was taken in the context of a situation in China in which the British and French were trying to maintain a measure of diplomatic and military collaboration to promote congruent but different objectives. The development of the Chinese crisis affected the timing, the scale and the immediate objectives of French intervention in Vietnam.

Reluctant at first to act together in China, British and French policymakers had come to find a common interest in coordinating their strategies of pressure on Peking by 1856. The British had long been dissatisfied with the terms obtained by treaty of Nanking in 1842. Although the constrictions of the Canton monopoly had been removed and a further four coastal ports opened to British traffic, all other ports had remained closed, and access to the interior was still forbidden. British mercantile interests, both local and metropolitan, were convinced that the bulk of the China market was still untapped, and their new commissioner at Hong Kong, Sir John Bowring, an apostle of Free Trade, upheld their case with fervour. The French however, were less acutely irked by current trade restrictions than the British, for French commercial enterprise had so far ignored the China market. They certainly aspired to commercial penetration, but their immediate grievance against the Chinese related mainly to the execution of a French missionary, Fr Chapdelaine in 1855. The beheading and mutilation of Chapdelaine by order of a Chinese magistrate was not merely a religious issue: it was a challenge to French prestige. It also represented a setback to the Canton legation's strategy for pursuing a range of ulterior commercial and diplomatic objectives through the medium of missionary expansion in China. French objectives may have differed from those of the British but they were not incompatible. Moreover both powers agreed in wishing to establish direct diplomatic contact with the Chinese court: they both aimed to force the Chinese t accept their permanent diplomatic representation at Peking.

The British Commissioner at Hong Kong, Sir John Bowring, and Consul Parkes at Canton led the way in bringing these issues to a head. For more than a year both British agents had been searching for an opportunity to renegotiate treaty terms, if necessary by provoking hostilities. By late 1856, as British and French diplomatic dealings with Chinese officials became more acrimonious, the diplomats of both powers received instructions to organise a joint intervention in pursuit of their respective aims. When the Arrow incident sparked off Anglo-Chinese hostilities at Canton in October 1857, the French instructed Admiral Guérin, the commander of the French Far Eastern fleet to deploy his forces complementarily with those of the British; but as the crisis deepened, his successor, Admiral Rigault de Genouilly, was told to operate in direct conjunction with them.

British and French coordination of their naval action against China was an encouraging circumstance for advocates of a French expedition to Tourane. British appreciation of French assistance against China could be expected to temper British annoyance at seeing the French establish a permanent footing in Vietnam. Still more encouraging for the French was the outbreak of the Sepoy mutiny in India in May 1857. The Mutiny not only forced the British to deflect some of their forces from the China expedition to India, so increasing their dependence on French naval and military assistance on the China coast; but with their own empire apparently crumbling, British policymakers would hardly be likely to show much concern at French intervention to protect their own beleaguered missionaries in Vietnam.

Even so, despite these favourable conjunctures, Napoleon III still hesitated to give final sanction to a 'Cochinchina' expedition. He was undecided as to how large an enterprise to make it. He also wanted to emphasise its character as an undertaking on behalf of religious interests. The decision partly depended on the course of military operations in China, which were dragging on through the latter months of 1857. When finally projected on 21 November 1857 the Cochinchina expedition was to be mounted on different principles from those originally proposed. The Brenier commission had recommended an independent force of 2,600 men and six vessels, operating concurrently with the Naval division in China. Instead it came to consist of a diversion by the whole Far Eastern naval division, which was to await the cessation of hostilities in China before taking action against Vietnam. Within days of this decision news arrived of the Vietnamese execution of a Spanish Dominican bishop of East Tonkin, Mgr Diaz. Napoleon seized the opportunity of Diaz' death to invite the participation of the Spanish government in the venture. Spanish military help was not expected to be particularly valuable - in the event it consisted of one vessel and approximately 450 troops; but Spanish diplomatic support offered valuable cover against the possibility of British objections.

Napoleon's uncertainty of purpose was reflected in instructions given to Admiral Rigault de Genouilly. The admiral could try to establish a full French protectorate over the whole of Vietnam, as the Brenier commission had recommended. But if need be, and depending on Vietnamese willingness to treat, and in the light of local conditions, he could settle for a commercial and religious treaty guaranteed by the installation of a naval station at Tourane **(Doc. 7).** In effect Rigault was given a free hand to pursue whatever degree of involvement he wished to undertake.

Further reading

(Cady, Taboulet I, and Vo Duc Hanh, as above.)

Alain Plessis, **The rise and fall of the Second Empire.** (Cambridge, 1985).

Henri Cordier, 'La politique coloniale de la France au début du Second Empire. (Indochine, 1852-1858.)', **T'oung Pao,** 2e. série, X-XII (1909-11).

Henri Cordier, 'La France et la Cochinchine, 1852 à 1858: la mission du **Catinat** à Tourane (1856)'. **T'oung Pao,** 2e. série, VII, (1906).

G. Frédet, **Quand la Chine s'ouvrait. Charles de Montigny, Consul de France, 1805-1868.** (Shanghai, 1943).

G. Taboulet, 'La première évocation de la question de la Cochinchine au Conseil des Ministres', **Bulletin des la Société des Etudes Indochinoises,** 1943, pp. 16-77.

P. Franchini, 'La genèse de l'affaire de Cochinchine', **Revue d'histoire des colonies françaises,** 1951, 4, pp. 427-59.

A. Debidour, **Histoire des rapports de l'Eglise et de l'Etat en France de 1789 à 1870.** (Paris, F.Alcan, 1898).

L.E. Louvet, **La Cochinchine religieuse.** (2 vols. Paris, Challamel, 1885).

3. Fr E. **Huc.** Note for the Emperor **Napoleon III.** Paris, January 1857.

...To sum up, it is extremely important for France to have a rich and powerful establishment in the Far East. From every point of view Cochinchina is the point which would best suit us. We have the right to occupy it, and an occupation would be easy to accomplish. It would cost France nothing, and it could not fail to bring a great return in glory and riches. The English have their eyes on Tourane and they would get in first if they knew of our rights and of any plan for occupation.... (Ministère des Relations Extérieures, Paris. Série Mémoires et documents, Asie: volume 27.)

4. **Sixth report** of the Proceedings of the Cochinchina commission, 16 May 1857.

Present at the Hôtel des Affaires Etrangères:
        Baron **Brenier,** President.
        M. **Cintrat,** Departmental director.
        Rear-Admiral **Fourichon.**
        M. **Fleury,** Director at the Ministry of Commerce.
        Captain **Jaurès.**
        M. **de Mofras,** Secretary.

Invited to appear before the Commission:
        Mgr **Pellerin,** Bishop of Biblos and Vicar Apostolic of North Cochinchina.
        Fr **Chamaison,** Missionary in Cochinchina.

.... The president asked His Lordship the Bishop of Biblos whether it would be enough for us to make a new treaty or whether it would be necessary to occupy the country.

Mgr Pellerin replied that as for the treaty, reaching Hue would be enough to constrain the king to sign it, to publish it by an edict and to order its execution.

Since MM. Cintrat and Fleury raised some doubts as to the adequacy of such a measure for safeguarding the interests of religion and of our commerce and nationals, the president repeated the question.

His Lordship the Bishop of Biblos repeated that his opinion, entirely personal it was true, and not shared by the other missionaries, was that the conclusion of a treaty signed by the king, the presence of a Consul, the opening of the ports, and the frequent appearance of naval forces would guarantee our interests for a while. However, an occupation or a protectorate would be much preferable.

Fr Chamaison was not entirely of this opinion, and said that if we merely confined ourselves to making a treaty, its execution could not be ensured except by the presence of a French agent at Hue and the permanent presence of respectable naval forces to uphold it if need be; and he added that make-believe demonstrations and half-measures had eroded our position and our age-old influence in these regions.

The president remarked that the cost of sending and maintaining a naval and military expedition limited to concluding a treaty would be the same whether we occupied the country or merely established a protectorate over it; and he asked Mgr Pellerin if, in presenting ourselves, we should argue the validity of the treaty of 1787; and finally, which of the two would be more popularly received, an occupation or a protectorate ?

His Lordship the Bishop of Biblos replied that besides the rights conferred by the treaty, we should rest our case upon the absolute necessity of redressing grievances such as the martyrdom of our missionaries, the refusal of provisions to them, the poisoning of their water by the mandarins, the massacre of those of our faith, the humiliation inflicted on our last negotiator and finally on the threat made by M. de Montigny of the anger and prompt vengeance of France. That as for the a total occupation and the deposition of the king, he thought that there would be advantage in deferring to national sentiment, otherwise some internal and external difficulties would arise, - and that it seemed to him much preferable to seize the person of the king on arrival and leave him nominal power; but that, since in all probability this prince would hang himself along with his first minister, one would be governing through his successor who would be unlikely to have the same motive of injured dignity as a spur to suicide. The retention of the king and the benefits which would immediately result from the fairness and integrity of an administration run by France would make her name blessed, and her protectorate would be accepted by the whole population. Mgr Pellerin intimated how much we would be helped in our civilising and regenerating endeavours by the six hundred thousand native Catholics and by the numerous catechists educated by our missionaries, familiar with our ways and habits and almost with our language, for they all spoke and wrote Latin fluently. These catechists could form the seed-bed from which we would draw new mandarins. Through them we could deliver a population of 40 million souls from the opression to which their present leaders subject them....

.... M.Jaurès wanted to know if it would be easy to raise taxes, of what kind they were, and how they were paid.

Mgr Pellerin replied that tax was of two kinds: capitation of one ligature of sapeke (1 fr. 25) per annum per man - women and children being exempt; and a land tax of one bushel of rice weighing 150 lbs from each hectare or measure of land yielding 25 bushels. The administrative division of the country, which was almost the same as ours, would make tax gathering very easy. Moreover we would find at Hue, in the palace where the king lived alone with his five thousand wives, a treasury which one might reckon at <u>fifty million francs</u>....

.... The president invited Mgr Pellerin to furnish some details on the commercial question.

From the information thereupon given, it appears that the land in Cochinchina is healthy, very fertile, intersected and watered by rivers and numerous canals; that the country furnishes an abundance of silk, sugar, cotton, rice, fruit, vegetables, tobacco, indigo, building timber, teak, ironwood, canelle, oleaginous plants; that coffee grows well, that some rivers are full of gold, that the mountains contain coal,copper, iron and other minerals. The country produces good horses, though of a small breed, pig, beef, buffalo, buck, stag, wild boar and all kinds of fowl. The coast and the rivers are full of fish; alcoholic liquors, arrack and rum, are fermented from rice and sugar cane - in a word the provender is varied, healthy, abundant and very cheap, all important points for an expedition and for a permanent establishment.

The export of these products would be easy, the security of property and the certainty of selling would increase its quantity and number.

As for importation, the people are not industrious at all and they would be prompt to adopt our wines, our cloth, our velvets, our cottons, our ironmongery and a thousand other Parisian products of which they know nothing.

Mgr Pellerin gave details of the decadence of these people in the matter of industry....

After (Pellerin and Chamaison) had retired, the president reiterated to the Commission that if the government decided to mount an expedition it should take care to avoid any plausible objections on the part of England, and he directed the Commission to give attention to this important and difficult point.

M. Cintrat thought that if an expedition to Cochinchina were decided, it would be unwise to raise the matter with England. Such a communication could evoke complaint and cause some wrangling. England would probably take offence at seeing us enter Cochinchina on our own, whereas it was important that we should go in alone. If we notified her of our intentions and then went our way without taking account of her reactions, other difficulties could arise which would need to be avoided. If therefore we did decide on an expedition, it would seem preferable to undertake it without prior notification to the English cabinet, and act resolutely and forthrightly in the matter....

M. Fleury thought that one of the determining motives for our expedition should be the notification given by M. de Montigny who had, after a fashion, warned the Hue government of the likely despatch of an imposing force.

The president thought that for the time being the treaty of 1787, despite being the starting point of our deliberations, would have to be set on one side; that the failure of M. de Montigny had changed the situation and the nature of our rights; that a negotiation would perhaps oblige us to consult and heed other opinions; and that we should guard ourselves against anything which hindered France's independence of action. He thought that we should make this an entirely French business, an affair that was both political and religious whose purpose in exacting retribution for long endured persecution and for the recent murders of our French missionary compatriots, was to form a political establishment which would safeguard all our interests.

The president realised that we would inevitably have to face some comment and expression of surprise from England; and added that the government wanted the opinion of the Commission precisely upon this question of the effects of her presumed attitude. He finished by saying that this affair, and the expedition to China, were matters which should be kept separate. A Cochinchina expedition, if it took place, should depart secretly and as an integral force and that the failure of M. de Montigny had given us full freedom of action....

In sum, the Commission pronounced itself in favour of the establishment of a protectorate as incorporating the conditions most favourable to our interests, and as a measure which could be executed without difficulty.

Captain Jaurès read out a complete military, naval and financial plan for an expedition of 2,600 men drawn up by himself and Admiral Fourichon on the basis of official figures.... (Ministère des Relations Extérieures, Paris. Série - Mémoires et documents: Asie. Volume 27 bis.)

5. **Appendix** to the minutes of the Seventh meeting of the Cochinchina Commission. Paris, 18 May 1857.

The Commission was charged with examining a project submitted to the Emperor, begging him to require the King of Cochinchina (otherwise Annam) to implement a treaty concluded in 1787, by which the reigning king's forebear conceded to France, in exchange for help with troops, ships and munitions, certain territorial footholds together with some commercial privileges.

The Commission needed to examine firstly the question of Rights, that is to say the current validity of the treaty on which French claims are based, a matter which is related to historical facts....

...on the question of Right, the Commission had to admit that from the point of view of common law, the treaty of 1787 was too imperfect a basis for issuing a demand for its strict execution. However, the Commission, unable to disavow the influence that the Bishop of Adran, the French officers, and the help given by Louis XVI had had upon an outcome so profitable to King N'guyen-han and his successors, thought enough could come out of all this to give the treaty of 1787 a certain value. Neither in Europe nor especially in Cochinchina could it be considered excessive that France, by reason of an undoubtedly sound tradition, should issue a request to the descendants of King N'guyen-han to fulfil the obligations contracted by the dynasty, if not towards France, at least to those who personified her and who had fulfilled the intentions of King Louis XVI successfully and to the limit.

CIRCUMSTANCES PROMPTING THE FOUNDATION OF AN ESTABLISHMENT IN COCHINCHINA.
Rights based on facts and on religious and political considerations.

In the light of this situation the Commission wondered if there were no circumstances which could give France a new right, not only to negotiate on the basis of the treaty of 1787, but also, in terms of the question submitted to it for enquiry, to create a base in Cochinchina.

It recognised that now that England had begun making acquisitions in China, there was political opportunity for playing our own role, not in China where we would only encounter jealous rivals and perhaps great difficulties, but in a country a little apart from China, which offered considerable maritime and commercial advantages, where we would encounter neither resistance nor competition, and where we would be spared immediate contact with the English. Moved by the idea that if France had lost her great colonial possessions she should, in favourable circumstances, seek to restore the losses which her great political disasters had cost her, and associate herself with the great movement of progress, civilization and commercial expansion of which China would soon become the theatre, the Commission looked carefully into the circumstances which could justify our establishment in Cochinchina. It recogised that France has duties to fulfil to herself, to religion and to civization, and that since the King of Cochinchina had refused to negotiate treaties, mistreated and killed several of our missionaries, and insulted our officers and recently our Envoy, these circumstances justified our forcible intervention to our own commercial and political profit and for the good of religion. And that to these considerations of special interest should be added others relative to the general political situation: that with all maritime powers possessing territory in the region between India and China, France should not remain in a state of inferiority painful to her dignity and injurious to her commercial prosperity as much as to her right to the share of political influence which she should be enjoying in a region in which great events are in the making. So the Commission finally agreed that if the occupation of one or more footholds in Cochinchina could be carried out without much difficulty, and if this occupation were to be justified to the maritime powers as being provoked by acts akin to those which prompted the expedition to China, and in terms of our traditional relations with Cochinchina, and finally by her recent refusal to treat with us, there would be no reason to expect serious opposition. On the contrary several powers would note with satisfaction France's contribution to the work resulting from the struggle over many years between the West and the Far East.

Survey of our situation
in regard to England.

A single difficulty concerned the Commission: it wondered if the communications which took place between Sir John Bowring and M. de Montigny over the latter's subsequent mission to Cochinchina did not sacrifice some of our freedom of action; and whether, after obtaining the good offices of Sir John Bowring for the conclusion of our treaty with the kings of Siam and asking his cooperation in the negotiation of the treaty with Cochinchina, we could act alone without breaking a kind of implied agreement between England and ourselves to act together in the affairs of the region between India and China.

The Commission examined this point with the same concern which it felt about the well known antipathy of England towards any power wanting to obtain a preponderance in the seas and territories which she has so far been accustomed to dominate and trade with exclusively. The Commission thought that the situation had returned to its original position with Mr. de Montigny's failure, and that we are not bound by Mr. (sic) Bowring's wish for a joint negotiation now that the means of negotiating used by us has failed; that this new failure becomes France's grievance alone and that it is up to us to obtain redress for it on our own; and finally that if England obtains, as is probable, the possession of Chinese posts and territory, we would be all the more justified in taking in Cochinchina the compensation to which we can, after all, lay legitimate claim for all the reasons recounted above....

Commercial interest.

Finally, from the point of view of commercial interest, the Commission was unanimous as to the advantages of occupying a country of 20 million (Mgr Pellerin says more than 20 million), that is fertile, healthy, and contains numerous safe ports. The range of the country's primary produce is considerable and meets the keenly felt needs of our industry: cottons and silks abound in Cochinchina; sugar and rice are cultivated here in great quantity; the mountainous terrain contains forests rich in building timber, in metals, in all the primary and edible products which France needs.

Implementation.

So, in sum, our political and commercial interests coincide in justifying the formation of an establishment in Cochinchina which could assure the exploitation of a country that is as richly endowed as it is happily placed to give us, for the future, a basis for action from which, if necessary, we could follow, usefully and closely, the development of events in China. This way France would accomplish an enterprise both helpful to her interests and in line with the principles of religion and civilization which she seeks to spread throughout the world. The examination of this question has been extended to cover the conditions and means of execution that should be employed to mount the expedition and form an establishment. This plan consists of the despatch of an expedition consisting of, at most, 2,600 men, four mixed transports and an expenditure not exceeding four millions.

Once the establishment is formed it would perhaps have to defend itself in case of war and local revolt. The prospect of revolt seems unlikely and the outcome not dangerous: the people would be easy to subdue; our domination would be a deliverance for them from a hateful yoke and it would not occur to them to resist a regime which brought them all sorts of help. Moreover, one can presume the support of the Christian population, which consists of 300,000 souls according to documents which are already out of date, and 600,000 according to more recent information.

In war it is obvious that our establishment would be open to attack; but we have suggested that one of the first priorities of our establishment should be to devise an easily executed system of defence, the principal towns being almost all situated on rivers in the interior. Tourane itself is easy to fortify in such a way as to resist attack from the sea. Also it has been said that if we confined ourselves to a protectorate, the disadvantages of its possession in time of war would be mitigated. Moreover, while we are responding to the need to acquire Cochinchina, our first concern should not be with the danger of losing it. However, the Commision understood that the solution of this question rests entirely with the Government.

ON THE TYPE OF ESTABLISHMENT TO FOUND IN COCHINCHINA.

It remains to determine the nature of the establishment which we would have to form. Should it be based on total or partial occupation, or should it be a mere protectorate?

Before deciding its opinion on this issue the Commission wanted to hear Father Huc, a China missionary; Mgr Pellerin, Bishop of Biblos, who has spent twelve years in Cochinchina; Mr. Godeaux, attached to the mission of M. de Montigny; and Fr Chamaison, a former missionary in Tonkin (sic).

After listening to these gentlemen... the Commission deliberated, and after deeply considered enquiry concluded:

1/. That we must reject the negotiation of a treaty if it is to be based on the conditions of 1787; that such a treaty would lead to the inconvenience of a partial occupation without the advantages of possession or of a protectorate, and would guarantee neither the future nor the security of the Christian community.

2/. That a total occupation would have the drawback of raising political difficulties, and perhaps some discontent on the part of a people who, however fully subject and sympathetic towards France, would not pass from the sovereignty of a native dynasty into foreign subjection without some regret. But they would cheerfully welcome those who would make use of a position of permanent power to deliver them from intolerable oppression and return them to some prosperity.

3/. That a protectorate would have the advantage of soothing the anxieties of England and of offering us all the profits of formal possession without the drawbacks; that it would secure us the free exploitation of the country, and open it fully to religion and civilisation; that as masters of the government in the person of the king we could better judge how far to allow the interests of other maritime powers a footing; and also that this constitutional model has precedents which can explain and if necessary justify what we wish to do in Cochinchina; and finally that even if policy and commercial interest did not make it a duty, humanity and our religious belief would prevent us from abandoning an enterprise that is to the glory of Christian civilization and upon which hundreds of thousands of Christians who have been compromised by M. de Montigny's mission depend.

Mgr Pellerin and Fr Chamaison have confirmed what the Commission already knew as to the ease with which this enterprise could be carried out, the sympathetic reception which we would receive from the whole population, the fertility of the soil and the richly forested mountains.

Everything would be there on arrival. There is nothing that needs creating. It would be enough to replace a few senior mandarins. The country, as an administration, is akin to that of France, with Prefects, sub-Prefects and Mayors, and we would find our mandarins - that is to say devoted and efficient civil servants - among the Cochinchinese Christians. In a word we could substitute a protectorate for the present regime almost instantly.

The Commission added a few general considerations on the question.

GENERAL CONSIDERATIONS.

Force of circumstances seems to have confined France to the European territories which she possesses today. Hence it would be unacceptable if, denied expansion in Europe, she were forced to restrict her capabilities for action to these narrow confines while other maritime nations try to strengthen their power and resources in regions which Providence seems to have held in reserve to receive the superabundant expansionary capacities of Europe while inspiring true civilization with the legitimate aim of trying to penetrate them.

One can no longer say today that colonies are useless, and, because the dismemberment of colonial France always followed upon continental setbacks, the moment to repair the damage is now, while France holds such an eminent position on the continent. For her power, based on peace, now endows her with means of preserving colonies undreamed of at a time when distance and difficult communications as much as political weakness prevented her from keeping her overseas possessions secure.

It is pertinent to note one fact which will carry considerable weight in the balance of European interests. England seems to have made up her mind to abandon her preponderance in, or even ascendancy, over the republics and Spanish possessions adjoining the United States. The Monroe doctrine carries all before it, but only as long as England can recoup her loss in India, in China and in Australia, thereby absorbing - like the United States - one of the two great branches of world trade. We can only aspire to equality with the great maritime powers and aggrandise and enrich ourselves like them by acquiring territory, productive capacity and primary materials in that part of the world where these will meet our needs naturally.

CONCLUSION.

For all these reasons the Commission firmly concludes that even if our rights are not unchallengeable, there is enough reason in terms of past claims and present grievances to justify what we are going to do to put things straight and place Cochinchina under our control. All things considered, it believes a protectorate is less of a hindrance, keeps our options open and silences those who might be jealous of our setting foot in Cochinchina; that this protectorate, equivalent to a possession, would carry with it no immediate danger; that no one could challenge our right to intervene in a country which our missionaries have already acquired, so to speak, for France, spreading Christianity and the authority of our name at the cost of their own blood, toil and suffering; and that if we allow the maritime powers to share in its trade, their main interest would be satisfied and their opposition, if it exists, counteracted.

So this project is politically quite honourable, useful for religion, and favourable to trade and to the general interests of the country. Circumstances make it opportune,and its execution will be cheap and easy. So it seems to combine all the features which enable us to commend it to the Emperor. (M.R.E. Mémoires et documents: Asie, vol. 27 bis)

6. Count **Walewski,** Minister of Foreign Affairs, to the Emperor **Napoleon III.** Etiolles, 16 July 1857.

I spoke to the Council of Ministers about Cochinchina, but the Cochinchinese question did not find favour with my colleagues.

First of all Fould (Minister of State) told us that he did not know where Cochinchina was, nor what it was; that, moreover, since Your Majesty was referring the matter to the Minister of Finance for examination You were not bothered about it, for the Minister of Finance could scarcely favour an expenditure of six million (sic). As to whether it was opportune or necessary to assemble at least two thousand six hundred invasion troops, Fould declared that that was the least of our concerns.

Billault (Minister of the Interior) on the other hand made three points to show that the opinions of sailors, missionaries and in short anyone who had been there, lacked any common sense and should be ignored.

The sceptical Rouher (Minister of Agriculture, Commerce and Public Works) admitted the commercial and political interest of the scheme, but denied all the rest.

They tried to catch Abbatucci (Minister of Justice) off guard by representing the enterprise as the cover for a murky Jesuit plot.

Rouland (Minister of Education and Religion) made a great effort to avoid taking an initiative or even risk complicity in a question touching the interests of the Church.

Vaillant (Marshal, Minister of War) recognised that there was no question of damaging English interests there because she had none, but simply of seizing a favourable opportunity of bringing off, this time by chance, what England never fails to accomplish routinely.

As for Hamelin, (Admiral, Minister for the Navy) he resorted to quips: he told us that we would find an important outlet there - for our gold.

He cast doubt on the opinions of your delegates, his own assertions,the evidence of the Commission, in fact on everything that formed the basis of Your Majesty's opinion.

That only left me, Sire, to remind the Council that Your Majesty had weighed up the business carefully, and that if everyone's mind was made up it was merely left for me to report the outcome of the discussion to the Emperor. I recalled in conclusion that there was no question of making elaborate preparations to accomplish a fully established plan of conquest, simply a relatively minor expedition whose commander would have flexible instructions which would permit him to respond to circumstances, and which confined him, if our information proved correct, to occupying Tourane to obtain both redress for our grievances and undertakings for the future.

All my colleagues then associated themselves with this explanation and found that, put like that, it was all quite different, and that the question was worth serious examination in these terms. (G. Raindre, 'Papiers inédits du Comte Walewski', Revue France, 1 Mars 1925, pp. 53-54.)

7. Count **Walewski**, Minister of Foreign Affairs, to Admiral **Hamelin**, Minister for the Navy and Colonies. Paris, 25 November 1857.

The Emperor has decided that the Commander-in-Chief of His Majesty's naval station in China shall be instructed to use the means at his disposal to redress our grievances against Cochinchina and establish relations on a favourable footing with that Kingdom. In consequence I hereby notify you of the arrangements which, as far as they concern my department, this general officer should make to achieve both these objectives....

The Emperor has judged that we will prejudice our authority if we wait any longer to take steps for the protection of our interests and the rights of civilisation.

As you know, a Commission composed of officials belonging to both our departments has undertaken a special examination of the circumstances. I have the honour of enclosing its report whose contents and conclusions may profitably be consulted by Admiral Rigault de Genouilly.

As the Commission has amply demonstrated, we would expose ourselves to certain defeat if we simply proposed to renew negotiations for opening relations with the Court of Hue: the many wasted efforts we have already made to do this have shown the necessity of asking Rear-Admiral Rigault de Genouilly to find surer and more promptly efficacious means of achieving our ends. To fulfil the mission which the Emperor has entrusted to his experience and skill, this general officer should, on arriving off the Annamese coast, occupy the bay and territory of Tourane. Once in control of this position he should make enquiry and gather information on the spot, and after weighing the importance of the objective against the odds of success and the probable sacrifice, he should decide whether to attempt to establish a French protectorate over Cochinchina or merely confine himself to concluding a treaty of friendship, commerce and navigation, containing stipulations as to proper compensation for the persecution of our missionaries whose future security must be the object of a formal stipulation. The Emperor intends to leave the choice between these alternatives entirely to the judgement of M. Rigault de Genouilly, who must of necessity confine the scope of his action to the means available for achieving one or other of these results.

If, once in control of Tourane, the Commander-in-Chief of His Imperial Majesty's naval forces decides that he can, with every prospect of success, attempt to establish a protectorate by a solemn and formal treaty, he should not lose sight of the fact that a protectorate necessarily implies our direction of the relations which a protected state may eventually develop with foreign powers, together with favourable fiscal treatment for the traders and navigators of the protecting state, and exclusive jurisdiction by the Agents of the protecting power over its own nationals without distinction and in all matters. M. Rigault de Genouilly should construe and detail these terms in any way that tends to consolidate the authority which France is called upon to excercise in Cochinchina.

If Rear-Admiral Rigault de Genouilly chooses to discard this option and thinks he should confine himself to negotiating and concluding a treaty, he should make every effort to ensure that the agreement conforms to the draft of which a copy is enclosed and which seems to contain all the advantages we could expect from such an arrangement. He may, in any event, modify any of its dispositions which seem to him capable of being recast into a form more advantageous to our interests, or even attenuate its scope if he is forced to do so by circumstances, so long as he does not sacrifice those clauses which are indispensible to the extension of our commerce and for the security of our missionaries.

Finally, whichever course he chooses, whether the recognition of a French protectorate or simply the signature of a treaty, Rear-Admiral Rigault de Genouilly must retain control of Tourane as a guarantee for the full execution of undertakings made by the Annamese government. It is for you, my dear Admiral and Colleague, to give him on this point and on any other matter concerning naval and military operations, any instructions which you consider appropriate..... (M.R.E. Mémoires et documents: Asie. Vol. 27, pp. 330-341)

After the temporary cessation of operations in China following the signature of the first treaty of Tientsin in June 1858, Rear-Admiral Rigault de Genouilly set off for the coast of Vietnam hoping to force the Vietnamese court to sign a treaty by investing the port of Tourane (Da Nang). He took Tourane in September 1858 but was unable to compel the Emperor Tu Duc to come to terms. With his troops becoming progressively enfeebled by cholera and dysentery and lacking shallow draught boats capable of penetrating the interior, Rigault decided not to attempt an assault up river on Hue, the Vietnamese capital. His earliest despatches from Tourane angrily repudiated the Brenier commission's prediction of an easy conquest. He particularly derided the information supplied by Mgr Pellerin **(Doc. 8).** Instead of the 600,000 Christians promised by the bishop, only a handful of volunteers – enough for two small detachments – had presented themselves, with a few more offering their services as guides and porters.

Rigault de Genouilly's problem was his inability to deliver a blow sufficiently decisive to bring the Vietnamese to terms. The missionaries continued to press for an assault on Hue, and failing that, for a campaign in Tonkin in the north, where the claims of the Lê pretenders to the Vietnamese throne were popularly supported and where imperial authority was said to be exceptionally weak. But Rigault de Genouilly judged that fighting conditions in the north, especially during the monsoon season, would be beyond the capabilities of his small force. Instead he settled on a strategy of economic strangulation to force the Hue court to come to terms. He decided to secure control of the provinces of the Mekong delta in the far south – the ricebowl of Vietnam from which the Vietnamese army received the bulk of its food supply **(Doc. 8).** But when attempted, this strategy too, proved an illusory expedient. The Vietnamese forces in Cochinchina were too solidly entrenched for a rapid French conquest of the delta. Far from cutting the Vietnamese rice supply, the French attack stalled in the face of dogged resistance. After burning the delta port of Saigon, Rigault de Genouilly withdrew to Tourane leaving behind a beleaguered garisson under Captain Jauréguiberry. While still reconsidering the possibility of an assault on Hue, Rigault de Genouilly was withdrawn and replaced as commander-in-chief of the China expedition by Vice-Admiral Charner. Since Charner chose to return to the China coast, responsibility for the Cochinchina expedition devolved upon his subordinate, Rear-Admiral Page.

On the advice of Page **(Doc. 9)** Napoleon III decided not to seek the capture of Hue, ordered the French force to retire from Tourane, and nominated the hard-pressed garisson at Saigon as the headquarters of the Vietnam expedition.

The return of Page's superior, Admiral Charner with detachments released by the ending of the war in China, enabled the French to break the seige and blocade of Saigon by defeating a Vietnamese army of 22,000 at the battle of Ky Hoa in February 1861. In a further series of operations culminating in the capture of My Tho, Charner widened the zone of military security around the town. The arrival of Admiral Bonard as Charner's replacement later that year saw the capture of the island of Poulo Condore off Cap St Jacques and the seizure of Vietnamese military strongholds at Bien Hoa, Baria and Vinh Long in the central and eastern provinces of Cochinchina between December 1861 and March 1862.

The campaign as a whole had been regularly interrupted by the French government's efforts to secure a milder treaty than the version projected in Rigault's original orders. The occasional appearance at Tourane or Saigon of Vietnamese negotiators apparently ready to discuss terms sustained French hopes of a settlement. The repeated failure of these dealings was primarily attributed by Rigault, Page **(Doc. 9)** and Charner to the Vietnamese emperor's fear of the revolutionary implications of French demands for religious toleration. The missionary view, succinctly expressed by Bishop Lefebvre, Vicar Apostolic of West Cochinchina, was that the Vietnamese were merely using negotiations to procure tactical delays **(Doc. 10)**. Bishop Lefebvre may have been correct in his surmise. Emperor Tu Duc's decree of November 1860, coming two years after the start of hostilities, shows that, irrespective of the religious issue, the court's defiance, its commitment to full psychological and operational mobilisation, and its determination to resist were still remarkably strong **(Doc. 11)**.

The following year the new naval minister Prosper de Chasseloup-Laubat, accepting the view that the religious question was the major obstacle to a settlement, permitted Admiral Bonard to dilute the provisions of the religious clause in the French draft treaty of 26 February 1861. Chasseloup-Laubat argued that the permanent presence of a French force would be sufficient guarantee for the security of French missionaries: 'It is the French flag which best protects their apostleship.' But even with this clause on religion diluted, Bonard's overtures met with no success until early 1862. The Vietnamese court was finally forced to a composition as much by a renewed upsurge of antidynastic rebellion on behalf of the Lê pretender, Ta Van Phung, in Tonkin as by Bonard's succession of small victories in the eastern provinces of Cochinchina. By offering to remit a portion of captured territory (Vinh Long), Bonard finally obtained Tu Duc's assent to an agreement in June 1862. By this treaty the principle of religious toleration was proclaimed in terse, general terms **(Doc. 12).** The Vietnamese agreed to indemnify France and Spain in instalments, and confirmed French possession of Poulo Condore and the three eastern provinces of Cochinchina - Bien Hoa, Gia Dinh and Dinh Tuong (Mytho). The port of Tourane in Annam was also opened to French and Spanish trade, along with Balat and Quang An on the Tonkin coast.

The treaty of Saigon was a crushing disappointment to the missions, particularly since they continued to believe that the entire expedition had been mounted for the purpose of christianising Vietnam. Article 2 of the treaty signified an end to active persecution but left a range of Christian grievances unresolved. The imperial decalogue, the huan dich thap dieu, a body of moral and social precepts which which was recited in every village four times a year, continued to characterise Christianity as a proscribed cult. Missonaries under Vietnamese jurisdicition were not allowed to buy land or buildings, or preach and worship in public. Their movements were kept under hostile surveillance and the Christian communes (or chrétientés) remained subject to intrusive censuses, enhanced taxation and other forms of administrative pressure. Missionary reaction to the agreement was sufficiently vehement to cause the French authorities considerable apprehension; and Admiral Bonard, concerned to restabilise relations with the Vietnamese court, felt it necessary to restrain disappointed missionaries from provoking further conflict **(Doc. 13).**

For the Vietnamese the treaty of 1862 marks the moment when the Emperor Tu Duc began to part company with the opinion of the the bulk of the Vietnamese elite. Urged on the emperor by the peace party at court led by Phan Thanh Gian, the treaty of 1862 may have been intended as a temporary expedient, and it is possible that Tu Duc was temporising in order to reorganise resistance more effectively. After 1862, while still hampered by the campaign against Ta Van Phung, Tu Duc repeatedly sought a negotiated withdrawal of the French from Cochinchina in terms which suggest that he could not accept the stipulations of the 1862 treaty as final. But the large war party within the mandarinate and the broader educated class - the scholars - were mostly still intent on prolonging resistance and showed impatience with placatory tactics.

Further reading

(Cady, Taboulet and Vo Duc Hanh, as above)

Henri Cordier, **L'expédition de Chine, 1857–8.** (Paris, 1905).

Truong Buu Lam, **Patterns of Vietnamese response to foreign intervention,**
1858–1900. (Yale U.P., New Haven, 1967)
A. Baudrit, 'L'Amiral Rigault de Genouilly', **Bulletin de la Société des**
Etudes Indochinoises, 1933, III, pp. 5–22.
J.W. Cortada, 'Spain and the French invasion of Cochinchina', **The**
Australian Journal of Politics and History, XX, 3. Dec. 1974,
pp. 335–45.
Thomas R. Stanley, 'The diplomacy of imperialism: France and Spain in
Cochinchina, 1858–1863', **Journal of Modern History,** XII, 1940,
pp. 334–356.
L. Pallu de la Barrière, **Histoire de l'expédition de la Cochinchine en**
1861. (Paris, Hachette, 1864.)
G. Taboulet, 'Les débuts de l'Amiral Bonard en Cochinchine', **Bulletin de**
la société des Etudes Indochinoises, II, 1942, pp. 1–18.
Le Marchand de Trigon, 'Le traité de 1862', **Bulletin des Amis du Vieux**
Hué, 1918, pp. 217–252.

Documents

8.   Rear-Admiral **Rigault de Genouilly,** Commander-in-Chief of the
French and Spanish forces in Cochinchina, to Admiral **Hamelin,**
Minister for the Navy and Colonies. Tourane Headquarters, 29
January 1859.

... Dysentery is rife and spreading, and weakens those whom it doesn't
kill. The government was misled about the nature of the enterprise in
Cochinchina. It was represented as being a modest one: it can no
longer be characterised as such. Resources were said to exist which do
not. The disposition of the inhabitants is quite other than has been
predicted. The supposedly enervated and feeble power of the mandarins
is extremely vigorous. Armed troops, far from being non-existent, are
very numerous, and the militia includes all the able-bodied men in the
population. The healthiness of the climate was extolled... but one has
only to see the haggard and fleshless faces of missionaries coming from
different parts of the country to be certain that Tourane is no better
than Hong Kong, and Hong Kong is rightly reputed an unhealthy country.
Re-reading the report of the mixed commission convened at the Ministry
of Foreign Affairs one remains convinced that the question has been
swamped in erroneous assertions, and that the real difficulties were
left in the dark. It seems obvious to me that the interested parties
wanted to commit the government, knowing that once engaged it would be
difficult if not impossible to step back.

No serious land expedition is possible. However short the marches
the healthiest men cannot stand them. For an expedition against Hue to
be sure of success, gunboats of shallow draught such as those which were
sent to the Baltic would be necessary.... And Hue is the crux of the

problem.   I could not take responsibility for the enterprise without the forces I have just mentioned.

It is because I believe strongly in the success of the expedition to Saigon that I am going to that town.   Saigon has a river accessible to our corvettes and our transport ships.   The troops could be disembarked to the point of attack, so they would have no marches to undertake, nor supplies to carry.   This expedition is well within their physical capabilities.   I do not know whether Saigon will be well or poorly defended because missionary reports about this place are so confused and contradictory,   and   I   have thoroughly lost confidence in their information.   However that may be, Saigon is the entrepot for the rice traffic which supplies Hue and the Annamese army, and which should go to the north: in March we will halt the flow of rice.   Knocking out Saigon will also prove to the Annamese government that, while holding Tourane, we are capable of an external operation,   and this will humiliate them before their neighbours the kings of Siam and Cambodia, who detest them and will not be slow to take their chance to regain what has been seized from them.   The Hong Kong merchants were said to be pushing the English authorities to make a demonstration at this spot. It seems to me important to forestall the possible appearance of British troops within our sphere of operations.

On the other hand the government of the Philippines has made its views on Tonkin only too clearly known, and the Spanish Dominicans are proclaiming the conquest of this province as the only serious objective of the expedition.   We should set all such ideas aside.   Tonkin is impossible from two points of view: the first is that in this season of the year when the rivers are low and the silt is exposed, cholera is endemic;   the second is that to reach anywhere important, the troops would have to undertake impossible marches....

What Your Excellency may hardly believe is that this expedition to Saigon, demanded a month ago by Mgr Pellerin, Bishop of Biblos, who has come here merely as an interpreter, became, once decided upon, the subject of this prelate's sharpest and most virulent attacks and recriminations.   Won over by Fr Gaentza, the leader of the Spanish Dominicans who naturally dreams only of Tonkin and wants to carry the Spanish flag there in triumph, His Grace has preached publicly in the officers' mess-rooms against the Commander-in-Chief's plans, against his views, and has announced that I have misunderstood the intentions of the government, that he alone is cognisant of its thinking, and that I shall be brought to account for my conduct.   The situation was getting so tense that I was on the point of arresting Mgr Pellerin and sending him to Hong Kong.

However, before taking a drastic course so damaging to an expedition whose purpose is primarily religious, and which would cause consternation in France, I tried to get his missionary colleagues, particularly Fr Pelletier the divisional almoner, who has some influence over this impetuous prelate, to prevail on him to understand that he has made himself impossible and would be better returning to Hong Kong. After a lot of discussion about his supposed political mission these gentlemen succeeded in overcoming his resistance and he even asked me himself for permission to return to Hong Kong. By his proposals and by his attitude he has caused only confusion and embarrassment among us. He has involved himself in every intrigue and has given no useful service at all. Everything he has said, announced, promised, both here and before the Commission in Paris, has been found on experience to be false, always false, even the commonest things such as the nature of the climate and the direction of the rains, which persist.... Mgr Pellerin wanted not only to witness our operations but to be involved in them, to the point of staging a violent scene when he tried to impose his plans of campaign upon me.... The announcement of Mgr Pellerin's departure has discouraged the meddlings of Colonel Lanzarotte, and there is reason to think that these too were due to the disturbing and restless spirit of Fr Gaentza, who in reality influenced Mgr Pellerin more than he was influenced by him.... (Archives Nationales, Paris. Série BB4, vol. 769.)

9.   Rear-Admiral **Page**, Commander of the Cochinchina expedition, to the Minister for the Navy and Colonies. On board the _Primauguet_, 30 January 1860.

Negotiations have been broken off. So even the Emperor's last, very moderate terms for a certain freedom of conscience and some religious toleration were fruitless...

The real reasons are, as the mandarins know from sure instinct, the following: that the admission of missionaries would cause a popular uprising, a revolution; and that the free entry of English commerce would necessarily bring in its wake the English fleet, the invasion of the country and the destruction of the state...

The province of Saigon is the finest conquest, the most beautiful colony that France can dream of at present... If France rejects what Providence seems to press insistently upon her - not simply a colony but such a rich kingdom, which far from costing her anything will bring her profit - I can only bow my head. The Minister should reflect carefully on this new circumstance, that I am not merely passing on the information of missionaries, traders and tourists: it is your Admiral who is speaking. I know Cochinchina now, its inhabitants and administration. I am going to open the port of Saigon and the English flag will make use of it: if the French flag is withdrawn, the British flag will replace it...

Our Cochinchina expedition will have dealt a death blow to the King of Annam's authority over the provinces of the prosperous south. Who will reap the reward of this rich inheritance? Will it be France? Will it be England? I can say with certainty it will be one or the other. (M.R.E. Mémoires et documents: Asie. Vol. 27)

10. Mgr **Lefevre**, Bishop of Hauropolis, Vicar Apostolic of West Cochinchina, to the **Directors** of the Société des Missions Etrangères in Paris. Saigon, 2 February 1860.

... It is a wholly religious expedition and, please God, the government and its principal agents have no other purpose than to serve Providence. Unfortunately all those who were set at the head of this expedition are people who regard religion as a very secondary matter, barely worth their attention. When they have a service to ask of us, which only happens when they can't avoid it, they do not fail to say that they have come here for us, and when something happens like the death of an officer they are sure to say that he is the latest sacrifice for the missionaries. But when it is we who come to ask them for the smallest service on behalf of the church they declare roundly that they haven't come here for that; and they beguile themselves with listening to propositions from the Annamese mandarin about a peace treaty in order to give the lie to missionaries who keep repeating to them that no pact is possible with people who are totally on the side of the Devil. We put up with this and await the time when experience teaches them what we cannot make them understand. After all the lengthy negotiations and representations, not only of Admiral Rigault at Tourane, but of Commander Jauréguiberry here at Saigon, and of Admiral Page here again recently, they are beginning to feel disillusioned. Page flatters himself on being a cleverer negotiator than his predecessors, but he has been no more successful than they. Today it has become so obvious that he has lost his way that he has regretfully refused to prolong the armistice and has left this very morning with ten boats to attack the enemy's forts. The government was very much mistaken to send too few troops. It is true that despite the small number of soldiers it would have been possible and profitable to attack the town of Hue from the start; but for lack of adequate knowledge of the locality and with little confidence in the opinions and information offered by

Mgr Pellerin, they were excessively timid and did very little of what should have been done.... But now that the small number of troops despatched has been halved by disease and mortality, it would be impossible to attack the royal capital: it has been considerably strengthened while all this time was being wasted. (Archives de la Société des Missions Etrangères. Vol. 755, (Cochinchine Occidentale), 1845-1866. No. 148)

11. The Emperor **Tu Duc**. Decree of 4 November 1860.

Supreme Ordinance.

These tenacious overseas barbarians, like a swarm of disgusting insects, are accustomed to act underhandedly and perversely. After troubling Tourane they molested and partitioned Gia Dinh over a year ago. I have frequently sent military commanders to forestall this cruel race, and we have halted and surrounded them near our capital. These barbarians are incomparably skilled in warfare. Before bringing upset and disorder they sued for peace. If they had shown respect and observed convention we would not have hesitated to open relations with them, and we would, in the end, have bestowed Da Nang (Tourane) upon them, which is what they wanted, so that our soldiers could enjoy a break from their operations and hardships. But I have seen clearly that it is not possible to put faith in people with the hearts of dogs and goats. Accordingly, I have ordered all those who inhabit the coast to build forts and defence works, and to guard them carefully with a view to repelling by force the barbarian attempt to invade us. At present these men, who only seek for gain, are becoming more and more demanding.

If we gave in to their desires what would happen to this kingdom and what hope would be left to us after that? So I have taken care to multiply our means of expelling them to cut short their exorbitant demands. But see how, frustrated in their hopes, they show more and more evidence of bad faith. Little by little they search about for a flaw in the strategy of the Governor of Quang Nam in order to destroy his army by a sudden, violent assault. The feverish aggression which makes the barbarians behave like this is really execrable. I am at the moment ordering everyone in charge of openings to the sea or other defence points wheresoever, to double their vigilance so that nothing will need to be redone....

What scholar or common man is there who does not grind his teeth with rage, or who, thinking of eating meat still wastes time taking off the skin? That is why it is not a matter of waiting for a particular man, or a particular morning or evening before acting! Is there anyone who, in return for living off the fruits of the earth, will not recollect his loyalties and obligations? I am ordering every provincial official to do everything to mobilize the scholars and common folk in his district to rise up and resist. It is necessary now to abandon the language of ambiguity and equivocation. Only when there is nothing to fear can each man rejoice, plough, cultivate, look after his own and help his neighbour. But in the face of imminent danger one must rally round and support the whole community to enable it to find ways of resisting and repelling danger. Moreover, now is the time that all men of experience and ability in the country should make best use of their gifts. Any village of ten houses will certainly contain at least one man who inspires confidence. How in those thatched huts can any merit or distinction remain unnoticed...? How can it be discerned?

We order all authorities other than the communal authorities, from Prefects and Sub-Prefects of the first (sic)$^{(1)}$ and second rank downwards, to investigate and find any who can come up with good strategies for destroying and expelling these mad barbarians. The local official will report to me, and I will make the selection. However, those who send the information should be careful not to exhaust the couriers unnecessarily. I am also notifying both civil and military mandarins in all districts that anyone who is really intelligent, efficient and practical, and who possesses the will and the means to destroy these brigands, should ask to follow the military officials; and the local officials should situate him properly, first by finding out which corps such a man should belong to, then by recording his name. The six southern provinces with Binh Thuan and Khanh Hoa will obey the military commander of Gia Dinh. All the provinces between Binh Dinh and Quang Nam must obey the commander of Quang Nam. Thua Thien and all the northern provinces down to the capital will conform to the instruction issued for repelling attack. Afterwards all those who have won the country's gratitude will be praised by the Court and generously compensated for their work. (From L. Pallu, Histoire de l'expédition de Cochinchine en 1861, pp. 291-3.)

(1). Prefects were not mandarins of the first Rank.

12.   **Treaty of Saigon**, 5 June 1862.

Article 1. Henceforth there will be perpetual peace between the Emperor of the French and the Queen of Spain on the one hand, and the King of

Annam on the other. Friendship will be complete and likewise perpetual between the subjects of the three nations wherever they find themselves.

Article 2. The subjects of the two nations of France and Spain may practice Christian worship in the kingdom of Annam, and subjects of this kingdom, without distinction, who are desirous of embracing and following the Christian religion, may do so freely and without constraint; but no one who does not wish to become Christian will be forced to do so.... **(L. de Reinach, Recueil des traités conclus par la France en Extrême-Orient (1684-1902). (Paris, 1902), p. 94)**

13. Rear-Admiral **Bonard,** first Governor of Cochinchina, to Marquis **Prosper de Chasseloup-Laubat,** Minister for the Navy and Colonies. Saigon, 24 July 1862.

Now that the situation of our Cochinchina expedition has been completely changed by the treaty concluded with the king of Annam, I think it my duty to give you an indication of what may be its consequences and what difficulties might arise from it, to forewarn and forearm Your Excellency against exaggerations which it will certainly provoke from those who intend to push the implications of the peace beyond the limits in which I think it good policy to confine it.

I am sure that the government, convinced for the moment that it cannot prevail against our cannons and that its own ruin would result from open hostilities, has sacrificed the ceded provinces to save the rest of Annam.

There are good grounds for hoping that if we keep to this programme with prudence and firmness, there will arise only difficulties of detail which we could settle locally without deploying much of our force.

The most serious complications might arise in regard to the missionaries if, for religious reasons, we support them in political activities designed to overthrow the established monarch, activities into which, unfortunately many of them allow themselves to be drawn too often, and which all of them are far from renouncing. We should confine ourselves to assuring them of a just degree of protection. It would be dangerous to support their interference, for they would become veritable troublemakers and not religious martyrs.

This assessment, Minister, is based on the following considerations. No one can deny that the war in Cochinchina was brought about to a great extent by appeals from French and Spanish missionaries who complained of the unjust persecutions to which they were subjected by the Hue government.

Now this is what the spirit and constitution of these religious are like.

Cochinchina is divided into several dioceses each managed by a bishop. All these prelates receive - perhaps, but I do not know - common direction from the main Society in Europe. But each in his own diocese does more or less as he likes, and is very jealous of the least interference by his neighbour in the vast district over which he has been appointed spiritual governor. All of them nurse the ambition of returning to the time when the Bishop of Adran was the real sovereign of Cochinchina, a time when nothing could be done without his advice and permission.

To achieve this goal the means employed are these. Some bishops, finding that the dynastic successors to Gia Long were obstructing their aspirations, have questioned their legitimacy and have sought to put forward a candidate who, if he overthrew the reigning dynasty, could offer them a better guarantee of achieving their ends.

The pretext invoked by one group to achieve the usurpation is that Gia Long designated his second son rather than his first to succeed him.

This is a familiar custom in the Far East, and the French missionaries of Lower Cochinchina espoused this idea and aligned themselves with the supporters of Gia Long's eldest son. Those from the part of Annam around Hue, a province between Tonkin properly speaking and Cochinchina, went further in contesting the legitimacy of the ruling branch: they regard Gia Long himself as a usurper and produced a pretender from among the descendants of the Lê dynasty whose kings, losing the will to rule were dethroned by one of their court chamberlains.

I think that the Spanish Dominicans, even more ardent and fanatical than the French missionaries, belong to this party.

A descendant of the Lê family, perhaps real, perhaps false, was found in a Chinese convent; and after overwhelming him with humiliations to the point of making him a monastic porter, these ecclesiastical radicals have made him a candidate for the imperial purple, feeling sure of their influence over him if they succeed in their projects.

In the present state of things, and according to the words and actions of these different categories of missionaries, it seems obvious to me that the majority of French missionaries in French Cochinchina tend to fall short of their pretended political aims: they hope that the influence conferred by our occupation and possession, though it does not match the absolute power enjoyed by the Bishop of Adran, will enable them to excercise a substantial preponderance. They seem happy with this for the present.

So one can expect, with firmness and caution, to force them to confine themselves to the reasonable limits of the influence which they claim.

The missionaries of the area around Hue are far from approving of this measure of conciliation. Some of them agree to it passively, but the majority tend to show both in speech and action that they have not abandoned their radical notions. The Bishop and some of his most intelligent colleagues, submitting to my advice not to start anything, are still in Cochinchina and have promised to behave prudently when they go back to their dioceses once peace is more fully established.

But the more enthusiastic have left already, making the Sign of the Cross and in the company of some veritable bandits. Grave complications could arise from this if we are not exceptionally cautious in responding to their demands for protection as French citizens and Christians, which they will certainly make once they have involved themselves in political activity against my express advice.

As for the Spanish Dominicans who are generally situated in upper Tonkin, they are even more unmanageable: zealous and fanatical to the last degree, a fair number of them are ex-guerillas and Carlists who have taken up the sabre and musket with the crucifix and are committed body and soul to the revolt afflicting Tonkin.

I think that the difficulties which they are creating for the government of Her Catholic Majesty require that the treaty concluded with Hue by France and Spain conjointly should be executed by each power separately or it will lose all the material benefit which ought to stem from a frank commitment to peace.... (M.R.E. Mémoires et documents: Asie. Vol.28, pp. 85-8)

The Cochinchina expedition had been a far more difficult and expensive enterprise than was first anticipated. Reluctant to see French military and financial commitments escalate, Napoleon III had given only grudging assent to the occupation of the three eastern provinces in 1861. Over the following three years, supporters of the French invasion found themselves repeatedly forced to defend the existence and development of the new colony against its detractors.

They had a difficult case to make. In its first years as a French possession Cochinchina showed little revenue return, and the defence of the eastern provinces surrounding Saigon remained an indefinite burden on the French domestic budget. Moreover, in France the influence of an important segment of political support for the colony had declined. The clerical lobby, active in provoking intervention in 1857-8, could no longer claim the emperor's consideration on behalf of missionary interests after 1860. For Napoleon III's opposition to papal policy in the Italian war of 1859 had led the French Catholic hierarchy to articulate the first public criticisms of the Bonaparte regime. The Church thereby sacrificed much of its political leverage. As the broader financial and foreign policy difficulties of his regime accumulated, the emperor viewed the problems of the new acquisition especially its continuing tendency to expand - with increasing hesitancy. In the early 1860s the survival of French Cochinchina as colony remained in doubt.

However, the colony's interests were powerfully and successfully defended within the Council of Ministers by Prosper de Chasseloup-Laubat, Naval Minister for an unusually long duration (2 November 1860 - 20 January 1867). A convinced and dedicated exponent of its commercial and strategic potentials, **(Doc. 14)** Chasseloup-Laubat faced major problems in renewing the French Emperor's commitment to Cochinchina.

The protectoral treaty with Cambodia, 1863.

Chasseloup-Laubat's first crisis occurred in 1863 when Admiral Bonard's successor, Admiral de la Grandière (1863-8) seized an unexpected chance to expand the zone of French influence northwards by establishing protectorate over Cambodia. Without reference to Paris, La Grandière had responded promptly to an appeal from King Norodom of Cambodia for help in resisting political intimidation by Siam. A secret treaty mediated in part by Mgr Miche, Vicar Apostolic of Cambodia, was concluded on 11 August 1863. It pledged French support for King Norodom in return for France's assumption of full control over Cambodia's foreign relations. When the treaty was referred to the Quai d'Orsay for ratification the French Foreign Minister, Drouyn de Lluys, pressed for its repudiation on the grounds that the British would find a French protectorate over Cambodia highly objectionable. However, Chasseloup-Laubat obtained Napoleon III's reluctant endorsement of the agreement by urging the importance of a Cambodian protectorate for the commercial viability as well as for the strategic defence of Cochinchina. The naval minister took the opportunity to paint a glowing picture of Cochinchina's future prospects; and among other arguments extolling its importance he laid considerable stress on the political value of Cochinchina's potential for mass christianisation **(Doc. 15)**.

Chasseloup-Laubat's defence of the Cambodian agreement had been a relatively brief tussle. Later in 1863 a more serious and prolonged challenge to Chasseloup-Laubat's policy of developing the colony of Cochinchina occurred when the Vietnamese court despatched an embassy to Paris with an offer of 85 million francs, payable in instalments, for the retrocession of the three eastern provinces of Cochinchina to Vietnamese sovereignty. Since Napoleon III himself found the financial terms particularly alluring, the proposal became a threat to the very retention of the new possession. With the Mexico adventure now running into expensive difficulties and a policy of general budgetary retrenchment in operation, the prospect of immediate financial returns from this costly asiatic acquisition could not be ignored. On 5 November 1863 Captain Aubaret was authorised by the Quai d'Orsay to negotiate a treaty of retrocession at Hue. Hence Chasseloup-Laubat lost ground in the early stages of official deliberations on the Vietnamese offer. At the court of Hue, Tu Duc's appeasement policy seemed on the point of vindication.

While negotiations were in train Emperor Tu Duc sought to maximise the chances of obtaining French ratification by proclaiming a drastic adjustment in official policy towards Christians in July 1864 **(Doc. 16)**. His decree, cast in homiletic form, no longer characterised Christianity as a heterodox and subversive practice; and it enjoined Christians themselves to show filial obedience to imperial authority.

Tu Duc's conciliatory proclamation failed to stave off opposition to retrocession from missionary bishops in Annam, however, and Admiral de la Grandière took up their arguments in his own vigorous denunciation of the retrocession project. When Aubaret's draft treaty was remitted to Paris for consideration, Chasseloup-Laubat drew from the Admiral's despatch in composing his own lengthy memorandum urging its rejection. The naval minister again rehearsed the potentials of the colony at length, making much of the argument that the abandonment of France's Vietnamese collaborators - Christians in particular - would inevitably expose them to savage reprisals **(Doc. 17)**. With support in the Cabinet from Victor Duruy, currently Napoleon III's most influential adviser and an ardent enthusiast for colonial expansion, Chasseloup-Laubat finally secured the rejection of Aubaret's treaty of retrocession, and the Vietnamese offer lapsed for the time being.

French conquest of the western provinces of Cochinchina. June 1867.

Popular Vietnamese reactions to the failure of Emperor Tu Duc's retrocession gambit helped to provoke France's final expansionary move in the Mekong delta. The collapse of Tu-Duc's negotiating strategy weakened the Hue court's capacity to restrain a growing movement of guerilla activity against French territory organised by Vietnamese irregulars from bases in the western provinces of Cochinchina. These provinces - An Giang, Vinh Long and Ha Tien - were still under Vietnamese authority. But, situated between the French protectorate of Cambodia and the French zone of occupation, they were cut off from the rest of Vietnam and were especially vulnerable to French absorbtion. Vietnamese guerilla infiltration of the French colony in 1866-7 drew a devastating French response. Admiral de la Grandière launched a brisk and bloodless seizure in June 1867 and the western provinces succumbed to French domination. With the French government now committed to the retention of eastern Cochinchina, Admiral de la Grandière had little difficulty in obtaining retrospective sanction from Paris for the occupation of the western provinces. France now controlled the whole of Cochinchina.

Scholar-led popular reactions to French seizure of the western provinces, 1867-1869.

Technically the treaty of 1862 was now inoperative; but the French move did not provoke a resumption of hostilities by the Vietnamese. Although the loss of the western provinces prompted a wave of patriotic fury **(Doc. 18)** in Tonkin and Annam, the Vietnamese court remained placatory in its dealings with the French. Tu Duc at first deferred to popular fulminations against the French by issuing an edict of general mobilisation. But the gesture was merely a palliative to appease patriotic opinion, and no further action followed. The · tragic divergence between a scholar elite passionate for a policy of continued resistance and a Vietnamese monarchy doggedly pursuing a face-saving settlement with France became increasingly evident from the end of the

1860s. The court held back from attacking French territory, but it could not restrain the scholar elite in parts of rural Vietnam from expressing its antagonism. Missionaries and their Christian converts in Annam-Tonkin found themselves at the focus of the ensuing crisis, scattered as they were among the mass of the population. In the vicariate of South Tonkin thirty Christian communes were reported destroyed in 1867-8 by groups under scholar leadership, and at Hue a similar pogrom was threatened. In 1869-70 missionaries in Tonkin were still reporting harassment from bands of Vietnamese villagers under the leadership of scholars, a class which the emperor needed to manage with increasing circumspection **(Doc. 19)**.

Tu Duc's final attempts to regain sovereignty over Cochinchina. The negotiations of 1868.

But Tu Duc refused to be deflected from his continuing hopes for a negotiated retrocession. The vital issue for a monarch insecure in his claim to the throne was to regain at least nominal sovereignty over the lost provinces. Averse to those court mandarins and provincial officials and scholars who were pressing for the resumption of hostilities, Tu Duc proposed to La Grandière in 1868 a form of protectoral arrangement by which sovereignty and administrative control of all six provinces would be retained by Vietnam in return for an annual rental to France amounting to the entire annual surplus of Cochinchina's revenues. Once more Tu Duc appears to have considered it important to accomodate the missionary interest. Victims of popular antagonism, missionaries were evidently destined to become major beneficiaries of treaty and legal arrangements between the two governments **(Doc. 21)**. According to the report of the French administration's interpreter, phu Ba Tuong the Vietnamese ambassadors in the talks of 1868 at Saigon seemed prepared to accept a wideranging clause on religious worship drafted by La Grandière. This clause elaborated new guarantees for the missions and even permitted the entry of qualified Christians into Vietnamese higher administration **(Doc. 20)**. However, Vietnamese counter-proposals on other issues were rejected by the French, and negotiations had already lapsed by 1870, when the Franco-Prussian war began. The war democratised the French policymaking apparatus and altered the financial and diplomatic postulates of French policy in the East beyond all previous recognition. The collapse of the Second Empire therefore marks a major hiatus in Franco-Vietnamese political dealings.

Further reading

P. Cultru, **Histoire de la Cochinchine française des origines à 1883.** (Paris, Challamel, 1910)

P. Vial, **Les premières années de la Cochinchine française.** 2 vols. (Paris, 1874).

C. Meyniard, **Le Second Empire en Indochine. (Siam, Cambodge, Annam.) L'ouverture du Siam au commerce et la convention de Cambodge.** (Paris, 1891).

Milton E. Osborne, **The French presence in Cochinchina and Cambodia. Rule and response (1859-1905).** (Cornell, 1969).

Ngo Dinh Diem, Nguyen Dinh Hoc et Tran Xuan Toan, 'L'ambassade de Phan Tan Gian (1863-4)', **Bulletin des Amis du Vieux Hué,** VI, (1919); VIII, 3-4, (1921).

A. Delvaux, 'L'ambassade de Phan Tan Gian en 1863 d'après les documents français', **Bulletin des Amis du Vieux Hué,** XIII, 1, (1926).

P. Boudet, 'Chasseloup-Laubat et la politique coloniale du Second Empire. Le traité de 1864 entre l'Annam et la France'. **Bulletin de la Société des Etudes Indochinoises,** n.s. XXII, 2, 1947, pp. 17-74.

A. Duchêne, **Un ministre trop oublié: Chasseloup-Laubat.** (Paris, 1932).

K. Stanley Thomson, 'France in Cochinchina: the question of retrocession, 1862-65', **Far Eastern Quarterly,** VI, 4, Aug. 1947, pp. 364-378.

Nguyen The Anh, 'Traditionalisme et réformisme à la cour de Hué dans la seconde moitié du XIXe siècle,' in P. Brocheux (ed.), **Histoire de l'Asie du Sud-Est: Révoltes, Réformes, Révolutions.** (Presses Universitaires de Lille, 1981).

Documents

14. Marquis **de Chasseloup-Laubat,** Minister for the Navy and Colonies, to a private correspondent. Paris, 14 February 1862.

...We have just enjoyed some fairly considerable successes in Cochinchina. I have a great responsibility there, I feel. I want to create for my country a veritable empire in the Far East. I want our Christian civilisation to have in its new conquest a formidable establishment from which she can radiate (her influence) over all those territories. A lot of people doubt the possibility of achieving this; and others are bothered by the cost. So I have some big hurdles to surmount, but I have faith: I proceed as if certain of success....

(J. Delabre, <u>Le Marquis P. de Chasseloup-Laubat, 1805-1873.</u> (Paris, Challamel,1873) p.130)

15.   Marquis **de Chasseloup–Laubat,** Minister for the Navy and Colonies, to **Drouyn de Lluys,** Minister for Foreign Affairs. Paris, 10 December 1863.

I know that the policy of France has wider and more immediate interests which occupy the greater part of your time; but permit me to tell you that in my eyes either the Emperor's government must take the utmost care to study what Providence has given us in Cochinchina or we must abandon all means of creating an influence for our country in the Far East. We have found an admirable position.   We have before us populations which accept Christianity.   We have beneath our feet the most fertile territories on earth.   The remaining traces of an exceptionally advanced civilisation show us what riches our own civilisation may create there.   In a word, if we know how to make use of it, if we do not compromise the future, French influence must one day radiate throughout the East from here.
The Dutch have Java.   But the Dutch have not Christianised the Javanese and they will perhaps see more dangers arise there than they expect.   The English in India are every day exposed to the revolts which a fanatical Islam can inspire and which can only be suppressed by force.   In the Philippines the Spanish, who knew how to attract the inhabitants to their religion, hold sway without apprehension.   As for us, we are dealing with populations of which some had embraced Christianity even before we began our conquest.   That was an important factor in our success.   So let us seek to found an establishment which might become yet another fine page in the history of a fine reign....
(Archives Nationales. Section Outremer, Paris. Indochine (Anciens Fonds) Carton 37, Dossier B30(1).)

16.   The Emperor **Tu Duc.**   Royal Edict concerning Christians. July 1864.

While still young and unworthy we inherited power from our royal ancestors and became father and mother to ten thousand peoples.   That is why we consider them all our children.   Sometimes children are good, though when they are bad it is the duty of parents to chastise them. But after chastisement they must be loved as much as before.   They are only beaten to show them their faults and how to correct them.
For their part children should love eachother, behave themselves and avoid quarrelling for fear of displeasing their parents.   It is all the more important that they do not give way to annoyance at paternal correction.   That is how all our people should behave.   Our own duty

is to make clear to them our opinions.

Some years ago the French and Spanish arrived unexpectedly in our land. Our people had to remain under arms and undergo all manner of stress in mounting a resistance to them. The mandarins then told them: 'The Christians called in the French because they were unable to practise their religion freely.' They also said that many of the leaders of this religion had contact with the Europeans and helped them as much as they could. That is why the mandarins proclaimed: 'To avoid all misfortune the Christians should be scattered and imprisoned.'

Poorly informed and present at discussions where opinion was divided, we were unable to disentangle the truth. Not knowing what course to pursue, we were forced to follow the advice of the mandarins and take harsh measures. We had only one object in mind: to restrain our people and ward off the evils which fate had in store. We hoped that the Christians would change their behaviour, or that their innocence would be recognised sooner or later, and that then, better informed, we could put right the damage done to them. Could we ever abandon our paternal feeling and let our people perish? No. And here is proof of it.

There were some mandarins who were calling for the massacre of all the Christians, and others who, from the beginning, instantly demanded their dispersal and imprisonment in the non-Christian villages. Our paternal heart could not face such measures. For three or four years we put off their implementation. Finally we took the mildest course, that of dispersal. See how merciful we were! The facts speak for themselves But who would believe it! Those who carried out our will exceeded their orders. There were some moderate mandarins, but there were others who were cruel and tormented our people exceedingly, to our great displeasure and in contravention of our wishes. When peace was established, we made haste to return the Christians to their homes so that they could resume their work and follow the dictates of their religion. We were harsh or merciful according to circumstance. There is a proverb which says: 'If the King is mistaken his subjects should not be annoyed with him: a father's unkindness does not justify a son's ingratitude.' All the more so when a father has no evil intent.

We thought hitherto that our people were at peace, that everyone was going about his own business or following his profession equably, that there were no factions, that our wishes would be fulfilled, and that our people were beginning to enjoy the fruits of peace and prosperity. But believe it or not factions still abound.

One of them, confident of support, has become arrogant and contemplates revenge: it has brought public indignation down on itself and this shows how short-sighted its members are.

The other group hates it and persists in harassing it in every way. This is also reprehensible. And so everyone is following opposing tendencies and this is tearing our entrails apart. How can such blindness be explained? Some people say: 'It is the Christians who have called in the Europeans.' I do not know whether this is a true assertion. All the same the Christians are our subjects: they should follow the religion of the State, and if they do not how can they be free from fault? That is why those who had power before, even though they exceeded it, should not be the objects of vengeance. Here are the reasons.

There was cause to suspect the Christians, for their unusual practices differed from those of the Nation. Our other subjects were obliged to make war and bear all the burden of it for four or five years. They lost their fathers, their children and their possessions. Dragged away from their work they experienced all manner of calamities. How could one compensate them for such losses? Only the Christians escaped suffering.

So you Christians, your position was certainly very awkward, but you always persevered in following your religion while remaining true to the laws of the kingdom, and for this we can only congratulate you. We will remember it always. All the more reason for us to treat Christian and pagan (sic) alike after showing mercy to the former and setting them free. You should be extremely grateful to us. If you are hiding any thoughts of vengeance in your hearts you will not be showing obedience to the King: if you do not obey the King you will be outlaws; if you become outlaws, how can you call yourselves Christians? Clearly you should set all rancour aside: vengeance is not permissible. Strive only to become perfect so that your prayers may be more easily answered.

You should pay no heed to glory or shame, fortune or misfortune, or the various ups and downs of life.

The duty of everyone under the sun is to obey a king. Inferiors should obey superiors, the small should defer to the great. That is what good sense tells us, and that is what has always been done down to the present century. Men should keep their eyes fixed on the paths followed by their ancestors. Be like the fox who dies with his head bowed over the earth of his forefathers.

As for those who contemplate revolt, they should know that not everyone can achieve power. Out of a hundred or a thousand only one or two succeed. There can never be honours enough for all. That is the normal course of things. We are telling you truths which anyone can understand. Why not reflect on them instead of giving way to arrogance? Not only is it impermissible to demonstrate openly, but it is bad to store up evil intentions in your heart. If you stifle your anger and

75

allow none of it to show, no one will treat you with suspicion.   But if you murmur loudly you will be acting provocatively.   You have suffered much: if you murmur you will lose the merit of those sufferings.

From what we have just said it is easy to see that we in no way condemn the Christian religion, but only arrogance and revenge.   If we avoid being carried away by arrogance we will not provoke others to anger.   If we do not provoke others to anger we can live in peace with them.   If we live in peace we can follow our religion in full freedom, because religion does not contradict moral principles.   What is there then to fear? (Quoted in Fr P. Bernard to Mgr Sohier. Hue, 17 September 1864. Published in <u>Annales de la Propagation de la Foi</u>, vol. XXXVII, 1865, pp. 325-7.)

17.   Marquis **de Chasseloup–Laubat,** Minister for the Navy and Colonies,
to the Emperor **Napoleon III.** Paris, 4 November 1864.

... As far as Christian worship is concerned the new (Aubaret draft) treaty adds nothing to what was stipulated by the treaty of 1862, which authorised the Annamese to embrace Christianity; but a new article, full of pitfalls, seems to have been inserted by Hue to narrow interpretation of the scope of this stipulation.

While on the one hand the treaty allows the Annamese to become Christians, on the other it punishes Annamese who violate the laws of the kingdom, and among these laws is one forbidding them to become Christians: it has been the pretext for persecutions in defiance of the treaty of 1862....

And what of the people who have loyally accepted our domination, who have denounced, attacked and killed the organisers of revolt, and who despite requests from Hue have remained faithful to us and still give us proofs of their devotion today?   In giving them back to Hue we should be abandoning them to the revenge of the mandarins who will have become more influential than ever.

'Believe me', the admiral wrote on 30 May, 'the bad faith and cruelty of the mandarins towards the Christians and those who have served us will soon force us to recommence the war and resume an appropriate role for France in Cochinchina....'

One cannot hide the fact that we undertake a grave responsibility in abandoning those people whom we have compromised, some of whom were or became Christians and who have proved their genuine devotion to us.

Lastly, if, one day, following the violations of this treaty and outrages which our occupation will have to suffer we have to resume this war, what support may we hope for from people who who will have th right to reproach us for all the evils which we will have caused them twice over, first by our conquest and then by our withdrawal? (Quoted in P. Vial, Les premières années de la Cochinchine, colonie française. (Paris. Challamel ainé, 1874). p. 299)

18. Mgr **Sohier**, Bishop of Gadara, Vicar Apostolic of North Cochinchina, to an unknown correspondent. Hue, 28 December 1867.

We have come through the moment of crisis which I have been dreading for so long, the occupation of the three provinces surrounding the French colony. The admiral has seized them without firing a shot.

When the news arrived at the capital it caused a considerable sensation and high indignation. It happened at exactly the time when the scholars - approximately 5000 of them - had converged on the capital for the examinations. They uttered the most fearsome threats. It was rumoured that they were going to kill us, to burn us alive, and the days for killing us were fixed. They said that it was better to die than accept such shame, but that before restarting the war it was necessary to get rid of the Christians who were in league with the French, and that they should be dispersed, imprisoned and once again massacred. The scholars circulated anonymous letters accusing the king and mandarins of cowardice for letting the kingdom be partitioned. As a concession to these patriots an edict was issued which authorised the levying of a sizeable national guard from all the villages, and the forging of arms. The Christians, who were excluded from this national guard, believed that all these arms were intended for use against them... but, thank God, our panic has abated. Little by little the fulmination has died down and no harm has come to us.... (Georges Taboulet, La Geste Française en Indochine, (Paris, Maisonneuve, 1955). Vol.II, p. 516. From the original in the archives of the bishopric of Hue, copied by Father Delvaux.)

19. Mgr **Theurel**, Bishop of Acanthe, Vicar Apostolic of West Tonkin, to the **Directors** of the S.M.E. West Tonkin, 18 February 1868.

I have already mentioned how little sympathy the scholars have for association with the French or for religious liberty. This repugnance has merely grown since the occupation of the three provinces of Lower Cochinchina. On pretext of preparing for a dogged resistance against a possible French invasion of Tonkin they have formed a mobile militia commanded by retired mandarins in the provinces of Nam Dinh, Ninh Binh and elsewhere.

At Nam Dinh this militia, composed of four regiments, has as its general an old scholar-mandarin who was previously in disgrace for some unknown misdemeanor, and who is now highly influential because his former pupils include practically all the graduands and graduates of the province and even some serving mandarins. The militia I refer to has never had government authorisation, although the mandarins have delivered mandates to the village chiefs to raise money. Some mandarins have told me that an order has even been sent from the capital to dissolve it, but it has been ignored.

As we expected, the scholars have sent these formations organised for brigandage against us and against the Christians. They were due to attack us in the village of Ke-Trinh when I was in Nam Dinh province. The plan failed on two occasions at the moment of attack because the bandits were afraid of being the weaker force. But after being strengthened with a few new companies, they fell on Ke-Trinh two days after we left, on 14 January, in the middle of the night: first they pillaged everywhere, then they burned the church, the convent and thirty Christian houses.... The sacked village asked for justice and compensation. I myself wrote three letters to beg the mandarins to deliver legal judgement on the affair and to warn them of greater evils to come if they did not put down this brigandage. But the mandarins simply folded their arms and replied that they awaited orders from the capital, orders which would not arrive. Meantime heads showed themselves again and the scholars took to the countryside like bandits. A dozen Christian hamlets were sacked. In order to avoid visitation from the plunderers, the pagan inhabitants of several villages razed the houses of Christians and put the latter to flight....

Are the mandarins inactive from weakness or through complicity? We will not know with any precision, but we think it likely to be a mixture of both. Nonetheless, seeing the scale on which the affair is developing the Prefect of Nam Dinh recently called the scholars together and exhorted them to stop or at least suspend their devastations until the Hue court makes known its views on the Ke Trinh affair. From a week ago the scenes of pillage have slackened off. Christian hamlets remaining to us in the Nam Dinh territory, not including those destroyed, contain about thirteen thousand souls: they await the fate of the rest. The scholars are openly advertising their intentions: 'Death to Europeans! Death to native priests! Destroy Christianity!'....

What will the Annamese government do? We do not expect it to mount a vigorous repression or give impartial justice because it has to deal carefully with the factious elements whose leaders belong to the class from which the civil mandarins are drawn. We would be happy to obtain some satisfaction and modest compensation for damages. As for French government intervention, this would only sharpen hostility at the moment and worsen our predicament. (A.P.F., vol.XL, 1868, pp. 441-6)

20. Report of the phu **Ba Tuong,** Prefect of Saigon, on the treaty discussions between Admiral **de la Grandière,** Governor of Cochin-china, and the hiep-bien-dai-hoc-si (Chancellor) **Tran Tien Thanh,** Ambassador from Hue. Second session, 29 January 1868.

... Article III (of the draft proposed by the French).
The Chinese text of this article states:
'The (Christian) religion may be freely taught; the practices of (Christian) worship will be authorised; Christians will have the right to build churches in any place; they shall be admitted to the competitive examinations for scholars, and to the mandarinate, and to public office; and they may not be persecuted. Christian mandarins may not be forced to do anything contrary to the doctrines of the Christian religion'.

The hiep-bien raised various objections relating to the characters used in drafting the Annamese text. These are as follows:
The expression 'tuy-xu' (anywhere, in any place) used in relation to the right accorded to Christians to build churches may give rise to interpretations which appeared dangerous to the hiep-bien. The Annamese government wished to reserve certain lands, certain places, and forbid anyone to construct anything there. So the hiep-bien asked for the suppression of the two characters 'tuy-xu'.... (T)he admiral agreed to remove the characters 'tuy-xu', which should simply be regarded as a discrepancy in translation.

The hiep-bien considered insufficiently explicit the phrase of the Chinese text which deals with the admission of Christians to the scholars' and mandarins' examinations. This phrase could, according to him, give rise to ambiguity.... The Annamese government wants to...allow Christians to enter public office, but that did not mean that they should be let in unconditionally. They must conform to present regulations; they will have, like anyone else, the right to sit the examinations.... Their faith will be no obstacle to their careers, but their character as Christians must not give them the right of admission to public positions if they are not capable of filling them competantly.

The Chinese text says that Christian mandarins may not be forced to do things contrary to the doctrines of the Christian religion. The

<u>hiep-bien</u> finds this expression far too vague. He asks us to be specific: that if, by 'things contrary to', one means Buddhist or Confucian practice, there should be formal mention of this in the Chinese text; or else we ought to enumerate all the things contrary to the Christian religion which Christians, even when they are mandarins, must not be forced upon any pretext to do.

The admiral declared that the purpose which this stipulation has in view is simply to prevent mandarins who are Christians from being forced to take part in pagan ceremonies, such as the practices and salutations of the Phat cult, by reason of their official responsibilities. This clause, as well as the one relative to the admission of Christians to the examinations and to the mandarinate have been prompted by the admiral's wish to see freedom of worship established in Annam as it is in France. The two draft clauses which the <u>hiep-bien</u> had just criticised tended solely to ensure the achievement of this purpose, and can signify no more than this, nor give rise in the future to any false interpretation.... (Quoted in P. Vial, <u>Les premières années de la Cochinchine</u>, pp. 206-9)

21.　　Note by Admiral **de la Grandière** to Admiral **Rigault de Genouilly**, Minister for the Navy and Colonies. April 1870.

One can get some idea of the King's opinion of us and that of the mandarins by what can be seen today situated at the doors of the Hue citadel: the big orphanage founded in 1867 by Mgr Sohier contains a hundred and seventy children, and princes are sent there to be educated and looked after when they are ill. At an awkward moment, when the mission was short of money because communications with its Procurator at Hong Kong were uncertain due to piracy, it was authorised to borrow sixty thousand francs from the royal treasury as an interest-free loan. This act shows beyond doubt a real and almost unbelievable improvement, especially if one recalls that a few years ago Tu Duc issued three edicts putting a price on Mgr Sohier's head....

Since the attitude of the Hue court towards us has changed, we should make use of this to extend our influence and our commercial relations and for this purpose ask for a treaty agreement opening all our ports in reciprocity with those of the kingdom of Annam. (A.O.M. Aix. Indochine, G.G 10,581. Quoted in full in Vo Duc Hanh, <u>La Place du Catholicism dans les Relations entre la France et le Vietnam de 1851 à 1870</u>. (Leiden, E.J. Brill, 1969). Vol. II, pp. 248-9)

II

MISSIONARIES AND GOVERNMENT IN FRENCH COCHINCHINA UNDER THE ADMIRALS, 1859-1879.

II A   MISSIONARY ADJUSTMENT TO THE NEW ORDER, 1859-1870.

The first decade of crisis and improvisation in Cochinchina was an acrimonious one for relations between the colonial administration and the mission. Friction reflected disappointed missionary expectations of unstinting official support on the one side, and official annoyance at missionary indiscipline and political and administrative interference on the other. These initial tensions were transitory. They reflected a mutual incomprehension of roles and marked stages in adjustment to a working relationship. Both mission and French colonial administration pursued fundamentally congruent objectives, but both began with absurdly high hopes of mutual collaboration.

From Paris, the Minister for the Colonies, Chasseloup-Laubat, taking the peaceful Spanish Philippines as a model, looked to mass christianisation as a prescription for political stability in the long term. (See supra **Doc. 15**). Not only was the total christianisation of Cochinchina seen as a political necessity **(Doc. 22)**, it was also thought of as a real possibility. This had always been the fundamental aim of the mission itself.

But in Cochinchina the mission was small in the early 1860s. Mass conversion was still only a distant prospect, and meantime the French garrison and administration were under constant threat from insurrection. The first years of cooperation between the mission and the colonial authorities were characterised by short term emergency measures taken in the context of shifting experiments in administrative control. Friction was frequent because interdependence was closer than suited either mission or colonial authorities. Naval governors, deeply disappointed at the lack of mass Christian support promised by Bishop Pellerin and his colleagues, reproached the mission for mendacity and lack of support. Such Christian Vietnamese collaborators as the French administration could find or steal from the missions lacked the training and social authority to make adequate substitutes for those higher Vietnamese officials who had fled to Annam, in the wake of French conquest. Missionary grievances against French officialdom were even more acute. When the naval administration began inducing the mission's Vietnamese catechists and priests to abandon their religious duties and act as interpreters and minor officials, the mission's vital reserve of intermediaries was seriously depleted **(Docs. 23, 29)**. This had adverse effects upon its ability to minister to the Christian communes. Missionaries also jibbed at the effect which the materialistic culture of the new colony - and particularly the disorderly morals of its French personnel - was having upon their Vietnamese converts **(Doc. 25)**. Hitherto, Vietnamese converts had regarded Catholicism as a specifically French, not a universal, religion. The scandalous behaviour of the French fleet and administration eroded the idealised view of French civilisation hitherto purveyed by missionaries and was said to be destroying the religious commitment of Vietnamese converts. At the level of local administration, the reportedly anticlerical attitude and behaviour of the Inspection des affaires indigènes particularly galled missionaries and demoralised their proselytes **(Docs. 28, 29)**. Local officials for their part complained frequently that missionaries were usurping the functions of civil administration in seeking unwarrantable autonomy for their communes and infringing a variety of newly imposed regulations.

Admiral de la Grandière's governorship (1863-1868) should have marked a departure from the pattern of recrimination which had developed from the first moment of Admiral Rigault de Genouilly's arrival in 1858. For the new governor departed from the embattled attitude of his predecessors and declared himself to be wholly committed to the furtherance of the mission's aims and work **(Doc. 26)**. He had been ordered by Chasseloup-Laubat 'not to tolerate scandals which would, beyond any doubt, alienate the native populations' who should 'not be exposed to acts of which Christian civilisation disapproves.'$^{(1)}$ On arrival in Cochinchina de la Grandière accordingly sought to enforce higher standards of personal morality in the administration. Initially gratified, missionaries soon became sceptical of the effectiveness of this policy and complaints at the behaviour of French officials continued to accumulate. Meantime de la Grandière's autocratic style, his obdurate resistance to Bishop Miche's unsolicited advice, and particularly his threat to break the monopoly of the Société des Missions Etrangères by inviting new missionary orders to set up in Cochinchina, drew pained denunciation from the mission hierarchy **(Doc. 31)**.

Some of these grievances had disappeared by the end of the 1860s, along with the absurder hopes and expectations of the initial period of conquest. In the 1870s the mission of West Cochinchina was to find itself not only materially supported by the government of the colony, but still exempted from direct administrative controls. Disputes continued to arise between missionaries and colonial administrators over issues such as the objectives of colonial education and the security of missionary property rights. But such disputes produced no movement on the part of colonial administration to force missionaries into formal dependence upon government. They were resolved by decisions which, while continuing to acknowledge the mission's independent role, implied the abandonment of any serious effort at collaboration.

(1). P. de Chasseloup-Laubat to Admiral de la Grandière, 17 June 1863. (S.H.M. Vincennes. Papiers La Roncière le Noury, GG²/81.)

Further reading

P. Cultru, **Histoire de la Cochinchine française, des origines à 1883.** (Paris, Challamel, 1910).
M. Osborne, **The French presence in Cochinchina and Cambodia. Rule and response (1859-1905).** (Cornell, 1969).
G. Francis (Francis Garnier), **La Cochinchine française en 1864.** (Paris, E.Dentu, 1865.)
L.E. Louvet, **La Cochinchine religieuse.** (2 vols. Paris, Challamel, 1885).
J.B. Piolet, **Les missions catholiques françaises au XIXe siècle.** (6 vols. Paris, A.Colin).
E. Luro, **Le pays d'Annam. Etude sur l'organisation politique et sociale des annamites.** (Paris, 1878).
J. Silvestre, **L'empire d'Annam et le peuple annamite.** (Paris, 1889).
P. Vial, **Les premières années de la Cochinchine française.** (2 vols. Paris, 1874).

Documents

22. Captain **Gabriel Aubaret,** interpreter and political counsellor to Admiral **Bonard,** Governor of Cochinchina. Note on Cochinchina, c.1862-3.

We are absolutely convinced that Cochinchina will never really belong to us until it is Christianised. That is the surest and most durable of all means of conquest.... On the subject of the Christian religion, we must be particularly careful to avoid appearing to give special protection to those who embrace this religion. The Annamese character is so accustomed to dissimulation that we would be exposing ourselves to some serious miscalculations. Best to leave the missionaries a free hand and never raise the religious question in administrative matters....(Service Historique de la Marine, Vincennes. Papiers La Roncière le Noury, GG² Carton 81.)

23. Fr **Barou,** a missionary in West Cochinchina, to the **Directors** of the S.M.E. Saigon, 3 March 1860.

It is rather difficult living under the aegis of a protestant, apostate, masonic senior commander (Jauréguiberry) who behaves like a fanatic, crosses us at every opportunity, (and) speaks only of replacing us with (Protestant) ministers from Singapore.... Are the subordinate officers made of any better metal? Alas! Jauréguiberry himself avows that he was not able to move back the occupation posts because he had no officers on whose morality he could rely. We think the same. Mass is attended only by the Annamese and Spanish when we say it regularly on Sundays in the French and Spanish camps respectively.... On Sundays officers and soldiers get plenty of leave to go anywhere on land, but these furloughs are employed in pursuing women.... It is a veritable calamity, for all this seems to be sanctioned by the authorities.... They speak of the licentiousness of the camps, but that of a fleet as demoralised as ours is certainly worse.... We had language teachers who had graduated from the Penang seminary: they have been brutally and forcibly taken away from us to become interpreters on board the ships. Some of these thay (catechists) have already succumbed to corruption in such an ambience, and the remainder are in danger of becoming equally debauched. (A.S.M.E. Vol. 755, (Cochinchine Occidentale), 1845-1866. No. 151)

24. Fr **Wibaux,** Provicar of the vicariate of West Cochinchina, to Rear-Admiral **de la Grandière,** Governor of Cochinchina. Saigon, 30 December 1863.

It is difficult to give even an approximate estimate of the present number of Christians in the three provinces (of French Cochinchina). The war has caused so much dislocation that our old registers are useless, and the recent massacre of a sizeable number of the faithful at Bien Hoa and Baria has notably diminished the number of Christians. However, their number has increased since French occupation: in the last three years we have obtained 3000 conversions. I think, however, that one can, without exaggeration, estimate 10,000 Christians for the province of Saigon, 7000 for Bien Hoa and about 5000 for My Tho.

Twenty missionaries scattered around seventeen different posts are responsible for administering these Christians... The number of our native priests has declined since the beginning of the war. Three were martyred shortly before the French occupation, and you know of the unfortunate defections which have deprived us of the help of many

others.   However, eight of them are left, have remained faithful and
still perform their ministry in the three provinces. (A.O.M. Aix.
Indochine, Amiraux 12,203)

25.   Fr **Wibaux**, Provicar of the vicariate of West Cochinchina, to
the **Directors** of the S.M.E. Saigon, 25 January 1863.

...Of the twenty-one (Annamese) priests whom we had four years ago, only
six (sic) remain.   Even among these, many are not without reproach.
The others are a scandal, they indulge in trade and worse.... The sight
of our civilisation, trade with Europeans, the ease with which they
discover more attractive paths opening before them as a result of our
very training and education, all this is making them leave us one after
the other....(A.S.M.E. Vol. 755, (Cochinchine Occidentale), 1845-1866.
No. 297)

26.   Fr **Wibaux**, Provicar of the vicariate of West Cochinchina, to
Father **Osouf**, Sub-Procurator at Hong Kong. Saigon, 28 March 1863.

...Now Fr Pernot (Procurator for Receipts, Paris) writes to me that
Admiral de la Grandière is a believing and practising (Catholic), a man
who goes to mass every day when in France. The Emperor has chosen him
with the avowed intention of inaugurating a new policy in Cochinchina.
This admiral has selected a staff of believing and practising
(Catholics). The new admiral has sent his aide de camp to tell the
gentlemen in the Seminary that his plan is to work for the conversion of
pagans - or rather to help us to do so with all his might; to induce
respect for morality, a matter over which he is resolved to be ruthless
in sending back to France any officer who gives cause for scandal; and
to deal with the Annamese in ways which will help them turn back to
us.... (A.S.M.E. Vol. 755, (Cochinchine Occidentale), 1845-1866. No.
309)

27.   Fr **Wibaux**, Provicar of the vicariate of West Cochinchina, to M.
Ansart, aide de camp to Rear-Admiral **Bonard**, Governor of
Cochinchina. Saigon, 16 January 1863.

You ask me, Sir, what one is to think of the rumours circulating about
the antipathy of the native clergy towards us, and especially towards
the missionaries.   As can easily be imagined, the deserters whom I have

referred to are neither our friends nor yours. One of them whom our officers had shocked very deeply, whose patriotism and antipathy towards the French had been extolled and applauded (he is currently under an interdict), has done a lot to give his colleagues a reputation which they did not deserve. The fifty or sixty native priests martyred in the missions since the beginning of the war were persecuted not simply as Christians but as friends of France.

Nevertheless it certainly cannot be denied that there are certain racial antipathies - quite natural in a conquered people - and which even the Christians, even certain of our priests, still feel; but I know some who are completely devoted and are French at heart.... (A.O.M. Aix. Indochine, Amiraux, 12,185.)

28.   Fr **Thiriet,** teacher at the Saigon seminary, to Father **Albrand,** Superior of the S.M.E.   Saigon, 20 April 1866.

The conduct of the government is far from persuading the Annamese to convert to Christianity. It is not the fault of the admiral exactly - he is at least of the faith, even if lacking in good works - but of his agents who do everything and are mostly miscreants who persecute the Christian religion in a more malicious and disastrous way than the mandarins.... (A.S.M.E. Vol. 755, (Cochinchine Occidentale), 1845-1866. No. 552)

29.   Fr **Colombert,** Procurator and private secretary to the bishop of West Cochinchina, to Fr **Péan,** a director of the S.M.E. Saigon, 18 August 1868.

Most of our Inspectors hate (the Annamese Christians) and calumniate them. All too often in these gentlemen's eyes being a Christian is enough to merit a suspension of rights. It is notorious that Christians have never betrayed the French cause, but (the French) are training up pagans - even ex-rebels who will take the first opportunity to betray them, as in the Rach Gia incident...

I take no pleasure in seeing Christians enter the administration: it causes them to turn hostile towards us, gives them opportunities for oppressing their own people, and this in turn exposes them to prosecution and exile. Best not to say this too loudly because not all missionaries agree, and the government would be hurt by such language.... (A.S.M.E. Vol.756, (Cochinchine Occidentale), 1867-1889. No. 85)

30. Marquis **de Chasseloup-Laubat**, Minister for the Navy, to Rear-Admiral **de la Grandière**, Governor of Cochinchina. Paris, 18 November 1864.

Finally I come to the question of the clergy. It is a truly difficult problem whether to found an episcopate as in Réunion or the Antilles. We would have to negotiate with Rome, and then afterwards we will no longer be masters in our own house. Missionaries are often enfants terribles, but we could perhaps begin by introducing religious orders. We have nothing to fear from these in Cochinchina, I imagine. Anyhow, I will send you friars and nuns. This carries no risk, and there is something so sublime in their devotion that it is truly good to give them a share in our conquest, which seems to be undertaken more on behalf of Christian than of French civilisation, though only France is capable of managing it. (S.H.M. Vincennes. Papiers La Roncière le Noury. GG²/81.)

31. Mgr. **Miche**, Bishop of Dansara and Vicar Apostolic of West Cochinchina, to Fr **Pernot**, Procurator of the S.M.E. Saigon, 27 September 1864.

(La Grandière) plagues us in every way. He has some religion but understands it poorly and this leads him to try to impose his will on the Church, to make it serve him rather than submitting himself to her. He wants another sort of clergy together with the Sisters of Charity or even the good sisters of St Paul who are having the most astonishing success everywhere in hospital and orphanage work.... (A.S.M.E. Vol. 758, (Cochinchine Occidentale), 1843-1880. No. 44)

32. Bishop **Miche** to Fr **Pernot**. Saigon, 29 April 1865.

(If La Grandière brings in the Jesuits and Lazarists)...I will give them no power without an express order from Rome, and if this happens I will give them more than power, I will give them my place and will go and pitch my tent elsewhere... (A.S.M.E. Vol. 758, (Cochinchine Occidentale), (1843-1880). No. 56.)

Despite many disappointed expectations, naval governors of Cochinchina continued to proclaim the need for mass christianisation in conformity with the general policy laid down by Chasseloup-Laubat, and gave considerable, if somewhat miscellaneous, material support to the mission throughout the period of naval rule.

This support was optional. The Cochinchina administration had no constitutional obligations towards the colony's clergy. Following the cooling in relations between the Bonapartist regime and the Catholic church after 1860, Chasseloup-Laubat had recoiled from extending to Cochinchina the concordatory arrangements with the Papacy which prevailed in France and in some of her older colonies. He was anxious to prevent papal interference in any part of the colony's administration **(Doc. 33)**. A concordatory agreement would have placed the naval government in Cochinchina under an obligation to create an episcopate and a parochial system staffed by secular clergy. The Ministry of Cults could nominate clergy to posts but the Vatican retained the right of appointment. Regular intrusions from papal bureaucracy would ensue. There were material disadvantages too, in a contractual relationship. While the Concordat certainly gave civil authorities a high degree of control over secular clergy, it also obliged the state to pay their salaries and meet the entire cost of maintaining clerical establishments. In the colony this obligation would have diverted scarce resources from missionary enterprises in order to support a purely parochial facility for which there could be little demand until a sizeable proportion of the population had become christianised.

By avoiding an extension of the Concordat to Cochinchina naval authorities retained full administrative initiative in deploying their budget for religious affairs. The most significant element of official assistance was the allocation of annual salaries to all French missionaries: in 1864 40,000 frs was allocated from the colony's budget, a subsidy which had risen to 145,000 frs by 1879. Under La Grandière only French priests received salaries; but later governors acknowledged the mission's need to train and provide for Vietnamese catechists and priests. By 1879 the annual allocation had been expanded to cover not only the salaries of Vietnamese teachers in fifty-four parish schools, but the needs of the Saigon seminary, the construction and upkeep of chapels and churches, and the pay of twenty-six Vietnamese priests at the rate of $9 (piastres) or 45 frs per month. Relieving the mission of the salary burden made possible the diversion of its own resources into wider activities. By 1879 the mission's additional annual grant of approximately 55,000 frs from the Propaganda Fide and its revenues from property and alms of approximately 22,000 frs were being spent on the two seminaries at Saigon and Cai Nhum , on a school for catechists, on the mission press, on monasteries for Vietnamese Carmelite clergy dependent on the mission, on some of the costs of travel, on the building of new churches and chapels, and on assistance to some Christian communes **(Doc. 36).** During the 1860s, a decade of high inflation consequent upon French conquest, the authorities also tempered the persisting financial difficulties of the mission by measures of indirect support, some of which remained in force until the 1900s: some land tax and customs exemptions, free postal facilities, free travel on the shipping of the Messageries Maritimes, and free treatment in the colony's hospitals. The Pauline nursing sisters received free rations, and individual missionaries were encouraged to supplement their meagre incomes by part-time employment as teachers, almoners and interpreters on government contracts. A small number of ex gratia contributions were occasionally made for the construction of churches and schools. Building works of exceptional scope also received exceptional support: in the mid 1870s the authorities were to contribute heavily towards the building of Saigon cathedral, which cost 2,500,000 frs to construct.

However, some of the administration's incidental subventions to clergy were not primarily intended to serve the interests of religion, but to encourage mission-organised social assistance. Support for the clergy's social work was the most cost-effective means of meeting one of the ackowledged responsibilities of government. The sheer cheapness and availability of clerical personnel determined support for the orphanages and Vietnamese schools of the Ste Enfance, and for the native hospitals and dispensaries of the nursing order of St Paul de Chartres. Clerical teaching contracts for the colony's non-denominational schools cost approximately a quarter of of the cost of contracts demanded by lay staff, who were usually of low quality and difficult to obtain; and lay nursing staff for some hospitals - especially leprosaria - were almost impossible to secure.

In the early 1870s a reaction began to set in among higher administrators against the terms on which material support for the mission was to continue. While still plainly keen to promote christianisation,**(Docs 34, 37)** naval governors began to balk at some of the implications. In particular, they began to show hostility to the apparent growth of the mission as a property holder. By 1874 the vicariate of West Cochinchina had acquired the reputation, almost certainly unmerited, of being rich in land and property, of benefitting immoderately and improperly from the legacies and gifts of its converts, and of entrenching its economic power through the process of mortmain **(Doc. 35).** If a concordatory agreement were ever to be contemplated, mission property holdings, especially in the Christian communes, would have to be bought out by the colonial government on behalf of a secular parochial clergy. This prospect seemed to pose a particularly daunting problem for the future. While acknowledging that the mission's proselytism had to have an economic basis, the administration began to emphasise the distinction between the communal property of the Vietnamese chrétientés, which it wished to treat as autonomously held and was happy to see increase, and the property of the Société des Missions Etrangères, which it wished to restrain from growing further (Doc. 38). For its own purposes the mission sought maximum flexibility in deploying resources, and made light of the distinction between commune and mission property. At least two naval governors, Admiral Krantz and Admiral Duperré, tried to exploit the irregularity of some of the mission's property titles to prevent the patrimony of the mission growing any further. In this they met strong resistance from the mission, and by 1878 Bishop Colombert had succeeded in convincing the pro-clerical Admiral Lafont that rumours of the mission's immoderate wealth were exaggerated. The Bishop obtained sanction for procedures to regularise mission property titles, essentially to shield the mission from the hostility of any future administration. The thorny issue of the distinction between commune and mission property was finally resolved in the mission's favour: the mission was empowered to continue accepting legacies of under 10,000 frs - enough to meet nearly all cases - without reference to higher authority (Doc. 39).

Set entirely within the boundaries of French colonial dominion, West Cochinchina alone of all the Apostolic Vicariates in Vietnam benefitted from regular official support. Vicariates in Cambodia, Annam and Tonkin were left to fend for themselves on what support they could generate locally and on what the Propaganda Fide could provide. By 1879, when the regime of the admiral-governors ended, the mission in West Cochinchina was in a more advantageous position in its relations with the colonial administration than it would ever be again. The mission was unhampered by the administrative controls which a concordatory agreement would have given to the colonial government. It benefited nonetheless from financial arrangements to which, as a non-concordatory clergy, it was not constitutionally entitled. It remained directly dependent on the papacy, which meant, in practice, that it enjoyed a high degree of canonical autonomy. Its personnel was extensively employed in official schools and hospitals, and enjoyed a range of modest privileges and gratuities. Finally, all its property titles had been re-registered and its power to dispose of the property of Christian communes had been confirmed.

Further reading

(Taboulet and Osborne as above.)

L. Louvet, **La Cochinchine religieuse.** 2 vols. (Paris, Challamel, 1885).
P. Vial, **La Cochinchine française. Rapport sur la situation de la colonie, ses institutions et ses finances.** (Saigon, 1867).
G. Taboulet, 'Les débuts de l'Amiral Bonard en Cochinchine'. **Bulletin de la Société des Etudes Indochinoises,** 1942, II, pp. 1-18.
Un officier de Marine (Admiral-Governor Dupré), 'La Cochinchine en 1872', **Revue des Deux Mondes,** 1 janv. 1872, pp. 204-18.

Documents

33. Marquis de **Chasseloup-Laubat,** Minister for the Navy, to Rear-Admiral de la **Grandière,** Governor of Cochinchina. Paris, 18 November, 1864.

Finally I come to the question of the clergy. It is a truly difficult problem whether to found a (Concordatory, salaried) episcopate as in Réunion or the Antilles. We would have to negotiate with Rome, and then afterwards we will no longer be masters in our own house. Missionaries are often enfants terribles, but we could perhaps begin by introducing religious orders....
(S.H.M. Vincennes. Papiers La Roncière le Noury. GG^2/81.)

34. Rear-Admiral **Dupré,** Governor of Cochinchina, to Vice-Admiral **Pothuau,** Minister for the Navy.

Survey of the situation of French Cochinchina, 1 February 1873.

...Worship.

The great, indeed the immense majority of the population is Buddhist, at least nominally, for there prevails among the Annamese a considerable religious indifference. Its practices tend towards superstitious credulity rather than towards religious inspiration. The educated adhere to the doctrines of Confucius and the Chinese philosophers. The only practice universally honoured is ancestor-worship.

By contrast the Cambodians remaining in our territories are very attached to Buddhism, and very few of their villages lack a Buddhist temple. According to the missionaries they are obstinately hostile to the preaching of Christianity which makes, by contrast, some inroads into the Annamese population. The number of native Catholics (in Cochinchina) is about 45,000. The European clergy belong to the order of the Missions Etrangères, which is supported by a native clergy whose contribution is found very useful.

At the time of Annamese domination the missionaries, despite the dangers to which they were too often exposed, enjoyed considerable independence in their communities, whose supreme magistrates they were. A few difficulties arose and some resistance during the early years of our occupation when it became necessary to appoint lay magistrates over Christian as well as non-Christian villages. All that has been settled now, thanks to the elightened cooperation of Mgr Miche, Bishop of Lower (recte West) Cochinchina, and Fr Aussoleil, Apostolic Provicar of the Cambodia mission, both of whom understand what the role of a clergy can and should be in a colony.

The administration supports and subsidises the clergy. To the resources furnished by the Propaganda Fide it adds an allowance of 112,000 frs for the personnel and about 40,000 frs for the erection and maintenance of chapels. And justly so, for even if this clergy is not subjected to the rules of the Concordat and enjoys completely independent scope, the colony has an interest in seeing an increase in the number of Christians. They are assuredly loyal and have everything to fear from the return of Annam's dominination.

The example of the nearby Spanish colony (the Philippines) could arouse fears that the independence of a clergy which will recruit more and more among the natives might eventually become a danger to our authority. But in any event this danger would only occur when the great majority of the population is is converted, and that day is still far off. Until then our political interest, in conformity with the interests of civilisation and of the subject peoples themselves, compels us to favour missionary efforts as much as we can, short of violating the general population's sentiments and beliefs. (A.N.S.O.M. Paris. Indochine (A.F.) 5/A20 (14))

35. Rear-Admiral **Krantz,** Governor of Cochinchina to Admiral Marquis **Montaignac de Chauvances,** Minister for the Navy and Colonies. Saigon, 8 September 1874.

I have the honour to notify you of a problem which frequently occurs in this colony.

Native Christians sometimes make gifts of fixed property either while alive or at the moment of death, to the Christian commune to which they belong, to the missionary in their locality, or to the bishop in charge of their mission.

The donors certainly have the right to dispose of their property as they wish; but generally they do not know the difference that exists between a gift made to their community and a gift made by name to the missionary of their choice or to the bishop. The effect of this ignorance is that very often donors who believed that they were conferring part of their property upon their Christian commune have seen the same property fall into the hands of the mission once it has left the ownership of the donor.

...Since the titles of such properties are Annamese titles which have no legal standing until they are replaced by French titles, the mission has frequently asked the colonial administration for their transfer, or else quite simply to be registered on the village tax rolls in place of the donors. Sometimes these requests for the transfer of title have been refused because the donors expressed a clear intention to give the property to the Christians of their community and not to the mission....

The number of properties which the Cochinchina mission holds by such means is considerable, and tends to grow daily. The moment is not far off when it will be the proprietor of all the properties devoted to the excercise of worship within the colony.

This, Minister, is the state of things to which I wish to draw your attention. For if the missionaries come to be replaced by a regular (parochial) clergy, the colony will be obliged to buy the relevent property off the mission at a very high price. I think that to avoid all future difficulty, French title should be established in the name of the Christian community of the village in which the property is situated. (A.N.S.O.M. Paris. Indochine, (A.F.) 28bis/A90(3).)

36. Mgr **Colombert,** Bishop of Samostate, Vicar Apostolic of West Cochinchina, to Rear-Admiral **Duperré,** governor of Cochinchina. Saigon, 23 July 1875.

I have the honour to enclose a copy of the reports which I have sent to the Directorate of the Interior for the purposes of the 1876 budget. I request permission, at the same time, to describe the requirements and the resources of the mission of Western Cochinchina. Public opinion considers that the mission has a large revenue; and I know that the rumour of this opinion reached one of your predecessors. I think it helpful to give you exact details on this point. There are in Saigon some ecclesiastical properties belonging to the Cambodia and Binh Dinh missions. The mission in Western Cochinchina only possesses a few gardens and rice fields whose annual revenue varies between $1000 (1) and $1100. The other resources consist of a subsidy from the Propaganda Fide of less than $3000 a year, and Lenten alms to a figure of between $300 and $400. The total annual resources of the mission, apart from the government's contribution, is never more than $4,500. With this sum the mission has to meet the following expenses: a supplement for the Saigon seminary, $2000; travel expenses for sick missionaries returning to Europe (in '72 and '73 this expenditure reached $1200); supplements to native priests for their chapels; expenses for the chapels of new priests ($100 each); assistance for churches, chapels and presbyteries (according to availability); upkeep of the press and establishment at Tan Dinh; foundation of schools etc. You can easily appreciate, Governor, that our modest revenues are quickly exhausted and that the mission has no other important resources except for the government subsidy. To put it plainly, if the mission's operations have expanded in the last 15 years, it is essentially thanks to particular gifts or personal sacrifices on the part of missionaries themselves. Thus, the seminary is the work of M. Eveillard (sic); the little seminary at Cai Nhum (the gift of Mgr Miche); the Taberd school was founded by M. Kerlay.... (A.S.M.E. Vol.758, (Cochinchine Occidentale, 1843-1880). No.417)

(1)   One piastre ($) was worth a little over 4 frs during the 1870s.

37.   Rear Admiral **Duperré**, Governor of Cochinchina, to Mgr **Colombert**, Bishop of Samostate, Vicar Apostolic of West Cochinchina. Saigon, 29 July 1875.

...I know that the support of the administration has always been, and still is, indispensible for the accomplishment of the work it is undertaking, and Your Grace may be assured that I truly appreciate the need to subsidize such eminently useful expenditures handsomely.... (A.S.M.E. Vol.758, (Cochinchine Occidentale, 1843-1880). No.418)

38. Rear-Admiral **Duperré,** Governor of Cochinchina.

Note on the organisation of worship. (1877)

... I have named a commission to regularise a totally abnormal situation concerning the property of the mission. The mission has the right to possess property, but only on certain conditions which have not always been observed. Moreover, scattered all over Cochinchina are church properties, properties belonging to Christian communes (chrétientés) and gifts of property made to particular missionaries. All this is illegal. For there are no (regularly constituted) parishes, no vestry councils, and missionaries cannot possess property in the name of the mission. So all titles of property ownership must be looked into and regularised, without of course our intending to resort to any confiscations. It has been agreed that we would shut our eyes to the means by which possession has been obtained and to the value of contents, but we will be insisting that all legal formalities be observed in future. We will therefore be settling matters legally in a way that is profitable to the mission. The emotions aroused by this enquiry will have the effect of showing the Annamese that we are not indifferent to the behaviour of the missionaries. That will encourage those among (the Christians) who were half disposed to imitate their forefathers by aggrandising the mission's property holdings, to resist doing so.... (A.O.M. Aix. Amiraux, 10,273)

39. Mgr **Colombert,** Bishop of Samostate, Vicar Apostolic of West Cochinchina, to the **Directors** of the S.M.E. Saigon, 7 August 1877.

I want to raise a rather important material question with you. Until now it has been a source of awkwardness and conflict which I want very much to bring to an end. I speak of the matter of Ecclesiastical Property in the colony, and of the altogether special situation we occupy in relation to French legal practice.

In short, we are faced with the question of principle at the moment. Have we the right to own property in Cochinchina ? Common sense and reason would say: Yes. But our French jurists say: No.

Hence our precarious situation, which it is interesting to compare with the situation of our missions in Annam's territories. These, in virtue of a treaty imposed by France, have the right of ownership and effectively do possess (property).

In examining the letters patent of the Society we find that these do not stipulate that each mission has a separate legal identity: they stipulate that the Paris office alone has this right in French territory. So, in the eyes of French law, the West Cochinchina mission has no right to possess its own property. But if perforce, and by a somewhat irregular exception the Vicar Apostolic may nominally possess the mission's property, which is after all a part of a legally recognised society, there is still another category of property, that of the Christian communes. The communes have absolutely no legal existence, since parishes and vestries neither are, nor can be, established in the present state of the colony.

This is the legal position and these gentlemen of the Native Affairs (Inspectorate) want to apply it against us. Tormented as they are by the frightful nightmare of mortmain property and clerical encroachment they wish to withhold recognition of our capacity to claim rights over the Christian communes and to administer their property.

I cannot describe the number of difficulties which have recurred time and time again for us over the last ten years as a result of our irregular position in relation to the French legal code. We are, in some circumstances, at the mercy of the Native Affairs Inspectors. They operate like the Bureaux arabes with whose tendencies you are familiar, and from which even the goodwill of the higher administration cannot protect us.

When a dispute arose six months ago over an old legacy to a Christian commune which was belatedly contested by a descendant of the donor, it caused real embarassment to the higher administration which was convinced of the legality of our rights. At the time the governor (Admiral Duperré) declared to me that the mission should try and get out of its impasse and obtain a legal identity for the future, not only to avoid new difficulties but also to have legal grounds for opposing any potentially hostile future administration which might wish to resort to direct or indirect confiscation on the grounds that we lack regular property titles.

One solution is obvious: to have the French government acknowledge a legal identity for the mission, just as it does for the diocese in France. But it appears that a request to the Conseil d'Etat in present circumstances would meet with a categorical refusal, or will encounter a danger which in my opinion should be avoided at all costs - namely that the government might propose to turn the mission into a regular (Concordatory) diocese. So this solution did not seem possible. But how to get out of the difficulty?

The colonial government, by prior agreement with me, nominated a commission to study the question. This commission was composed of French magistrates, missionaries and high officials in the Native

Affairs Inspectorate, and its president was the Procurator-General whose fairness and Christian disposition are beyond doubt.

The commission has studied the situation in depth. For my part, I studied it with my colleagues and we were all unanimous in recognising that only one solution is possible, namely to establish ecclesiastical property on a fully legal basis by putting it in the name of the <u>Missions Etrangères</u> whose vicars-apostolic at Saigon will be the proxies normally designated, and in this way property of all kinds - that of the mission as well as that of the communes - would be held in the Society's name....

The commission, the governor and my council are adopting this measure as the easiest, the surest, the sole solution; and I ask you, gentlemen, to be kind enough to examine this project closely....

As for the other formalities and hindrances to which we are subjected in France, the colonial administration in no way claims to impose these on us. Its only purpose is to create for us a legal right to own property, and once this is formalised it will give us full power to buy and sell <u>ad libitum</u>. The administration only reserves the right to endorse legacies which, if in excess of 10,000 frs will have to be authorised by the colonial governor. I can confirm that this condition in no way hampers me in the new situation we occupy....

(S)o long as strict legality is adhered to, we would derive immense advantage from being safeguarded by the Society's name in having an incontestable right to manage our property, and could offer resistance if need be to a hostile administration which would no longer dare to violate a right sanctioned by law....

Moreover, gentlemen, all the property of the mission and the parishes (sic) taken together does not amount to much. I have just drawn up an exact survey of our official property titles. The mission owns 400 hectares of land. The parishes own 600 hectares - a total of 1000 hectares. Approximate value, 50,000 frs. Maximum annual revenue, 20,000 frs An ill informed governor, by the way, was so bold as to spread the word here and at Paris that we were about to swallow up the whole of Cochinchina. The present governor wanted to clear the matter up: I put all my cards on the table and they were astonished to find that for all the operations of the mission and the parishes (<u>sic</u>) we had no more than 20,000 frs of territorial revenue. That is exactly the pay of one Inspector of native affairs. This revelation has reversed opinion in our favour, hence the fairly benevolent attitude being shown to us at the moment. I am trying to benefit from this transitory goodwill.... (A.S.M.E. Vol.756, (Cochinchine Occidentale, 1867-1889). No.589)

II C THE MISSIONARY ROLE IN EDUCATION AND SOCIAL PROVISION IN FRENCH COCHINCHINA.

The essential purpose of the Société des Missions Etrangères was to obtain mass conversions. Since their evangelising evoked readiest response from among the impoverished and socially marginalised, their strategy for obtaining conversions tended to be primarily economic: as far as possible they aimed to assemble Christians into self-supporting communes. Since the number of French missionaries was limited they depended heavily upon a large body of Vietnamese intermediaries - priests and catechists - to contact, indoctrinate and organise converts and administer their communes **(Doc. 40)**. All this influenced the character of missionary education, for which resources were limited. The scope of missionary education was normally narrow and highly directional. In the seminaries it consisted of the training of priests and catechists in Latin, religious doctrine and quoc ngu, the Latin character form of Vietnamese invented by missionaries in the seventeenth century. In the schools of the village communes it consisted of the teaching of quoc ngu for the transmission of devotional and catechising works, and training in basic craft and agronomic skills.

This was not a system suited to the needs of colonial administration. Both government and mission sought to educate for dependency and control. But the general purpose of the mission was to retain a moral ascendancy over Christians by containing them as far as possible within the physical environment of the mission system, limiting their social mobility and confining them to their communes **(Doc. 52)**. The general objective of the colonial government on the other hand, was to elicit political and economic collaboration from the elites of the non-Christian majority, a more complex process for which it was considered essential to meet a broader set of educational needs **(Docs 42, 44)**. Hence even though the Admiral-Governors were manifestly keen to promote missionary work in the hope of inducing mass christianisation, they also pursued what seemed to missionaries to be the contradictory aim of making alternative provision for popular secular education.

There was certainly some initial cooperation between mission and government over education in the early 1860s. At a time when the need for interpreters and language training was particularly acute, the missions played a role in staffing an Interpreters' College for teaching administrators quoc ngu **(Doc. 42)**. Here, two of their ablest seminarians, Petrus (Truong Vinh) Ky and Paulus (Huynh Tinh) Cua began their long careers as educational collaborators for the French administration. The mission also set up the Collège d'Adran which was

primarily intended for teaching French to Vietnamese Christians
(**Doc. 41**). This institution provided the first generation of teachers
for the government schools set up in 1864. However, the Interpreters'
college was shortlived, and the Collège d'Adran was soon handed over to
a specialised teaching order, the Frères des écoles chrétiennes,
operating under government contract from 1866. From then on the
mission's schools and seminaries were run separately from the colony's
educational establishment.

After 1870 the divergent values and aims of missionary and government
educational systems led to open friction. In the early 1870s the
unpopular, non-denominational écoles d'inspection, where the inspecteurs
des affaires indigènes supervised the teaching of French, competed
openly with the mission for schoolchildren and gave rise to some
celebrated incidents (**Docs 44–47, 49**). In the missionary view, colonial
education was becoming pervaded by the tainted secular and materialistic
values of a politically changing and increasingly anticlerical France
(**Docs 45, 46**). Missionary education, on the other hand, was seen even
by well-disposed Admiral-Governors as too rudimentary and narrowly
specialised to meet the government's need for trained personnel
(**Docs 44, 48**). By the largely anticlerical Inspection des affaires
indigènes it was criticised for alienating Vietnamese notables (a charge
which was returned with interest by the mission). Finally, the staunch
Republicans of the Saigon municipality who had set up their own 'Ecole
municipale' in 1868, attacked missionary education in the press as being
retrograde, obscurantist, and socially and politically disruptive to the
Vietnamese family and commune. Their views (**Doc. 43**) offer a foretaste
of the neo-positivist, laic ideology which was to prevail in the
colonial education system by the 1880s.

The debate in the colony on education related not only to the
divergence between secular aims and religious values, but also to the
political problems posed for mission and government alike by the
traditional Vietnamese system of education. In the sinicised culture
of Vietnam respect for Chinese classical learning was notably intense.
Study of the classical texts reinforced popularly shared moral, social
and political values and religio-cosmographical precepts (**Docs 48, 50**).
Popular pursuit of Chinese learning was encouraged by the social
competition engendered by the use of classical texts in competitive
examinations for entry into the mandarinate. Missionaries rightly
identified the Vietnamese elite - not merely the higher officials of the
mandarinate but also the far larger caste of classically educated
literati, or scholars - as the main source of resistance to
christianisation. Hence the indigenous educational system sustaining

their culture became a consistent target for missionary attack **(Docs 41, 51)**.

But for a French colonial government experimenting with different methods of inducing Vietnamese political collaboration, the issues raised by the tradition of Chinese learning were more complex, and depended partly on the changing political strategies employed. Under the regime of the Admirals (1859-79) the colonial government shifted its position considerably. Admiral Bonard, who sought to construct a cheap system of indirect rule in the three eastern provinces of Cochinchina by re-employing Vietnamese officials, tolerated the teaching of Chinese for the purpose of training up new officials in traditional form **(Doc. 42)**. But the 'flight of the mandarins', who abandoned the colony in successive waves after each phase of expansion in the 1860s, undermined this attempt at constructing a collaborating class. Bonard's successor, de la Grandière, was forced to resort to a more expensive system of mixed direct and indirect rule. He was freer to follow his inclination to 'combat mandarinism' by excluding the teaching of Chinese from the curriculum of the first largescale system of schooling set up by the administration in 1864. However, the new educational system proved unpopular, particularly among Vietnamese notables. The mediocrity of students emerging from these écoles d'inspection **(Doc. 48)**, the lack of ethical content in the secular quoc ngu curriculum, and the tendency of parents to send children back to the Chinese language schools of the villages, prompted a further revision of official policy. Although there was now less requirement for a Vietnamese higher administrative class, it was still considered politically desirable to foster the confidence of Vietnamese notables in government schools. An educational commission of 1873 argued that official schools were unpopular with the notables because the absence of classical Chinese from the syllabus tended to cut off the colonially educated écolier from what seemed bound to remain the prime language medium in general legal and commercial use in the colony **(Doc. 48)**.

Luro, one of the members of the 1873 commission, later proposed a strategy for reconciling all sides in the education debate. He advised reinstating Chinese studies, while drawing the resources of missionary schools into the mainstream of colonial education. He suggested that if, in addition to religious studies, missionaries taught the Chinese language together with the modern sciences they would expose the classical learning of the scholar class as redundant. This would attract the Vietnamese scholar elite itself to modern learning. This in turn would harness its social leadership to the cause both of christianisation and political cooperation with the French authorities **(Doc. 50)**. But as Bishop Colombert's memorandum of 1880 on Chinese

learning indicates, Luro's scheme expected too much of the mission
(**Doc. 51**).

Recent political change in France was, in any case, making it
impossible to produce an integrated educational system. The victory of
the moderate Republicans in the French domestic elections of 1877 was
to ensure the eventual triumph of the values of the Saigon municipality.
A different sort of compromise emerged which left the administration and
the mission free to go their separate ways. In April 1878 quoc ngu was
declared to be an official language of government in addition to French,
as the mission fervently wished. But, against missionary protest and in
conformity with the policy of encouraging Vietnamese notables to show
confidence in the colony's schools, provision was made through the
budgets of the arrondissements for the teaching of Chinese. Finally, in
1882 missionary education was cast adrift to fend for itself without
benefit of subsidy.

Further reading

P. Cultru, **Histoire de la Cochinchine française, des origines à 1883.**
   (Paris, Challamel, 1910.)
M. Osborne, **The French presence,**(esp. ch.8, 'Education and **quoc ngu** - a
   qualified triumph'.)
G. Taboulet, **La geste française,** II, pp. 589-600.
J.B. Luro, **Le pays d'Annam. Etude sur l'organisation politique et
   sociale des annamites.** (Paris, 1878)
P. Vial, **Les premières années de la Cochinchine française.** (2 vols.
   Paris, 1874)
H. Cordier, 'Petrus Truong Vinh Ky', **T'oung Pao,** série II, 1 (1900),
   pp. 261-8.

Documents

40.   Fr **Wibaux,** Provicar of the vicariate of West Cochinchina, to M.
Ansart, a.d.c to Rear-Admiral Bonard, Governor of Cochinchina.
Marked 'Rép.(onse) X Dec.' (probably 1862 or 1863)

Note on secondary education and the college established at Saigon.

...The (seminary) college existed before the French occupation. The
main purpose of this establishment is for the training of a (native)
clergy by the French missionaries. Experience has shown that religion
cannot be established on a sound footing in a country until a native
clergy is formed. France cannot possibly supply enough priests to
cater for all the work entailed in converting such a vast country. As

far as Cochinchina is concerned, we hope that in a few years the harvest will be sufficiently extensive to absorb the enthusiastic endeavours of clergy enough for two or three dioceses; but we cannot expect France to supply them all. We simply deduce that the future of religion in this country lies with the foundation of this seminary college.... In working to train a native clergy it could be that we are anticipating the views of a government which wants to open administrative and civil careers to the natives, and which may approve of our offering them an opportunity for an ecclesiastical career as well.... (A.O.M. Aix. Indochine, Amiraux 12,203)

41.   Fr **Wibaux,** Provicar of the vicariate of West Cochinchina, to Rear-Admiral **de la Grandière,** Governor of Cochinchina. Saigon, 30 December 1863.

Collège d'Adran

... Despite our inadequate means we can soon hope to make the speaking of French common among the more advanced of our pupils, and that will be the start of more obvious progress.... We may consider this school as the means of forming a new class of scholars and even of officials to set against the mandarinate, which will never be more than a caste and a focus of opposition and rebellion. The French college will have fulfilled this purpose once the learning of the scholars acknowledges its own impotence and is seen to be useless.... In taking charge of its direction we have begun a work which is not really within our scope. But at least we will have wasted no time and we will be happy to hand over the basis of a useful institution to the Christian Brothers, whose imminent arrival is expected.... We hope to create a similar type of school on a more modest scale in the town of My Tho, but we are waiting for the government to give us an appropriate piece of land in a healthy area before setting it up... (Such) schools may eventually be multiplied in all the centres of population. If they merely have the effect of transferring to Latin characters the regrettable prestige which attaches to the knowledge of Chinese characters they will already have rendered an inestimable service.... (A.O.M. Aix. Indochine, Amiraux 12,203)

42.   Paulin **Vial,** Director of the Interior for Cochinchina, 1864-1869.

Public education in Cochinchina.

We could not at first communicate with the natives except through the mediation of the missionaries and their pupils, who were happy to help us as interpreters. But after Ky Hoa was taken, which gave us a considerable territory to administer, Admiral Charner, assisted by Commander Ariès, Director of the Civil Services, sought to provide teaching of Annamese to the French, and a French school for the natives. A school founded under the name of the Collège d'Adran by Mgr Lefèvre, Bishop of Saigon (sic), received a subsidy of thirty scholarships for teaching the equivalent number of young Annamese, while another establishment was founded to train French interpreters where public courses in the Annamese language were given by a talented young missionary.

In the same period Captain Aubaret, a superior officer exceptionally gifted in oriental languages, took only three or four months to write and publish an abbreviated French-Annamese, Annamese-French dictionary. This work... was printed at Bangkok by the Catholic mission press.

In taking command at the end of 1861, Admiral Bonard, responsible for founding a large colony in Cochinchina, promptly set to work to develop institutions of public education. He raised the number of students at the Collège d'Adran to 100, he created a hundred scholarships for orphans at the Sainte-Enfance, he reorganised the Interpreters' College in its entirety, and he even wanted to restore the teaching of Chinese as it had existed before our arrival.

This last attempt to revive in our own territory institutions which were frankly hostile to our dominion had no practical outcome.

Such endeavours, moreover, held little attraction for literate natives: they were attached to their national government, and they were not inclined to make great efforts to reach secondary positions under us while their equals among the Annamese could aspire to the highest offices of state. It is also probable that their cooperation would have greatly embarassed us, for there were few French able to supervise their studies and their publications, through which some teachers would certainly have tried to rouse the population and excite them against us....

At this time we had to take exceptional pains to enable the Annamese to understand the principal administrative enactments of the government through an official bulletin published in Chinese. For this script, eloquent as it is for the expert to use, remains vague and confused when used by those who have not dedicated their whole existence to mastering its intricacies. Admiral de la Grandière, to whom we owe the retention of Cochinchina, thought it indispensible that the masters of the country should have the means to make themselves clearly and directly understood by the population. He also wanted to restore the use of their own tongue to the natives, individualise them as a nation and free them from their subjection to Chinese works....

One might have assumed that a people with no national literature would respond fairly willingly to a system of writing (quoc ngu) which enabled it to transmit accurately its impressions, its most cherished notions and the experiences of its intimate life into its own books and writings. Nonetheless, it was a bold enterprise to confront an ancient civisation of inveterate habits with changing the official literature and with destroying the prestige of its scholars by bringing its children new and unknown learning different from that of the mandarins. There was no mistaking it, we were going to encounter covert and active opposition from the natives of the élite classes, even from among our own supporters.... On 16 July 1864 a Governor's decision created primary schools in all the major centres of the colony. Writing, elementary mathematics and geometry were to be taught in them. Model writing texts and two abridged arithmetic and geometry books were hastily printed; and a monthly paper (Gia Dinh Bao) containing colonial news and a few articles of interest to natives was circulated in all our schools.

The government's interpreters were the first teachers, the Inspectors of Native Affairs supervised their work, and the Governor himself followed the enterprise with passionate interest.... In a short time there were remarkable results. The children, flattered by the attention given them, showed themselves both talented and exceptionally amenable to study. Almost all the pupils entering the first schools of 1864 learned to write and understood the four basic rules within three or four months. It only remained for this precious seed of the intellectual conquest of the country to be made to develop.

By the terms of the edict of 16 July the students who proved sufficiently qualified were authorised to open new schools These establishments, numbering fifteen at first, were increased to thirty in 1865 under Admiral Roze. In 1866 there existed forty-seven, with 1,238 pupils. Often the new teachers had the youth and bearing of schoolboys, but supervision by village notables and innate Annamese respect for anything to do with study offset the inconvenient lack of personal authority attaching to these improvised pedagogues.[1]

Although the ancient Chinese university of Saigon was not reestablished, it would misrepresent the liberal tendencies always shown by the colonial government to suppose that any obstacle was ever put in the way of studying Chinese....

Here is a table showing the progress of our schools in Cochinchina from 1866:

In 1866

49 schools (2 of them French, run by the Christian Brothers): 1,238

pupils.

In 1867

58 schools (2 of them run by the Christian Brothers): 1,368 pupils

In 1868

116 boys' schools (4 of them Christian Brothers'): 3,067 pupils. In addition 4 schools for little girls run by the nuns of St. Paul de Chartres, with 372 pupils.

In 1869

I26 boys' schools (including the lay Saigon municipal school and 4 Christian Brothers' schools) totalling 4,760 pupils. In addition, 8 schools for little girls with 500 pupils.

In 1870

131 schools (including the seminary, 5 Christian Brothers' schools and the municipal school) with 5000 pupils. In addition 8 girls' schools with 530 pupils.

The Saigon municipal school was created by an edict of 10 February 1868 by Admiral de la Grandière for European and Asiatic children of all nationalities inhabiting the capital. On the same seats one could see young Europeans, Chinese and natives. This foundation which met quite special needs, has increased in importance as the town has developed and gives good results.... (P.Vial, 'L'instruction publique en Cochinchine', Revue maritime et coloniale, (Paris, Challamel, 2d. ed., 1872), pp. 708-16.)

(1). Probably a reference to the official school for Chinese learning at Gia Dinh, headed by the doc hoc, or Director of Education, before the conquest.

43. Jules **Blancsubé**, Mayor of Saigon from 1879-1881 and Deputy for Cochinchina, 1881-1888.

The purpose of the city council of Saigon in creating...the municipal school (in 1868) was to create an institution in which we would promote, among the populations around us, a knowledge of our writing, our mathematical sciences, our decimal system, where we could teach the elements of geography, natural history etc. and where we would frequently call to mind the great principles of universal morality which is not the monopoly of any religion.... The municipal institution... in

105

a town where so many different religions live side by side, should remain neutral ground, the exclusive domain of science and morality. Intolerance is for others! No French authority of whatever kind should be allowed to champion any religious sect. It owes equal protection to all those who neither disturb public order nor good customs. This is the duty followed by the (Municipal) Council in its deliberations.... (Jules Blancsubé, 'L'invasion cléricale.' (15 October 1871). Articles publiés dans l'Indépendant de Saigon de 1870 à 1877. Saigon, 1880)

44. Gibert **des Molières**, Director of the Interior, to General **d'Arbaud**, Acting Governor of Cochinchina. Saigon, 29 August 1872.

In reestablishing public education in Cochinchina, your predecessors, particularly Admiral de la Grandière, wanted to spread as widely as possible among the recently conquered populations the elements of European civilisation and, at the same time, an understanding of our language. To achieve this promptly we knew that, while making education obligatory, we had to avoid anything that could upset the religious feelings, customs and usages of the Annamese people. The native schools founded in 1865 (sic) on these principles still operate, along with the courses in French begun wherever the headquarters of the inspectorates were situated....
(A.S.M.E. Vol. 758, (Cochinchine Occidentale) 1843-1880. No. 238)

45. Mgr **Miche**, Bishop of Dansara, Vicar Apostolic of West Cochinchina, to an unnamed correspondent. Saigon, 12 September 1872.

.... Before leaving us, the Director (of the Interior) endowed us with atheistic schools run by materialists well known for flaunting their concubines in public.... Free, lay and compulsory - that is to say impious - education: no talk there about God, or his religion or worship: no one to have access to these schools, where Christians and pagans are indiscriminately piled together, without the Inspector's permission - (a shot aimed at the missionary). I said that these schools are free, but not for the poor people who have the misfortune to be charged 7 fr. 50 per person in the village register to furnish what is needed for these atheistic schools!! Of course we have complained and protested against these illegal measures which are an outrage against freedom of conscience, but in vain....

The socialists who govern us have the power they need, and in Cochinchina as in Europe itself they carry the law with them. And that is how our dear compatriots can demolish in a few days what the poor missionary has spent sweat and blood building up for so long....

In France they don't understand what a state our colony is in. The Journal de Saigon is the most mendacious of newspapers. According to it everything is going well, peace reigns everywhere, the people likes its new masters very much, whereas it hates them and insurrections are the order of the day. We have 60 inspectors in the provinces. Out of these, 58 live openly with mistresses. One of the two others is married and lives with his wife. So all these inspectors have harems, and such are the means used by our satraps to civilise the Annamese people which, up to now, has learned nothing from the French but their vices. So let there be a reform in the Directorate of the Interior. It is much desired. To be nominated as Inspector it should not be enough, as in the past, to have a stripe on one's sleeve and make a parade of strong hostility to God and his church.... (A.N.S.O.M. Paris. Indochine (AF), 327/Z 00 (8))

46.   Mgr **Miche** to General **d'Arbaud**, Acting Governor of Cochinchina. Saigon, 22 September 1872.

The My Tho case.

Is (Father) Lizé to be blamed for having protested against the way the (Inspection) school at My Tho is run? Let anyone dare! For my part, far from condemning M. Lizé for anything, I congratulate him for having done his duty conscientiously.... Even though they are voltairian freethinkers, the Inspectors realise that the Catholic religion puts fathers and mothers under a strict obligation to secure a Christian education for their children, especially at the age when evil passions begin to develop and break out. But even if they do not realise it, the priest for his part knows that he has to defend youth from the dangers besetting it, and prevent it from drinking at the poisoned wells of vice. Now, a school has been established at My Tho. Its programme is atheistic: 'It is forbidden to make any mention here of the dogma of any religion.' Very probably this programme will not even be respected and, as has happened at an establishment which we all know, we will soon find the most sacred teachings of the Catholic religion ridiculed. Added to that, this lavishly endowed school is to be directed by someone who lives openly with a concubine, one of these men whom Annamese law, pagan though it is, punishes with exemplary severity. And are Christian parents to be forced to send their children to such a school?

(What truly French heart would not tremble at such a thought!) An institution such as this does not deserve to be called a school. What will emerge from it? Young people with a smattering of French but with no serious knowledge, full of arrogance and with a pronounced vocation for prison. I am afraid our magistrates will, before long, be compelled to issue these communards with a new type of passport - one for (the penal colonies at) Poulo Condore and Bourbon.... If, considering all this, M. Lizé had not felt some emotion he would not have had a priest's heart and I should have repudiated him....

Must a pagan's freedom of conscience enjoy preference over a Christian's? Is a Catholic father not free to give his son a Catholic education? Is he to be forced - in disregard of his rights - to place his child in an establishment where he will hear not a word about the religion he wants him to follow? Has he to deliver his own child up to atheism, to materialism, to moral corruption! This is asking too much and shows too much contempt for the indefeasible rights of conscience. And don't imagine that I am exaggerating, Governor. What is happening at our very door? Three quarters of the children at the école normale (teacher training school) are Christian: what religious education are they being given?... Where are the teachers? Where are the catechisms?...

In moments of political upheaval, has a pagan village ever sided with us? The Christians show that they are for us and only ask for arms to repel the common enemy. Did not the Catholics at Cai Nhum and Cai Mong, led by their missionaries, paralyse the whole rebel force in the Inspectorate of Mong Cau? At Bay Xau, Giong Rum and Mac Bac they performed just as vigorously. Actions speak louder than words, and we would have to cover our ears not to hear what they shout at us.

You must believe this, Governor: neither our religion nor its ministers preach any kind of insubordination. But our obedience will not be blindly given. It has its limits and these are defined by the law of God and the obligations of conscience. We avoid struggle and conflict as much as we can, but if an authority which is in no way infallible loses its way and violates divine law we have to tell it so, as the apostles did to the Jews.... When the laws of temporal authorities are in opposition to those of God, their sanction evaporates along with our obligation to obey. While we are always as obedient as ever in all other respects, we have to oppose irreligious directives, not with insurrection but with passive resistance, not with revolt but with martyrdom.... (A.S.M.E. Vol.758, (Cochinchine Occidentale), 1843-1880. No. 241)

47. General **d'Arbaud**, Acting Governor of Cochinchina, to Mgr **Miche**, Saigon, 5 October 1872.

The My Tho case.

Above all, I hasten to assure you of my most firm belief that the spread of the Catholic religion is the surest guarantee of our conquest, and knowing this more and more each day I feel a corresponding admiration for the patriotism and zeal of our missionaries....

I have also told you that I did not at all approve of the orders contained in the circular of the Inspector at My Tho and that I find it naturally preferable to send Christian children to Christian schools. I also recognise that Father Lizé had the right to complain and protest, though I am not happy with the manner in which he did this, nor at the advice he offered. (A.S.M.E. Vol. 758, (Cochinchine Occidentale), 1843-1880. No. 243)

48. Rear-Admiral **Dupré**, Governor of Cochinchina, to Vice-Admiral **Pothuau**, Minister for the Navy. Saigon, 1 February 1873.

...... Public Education.

I regret to say that in the important area of Public Education we are still searching and feeling our way.... After the occupation we found that the numerous schools in existence had all been dispersed and that we had to start from scratch. We wanted to profit from this by replacing Chinese script, which the Annamese use, with the European characters long used by missionaries to convey the sounds and tones of the Annamese tongue through a complicated system of accentuation. (Missionaries) had made great progress in replacing the myriads of ideographic characters used by Chinese and Annamese scholars with 26 letters and half a dozen accents. So we ceased teaching Chinese characters in our new schools and taught children to read and write in our own alphabetic system. But the reform was premature. There was nothing to teach children after reading and writing, for books were lacking and so were teachers. Before, in studying Chinese, they learned at the same time a few moral precepts, some principles of law and a few episodes of history drawn from classical authors. This knowledge was rather limited but regarded as indispensible, and we were accustomed to finding it among children emerging from the most elementary schools. Their parents were astonished to find it completely lacking in those who attended our new schools. Nothing further was needed to dissuade them from sending their children to us. All our efforts resulted in attracting only 3,000 or 4,000 children whose parents were subsidised by the villages in return, as it were, for the sacrifice they were making in sending them to us.

To revive education we should put into reverse the over-rapid revolution which we were claiming to have wrought in forbidding the study of Chinese, the consequence of which has been to deter children from entering our schools. We should, as soon as possible, furnish these with a few good Annamese books transcribed into Annamese characters and train some instructors. We have provided for the latter requirement by creating an éc3ole normale at Saigon a year ago, which promises favorable results. As for the rest, a commission composed of the most competent people is studying the important issues relating to this....

Other than the native lay schools, indispensable in a country where the immense majority of the population is not Christian, the colony subsidises four Christian Brothers' schools, attended mainly by the children of Christian families, the seminary college at Saigon, and three girls' schools run by the sisters of St Paul de Chartres. In addition we maintain scholarship boys in France. Finally the town of Saigon has founded and maintains a municipal institution in which, along with French and Annamese, we teach a little history, geography, calculus and the elements of geometry.

The total budget for public education is 362,000 frs. (A.N.S.O.M. Paris. Indochine (A.F.) 5/A20 (14))

49. Fr **Thinselin,** missionary at Bai Xau, to Fr **Voisin,** Professor of Theology at the Paris seminary of the S.M.E. Saigon, 10 March 1875.

We are being more or less harassed by the civil administration which is far from being favourably disposed to us. A little over two years ago the government established some écoles normales which they forced our young Annamese to enter, financed of course by the villages which paid for the upkeep of their pupils. The directors and teachers at these schools were the most degraded individuals it is possible to imagine, so that about half the children leaving their care were corrupted. These teacher training schools were scrapped and for a time they thought of handing public education over to the missionaries, but the freemasons of Saigon have again succeeded in making the government try again. So they created (five further) central schools in all the Cochinchina inspectorates. They spent an insane amount of money on this.... And note that the decree which established these central schools says formally that the Annamese will be free to attend or not as they wish.

Well, they are coming over to grab our children by the scruff of the neck to force them into these establishments where they are going to be corrupted. And I, who have some of these schools in my district, I am obliged to let my children go without saying a word.... (A.S.M.E. Vol.756, (Cochinchine Occidentale), 1867-1889. No. 544)

50. J.B.Eliacin **Luro,** head of the bureau of Native Justice and Director of the Collège des Stagiaires at Saigon.

Missionaries and education (c.1876-7)

Until now our priests have confined themselves to the study of the common (Vietnamese) tongue and to teaching religious doctrine. This is not enough to convert the Annamese, if a layman may repeat Francis Garnier's advice. The Annamese are an essentially practical people. Certainly their minds are receptive to religious ideas, but they welcome scientific learning relevant to their daily lives even more. The Catholic schools should expand their syllabus to make their teaching more popular and even include the study of Chinese characters. Otherwise Catholics will be left in an inferior position to the majority of the population and incapable of responding to the needs of commercial life.

The study of Confucius should not be set aside. According to the most eminent missionaries, his moral teachings contain nothing inimical to Christian doctrine. By making this concession to the prejudices and material needs of the natives, and by encouraging the practical study of the European sciences whose application does most to enrich any people, the school could become, in the hands of our missionaries, the most powerful of all their means of conversion. Missionaries would have to begin reading scientific works unfamiliar to them and submit to the drudgery of studying Chinese characters, which they have consistently neglected in Annam. But by combining these two types of learning they could ensure their supremacy over the traditional educators of the people, the scholars, and even over the teachers in the lay schools run by the government. If they fight the scholars with their own weapons, as the Jesuits did in the seventeenth century, they would soon defeat them. For they will have combined the rational moral philosophy of Confucius with a Christian morality which comes from the heart, and they will have humbled the scholastic learning of China before the positive sciences of the West. The scholar, accused of inadequate intelligence and condemned for propagating false learning, would be drawn to us by his own self-interest. He would bring with him the most recalcitrant elements of the population who, still modelling themselves on his example, will always hesitate to liberate themselves so long as he remains unreconciled.   God wants the religious, moral and scientific instruction of the people to be concentrated in the hands of our missionaries who are so devoted to their civilising task and so worthy of our esteem and respect.   When that day comes the assimilation of the Annamese will at last be achieved!   (E. Luro, Le pays d'Annam. (Paris, E. Leroux. 1878) pp. 58-60.)

51.   Mgr **Colombert**, Bishop of Samostate, Vicar Apostolic of West Cochinchina.   Note to the Governor, (Charles **Le Myre de Vilers**). Saigon, 1880.

Public education.

In consolidating French domination over Cochinchina it would have been very desirable to have imposed our own language on the conquered population at the same time.   But since that was really impossible to achieve, it still seemed useful to prescribe the use of Latin characters (quoc ngu) for the Annamese language....

1º Chinese characters are as dark as night to use in practice.   It is a notorious fact that two scholars cannot agree in their translation of a text of any importance and, if they do not consult eachother, they sometimes hit upon exactly the opposite sense.   In lawsuits administrators are obliged to accept these translations, which have sometimes been corrupted by the money of interested parties.   But administrators can easily understand administrative texts for themselves when these are in Latin characters and in ordinary language;   and if this came about generally, the door would be closed to many abuses, and administrative business would be expedited with greater promptness.

2º Moreover there is a very sure link between Chinese characters and the idea of a return to Annamese domination.   That is how the whole population understood it when a few years ago the study of characters was forbidden and then honourably reinstated, and it was for this reason again that the Annamese ambassadors for the treaty (negotiations) of 1874 set so much store by the stipulation that a school should be founded by them at Saigon, because His Annamese Majesty feared that the people of Dong Nai (the South) might forget the national characters.
So it seems useful 1º to set aside Chinese characters by ceasing to favour - but not actually prohibiting - their study; 2º to make the study of Latin characters necessary by declaring that from a prearranged time it will be the only script allowed in administrative matters.

Without doubt there will be plenty of practical difficulties to start with; but these will be quickly overcome and will, in any case, be amply offset by the long term benefit.

When this measure was first attempted ten years ago we saw how villages in several districts spontaneously started up well run schools and supported them at their own expense and at no cost to our budget. So it seems that in going back on this measure a politically retrograde step was taken and the budget was burdened with considerable expenditures which failed to bring all the expected results. For we are embarking on our third attempt at organising public education.

In making a knowledge of Latin characters necessary for administrative business we will be attracting the children of notable families, the sons of landowners, to Latin character schools. For (at present)...the administrations's schools are regarded by the pagan population as a corvée, and that the villages hire out the children of poor families for money to go and study, as if for military duty or labour service. As soon as the notables sense the danger of seeing the village administration fall into the hands of these children of low degree, they will certainly forget their indifference and send their own children to the administration's schools. So long as the use of Chinese characters is retained in administration they will never make any effort to resist their old routine or their repugnance for the new characters. (A.S.M.E. Vol. 758, (Cochinchine Occidentale), 1843-1880. No. 612)

52. J.L. de Lanessan, Governor-General of Indochina (1891-1894).

I have at hand a note by Bishop Puginier in which the purpose of (teaching quoc ngu in preference to Chinese) is very clearly explained. In it he says that by substituting quoc ngu for Chinese characters the mission sought to keep Christians isolated. The latter are, in fact, incapable of reading the most elementary texts or entering into written correspondence with any Chinese or Annamese scholars. Brought up in this way, native clergy are confined to reading the very few works dealing with religious subjects which the missionaries have translated into quoc ngu for their own use. It is difficult to deny that the missionaries have found it advantageous from a Catholic point of view to act like this. Since their sole purpose is 'to make converts and since their tactics are to keep these Christians under religious authority by keeping them as far as possible away from contact with pagans, it is obvious that the substitution of quoc ngu for Chinese characters would naturally favour their work.... (J.L. de Lanessan, Les missions et leur protectorat. (Paris, Alcan, 1907), p. 52)

II D THE END OF THE REGIME OF THE ADMIRALS, AND THE REDEFINITION OF THE MISSION'S RELATIONSHIP WITH THE COLONIAL ADMINISTRATION, 1879 - 1882.

The electoral victory of 1877 which saw the Centre Republicans into power by 1878 brought a succession of changes to the French system of colonial administration which were to have important local implications for the mission in West Cochinchina. From the outset the Republicans in France set about purging central administration of its more overtly Bonapartist and pro-clerical adherents. All parts of the French bureaucracy - military, naval, civil and diplomatic - were to some degree affected. In the mid 1870s the Navy Ministry - generally characterised as a bastion of clericalism - had been criticised by Republicans of the Centre and Left for having been insufficiently answerable to parliament; and the naval government at Saigon was condemned by local Republicans of the municipality for reflecting the pattern of Bonapartist authoritarianism too closely in its despotic style of administration. Although the Navy retained overall responsibility for the colonies after 1879, the system of Admiral-Governors in Cochinchina was locally reformed and replaced by a civil government. The most significant aspect of the reform was the exposure of the administration of Cochinchina to the influence of the local French community and to closer parliamentary scrutiny.

The new civil governor's powers were qualified in two important respects. In order to make him financially answerable to the French community of the colony, an elective Colonial Council was created with broad powers of control over taxation and revenue expenditure. This measure transferred considerable influence to the dominant commercial and professional elements of the municipality of Saigon. For the first time their normally anticlerical sentiments found scope for economic expression. Meantime, in order to expose the management of the colony to the broader democratic process, Cochinchina along with a handful of other colonies, was given a parliamentary seat. The new deputy, first elected in 1881, was free to promote or frustrate the civil governor's policies, not only in parliamentary debates but by intervening directly with ministers in Paris.

Both the Colonial Council and the parliamentary constituency of Cochinchina fell into the hands of a local republican clique led by Jules Blancsubé, a lawyer, freemason and anticlerical, who had risen to prominence in the Saigon municipality during the early 1870s. An intimate of Léon Gambetta - leader of one of the two most powerful parliamentary factions of the republican Centre - Blancsubé's influence in the colony was to be particularly strong until the death of his political patron in December 1882.

The first civil governor appointed under the new dispensation, Charles Le Myre de Vilers, a devout Catholic, was mildly soiled with the taint of Bonapartism from previous administrative appointments. Forced to tread warily in dealings with Blancsubé and the Colonial Council over the missionary question as over other issues, Le Myre de Vilers was unable to offer the Bishop at Saigon overt official support during the period of Blancsubé's most active machinations against the West Cochinchina mission, from 1880-82.

Blancsubé's attack on the mission focussed on the anomaly that clergy in Cochinchina were officially subsidised while remaining exempt from the operation of Concordatory controls. In general terms, Blancsubé favoured the early abolition of the Concordatory system in France, essentially to deprive the Church of material support from the State **(Doc. 53)**. But pending the passage of a Law of Separation, Blancsubé argued that in Cochinchina the administration should insist on imposing Concordatory controls in return for the continuance of subsidies to the local clergy **(Docs 55, 57)**. An important consequence of this proposal would have been the diversion of the official subsidy away from missionary work towards the upkeep of a new, non-proselytising parochial clergy.

But Blancsubé's preference for an early Law of Separation ran counter to the gradualist policy of the republican Centre. As a domestic political issue in France, the question of the Concordat was far too complex for brisk disposal. The leadership of the republican Centre favoured retaining the useful administrative controls which the system embodied until the work of dismantling the social and institutional power of the Church was complete. Léon Gambetta and Jules Ferry, the leaders of moderate republicanism, expected this to take years, and only the Radical Republicans were pressing as a group for immediate abolition.

While Blancsubé was coming to terms with the drift of his party's thinking on the Concordat issue, he appears to have used his influence with the Colonial Council to press for the withdrawal of the West Cochinchina mission's official subsidy. Supported by the votes of the four Vietnamese members of the Colonial Council, the motion for abolition was passed and the subsidy withdrawn from 1 January 1882 **(Docs 54, 56)**.

Bishop Colombert reacted vividly both to the threat of Concordatory controls and to the withdrawal of the subsidy. He expressed his fury at the extinction of the subsidy in terms sufficiently detailed to show its current importance for the development of the mission's various enterprises. Although the subsidy was not exceptionally large in administrative or commercial terms, its utility to the mission was magnified by the rigorous thrift of the vicariate's financial management. Moreover, the very abruptness of the revocation maximised the damage of withdrawal. As for the prospect of Concordatory controls, Bishop Colombert wrote to his canonical superior, the Cardinal Prefect of the Propaganda, in the hope of mobilising papal opposition to any French government proposals. The length and prolixity of his argument shows the importance he attached to the mere absence of administrative interference as a condition of the mission's effective operation (Doc. 57).

According to Colombert, Governor Le Myre de Vilers, despite his posture of formal aloofness towards the mission, finally played a vital part in dissuading the metropolitan authorities from instituting the Concordat (Doc. 58). Official archives however, throw no light on this point. On the withdrawal of the subsidy the governor appeared to react neutrally in his official report. He avoided mention of Blancsubé's influence over the Colonial Council's vote, but he reflected on the possibility of adverse reaction from Vietnamese Christians in Tonkin at a moment when the renewal of French intervention might have made their collaboration seem advantageous. If he hoped for ministerial intervention he was to be disappointed. The Naval minister, Admiral Jauréguiberry, - the 'protestant, apostate, masonic' former commander of the Saigon garrison in 1860, and an old adversary of Bishop Lefebvre - gave the missionary case short shrift.

From 1882 onwards, therefore, the West Cochinchina mission, like all other vicariates in Vietnam and Cambodia, operated without a regular, uncovenanted subsidy. If subsidies were later reinstituted, they operated as fixed contracts for specific educational services only. Church and State in the French colony had never been formally linked, so Blancsubé could not claim to have effected their separation. But the economic dependence of the mission on the colonial administration was now ended. This, for the time being, was welcomed by anticlericals as a practical expression of their ideal of State neutrality in religious affairs.

Further reading

J-M. Mayeur and M. Rebérioux, **The Third Republic from its origins to the Great War, 1871-1914.** (Cambridge U.P., 1984).

P. Cultru, **Histoire de la Cochinchine française, des origines à 1883.** (Paris, Challamel, 1910).

L. Louvet, **La Cochinchine religieuse.** (2 vols. Paris, Challamel, 1885).
C. Le Myre de Vilers, **Les institutions civiles de la Cochinchine (1879-1881). Recueil des principaux documents.** (Paris, 1908).

For biographical material on Jules Blancsubé and C. Le Myre de Vilers see:

A. Brébion et A.Cabaton, **Dictionnaire de Bio-bibliographie générale, ancienne et moderne, de l'Indochine française.** (Paris, 1935).
A. Pavie, **Le Myre de Vilers.** (Paris, 1918).

Documents

53. **Jules Blancsubé**, Deputy for Cochinchina, to **M. Barodet**, Chairman of the Parliamentary Election commission. Toulon, 14 April 1882.

On two occasions, in public meetings, I have declared myself in favour of the separation of Church and State. However, I said that I would not vote for this measure until after (church) privileges had been removed, until all Frenchmen without distinction had been made liable for military service, until all mortmain property had been returned to commercial use, until all catholic clerical privileges in the matter of charity work and cemetaries abolished, and above all until the law on primary education had been passed. But I also said that all this should be done during the current legislature, and consequently that the separation of Church and State should also be achieved under this legislature.... (M. Barodet, Programmes, professions de foi et engagements électoraux. Elections législatives du 21 août, 1881. (Paris, Quantin, 1882.) Tome XIII, vol. 2)

54. Mgr **Colombert**, Bishop of West Cochinchina, to the **Directors** of the S.M.E. Saigon, 29 December 1881.

The fears which I expressed in my report of 15 October last have been realised all too soon. My telegram of 27th. has already informed you of the suppression of the subsidy for religious worship in Cochinchina. Our subsidy, proposed by the administration and passed by the Special Budget Commission was, against all expectations, rejected by the Colonial Council (of Cochinchina) on 23 December. Not even the subsidy for the cathedral has been maintained. It is a blow aimed from below, but prompted by the governor and the parliamentary deputy, Blancsubé. The former saw it as a means of saving a quarter of a million on the budget (and of earning a word of praise from Paris); the latter is satisfying a personal grudge. They pressured the pagan Annamese councillors, who were not hostile, into voting against us. They did not even take the trouble to give reasons for such a grave measure. The motion was proposed out of the blue and the vote was rushed through, nine against three. Now that public opinion has reacted with indignation it seems that no one wants to accept the blame. But it is a _fait accompli_. The decision is final and, for us, all the more disastrous for being totally unexpected and for being taken six days before the end of the year.

It deprives us of exactly two thirds of our resources, and since we have arranged no loans it forces us to curtail or abandon entirely the greater part of our activities. We do not even have the means to keep them going for a year while waiting for help from abroad.

After giving ten piastres a month each to the missionaries (the pay of a second class domestic servant at Saigon) and only five piastres to each native priest, and after paying for a hundred students at the seminary, there will be nothing left. So we will disband the little seminary at Cai Nhum, send back 150 pupils from the big seminary at Saigon, and abandon the primary schools in the Christian communes along with the 4000 pupils who attend them. We will found no new Christian communes, or build any more churches and we will be letting those which exist fall into decay along with their presbyteries and all the other buildings of the mission. These are the steps which we have to take immediately, from 1 January 1882.

We are literally in the position of ruined men.... (A.S.M.E. Vol.756, (Cochinchine Occidentale, 1867-1889). No. 683)

55.   Mgr **Colombert**, Bishop of Samostate, Vicar Apostolic of West Cochinchina, to Cardinal **Simeoni**, the Cardinal Prefect of the Propaganda. Saigon, 3 January 1882.

...But at least some good can come out of evil. I have to inform Your Eminence of one very important consequence arising out of our execution. The deputy Blancsubé, a defrocked Lazarist sent by the colony as its representative to the French parliament, had the publicly announced project of bringing a colonial clergy to Saigon in order to sow confusion among the clericals by mixing jurisdictions, or at least to have the missionaries converted into a concordatory clergy. I have

already notified Your Eminence of this project through the medium of the procurator of the Missions Etrangères in Rome. Now that the colony, whose budget of 24 millions benefits from a considerable surplus, shows no scruple in throwing the missionaries overboard, snatching the bread from their mouths (which is literally true), it forfeits any right to interfere in their business and has given them entire and complete independence from any administrative attachment.... It is a piece of first rate political ineptitude: the development of public education, and the use of European characters for the Annamese language are both due solely to the missionaries. Our rulers want to assimilate this people, but they repudiate the only means of assimilation - religion....
(A.S.M.E. Vol.756, (Cochinchine Occidentale, 1867-1889). No.684)

56. Admiral **Jauréguiberry,** Minister for the Navy and Colonies, to **Charles de Freycinet,** Minister for Foreign Affairs. Paris, 27 February 1882.

By a letter of 5 January last, M. Le Myre de Vilers informs me that during the course of its last session the Colonial Council (of Cochinchina) has suppressed the (annual) subsidy of 170,000 frs accorded to the missions of Cochinchina and Cambodia for the expenses of worship. M. Le Myre de Vilers attributes this vote to the four Annamese members who, on this issue, abandoned their normal calmness and moderation.

Since this was a discretionary grant, the Colonial Council was within its rights and the local government had no grounds for intervening. All the same, the governor wonders if this radical measure might not give rise to complications. In Cochinchina and in Cambodia there is no reason to fear difficulties. But one cannot be sure that it will be the same in Tonkin where there are a large number of Christians of which half are supervised by the <u>Missions Etrangères</u> and consider themselves under the direct protection of France.

M. Le Myre de Vilers adds that perhaps this part of the Tonkinese population, upon whom we relied at the time of our first intervention in Tonkin and who suffered by it, might consider the withdrawal of the subsidy as a change in our policy, and might become less disposed to give us its support when we put our plans for Tonkin into effect. It is more probable - and the attitude of the Annamese members of the Council should enable one to presume - that the majority of Tonkinese will be grateful to us for being placed beyond all issues of religion and will show us all the more confidence as a result. Since the Tonkin mission is not subsidised by France, the impression produced by the measure in question could only have indirect repercussions upon it.

However, because the treaty of 1874 has given us the role of protecting Christians, it could happen that the interested parties might pretend to misunderstand the nature of a measure which affects them indirectly. After considering this question I beg you to let me know what views you may have on this particular point. (A.N.S.O.M. Paris. Indochine (A.F.) 28bis/A90(9).)

57. Mgr **Colombert**, Bishop of Samostate, Vicar Apostolic of West Cochinchina.

Note on the plan to submit the mission
to the Concordatory regime. Saigon, 10 August 1882.

1°. The project of submitting the mission of Western Cochinchina to the Concordatory regime has, in the mind of the French government, the purpose of subjecting and regulating a clergy which has, until now, been independent of the temporal authorities. They want the bishop of Saigon to be a temporal official, answerable like all the other departmental heads to the governor; and for the missionaries and native clergy to be answerable to the civil administration as much as to ecclesiastical authority. 'Until now we have not had enough leverage over these people'. The originators of this scheme have declared in public that they have had enough of a clergy which looks to Rome, is under foreign authority and independent of French power, and is in conflict with the masonic order and modern ideas: time to bring them under control, or disband them and pack them off to live among the savages. In a word they feel the need to turn current religious administration upside down, just as they have been revolutionising all the various administrative services of the colony for the last two years.

That is what they propose to do and it is fairly frequently repeated in official documents or in the minutes of meetings of the Colonial Council for 1880 and 1881, or in newspaper articles signed by the originators of the scheme. It is, moreover, so much of a piece with the centralising and authoritarian notions of the French administration that it seems superfluous to dilate upon it further...

However, it is very important to note that there is no unanimity of views on this issue in administrative quarters.

When I was in France four years ago I had the opportunity for discussion with the Directorate of the Ministry of Public Worship at Paris. I was told in the clearest terms that the government would make every concession to the mission rather than extend the Concordatory regime to it: (i). because, for a colony with such a deadly climate as Cochinchina, only a (regular) religious order is capable of recruiting clergy; (ii). because a regular clergy is more economical; (iii). because bishops belonging to the regular clergy remain at their posts until they die, whereas bishops appointed from French dioceses keep pressing to be returned to France....

Ideas have changed little in the Ministry's offices since then. However the project still exists in Cochinchina. I hear from the general currently commanding the troops, who is a member of the Private Council in Cochinchina, that the governor has recently declared in a council session that he did not, for his part, want a metropolitan clergy, which would cost a great deal and could set up opposition to him if given official standing; that he preferred to keep to present arrangements with the missionaries, who mind their own business, leave him alone and cost him nothing. The general who confided this to me can be believed, and is worthy of our full confidence. I am sure that this really is the governor's thinking, all the more so because, after attempting various projects, he is finding it very awkward to balance the colony's budget and certainly has no wish to open a new account for religious worship....

....3º. In anticipating every possibility, I have to consider a situation in which, while the missionaries are left free to pursue their work, another clergy is established in a few localities solely for the service of Europeans... The mixture of two jurisdictions in the same localities, often in the same churches would, one way or another, cause scandalous frictions. We have to take account of the situation prevailing in a number of places like Baria, Bien Hoa, Mytho, Vinh Long etc. where there are 100 or 200 Europeans and 600, 800, or 1000 Annamese Christians. To whom would the only church belong? To the Europeans? But they do not set foot in them, as at Vinh Long now, where out of 200 you never see a single one at a religious service. The Annamese have contributed substantially to the building of the churches - will they be expelled from them and rendered incapable of fulfilling their Christian duties ...?

....5º. Even in respect of temporal interests, a Concordatory regime would present very serious difficulties.

In the present situation ecclesiastical properties are regulated by the terms of a fairly favourable decree. The mission may acquire and dispose of fixed property with complete freedom on the same terms as any

French property owner, and in particular it may buy without difficulty the land needed for founding new Christian communes. Under a Concordatory regime it would revert to common law regulations, would become in consequence a minor, and therefore incapable of buying or selling a parcel of land, or of building a church, school or presbytery without prior permission from the government. Now such authorisation, considering the attitudes and prejudices shared by all our governments, would almost always be refused. We have had long experience of this, and if today the Vicar Apostolic wants to buy territory in the public domain, the governor refuses to sign the contract solely because the bishop is to become the owner. In its present state of independence the mission is in effect placed beyond the operation of common law by those who govern us: it cannot buy except through individuals, or by proxies when it has to deal with the State. All the same it manages to acquire regularly all the land it needs. But under a Concordatory regime, with all the obstacles and malevolent harassment of the administration which even the best governors do not refrain from, and with the iniquitous procedures which their subordinates do not scruple to use, the foundation of Christian communes here will become impossible, and the spread of conversions will cease. Unable to expand, this mission will become an etiolated diocese like Goa, Macao and others which have yielded such sterile fruit in the Far East....

...9°. Once governors have the right to stick their fingers into the Church's business, we can reasonably assert that they will soon be in it up to their elbows. Their habit of absolute despotism over the last 15 years provides irrefutable proof of this. There is not the least similarity between a prefet in France and a colonial governor who reigns 3,500 miles away from home with extraordinary powers over a society which is almost entirely pagan or freethinking. Armed with the Concordat and the Organic articles, the prospective regulations of Paul Bert and the whole arsenal of hostile decrees which infest French legislation, guided by his despotic whim, his ignorance or contempt for canon law, encouraged by the absence of control from a superior authority and by the bishop's inability to find effective recourse to the home authorities against him, always supported by public opinion and the servility of the administrative caste, there are no impediments which the governor cannot throw, day by day, into the path of the Bishop of Saigon's administration to hold up the progress of religion....
(A.S.M.E. Vol. 756, (Cochinchine Occidentale, 1867-1889). No. 692)

58. Mgr **Colombert**, Bishop of Samostate, Vicar Apostolic of West Cochinchina, to the **Superior** of the S.M.E. Saigon, 26 January 1883.

....4° M. Le Myre de Vilers has been dismissed for his doughty deeds. He has ruined Cochinchina, revolutionised the ideas of this people and lined his own pocket. I had not seen him for 14 months.... Before leaving, M. Le Myre de Vilers came to make his confession for an hour and a quarter. Since he did not get down on his knees, nor make the sign of the cross or an act of contrition, I am not bound to keep it a secret. He told me a lot of things, gave me a lot of information and handed over copies of his official despatches about us. I now know what course to follow over the Concordat. It was he who prevented it from becoming official policy, for the government had adopted Blancsubé's ideas. M. Le Myre de Vilers told the minister 'that the present state of the mission is best and that it is preferable to keep it that way; that there is no clerical question in Cochinchina, and that one should not start it up; that the missionaries have had the monopoly of spiritual care for two centuries and it would be rash to take it off them, especially if one wants to invade Tonkin; that to replace them with another clergy would be an act of extreme ingratitude, for it was through them and their Christians that France was able to instal herself in Cochinchina; that their very real influence is not dangerous for France', etc. He said all this to the Minister and said it all to me at even greater length. In short he is forced to regard us highly, and we are almost the only people (he respects) in Cochinchina. He recommended strongly that we never yield up the smallest part of our freedom to the government (etc.) He would be absolutely right if we had more material resources. Anyway, the Minister accepted his recommendations, so we can sleep easily for the moment. **(**A.S.M.E. Vol.756, (Cochinchine Occidentale, 1867-1889). No. 698**)**

III

THE MISSION AND FRANCE'S FIRST ABORTIVE INTERVENTION IN TONKIN, 1873-1879.

III A   THE MISSION AND THE GARNIER EXPEDITION, 1873-4.

The outcome of the Franco-Prussian war again raised Vietnamese hopes for an agreement involving at least partial restitution of sovereignty over Cochinchina. On the face of it their chances of success might have seemed favourable. France was recovering slowly from German occupation and paying off a huge war indemnity. Without allies in Europe or money to spare, the French government was currently expressing little interest in the development of colonies. However, the Vietnamese were dealing not with an indifferent metropolitan government in Paris, but with a colonial administration at Saigon to whom retrocession was anathema. From 1871-2 a series of diplomatic exchanges failed to bring agreement. Finally, in the autumn of 1873 the Emperor Tu Duc tried to despatch an embassy to France to undertake direct dealings with the Quai d'Orsay. Since the previous Vietnamese attempt at a direct approach to Paris in 1863 had narrowly failed to secure a retrocession treaty, the Saigon administration took pains to counter Tu Duc's move. Passing through Saigon on a preliminary visit in October 1873 the Vietnamese envoys were detained from proceeding to Paris by the current governor, Admiral Dupré. Dupré was determined to impose a settlement locally. But events had moved on a long way since the last episode of treaty discussions in 1868. Far from planning a mere resolution of current differences, Dupré's objectives greatly exceeded those of his predecessors. Since 1868 the direction of local French expansionary interests had shifted. They now extended to include Tonkin. In order to achieve a predominant French influence over Tonkin, Dupré developed the aim of establishing a protectorate over Vietnam as a whole.

The development of French interest in Tonkin.

Admiral Dupré's determination to obtain a treaty establishing French protectoral rights not merely over Tonkin but over Vietnam in its entirety was the outcome of a series of recent developments. It originated in the frustration of a previous scheme which would have projected French expansion along a completely different axis - up the Mekong river north of Cambodia - virtually bypassing inland Annam and Tonkin. This was the Garnier-La Grandière plan for opening a river route to the reputedly rich market of South-West China from the direction of Laos. The main attraction of the Mekong river was that it linked Saigon directly with Yunnan, supposedly the wealthiest of the southern Chinese provinces. Part of the appeal of the Mekong route had been the lack of Vietnamese interest in it. Above Cambodia the Mekong ran through an undemarcated, sparsely populated and apparently neglected zone of frontier territory joining Siam to Vietnam. The petty Lao principalities which lay astride the Mekong were only insecurely linked by loose ties of vassalage to Siam and Vietnam respectively. Hence the progress of French trade and influence up this river were expected to encounter little indigenous political resistance, still less European competition. However, when the Mekong came to be explored in 1866-9 by the Doudart de Lagrée expedition, it was found to be unusable for commercial purposes beyond the Khone falls. Returning via Tonkin, the Doudart de Lagrée mission had pointed instead to the potentials of the Song Coi or Red river as a possible alternative route into Yunnan. The Song Coi, running diagonally through Tonkin from the gulf to the China frontier, was a shorter route situated within easy sailing reach both of the China coast and of Cochinchina. It ran through a province which itself offered an attractive range of secondary objectives. Recent reports on Tonkin had stressed the volume of its inland commerce and the value and variety of its mineral resources. Even if the South-West China market remained the ultimate goal of French commercial aspirations, the facilities and resources of Tonkin itself were coming to exert increasing appeal for the small French community at Saigon. In Tonkin moreover, the French did not lack a local presence, for the province also contained the largest concentration of Christian missionaries and converts in Vietnam - approximately 400,000 by now - over half of them under the supervision of the Société des Missions Etrangères. The Catholic missions in Tonkin, from being a neglected element - indeed an unwelcome complication - in French official dealings with the Vietnamese court, appeared suddenly relevent to French commercial and political calculations as a potential source of influence, information and support.

But if the French at Saigon found the prospects for profitable establishment in Tonkin enticing, there were also daunting drawbacks. The major political difficulty was obvious: Tonkin was under Vietnamese sovereignty. If Dupré wanted to procure the necessary treaty adjustments to establish French preeminence in Tonkin, he would have to apply intense political - and probably military - pressure on the Vietnamese court. In current circumstances French government sanction for this would be unforthcoming. Moreover local conditions in Tonkin were unsettled. While the Tonkin gulf was infested by pirates, the upper Song Coi was currently overrun by mobile Chinese marauders - the Black and Yellow flags - residues of the Taiping rebellion spilling over from the Chinese border province of Yunnan. Finally the Song Coi route had not yet been tested for its commercial practicability. Like the Mekong, it too might prove to be unusable.

Admiral Dupré considers intervention in Tonkin: December 1872.

Still, Admiral Dupré believed that if the commercial future of French Cochinchina lay anywhere, it now lay in Tonkin. A year after his appointment as governor, Dupré had resolved in December 1872 to exploit the continuing disorders in Tonkin as a means of forcing the Vietnamese to extend treaty rights there to the French. In response to the conclusions of a reconnaissance report from a French naval commander in Tonkin, Captain Senez, Dupré proposed to organise a menacing demonstration in the gulf of Tonkin to subdue coastal piracy and overcome the Hue court's negotiating resistance. But this suggestion was rejected out of hand by the French foreign minister, Rémusat. The National government at Versailles, still traumatised by the economic and diplomatic effects of France's recent defeat by Prussia, and mindful of the recent Mexico fiasco, would not contemplate potentially expensive and compromising colonial adventures. Despite this rebuff Admiral Dupré continued to hanker after intervention.

The Dupuis commercial expedition proclaims the viability of the Song Coi.

Within months a French commercial mission led by Jean Dupuis reported success in using the Song Coi river to carry a cargo from Yunnan in South-West China down to Hanoi. Dupuis' success in opening the Song Coi created a crisis. Although it confirmed French hopes for the viability of the route, it also raised the spectre of foreign rivalry in Tonkin. For now that a major route linking the provinces of South-West China with the gulf of Tonkin appeared to be operative, the situation of local disorder in the region presented eager foreign interests with excuse for political and commercial intervention ahead of the French. Not only were foreign commercial interests showing excitement at news of Dupuis' success, but according to some reports British and even German involvement was being encouraged by the Vietnamese court. At the beginning of 1873 the British governor of Hong Kong, Sir Arthur Kennedy, had informed the French consul at Canton, Chappedelaine, of the Hue court's request for British protection in Tonkin. The British were expected to welcome such an appeal since it was already rumoured that they were about to place an agent at Tali-fu in Yunnan and that they had incited the Chinese to deploy a detachment of the imperial army to pacify disorder in Upper Tonkin. Meantime German agents in search of a Tonkin commercial agreement were reported to have been cordially received at Hue. The prospect of being preempted in Tonkin by foreign interests gave particular urgency to Dupré's calculations. It accounts for the sudden escalation of his ambitions.

By July 1873 both Consul Chappedelaine at Canton and Admiral Dupré were independently urging a preemptive expedition **(Docs 60 , 61)**. The arguments for their respective proposals were based on impressions conveyed to both by Jean Dupuis' agent, Ernest Millot. While Dupuis' trading expedition remained at Hanoi, Millot had been sent to Hong Kong and Saigon to seek capital backing for the next phase of commercial operations. During these excursions Millot interviewed both Consul Chappedelaine and Admiral Dupré. Urging intervention to both, Millot minimised the difficulties of a military operation, misrepresented missionary appeals for protection as demands for a French protectorate, and stressed the value of likely support from the Christian population.

Admiral Dupré urges the formation of a Tonkin expedition, July-October 1873.

Consul Chappedelaine proposed a military and naval expedition to seize Tonkin outright as a French colony. His suggestion was ineffective: it was simply set aside by the Quai d'Orsay. Admiral Dupré's role and opinions however, became focal to the ensuing crisis. In a long and confused despatch of 28 July, Dupré outlined the gravity of the current disorders and the reality of the threat from foreign entrepreneurs and their governments. The Saigon administration was incapable of mounting a full-scale conquest of Tonkin; but Dupré proposed to organise a sizeable expeditionary force to seize Hanoi. Holding Hanoi would enable him to step up diplomatic pressure on the Vietnamese to accept a treaty excluding all foreign interests other than Chinese and French from Annam-Tonkin. In short, he recommended that France should establish a protectorate over Vietnam as a whole. He emphasised the ease with which an expedition to Tonkin could accomplish his purposes. In terms reminiscent of the Brenier report of 1857, he laid particular stress on the prospective value of missionary and Christian support.

Dupré's ideas unnerved his superiors at Paris. The Navy minister, Admiral Dompierre d'Hornoy, jibbed at Dupré's strategy for coercion. In a powerfully argued rejoinder he tried to restrain Dupré by reminding him of France's continental isolation and dire postwar financial weakness **(Doc. 62)**. The minister did not however, oppose Dupré's wish for a protectoral treaty, **(Doc. 63)** so he exerted himself to obtain cabinet consent for this. On 22 October 1873 Dupré was formally authorised by the cabinet to offer back the three western provinces of Cochinchina seized in 1867, in exchange for obtaining full French protectoral rights over all the Emperor Tu Duc's dominions **(Doc. 66)**. Permission for an expedition was tacitly witheld.

However, by now Dupré had become sceptical of attaining his objective by mere negotiation. He had already begun preparations in early October for an expedition to Hanoi **(Docs 64, 65)** and, encountering no prompt or formal repudiation from Paris, proceeded briskly with the arrangements.

The objectives of the Garnier expedition.

The commander appointed, Captain Francis Garnier, appears to have balked at the radical character of Dupré's initial plans for an occupation of Hanoi. Garnier was contemptuous of Vietnamese military capabilities, and considered that a small expedition would suffice for Dupré's purposes. He persuaded Dupré to scale down the operation and to refine his political strategy. At Garnier's suggestion the proposed force of occupation was reduced to a token handful of men – in essence an armed escort. Garnier's official instructions **(Doc. 65)**, which he himself helped to draft, enjoined him to mediate between Vietnamese officials and Jean Dupuis, securing the latter's withdrawal from Tonkin. He was then to stay on to arrange for the provisional opening of the river to French, Chinese and Vietnamese commerce. Once Garnier had secured the consent of the Tonkin authorities to open the river to trade, Admiral Dupré would press the Vietnamese envoys at Saigon to authorise the fait accompli by treaty. No mention was made of using French troops in any form of military operation against the Vietnamese; but most authorities agree that Dupré almost certainly wanted Garnier to occupy Hanoi. Garnier's orders also referred to the probability that Tonkin would soon rise in rebellion against the court at Hue. His arrival may even have been expected to trigger this uprising. In the event of a general insurrection against Vietnamese rule he was to be ready to proffer or withold assistance to the Vietnamese authorities, depending on whether they cooperated with him. Such were his formal instructions. They were drafted in fairly precise terms, but it was intended that he should interpret them flexibly, for as Garnier reported in a private letter to his brother shortly before departure, he had been given 'carte blanche' by the Admiral.

Garnier seizes Hanoi, and occupies the delta provinces leading to the gulf.

Garnier's expedition, consisting of only three small ships and two companies of men, arrived at Hanoi in November 1873. Though successful in military terms, it ended by embroiling the French in a confused and humiliating political fiasco.

On arrival Garnier took an obviously provocative tone in his dealings with Marshal Nguyen Tri Phuong, the Vietnamese governor of Hanoi. He offered to remove Dupuis, but only in return for official permission to open the Song Coi river to commerce. The Marshal, correctly informed by the Hue court that Garnier's role was merely to enforce Dupuis' withdrawal, naturally declined the deal and insisted on Dupuis' unconditional removal. Garnier then departed altogether from the terms of his formal instructions. On 15 November he issued a unilateral proclamation opening the river to French, Chinese and Vietnamese commerce. According to Garnier's account, Marshal Nguyen Tri Phuong, receiving no order from Hue to withdraw in the face of Garnier's expedition, began preparations to attack the small and vulnerable French force from the vantage of fortified entrenchments in Hanoi citadel. On hearing rumours of these preparations Garnier then issued an ultimatum summoning the Marshal to disarm his troops and abandon the citadel. Presumably outraged, the Marshal declined to reply. In consequence Garnier's force assaulted the citadel in a suprise attack on 20 November and succeeded in capturing it. Along with approximately 2000 Vietnamese troops, the Marshal himself was captured and died of his wounds shortly afterwards.

Garnier decided at once to claim 'parallel' administrative authority to that of the Vietnamese hierarchy, and invited assistance in administering Tonkin from all elements dissatisfied with Vietnamese rule. In a proclamation of 21 November **(Doc. 67)** he denounced the tyranny of the current Vietnamese administration, and called for volunteers to take over the posts of all Vietnamese officials who refused cooperation with the French. This appeal was relatively successful: he received an immediate response from a group of 4-5000 Lê supporters and from approximately 1500 other - mainly Christian - volunteers. Further volunteers continued to appear over the course of the following month.

Garnier's initiative in seizing control of Hanoi citadel and proclaiming an alternative administrative regime severed his links with the majority of senior Vietnamese authorities. With most of the Tonkin mandarinate now refusing cooperation Garnier found his force cut off from access to the sea. Using Dupuis' band of approximately 100 irregulars and deploying his newly recruited Christian and Lê auxiliaries, he began establishing control over the delta provinces leading from Hanoi to the Song Coi estuary. In the wake of these delta operations Garnier improvised a rudimentary provincial administration composed mainly of untrained and overeager Christians. He was uncomfortable at having to rely on the support of Christians, whom he had come to regard as unreliable **(Doc. 68)**. Nonetheless he promised permanent appointments to all his auxiliaries once a treaty with Vietnam was concluded. By mid-December the French had come to control five major fortresses in the delta, and Garnier's operations had escalated far beyond the intended function of his precarious little squadron. His military expedition was no longer a garisson force for Hanoi but an army of occupation stretched perilously across several provinces.

The Philastre mission to Hue, December 1873.

Garnier's military success brought the crisis in treaty dealings with the Vietnamese to an immediate head. For Admiral Dupré decided that the improvised occupation of the Tonkin delta could not be protracted for long without serious risks. His strategy of intervention had been designed to apply pressure on the Vietnamese court to accept a protectorate: the negotiating procedure now went into immediate effect. Dupré decided to offer back Hanoi forthwith in return for Vietnamese submission to French protectoral control. To save time the proposal would be taken direct to the emperor at Hue. On 6 December Lt Philastre, the senior member of the Inspection des affaires indigènes was instructed to proceed to the Vietnamese capital to make the offer in formal terms **(Doc. 69)**. Philastre was further ordered to procure confirmation of the opening of the Song Coi to trade, and to demand the withdrawal of Vietnamese forces from between Hanoi and the sea. He was also to stipulate a general amnesty for all Garnier's Vietnamese auxiliaries. In bringing the French naval minister abreast of developments, Admiral Dupré declared on 9 December that if his demand for a protectorate were refused, he would take Garnier's recent advice to declare Tonkin independent and place a Lê pretender on the throne **(Doc. 71)**. To make this course more acceptable to the minister Dupré claimed that a Lê protectorate was 'ardently desired by all our bishops'. However, there is no evidence of missionary pressure on either Garnier or Dupré for this course of action. Indeed, in later correspondance Bishop Puginier vigorously denied having offered any sort of political advice. Three weeks after Dupré had despatched his letter to the minister, news arrived at Saigon that Garnier had been killed on 21 December in a casual skirmish on the outskirts of Hanoi.

Lt Philastre, a fervent opponent of the Garnier adventure, was a noted orientalist who had long risked unpopularity with the naval administration for openly expressing sympathy for Vietnamese diplomatic and political difficulties. Even before news of Garnier's death reached Hue, Philastre was evidently ill disposed to a prolonged occupation of Tonkin. In early December he had castigated Garnier in personal correspondance for undertaking a brutal, piratical enterprise. Philastre's orders were flexible enough to allow him to operate a French withdrawal from Tonkin before insisting on the protectorate which Dupré had wanted. On hearing of Garnier's death, Philastre deferred treaty negotiations indefinitely. From Hue he journeyed to Tonkin in the company of the 'second' ambassador of the Vietnamese treaty delegation, Nguyen Van Tuong. Ignoring appeals from Bishop Puginier to stay and defend the Christian communes from local reprisals **(Doc. 77)**, Philastre made two sets of agreements with the Vietnamese authorities to extricate the French military force along with Dupuis' irregulars - on 5 January and 6 February 1874 respectively.

Reprisals and recriminations after the withdrawal of the French expedition.

Despite the inclusion of a formal amnesty clause in these agreements, Philastre's withdrawal of all the French forces left Garnier's erstwhile auxiliaries exposed to reprisals, and the Christian community as a whole politically compromised. With a strong, scholar-led, popular reaction against Christian villages developing in early January 1874 Bishop Puginier sent reiterated appeals for protection to Philastre, to the Vietnamese authorities and to Saigon **(Doc. 75)**. Admiral Dupré remained inert. The Vietnamese were understandably unforthcoming. Philastre for his part declared himself incapable of offering help **(Doc. 76)**: French forces were too meagre and too thinly dispersed for effective action. By now French officials were anxious to dissociate themselves from the consequences of the Garnier adventure. In the massacres accompanying French departure from Tonkin over one hundred Christian communes were burned and several hundred Christians killed. Both French and Vietnamese officials laid the blame for the carnage upon the agressive behaviour of Christians themselves during Garnier's operations **(Docs 73-75)**. After the eventual signature of a Franco-Annamese treaty in March 1874, French naval officers acknowledged the new policy of diplomatic collaboration with Hue by helping the Vietnamese authorities in Tonkin to suppress Garnier's other auxiliaries, the Lê faction, some of whom were still engaged in besieging Haiduong **(Doc. 81)**.

In the aftermath of this disaster Admiral Dupré commended Captain Garnier's daring but repudiated his initiative in seizing the citadel at Hanoi. Dupré argued that Garnier had exceeded his written instructions. With Garnier dead and in the absence of documentary proof to the contrary, Dupré encountered no public contradiction. But Dupré also chose to blame Bishop Puginier for encouraging the attack on Hanoi citadel and for favouring the return of the Lê dynasty to power. This drew from the bishop a scalding rebuke in a private letter of 10 July 1874. Even allowing for its partisan, self-exonerating tone, Puginier's letter throws a degree of light on his own behaviour and attitudes at the time of the attack. Puginier repudiated the accusation of political involvement. He even claimed to have opposed Garnier's assault on the Hanoi citadel for fear of inciting a general uprising. He also assumed credit for restraining Garnier for five days from mounting the operation. Puginier admitted that he had begged Admiral Dupré to send reinforcements after Garnier's death to protect Christian communities from Vietnamese reprisals. (See **Doc. 72**). But he stressed that his motives had been humanitarian, not political. And he castigated the Admiral for himself espousing the possibility of restoring the Lê dynasty to power. Depite the bishop's private disavowals the opinion that nevertheless prevailed among French authorities in the later 1870s and 1880s was that Puginier had himself been primarily responsible for pushing Garnier to excess, and that he was therefore responsible in some measure for the resulting political fiasco.

The problem was that French officials would not distinguish Puginier's role from that of the many missionaries and Christians, who had certainly been overzealous in tendering assistance to the French expedition. Even Puginier was forced to admit that the retributive activities of some French missionaries and Christians during Garnier's occupation had discredited the French expedition **(Doc. 77)**. Admiral Dupré may have called for the support of all the Tonkin bishops at the outset of the Garnier enterprise; but he had also asked them to show a measure of restraint. And Garnier, even at the height of his difficulties, had been wary of the zeal of his Christian supporters. Far from being considered docile instruments of French policy, missionaries and Christians appear to have been regarded as unruly liabilities at most stages of this affair. This impression became widespread and influential among French civil and naval officials, and led them to tread warily in their dealings with the the French missions in Tonkin during the eventful years which followed.

By contrast the Spanish bishops in Tonkin were given credit by French officials for having maintained a posture of neutrality. (See **Doc. 98** infra). The commendation was perhaps ironic. If the Spanish bishops had held generally aloof from the French intervention it was because they found it politically unwelcome. Relations between the Spanish missions and the Vietnamese authorities had become relatively cordial in recent years, and virtually no reprisals were reported in the Spanish vicariates during or after the Garnier affair. The neutrality of the Spanish bishops, maintained through the 1870s and 1880s, stood them in good stead in dealings with both the French and the Vietnamese. Beneficiaries of successive Franco-Vietnamese treaties, they were to remain largely exempt from Vietnamese administrative and social harassments during the subsequent phase of French expansion in Tonkin.

Further reading

(Taboulet II, pp. 674-754)

H. de Villemerueil, **Explorations et missions de Doudart de Lagrée.** (Paris, 1883).
Francis Garnier, **Voyage d'exloration en Indochine. Effectué pendant les années 1866, 1867 à 1868.** 2 vols. (Paris, 1873).
M.E. Osborne, **River Road to China. The Mekong River Expedition, 1866–1873.** (London, Allen and Unwin, 1975).
G. Taboulet, 'Le voyage d'exploration du Mékong', **Revue française d'Histoire d'Outre-mer,** LVII (1979), pp. 5-90.
A. de Pouvoirville, **Francis Garnier.** (Paris, 1931).
M. Dutreb (Marthe Dubert), 'L'Amiral Dupré et la conquête du Tonkin', **Revue de l'Histoire des Colonies Françaises,** vol.11, (1923): part I, 3e trim. pp. 1-40; part II, 4e trim. pp. 177-247.
J. Dupuis, **Le Tonkin de 1872 à 1886. Histoire et politique.** (Paris, Challamel, 1910).
F. Romanet du Caillaud, **Histoire de l'intervention française au Tong–King de 1872 à 1874.** (Paris, 1880).
Ella S. Laffey, 'French adventurers and Chinese bandits in Tonkin: the Garnier affair in its local context'. **Journal of Southeast Asian Studies,** VI, 2 (Sept. 1975) pp. 38-51.
A. Rivière, **L'expédition du Tonkin. Les responsabilités.** (Paris, Bloch, 1886).
E. Millot, **Le Tonkin, son commerce et sa mise en exploitation.** (Paris, 1888).
A. Masson, **Hanoi pendant la période héroique (1873–1888).** (Hanoi, 1929).
A. Launay, **Mgr Retord et le Tonkin catholique.** (Lyon, 1893).
L.E. Louvet, **Vie de Mgr Puginier, Evêque de Mauricastre, Vicaire Apostolique du Tonkin Occidental.** (Hanoi, 1894).
Jacques Valette, 'L'expédition de Francis Garnier à travers quelques journaux contemporains'. **Revue d'Histoire Moderne et Contemporaine,** XVI, Jan-Mar. 1969, pp. 189-220.

59.   Mgr **Puginier**, Bishop of Mauricastre, Vicar Apostolic of West Tonkin, to Rear-Admiral **Dupré**, Governor of Cochinchina.   Ke-so, 16 November 1872.

As for us, we will try to bear these everyday vexations with patience in the hope that we will soon be able to enjoy in somewhat greater measure the generous protection which France would willingly give us.   **(A.O.M.** Aix. Indochine, Amiraux 10,785**)**

60.   M. **de Chappedelaine**, French Consul at Canton, to the Duc **de Broglie**, Minister of Foreign Affairs. Canton, July 1873.

To make Tonkin a French colony it is not necessary to send 2000 men and four vessels to the mouth of the Song-Coi, as Commander Senez advises, but a single vessel - one of those disarmed gunboats at Saigon - and one battallion of naval infantry.   Six thousand Catholics whom Mgr Puginier undertakes to find, trained by a few instructors, would be enough to guard the country against the Annamese, who can only enter from Hue through a single mountain pass which is easy to defend with a handful of men.... If with such slender resources it is possible to secure for France a colony of fifteen million inhabitants of whom 500,000 are Christians, would we not deserve to be reproached for timidity? ....There is no question of an expedition prepared in advance, but of a coup de main undertaken simply with the colony's resources, backed perhaps by a naval division...

We do not lack motives for prompting the expedition.   Apart from our longstanding grievances, what is more natural than to send a warship and a few invasion troops to take care of Hanoi citadel as a guarantee for negotiations pending at Saigon?   If things are not as M. Dupuis, his friends and the bishops of Tonkin represent, the temporary occupation of a point on the coast of Tonkin will pass unnoticed.

What can one fear, moreover, in a country which twenty-three Frenchmen and a few Malays and Chinese have just crossed with impunity?   The exposé of the situation which will be made to Admiral Dupré might suggest schemes to him for which only tacit acquiescence would be required. **(A.Rivière, L'expédition du Tonkin. Les résponsabilités.** Paris, Bloch, 1886. p. 3 **)**

61. Rear-Admiral **Dupré**, Governor of Cochinchina, to Admiral **Dompierre d'Hornoy**, Minister for the Navy and Colonies. Saigon, 28 July 1873. Confidential.

In different despatches I have had the honour of calling the attention of the government to the state of anarchy and poverty in Tonkin, to the inability of the Annamese government to impose respect for its increasingly shaky authority there, and to the dangers that the occupation of the territory by a European power – or even by the armies of one of the Viceroys of Southern China – would create for our nascent establishment in Cochinchina.

The situation as I have represented it can undoubtedly be discerned from the rather confused but undoubtedly consistent reports of Tonkinese merchants drawn to Saigon on business and from the correspondance of the leaders of the Catholic missions in the country, and also from the very detailed account made to me by Commander Senez of his visit to Tonkin at the end of last year.

In my report two months ago on the mission which this superior officer accomplished with so much daring and intelligence, I stressed the absolute necessity of establishing an immediate foothold in maritime Tonkin either with the consent of the Annamese government, or without it if the court of Hue, blind to the last, persists in its covert refusal to settle with us and finds new pretexts for repeatedly adjourning the despatch to France of the embassy which, according to them, must necessarily precede the commencement of serious negotiations.

I stressed particularly the necessity of recalling Captain Senez to Paris to enable the government to supplement, through the explanations of this officer, the inadequate information which I have been able to provide in my own correspondence. I hope that this last request has been welcomed and that you are now completely informed on the situation as it was some months ago.

The question has taken a new and important turn following the expedition undertaken by MM. Dupuis and Millot, who were charged by the Yunnan authorities with bringing up arms and munitions by way of Tonkin.

These gentlemen, officially commended to the good will and good offices of the Annamese government by myself and by M. Senez, who witnessed their arrival in Tonkin last November, have had to battle against obstacles endlessly thrown in their way by the Annamese authorities. The latter, too canny to declare positively that they were opposed to this expedition, hampered it all they could without being able to prevent M. Dupuis from reaching Yunnan with the arms or returning from there with copper and tin. Their malevolence was not, however, without effect: continually obstructed, the operation took eight or nine months instead of the two or three which would have been enough even without the Annamese government's positive support, whereas in fact every possible obstacle was thrown in its path. Far from being profitable as it should have been, the expedition found itself burdened with considerable expenses, and its doughty promoters are today liable to judicial prosecution for being unable to meet commitments which are about to fall due. The German houses in China have, it is true, pressed them with offers of help on advantageous conditions in order to share the benefits of an enterprise which has shown in practical fashion the relative ease of linking Southwestern China with the sea by the Red river or Song Koi.

MM. Dupuis and Millot feel a very natural distaste for involving foreigners, and especially Germans, in an operation which they are convinced would result in a claim for indemnities against the Annamese government, the direct author of the damages suffered by them. I approved of their sentiment and have ordered an investigation into ways of obtaining for them, with the colony's guarantee, the funds which they need most immediately, in return for a promise in proper form to repay part of this loan from the metals which are owed to them by the government of Yunnan under the terms of ordinary contracts. I judged this measure to be both an indispensible means of carrying this affair to the English courts in Hong Kong which would then be forced to intervene in the event of a default, and also as a means of fending off German speculators who are highly desirous of sharing in the enterprise.

After the positive results obtained by these gentlemen and as an assurance for the future, I thought I should not hesitate.

M. Dupuis' journal and M. Millot's verbal reports have given me a day by day account, as it were, of the frequently puerile and often machiavellian manoeuvres employed by the mandarins to prevent the success of the expedition. But having read and listened to them, I am more than ever convinced of the drastic impotence of an Annamese government which could not even prevent 25 Europeans supported by 100 asiatics from crossing the whole of Tonkin from the sea to the Chinese frontier.

After finishing his voyage M. Dupuis sent M. Millot back with some of his ships to Hong Kong and remained with the rest of the expedition at Ke Cho or Ha-Noi to keep communications open and prevent by his presence the barrage work which the Annamese would otherwise have undertaken in the rivers.

The arrival of M. Millot at Hong Kong and the publicity accorded to his journey had an enormous impact upon European commerce in China: petitions were addressed to the Governor of Hong Kong to have a point on the Tonkin coast occupied on the pretext that the English had previously had an establishment there. German commerce, always on the prowl for chances to expand its operations, lost no time in informing its government of the discovery of a practicable means of communication between the sea and Yunnan, a route (the Song Coi) which would render useless all the attempts made up to now by the English, with true British doggedness, to form an artificial link between Burma and this province. Finally, even the Chinese authorities of Yunnan, impressed by the astonishing advantages offered by this new and comparatively easy outlet for increasing the value of the rich products of their country began planning the despatch of an armed expedition to secure free enjoyment of it.

Such is the situation, Minister, in all its full and exact precision. It is, as you will see, in a state to preoccupy me greatly.

On the other hand, as you know, the Annamese government has asked me twice to intervene with M. Dupuis and request him to withdraw from Tonkin. His presence there is in fact contrary to the stipulations of the treaty. Since I had no knowledge, at that time, of the duplicity shown by the mandarins in all their dealings with M. Dupuis, I did invite the latter to evacuate a point (Hanoi) where he had no right to reside. This communication reached him through the agency of the Annamese government itself.

I warned M. Millot about it, and he told me that M. Dupuis could not comply and that he would be forced, in the current state of his affairs to stay at Hanoi.

What was going to happen? Would the Annamese government, emboldened by my assent, have the courage and the power to force M. Dupuis to evacuate? Or would it, in its usual feeble fashion, temporise and again appeal to me to intervene?

On the first hypothesis I was going to inform the court of Hue that I had received reports from our two nationals which directly contradicted the account of the facts it had offered me, and that in the absence of any regular and direct diplomatic contact, which it obstinately rejects, I had no other means of informing myself than by an enquiry on the spot.

On the second hypothesis I would, on the contrary, maintain that M. Dupuis had rejected my request and that I could only force him to comply by sending to Tonkin a force large enough to make my decision respected.

But whatever M. Millot's conviction, we should consider the possibility that M. Dupuis might obey the request I have made to him, and we should try to find a means of appearing in Tonkin without breaking openly with our perfidious neighbours. The distaste they plainly show for a rupture would help us achieve this.

It would be enough to maintain that according to trustworthy reports, confirmed by their own requests to have a mere adventurer evicted,

Tonkin is in such a state of anarchy as to raise fears that the king's authority will soon be completely overthrown there and that the country might consequently pass under foreign domination;

That this change would lose us the benefit of one article of the treaty opening Tonkin to our commerce, expose 500,000 Christians, whose protection is our responsibility, to the greatest dangers, and compromise both the security and the future of our establishment in South Cochinchina for which such great sacrifices had been made;

That, faced with such eventualities, we judge it necessary to obtain guarantees and occupy the citadel of Ke-cho or Hanoi (capital of Tonkin) and a point on the coast, with a force sizeable enough to check both the rebels on one side and the pirates on the other;

That I regret being forced to take this decision and to carry it out without the prior assent of the Annamese government, but was forced to act promptly by alarming reports I had received on the rapid progress of the rebels, by the appeals of the Christians and by successive delays holding up the despatch of an envoy to Saigon;

And that I will maintain this occupation until a proper treaty reassures me as to the fate of my co-religionists, offers security for trade and allows me to share at least indirectly in the maintenance of order in this profoundly and painfully troubled territory; and that my attitude remains as friendly as before, which they can ascertain when they finally send me a plenipotentiary.

Minister, whichever hypothesis is considered, there are adequate reasons for prompting our armed presence in Tonkin. It only remains to investigate and consider the consequences.

It is possible that this bold stroke will change the attitude of the court of Hue and cause a transfer of influence to men who support a new policy more in conformity with that adopted by China and Japan. That is even the more probable hypothesis, for it is impossible that the Annamese can have any illusions about it: their impotence is too obvious and can only be made more so by the appearance and enforced presence of a handful of Frenchmen in the heart of the country.

A treaty made in these conditions, after the easy success of such coup, can only end up as a fairly cleverly disguised - but real protectorate by France over the sovereign of Cochinchina. In exchange for the political and commercial advantages we secure from it, we will restore the king's authority on firm foundations by organising an army and a fleet for him, and by creating financial resources for him through the foundation of a customs service similiar to that which has revived the finances of the Chinese empire. The future of French power in the Far East would be secured for certain. I think it unnecessary to develop this point further.

But it could also happen that, before capitulating, the Annamese government might want to make a supreme effort and promote a general rising in the provinces which we occupy, at the same time as it directs the few forces at its disposal against the expedition which we disembark in Tonkin. The consequences of such a course would be disastrous for it: troublemakers, the dispossessed and the socially displaced might, it is true, recruit a few hundred vagabonds and malefactors and disturb the peace for a time in our provinces; but what could such bands, even if they became multitudes, do without arms, discipline or money against our powerful resources? A regrettable uprising of this kind, because it would entail fairly considerable bloodletting, would be promptly repressed - I would answer for that - and it could not compromise our domination.

As for the attack on our expeditionary corps, however small it be, can we be afraid of this when we know that Commandant Senez crossed the whole river delta with two boats and twenty men, made himself respected and held an exhasperated multitude at bay? And when one knows, too, that for eight months M.Dupuis maintained himself in the country with twenty-five Europeans and a hundred asiatics of every origin? Evidently such a danger does not exist and the only eventuality to be concerned with if the Annamese government loses its balance or its sanity, withdraws from us and refuses to treat, would be how to substitute our authority for theirs in such a vast and populous country. That would certainly be a problem, but it is far from insurmountable. Our mere presence would give the country a security it has not known for many a long year either on its coasts or in the interior. A large part of the population is profoundly hostile to the Annamese government whose ineptitude and impotence has plunged them into a state of misery which is almost unimaginable to those who have not witnessed it. We would not see all the high and influential figures in the country emigrate to Annam as happened here, (in Cochinchina) leaving us isolated in the midst of an ignorant multitude to whom all administrative ideas and practises are alien. From that point of view our position would be incomparably better than at the outset of our occupation in the South. Only the compromised mandarins would flee from general reprobation and Tonkin would promptly achieve a state of relative pacification.

I can only speak from memory of the 500,000 Christians, representing about a twentieth of the total population, whose active support is promised to us by their bishops. I know that there were grave miscalculations on this score when we declared war on Cochinchina: perhaps there will be again, but they would certainly be less, and probably the support of these Christians, so numerous in some provinces where some of them are enlightened, rich and influential, is not to be treated lightly. One could usefully employ the profound knowledge of the country acquired by bishops and missionaries who have lived there for many years and have been able to get about freely since being shielded from violent persecution. The missionaries of the southern provinces (Cochinchina) hardly knew the country we were going to any better than we did since they were forced to hide in the daytime and go out only at night in covered boats.

I have had to discuss this hypothesis. But I repeat that I consider it to be a very improbable one, knowing the timid and wily habits of the Annamese government. This is especially so after the decisive blow we will have struck, which I am sure will put an end to all prevarication and prompt it to begin negotiating with me.

In one eventuality or another we would have to get rid of the Chinese bands occupying the north and north-west of Tonkin. This seems less difficult to achieve after the information given to me by M. Millot on the rebel dispositions: some of them have already offered their submission in order to return home. Moreover I think that we could count on the cooperation of the two neighbouring Viceroys - that of the two Kwangs with whom I have the best relations, and that of Yunnan and Kweitchow who is not far from accepting the proposals for submission which were conveyed through M. Dupuis by the chiefs of the bands bordering on his part of the frontier.

I think, Minister, that I have examined the question in all its facets as completely as possible. I only hope I have enabled you to share my burning conviction, and that I have shown you in a fairly vivid way the immense advantages which we would gain from the demonstration which I propose to make, and the serious danger to which we would be exposed by abstaining from it!

My conviction on this point runs so deep that, fearful of approval being withheld, I would have taken the whole responsibility for the decision myself if my conscience had not told me that I have to refer to the government whose servant I am in a matter which can commit its future policy and means of action. I submit to an imperious duty in writing you this letter.

But I am ready, if any doubt remains in your mind or in that of the government, to take full responsibility for the consequences of the expedition I am planning, to expose myself to a disavowal, a recall, a loss of the rank which I think I can claim to have merited. I do not ask for approval or for reinforcements; I ask you to let me act but to disown me if the results I obtain are not those which I have indicated.

It only remains to let you know the means of execution which after close study and deep reflection I rely on using. I will profit from the presence in transit of the transport ship the Cosmao which left

Toulon on 20 July and which should be sent back to France from Japan at the end of August or the beginning of September. I shall add the **D'Estrées** to it and a certain number of gunboats and sloops intended to to make communication secure between the capital and Cat Ba, the port chosen as the expedition's base.

The troops to disembark will consist of two select companies of infantry, two companies of militia and a half battery of artillery - in all about 600 men, more than enough for occupying Hanoi (the capital) and Quang-Yen. They need no provisions other than wine and flour in a country so rich and fertile in resources. The Tarn will cope easily with the transport of provisions, arms, munitions and a large proportion of the men, for a short passage. It would be enough to buy the freight of one collier which we would send up to provide the resources necessary for the expedition.

The expedition would be placed under the command of Captain Senez who knows the area and who has told me that he would undertake to achieve the end we have in view with an even smaller force. That is why I had the honour of asking you to be so kind as to send this officer to Saigon by the steam packet of 3 August. I hasten to thank you, Minister, for the mark of confidence with which you honoured me in meeting my request without further explanation.

I have informed you, Minister, of the very meagre resources with which I am committing myself to secure for France the course of the Song Koi after that of the Mekong, and to lay the unshakeable foundations for an eastern empire which, in the natural course of things will one day extend from the Gulf of Siam to the frontiers of China, with a population of 30 to 40 millions, covering the most fertile territories in the world. A moment's hesitation could upset everything. I was a firm supporter of delay when I saw no danger in it; but the moment of crisis is upon us. If you have any doubt of it, withhold your approval but, I beg you, let me act. The outcome will be so magnificent, so advantageous for our unfortunate country. I would be unworthy of France if I were not ready to sacrifice everything to prove it to her....

P.S. I had just finished this letter when I received the coded telegram informing me of the illness of Captain Senez and asking me to make my plans known. My coded reply of today's date, is phrased thus:

'The opening of Tonkin is now a fact following the the success of the Dupuis enterprise whose boats have gone up the Song Koi river as far as the frontiers of Yunnan. Immense effect upon English, German and American commerce. Absolutely necessary to occupy Tonkin to secure this unique route for France before the double invasion by Europeans and Chinese which threatens this country. No help requested. Will manage

with my own resources.   Success assured.'
The delay caused by Commander Senez's sickness is infinitely vexing.
I need a man whom I can rely on for such a delicate enterprise.   If I
cannot find him and am obliged to delay the expedition I shall not be
able to undertake it until November after the arrival here of the
transport ship of the 20 September.   The assistance of a transport is
vital.   Also I shall then be deprived of the assistance of the Cosmao
which would have been valuable, and which I will not be able to retain
for that long.   I am going to think over this and will undertake
nothing before receiving the telegram acknowledging receipt of the
present despatch. (A.N.S.O.M. Paris. Indochine, (A.F.) 12/ A30 (18))

62.   Admiral **Dompierre d'Hornoy**, Minister for the Navy and Colonies, to
Rear-Admiral **Dupré**, Governor of Cochinchina. Versailles, 12
September 1873. Private.

...I understand the attraction of this Tonkin conquest, which amounts,
in actual fact, to the complete absorbtion of Annam.   It is possible
that in the future it would have given us a dominion like British India.
It is possible, even probable, that from your own resources you might
be able to seize Ke-cho (Hanoi).   But seizure is nothing.   Organising,
keeping, defending, that is the difficult and expensive part.
Cochinchina, as it is now, costs a round total of twenty millions.
It brings in fifteen.   It figures in my budget for five millions, and
then only after all your efforts to get as much as possible out of it.
But if you stretch it further, as you inevitably will with your project,
how much more will this immense expedition cost us after that,
especially in the early years ?   You will need troops and still more
troops, for instead of being bordered by the people of Annam... you will
have Yunnan on your frontier, which is far more bellicose;   and these
Chinese, who may not amount to much as fighters, will need to be kept
constantly in check as brigands and corsairs.   We would have to double
the administration, we would need to construct all sorts of buildings,
and it all takes money, money and more money.   But even that is not the
main drawback, in my view.   More dangerous still is the jealousy of
England and Germany at seeing our power expand in this way in the East,
and we are afraid that this will give rise to difficulties whose
consequences will be felt in Europe.....
(Trentinian Family Archives, quoted in G.Taboulet, La geste française,
II, pp. 699-700.)

142

63. Rear-Admiral **Dupré,** Governor of Cochinchina, to Admiral **Dompierre d'Hornoy,** Minister for the Navy and Colonies. Saigon, 11 September 1873.

I had the honour of informing you by telegraph that I received yesterday your coded telegram of the 8th of this month. I will conform as far as circumstances permit to the orders which it conveys. I will not lose sight of all the precautions which our present situation in Europe imposes upon us. As for our future in the Far East, far from wishing to compromise it, all my efforts merely tend to strengthen it more definitively. I am fully conscious of the weight of the responsibility I bear, and I will not venture it beyond what my duty plainly commands. You would not have thought me worthy of the position I hold if I were not prepared to sacrifice it to my strongest convictions.

This Tonkin question is very complicated. It is possible that I will be drawn unwillingly into assisting it towards a solution, and that the court of Hue will request my intervention to help it overcome the difficulties which it no longer feels strong enough to resolve. Our abstention in this circumstance would be an avowal of impotence which would irreparably damage our present and future interests. But be assured that if I feel forced to act, I will only do so with extreme prudence....

My object would be to make them ask for a French protectorate, which would entail for them the obligation not to receive any foreign diplomatic or consular agent; the presence at Hue of a representative of the Governor; the presence at the capital or in one or several of the ports of Tonkin and Annam of a French agent supported by a military force adequate for his protection; freedom of commerce at these various points; the suppression of customs duties and any obstacle to trade at inland frontiers; the opening of the Song Coi river to French, Annamese or Chinese commerce in return for payment of modest dues at the coastal and Chinese frontiers; freedom of worship for Annamese Christians and the complete abolition of all obstacles to the excercise of their religion. Finally, of course, the payment of what remains due of the Spanish indemnity.

Provided that these conditions are faithfully and conscientiously observed, and so long as there occurs no upheaval or rebellion in the three provinces in question between now and then, the French government would agree to restore to King Tu Duc the administration of these three provinces after...(blank)...years have elapsed following the exchange of ratifications. The French government would maintain at Vinh Long,

Chau Doc and Ha Tien a resident and garrison sufficient to assure the security of the Christians and all the Annamese who have served us faithfully, preserve the rights of the Cambodians, (and obtain) the complete opening of all roads, rivers, canals and communications in general.

In return for our expenditures upon these provinces the Annamese government would pay us an annual return of...(blank)...hundred thousand piastres.

For its part the French government would undertake to defend King Tu Duc against any attack from within or outside the country; assist him with our experience in giving direction to his policy and administration; place at the king's disposal experts who would restabilise his finances and regularise tax returns; and supply a customs service, military instructors to train an army, effective weaponry, well constructed ships with powerful cannons, and engineers and foremen to direct public works.

If they are as anxious for the return of the three provinces as I have some reason for thinking, they may possibly agree to these conditions. At the price of a considerable but probably temporary sacrifice we would close to all foreign influence the left bank of the Mekong as far as the sea - still the most important commercial artery of all the rivers in Tonkin. We would be giving a solid basis to our domination over all the territories forming the ancient kingdoms of Cambodia and Annam, over a population of 25 to 30 million men capable of education to a high degree of civilisation. And finally we would be ensuring as far as the instability of the things of this world ever permits, a glorious future for France in the Far East. (A.N.S.O.M. Paris. Indochine, (A.F.) 12/A30 (18))

64.   Rear-Admiral **Dupré**, Governor of Cochinchina, to Mgr **Sohier**, Bishop of Gadara, Vicar Apostolic of North Cochinchina. Saigon, 6 October 1873.

The Annamese government is threatened with losing Tonkin very soon. Its own existence will be in peril if it loses this rich and populous province. A handful of adventurers is holding it in check there, pirates are ravaging its coastline taking ships from under the king's nose, bandits are pillaging the countryside, and the government's incapacity to enforce respect for the law is now plain to see. It cannot manage this without our help, which will impose a heavy burden on us if we consent to give it. What compensation is it willing to offer us in exchange? What guarantees can it give to reassure us that its former antipathy will not revive?

I am ready to formulate such compensations and guarantees once the Court of Hue decides to begin negotiations on a serious basis and invests its ambassadors with the powers they require. I have taken pains to convince the latter fully of my benevolent feelings towards the government and peoples of Annam (and I think they no longer have any doubts on this score), to make them understand the advantages which their country would gain from a close and sincere alliance with France, an alliance in which the benfits are mainly theirs, the burdens mainly ours. I am patient and await the outcome of my efforts.

However the Court of Hue itself considers the situation in Tonkin to be sufficiently serious to ask me to intervene and order M. Dupuis to leave the country. The request was justifiable. Dupuis' position was irregular. I invited him to withdraw but he took no notice. The Ministry of Foreign Affairs renewed its insistance. I declined to give an adventurer a second opportunity to trample my orders underfoot, so I proposed to send an officer with an adequate force to impose respect for them. My offer was accepted, and the ambassadors are now strongly insistant that the expedition takes place as soon as possible. I think that this little expedition can set off on about the 11th. under the command of M. Garnier in whose prudence I have every confidence.

M. Garnier has orders to invite M. Dupuis to abandon his enterprise for the time being and resume it later on under regular conditions, and to force him to do so if he refuses; to insist, after the latter's removal, that the Red River be opened to Annamese, Chinese and French craft upon payment of moderate dues for ascent and descent; to enforce respect for the (treaty) stipulations protecting Christians, and to stay in Tonkin until the conclusion of the treaty.

My intentions are honourable: my purpose is to initiate Annam into Christian civilisation, to serve (the Annamese) as a guide and support, to help them to reform their administration and finances, to revamp their army and their fleet, and finally to restore security to Tonkin, which has for so long been ravaged by civil war, brigandage and piracy.

If the Court of Hue expresses frank willingness to travel the road I am opening to it, France will fulfil her undertakings faithfully; but if, misconstruing my truly Christian intentions to the end, it persists in closing its eyes, raising difficulties for us and resorting to ruses to avoid the obligations it contracts, we will withdraw the hand of friendship and it will go to meet its inevitable destiny without our being forced to use violence to hurry it on.

I have no doubt, Your Grace, that I will have your sincere cooperation and that of all your venerable colleagues in the endeavours I have embarked upon. I have no time to write to the authorities of each separate mission to apprise them of the situation, so I beg Your Grace to be kind enough to perform this task for me. (L.E. Louvet, Vie de Mgr Puginier. Hanoi, F.H. Schneider, 1894. pp. 215-17)

65. Rear-Admiral **Dupré**, Governor of Cochinchina, to Captain Francis **Garnier**, commander of the Tonkin expedition. Saigon, 10 October 1873.

....you should insist on the prompt departure of M. Dupuis, whose presence at Hanoi is in contravention of the treaty, but you may undertake to support his claims for compensation if you think them reasonable.

Your mission does not end there. Since the Annamese government is plainly impotent and since the ease of communications with Yunnan has been demonstrated, it is obvious that unless effective measures are taken the same disorders could recur either on M. Dupuis' account or on that of some other adventurer. So it is indispensible that your stay at Hanoi should continue after M. Dupuis' departure, and that measures be taken to prevent the repetition of similar escapades.

The most useful thing would be the promptest possible provisional reopening of the river to Annamese, French and Chinese navigation from the sea to the Chinese frontier, on payment of modest customs dues chargeable at Hanoi on the way up and at a post adjoining the frontier on the way down. There should be no delay over this measure. You should make every effort to have it promptly undertaken, and you should demand payment of a proportion of the customs dues to cover the cost of our expedition....

The various reports which I have recently received on the situation in Tonkin indicate that this unfortunate country is in a state of violent crisis. The population, overwhelmed by all sorts of calamities for years, appears to be on the brink of a general uprising. It seems to be thought that the mere news of our presence might set off this explosion. Perhaps these reports are exaggerated: you should endeavour to find out the real state of feeling. If the Annamese government gives us serious proof of its good intentions and of its sincere desire to cooperate and listen to our advice, I intend to give it loyal support and put all our influence at its disposal to pacify popular feeling and restore security to a country which has lacked it for so long. If, on the other hand, the Annamese persist with their customary duplicity, take advantage of our benevolent attitude, snatch back with one hand what they have so grudgingly offered with the other, and keep for themselves the benefits of the help we are giving while leaving us to meet the cost, you should avoid any intervention, let events take their course, and retain full freedom of action so that we can choose the most humane, just and profitable measures to take as circumstances dictate.

... Recommend (the bishops) to counsel their Christians to be patient and to show complete obedience to the authorities for the time being; and ask them to avoid any bombastic behaviour or premature reaction, or any act which might compromise me when I come to ask for acknowledgement of their full rights.... (Cited in full in M. Dutreb, L'Amiral Dupré et la conquête du Tonkin. (Paris, 1927). pp. 182-6)

66. Admiral **Dompierre d'Hornoy**, Minister for the Navy and Colonies, to Rear Admiral **Dupré**, Governor of Cochinchina. Paris, 22 October 1873.

'Authorisation to negotiate on the basis of your despatch of 11 September. The acceptance of a Protectorate in exchange for the restoration of the administration of the three provinces (to Annam) should be in reality, if not explicitly, an effective seizure of the Annamese empire. This condition is absolute, and you should only subscribe to it if all guarantees are given to you for it. Stipulate an annual rental equivalent, as far as possible, to the revenue of the three provinces less expenses....'

That (telegraphic) despatch, whose terms were agreed with the Vice-President of the Council of Ministers (Duc de Broglie, also Minister of Foreign Affairs) in the presence and with the assent of the President of the Republic, contains the essence of the Government's thinking with regard to the negotiation which you are about to undertake with the Emperor Tu Duc's embassy currently at Saigon. The only purpose of the present instructions is, in accordance with the views expressed by you, to expand on this thinking, and to outline for you the line of conduct to follow in order to reach an outcome satisfactory not only, of course, to the interests of our finances and the development of our commerce, but also of our influence in the Far East.

The successive communications which I have received from you concerning the rapidly increasing importance of French intervention in Tonkin, the arguments which you have used to support your insistent request for authorisation to take military action in this territory, did not fail to impress me deeply, and if I resisted such pressing arguments it is because I felt, on the one hand that our situation imposed on us the greatest caution in this matter, and on the other hand that the same result could perhaps be attained by peaceable means.

The negotiations which have now begun open up the latter course to us, and the Government does not hesitate to follow you in it, if the acceptance of a sort of Protectorate over the Empire of Annam can really secure us a preponderance without firing a shot, assure for our flag a direct and relatively easy route to Yunnan, and permit us to take a large share in the commerce of this rich province....

Within the framework of these principles I leave it to your discretion to profit from all the ensuing consequences. Moreover, your above-mentioned letter of 11 September contains indications to which I attach great value and which I approve of completely, notably concerning the advantages which will stem from the establishment of a sort of Protectorate and concerning the guarantees to demand from Tu-Duc, especially in favour of Christians. I know you to be fully aware of the grandeur of the task and animated by the profoundest patriotism. I am also confident that you will neglect nothing to bring to a successful completion an undertaking of the greatest importance to our colony, to our commercial interests and to the progress of civilisation in the Far East.... (A.N.S.O.M. Paris. Indochine, (A.F.) 12/A30 (20))

67. Proclamation by Captain Francis **Garnier**, Commander of the French expedition to Tonkin. Hanoi, 21 November 1873.

...The mandarins of Hanoi, unconcerned with the interests of the general population, have strewn our path with traps and pitfalls, behaving treacherously towards us in a host of different matters. So we were unable to tolerate their conduct any longer. After careful thought and after exhausting all other means, we seized the citadel and expelled from it all those officials who, having no love for the people, had no other concern than to take its property and suck the marrow from its bones. The punishment we have dealt them is a good deal less than their crimes deserve.

...Now let men capable of governing the people come and offer us their services, and we will accept them and give them posts to fill.

As to how they will govern, that is to be settled between us: such posts are important but easy to fill. Once we have appointed people to fill them, complete peace will descend upon you.

We will leave all governors and deputy-governors in their posts if they make their submission to us. Those who will not acknowledge us and choose to withdraw will be replaced by prudent men concerned for the well-being of the people.

We have no wish to seize Tonkin for ourselves and expel all officials. We wish merely to find men from this country to place in authority over the people. Then we will advise the king and his officials to treat the people as a father treats his children.... All officials whom we nominate will keep their posts and will in no way suffer harassment.... The scholars should stay quiet in their villages, and let them beware of trying to revolt....

(M. Dutreb, 'L'Amiral Dupré et la conquête du Tonkin', Revue de l'histoire des colonies françaises. 1923, part IV, pp. 196-7)

68. Captain Francis **Garnier,** Commander of the French expedition in Tonkin, to Admiral **Dupré,** Governor of Cochinchina. Hanoi, 3 December 1873.

The province of Hanoi is at this present moment pacified. The whole administration is in our hands and is beginning to operate regularly.... Although the Christians were the first to offer me their help, I took care to avoid relying exclusively on them.... I issued a proclamation inviting the scholars to come and find me, because I did not want them to feel I harboured any prejudice against them.... (A.O.M. Aix. Indochine, Amiraux 12,466.)

69. Rear-Admiral **Dupré,** Governor of Cochinchina, to Lt Paul **Philastre** Inspecteur des affaires indigènes. Saigon, 6 December 1873.

Your mission is a mission of peace and conciliation.... The main (negotiating) difficulty you will face concerns the term 'protectorate'. I am obliged to refer you to your own knowledge of Vietnamese to find a term which meets our purposes without offending Annamese sensibilities.... For centuries the court of Pekin has excercised a suzerainty more humiliating than that to which we aspire. Even today the King of Annam is held to be a subject of the Emperor of China. Annam has received no benefit from her position of inferiority. We are offering her a share in all the advantages of European science, industry and civilisation. In exchange we are asking her to be guided by us in her external policy. This seems to me an eminently fair exchange.... (A.N.S.O.M. Paris. Indochine, (A.F.) 12/A30 (19))

70. Rear-Admiral **Dupré,** Governor of Cochinchina, to Captain Francis **Garnier,**Commander of the Tonkin expedition. Saigon, 6 December 1873.

...Notify our bishops of the situation and beg them in my name to use

The government, I repeat, wants us to achieve the ends we are pursuing only by peaceable means. (A.N.S.O.M. Paris. Indochine, (A.F.) 12/A30 (19))

71. Rear-Admiral **Dupré**, Governor of Cochinchina, to Admiral **Dompierre d'Hornoy**$_{(1)}$ Minister for the Navy and Colonies. Saigon, 9 December 1873.

France has no claim upon Tonkin. She desires to see order restored and agriculture and commerce flourish there under the domination of the King. In France's name I am inviting the Annamese government once again, more insistantly than ever, to conclude this treaty. For the uncertain situation created by events cannot continue without endangering its authority. M. Garnier finds himself forced, for the moment, to take steps to ensure peace in the territory. The need for this must be removed as soon as possible, and it can only be done by this treaty.

If, to my great regret and despite my most persistant efforts and most pressing requests the (Annamese) government continues to remain deaf to my pleas, I shall be obliged to take steps to secure the independence of Tonkin.

The steps I shall take, Minister, are: the promulgation of the sovereignty of one of the members of the deposed royal family, which retains a large number of supporters in the territory from which the Viceroy of the two Kwangs has already withdrawn his troops at my request; and the guarantee of a protectorate over the sovereign placed by France on the throne. I am confident that this solution, currently recommended to M. Garnier and heartily desired by all our bishops, will give us no further problems or create more difficulties than a protectorate conferred upon the government at Hue, and that in virtue of this it will receive our approval. (A.N.S.O.M. Paris. Indochine, (A.F.) 12/A30 (19))

(1) This letter is actually dated 9 October 1873. But it is evidently not of this date, for it refers to events which took place in late November. It is marked as having arrived at the Naval Ministry in Paris on 14 January 1874. Since letters from Saigon normally took over a month in transit, I am assuming a clerical error and propose a date of 9 December.

72. Mgr **Puginier**, Bishop of Mauricastre, Vicar Apostolic of West Tonkin, to Rear-Admiral **Dupré**, Governor of Cochinchina. Hanoi, 25 December 1873.

Allow me to inform you of the present condition of the Tonkinese population, and explain what it will be exposed to if it is not given sensible, effective and powerful protection.

After the occupation of the citadels of Hanoi, Nam Dinh and Ninh Binh – a decision on which I am not competant to pass an opinion – ... all the administrators of the phu and huyen fled. As a result of this general flight of the mandarins, the provinces were bereft of their traditional rulers.

M. Garnier, in seeking to avoid unrest and keep the peace took urgent steps to provide for the territory under his occupation. At his request a large number of men came forward to fill the different posts and form a militia which had become indispensible because the old army had totally deserted. For that alone these men and a large part of the population found themselves compromised in the eyes of the Annamese government. The Christians, falsely accused by malevolent mandarins and scholars of having pressed the French to occupy the country, have become a particular object of the implacable hatred of all those who detest the French name. Several of their villages have been sacked and burned; the others are in serious danger of suffering the same fate. All these disorders are the work of the scholars and former mandarins who are hiring bands of thieves to spread terror and fulfil their perfidious ends. This is what decided M. Garnier to guarantee to maintain the rank and dignity of the new mandarins nominated by him, even after the return of the provinces to the Annamese government, and to extend French protection indefinitely over the population of Tonkin.

The great majority of the population joyfully welcomed the French flag, which proclaimed for them an era of peace and prosperity. The prestige of France was, and still remains high; but if this prestige is to be sustained, French protection has to be irrevocably guaranteed for the whole of the compromised population. It is no way my intention to press you to thoughts of conquest; that would not be worthy of my episcopal role. My sole purpose, a just and praiseworthy one, is to explain to you the current situation in Tonkin. It is exceptionally critical. If France withdraws or fails to act in response to circumstances, it would lead to the ruin of all the Christians and result in the greatest disorder in the country. All the people who rejoiced in the arrival of your envoy would lose their esteem for France; and their affection would turn easily to hatred if the

confidence which they placed in her were to end in grievous
disappointment. Only one thing can now keep the love of the Tonkinese
for our country, and that is our assurance of effective and durable
protection. It is in no way necessary to make war , nor to undertake a
conquest to ensure such protection: it is perfectly compatible with the
ideas of peace which inspire you and which are those of France herself.
But for protection to be effective in the situation of unrest and menace
in which the country now finds itself, it is necessary to back it with a
respectable number of troops - about a thousand men and two more small
steamships. The purpose of such troops would not be to make war but
simply to punish those who break the peace. Their mere presence would
contribute greatly to reducing disorder, even if they failed to to halt
it entirely. Your Excellency knows that the North of Tonkin has been
persistantly ravaged by Chinese warriors for several years, and that the
mandarins are powerless to stop them. This state of things will last
until the arrival of outside assistance to help with the pacification of
this country whose unfortunate population is always a target for pillage
and massacre.

I beg you, Admiral, not to accuse me of wanting to get mixed up in
these questions, for which I feel a considerable distaste. I have been
prompted to write to you so frankly only by my awareness of the critical
situation in which the population of Tonkin has been placed. (Archives
of Cochinchina. Cited in Taboulet II, pp. 732)

73.   Report by Dr **Harmand**, Governor of the citadel of Nam Dinh, to Lt
        Philastre, Commander of the expeditionary corps in Tonkin. Hanoi,
        15 January 1874.

Before my arrival at Nam Dinh and after the fall of the citadel, the
main leader of the scholars, the hai-phong tham-dam and the other chief
dignitary,the roan-que, put themselves at the head of the resistance.
They had both been identified as extremely active and dangerous
personalities, enjoying great influence - especially the former. They
have long been leaders of the party which dreams only of the expulsion
of Europeans and the extermination of Christians. M. Garnier put a
very high price on their heads - a thousand ligatures - a figure which
he even ordered me to exceed a few days later to be sure of catching
them. I lost no time in obtaining news of them: from the first day of
my command I received numerous complaints about the depredations and
ravages committed by armed bands in the villages. It was above all the
Christians who came to ask for help, speaking of 1000 men when there

were only 100 brigands. Familiar with Annamese ways I was careful not to be taken in and never sent anyone without securing information from someone reliable. On the 18 December, two days after arriving, I received a very important letter from Mgr Cezon, the Spanish bishop established a few miles from Nam Dinh, and sent him Quartermaster Boilève and the two fusiliers Pirot and Martin in a junk armed with four small canon with 100 of General Ba's men. Leaving without interpreters and taking every wrong turning, they were led in triumph through a host of villages, and despite my formal orders and their wish to fulfil them they were only able to return to Nam Dinh three days later. At the mission they were sent at the head of the whole Catholic population to capture and burn a pirate village. They killed ten men, one of whom was a chief; the wounded were martyred, drowned or burned alive, the pagodas destroyed. The men behaved bravely, but I have sworn not to let a shot be fired without me (despite the advice I have received) in order to counter such barbaric activities myself, and only to attack villages which are well and truly implicated, and prevent these fanatical Christians from exposing themselves to terrible reprisals in the event either of French failure, or of a change in policy. Meantime I continued to receive incessant visits: there was literally a queue at my door from seven in the morning till nightfall. I was obliged to receive this crowd even during my mealtimes. These were people who, having gathered men together (in reponse to the proclamation made by M. Garnier after the capture of the citadel) asked to be given arms, put themselves forward as officers and scholars, or even came asking to be made huyen or phu. They were nearly all Catholics, and a considerable number came from the province of Ninh Binh, sent by priests. The Christians showed themselves in all instances indecently covetous, and as incompetent as they were conceited. In their own interests I always tried to temper their ardour. I wanted to nominate as far as possible more pagans than Christians, mainly so as not to cause natural discontent in the area, but also because the Christians, almost all of low degree, are disregarded by the Annamese government, are not familiar with business matters, and are absolutely new to administration. Moreover they are rarely literate. Since I am sure of this, I must speak openly and without prejudice. It is certain that the Christians have served us well, and have greatly eased our task, but they have caused me a lot of worry. On our side, once the encouragement was given, we found it necessary to rely exclusively on them. But they have shown remarkable ineptitude. They have taken our arrival as the signal for revenge, and they have made it too obvious. If the missionaries ever gave firm directives they have not been well attended to. I have repeated twenty times a day: 'Do you think we have come here to make a religious war?

153

We have come purely and simply for commercial reasons. It does not matter whether you are Chinese, Christians, or pagans. We will no doubt be happy to be of service to Christians. But if we nominate some of them to important posts it is because it is indispensible, in the interests of public order, that these posts do not stay vacant, and that we keep the Christians in check. But let former mandarins come to us and we will be happy to prove our impartiality to them. Not all the French are Christians', an argument which disturbs them considerably. On one occasion a native priest burned a pagoda without provocation. On another, a French missionary was naive enough to put himself at the head of a band of 300 men and make veritable war. I kept the first in the citadel for several days; and I interviewed the other and gave him friendly advice, showing him how prejudicial his conduct was to his own religion, and that it was the best way to revive old grievances, create new hatreds, and perpetuate agitation in a country which it was above all necessary to pacify.

I do not know what the future holds for such a rich and at the same time unfortunate country. I do not try to pry or offer advice, but if in the course of events it should ever fall into our hands, we will need great patience with these delicate issues, and I am sincerely sorry for those who are called upon to administer the cantons in which Christians and pagans live together. It would be far more difficult here than in Cochinchina, and will cause a lot of friction.... (A.O.M. Aix. Indochine, Amiraux, 11,689/32)

74.   Extracts from the Journal of Jean **Dupuis**.

...14 January (1874). I saw Mgr Puginier today and he is very downcast.

While I was with him he received news of his Mission from an Annamese priest arriving from Nam Dinh. He was told that immediately after the departure of the Mang Hao and the Espingole with the French garrison, they began to pillage, demolish and burn the houses of Christians who had sided with the French. These acts of brigandage were committed by scholars aided by soldiers who had arrived to take possession of the town. If the mandarins do not openly command them they do everything they can to encourage them clandestinely. Three large villages close to Nam Dinh have already been sacked. It is said that inside the citadel a certain number of the militiamen who helped Garnier have been beheaded.

Soon after, Mgr Puginier received news from the outskirts of Ke-So. Here too several villages have been burned and a lot of people killed. So far more than thirty villages have been burned in his vicariate. He is prepared for anything since M. Philastre is of the opinion that these reprisals are just.

'What were they doing taking Garnier's side against their mandarins', M. Philastre has said. He shows no sympathy for the bishop or his Christians.

Mgr Puginier speaks only of his Christians; but all those who gave their support to the French, Christians or not, have been treated the same way....

....15 January... I went to see Mgr Puginier for news from the interior. It is worse and worse. There are more than fifty villages burned, and four or five hundred Christians killed, including three native priests and thirty catechists. More than thirty thousand Christians are in flight, not knowing where to find food and shelter.

While Mgr Puginier was telling me the foregoing, M.(Lt) Balézeau arrived. The bishop told him everything with tears in his eyes. The former replied that what is happening is not the fault of the mandarins who, on the contrary, are doing all they can to put things right; but that these are reprisals against the Christians for what they did during the French occupation. Mgr Puginier, hearing this, flushed with indignation. 'That is too much', he replied to M. Balézeau in high dudgeon, 'now it is we who are the guilty ones! I will be asking for an enquiry to be held to establish the truth'.

I have rarely seen a spectacle so harrowing for a French heart as this man of the sword's impassivity in the face of the bishop's description of the desolation of this unfortunate country, and then his using language to this prelate which made me blush for very shame...
(J.Dupuis, Le Tonkin de 1872 à 1886. Histoire et politique. Paris, Challamel, 1910. pp. 254-6)

---

75. Rear-Admiral **Dupré**, Governor of Cochinchina, to Lt **Philastre**, Commander of the French expeditionary corps in Tonkin. Saigon, 21 January 1874.

I have received a very alarming letter from Mgr Puginier. I fear that he has provoked the very dangers which he warned me against, and I shall remind him that when informing him frankly of the attitude which I had intended to adopt and maintain in Tonkin I enjoined him, together with his venerable colleagues, to show great prudence and the most extreme reserve. I regret that he has exposed himself to recriminations, even though he will be effectively protected against their expression by the amnesty which extends to all our supporters, Christian or otherwise....
(L.E.Louvet, Vie de Mgr Puginier, Evêque de Mauricastre, Vicaire Apostolique du Tonkin Occidental. Hanoi, F.H. Schneider, 1894. p. 246)

76. Lt **Philastre**, Commander of the French expeditionary corps in Tonkin, to Mgr **Puginier**, Bishop of Mauricastre, Vicar Apostolic of West Tonkin. Hanoi, 17 January 1874. 2 a.m.

....Your Grace will certainly know that the population of Tonkin is very divided between several parties, of which some are in despair at peace being made between the two governments, because this peace is the ruin of their secret hopes. So they would evidently interpret an intervention by French troops as a pretext and cause for new uprisings against the Annamese government. Even the strongest alliance would have difficulty in surviving a blow like the one whose effects we are unfortunately (feeling) at the moment. An intervention of this kind, even if it took place by agreement with the Annamese government, would present the greatest dangers to our two countries, and for ours in particular, which could be dragged without prior authorisation into a hasardous and impolitic enterprise.

So all false hopes should be abandoned and vanish from the minds of Tonkinese of all parties who dream of war between the two countries and the overthrow of the reigning dynasty in Cochinchina: then the intervention of French forces could take place without risks.

I beg Your Grace to note, moreover, that so far we have no troops available, and that there is no ship at Hanoi or within call. Only yesterday evening did reinforcements arrive at Hanoi; but they were intended to save an endangered situation if it proved necessary, and then be sent back to Saigon as fast as possible. So intervention is still materially impossible at the present time. Moreover this intervention cannot, if it takes place, be more than transitory, and if it is misunderstood or misinterpreted it would adjourn the danger without eliminating it, and the troubles would resume from the day, which is not far off, when the greater part of the troops leave for Saigon.

However lamentable the fate of the Christians may be in Nam Dinh and Ninh Binh at the moment, Your Grace will understand that I bear the burden of an immense responsibility and that I have to act with the greatest circumspection. I must avoid returning to past errors and risking even more serious calamities and disasters than before.

Six days ago, my lord Bishop, the condition of disorder was the same, the danger growing, and the commonest prudence forebade exposing to catastrophe two handfuls of men thrown boldly into the midst of the thousands of enemies whom Your Grace mentions. The departure of these men took place on the tenth. We have not even given the Annamese authorities the time they need to bring up the troops they require. Three days ago disorders broke out which could easily have been predicted and which the illusory occupation of the citadels of Nam Dinh and Ninh Binh could plainly no longer prevent.... These are the inevitable consequences of previous events, and we cannot possibly draw from them conclusions of any kind about the future.

In the circumstances it is impossible to undertake a campaign and place a post in every Christian village, which would be the only means of abruptly stopping the arson. So to my greatest regret I can do nothing of that kind.

The only thing I can possibly do is to put the Annamese government under urgent pressure. Your Grace may be assured that I will spare no pains in the matter.

Perhaps tomorrow, or this morning, I will be able to do more if the Espingole, which is beached in a bad position at the moment, is on its way back to Hanoi. In that case, but only in that case, will I be able, if not to stop the disorders, then at least to preserve one or two of the more important establishments of the Mission and show that French authority is concerned at the danger to Christians and is not abandoning them.... (A.S.M.E. vol. 816, (Lettres de Mgr. Puginier). No.5)

77.   Mgr **Puginier**, Bishop of West Tonkin, to Lt **Philastre**, Commander of the French expeditionary corps in Tonkin. Hanoi, 28 January 1874.

I have had the honour of informing you clearly in several letters of the disorders which the scholars are committing, and of the bands which they are raising against the Christian villages. I know for certain that the mandarins of the province are striving to deny or at least to minimise all these evils; but I persist in affirming that there is no exaggeration at all in the reports of pillage, arson and massacre that I have conveyed to you. I have taken soundings and unfortunately the information I have obtained makes it certain that the disasters are even greater than I thought....

The Annamese mandarins, if they are not conniving with the scholars directly, are certainly doing so indirectly. Ever since the formation of these bands which spread terror, pillage and death into Christian villages, the provincial governors have done nothing, or almost nothing effective to halt these disasters, especially in the province of Nam Dinh. They claim, first of all, that they have no troops: this assertion is false because some were brought down from Son Tay and Bac Ninh and some have come from Thanh Hoa where there was a considerable corps of them before the return of the citadels. What expeditions have these troops undertaken against the bands levied by the scholars? How many engagements have they fought?

A letter from two priests in the province of Nam Dinh informs me that some Christian communes in their parish are a target for frequent attacks, that until now they have held the advantage in repelling them, but that they had not received the least help from the mandarins and remain with their own forces exposed to the efforts of their enemies.

One effective way of stopping the trouble would have been to capture some of the chiefs and make a judicial example of them. I believe not a single one of the principal scholars has been arrested. Worse, everyone says that the mandarins continue to have frequent dealings with them. The priests of several parishes delegated Christians to present petitions to the mandarins from Nam Dinh province, but the latter sent them away with reproaches.

Mgr Cezon, Bishop of Central Tonkin, also issued a request for protection to the mandarins: they did nothing and replied using a scornful expression, saying: 'Anh giam muc' ('This brother of a bishop,' an insulting expression).

Yet when the Christians are accused of inciting disorder the mandarins attach the greatest importance to their acts and give them the greatest possible publicity, whereas they strive to conceal the brigandage of the scholars. I certainly do not wish to excuse culpable Christians nor blame the mandarins for punishing them, but I would wish them to act with impartiality and give strict justice to all. It is evident that the Christians are not only extremely unfortunate, but that they have also been abandoned by the mandarins, whereas the protection of the latter is all given to the scholars whom they seek to excuse....

An order has been issued to all the villages to hand in their arms. I would not deny the very serious problem there would be in leaving the people armed, but to disarm the remaining Christian villages at this moment is to expose them to inevitable destruction. Let the mandarins first of all disarm the scholars, disperse their bands properly, forbid any levying of the doan ket militias, of which the scholars or their associates were the leaders till now, and let them guarantee sincere and effective protection for Christian villages, and then these can be disarmed without problem. Finally I have heard it said that several Christian communes in Ninh Binh were required to hand in their arms and still have not done so. I regret this because they will be declared rebellious, and punished officially as such, but as a matter of natural right can one blame them for keeping these arms to defend themselves against their enemies when every day they see some villages being destroyed and others like Ke Nap being strongly attacked for the last fifteen days by the scholars without receiving the least assistance from the mandarins?

So if I denounce the duplicity of Annamese officials it is because I am convinced that that is what it is. Consult public opinion. All sincere and disinterested men will assure you of it, as I do. It is true that written proof is difficult to provide because letters are secret and sent by special means; but I have been kept informed of their intimate communications and moreover their behaviour towards Christians makes their sentiments plain.

In a word, there is not a single Christian village in the three provinces of Hanoi, Nam Dinh and Ninh Binh which is not fairly seriously threatened. There is general terror, and it is not without foundation....

Another business which everyone regards as very important and which people have been astonished to see passed over in silence up to now, is the armed recapture of the three <u>huyen</u> (sub-prefectures) of the province of Hanoi.

This reoccupation was conducted as much by the former sub-prefects as by the scholars and their bands after the handing back of the provinces of Haiduong, Ninh Binh and Nam Dinh. The <u>huyen phu xuyen</u> was even retaken on the sixteenth of the present month, three days after the return of Hanoi province. Then everyone was advised of the peaceable intentions of France. Orders were given officially to all the prefects and sub-prefects nominated by M. Garnier to stay at their posts until further notice. That was the moment when the former <u>huyen</u> (sub-prefect) of Nam Xang came with recruits from Hung Yen and the scholars of the place to attack the sub-prefecture. Once it was taken the bands went off to burn the Christian village of Phu Da and part of that of Tong Xa, where the parish houses were situated. I have heard tell that despite this outrageous act of hostility the same <u>huyen</u> was kept on at the sub-prefecture.

Over the same few days the sub-prefect of Binh Luc was attacked in his <u>huyen</u> and killed with his wife and children; and on the 16th. the <u>huyen phu xuyen,</u> as I mentioned above, was killed at his post with his brother and six men of his entourage.

I am not considering these facts as a bishop: the victims were official employees and it was as such that this atrocious revenge was taken against them. But as a Frenchman I have to give you this information because many of those who might have given it to you are dead.

I also have to tell you that the mandarins are apprised of all this and have done nothing to condemn or punish these acts, which were all the more hostile since they took place in the midst of arrangements for peace and were intended to sieze back sub-prefectures which you were on the point of handing back, or which you had already handed back in relinquishing the province.... **(**A.S.M.E. Vol. 816, (Lettres de Mgr Puginier). No. 12**)**

78. Rear Admiral **Dupré**, Governor of Cochinchina, to Admiral **Dompierre d'Hornoy**, Minister for the Navy and Colonies. Saigon, 26 February 1874.

It was urgent and indispensible to concentrate in one position so as to withstand an impending reaction. This reaction was prompted by the movement of our troops which to some seemed a withdrawal, to others a forced retreat presaging an early and complete evacuation. Passions already high, boiled over; and inexpressible disorders and deplorable excesses ensued.

The situation worsened over the next ten days despite the efforts of M. Philastre. On the one hand Philastre was inundated with appeals from bishops obsessively denouncing both the mandarins and his own companion (the second ambassador); and on the other (the ambassador) was pressing him to enforce the submission of the Christians.

In this awkward position he had to calm the terror of the bishops, moderate the Christians, fortify and even threaten the second ambassador who, still fearful of using his authority, was himself obliged to restrain the overzealous and secure their respect.

The ambassador's delays and hesitations were such that M. Philastre thought he might have to send gunboats and troop detachments to halt the burning and slaughter; but the Christians, as soon as they saw themselves protected and supported, resumed the offensive and took reprisals. One native priest raised a band of 200 armed men which he was persuaded only with great difficulty to disband. **(**A.N.S.O.M. Paris. Indochine, (A.F.) 12/A30(19)**)**

79. Mgr **Puginier**, Bishop of Mauricastre, Vicar Apostolic of West Tonkin, to Rear-Admiral **Dupré**, former Governor of Cochinchina, 'in Paris'. Saigon, 10 July 1874.

... You dared to say that if the Christians were suffering it was their own fault and that of the missionaries.... In what way are we the cause of all these disasters? What wrongs have Christians committed to draw down these misfortunes upon themselves? .... The true and only cause of the disasters of our Christians is the unfortunate turn taken in the affairs of Tonkin. After the seizure of Hanoi the mandarins of the province deserted their posts: M. Garnier, wanting to prevent the country falling into anarchy, appealed to the population and demanded the assistance of influential men to keep order. These put themselves forward only because of the formal promise that France would never abandon them; and when the provinces were handed back, the compromised (part of) the population was abandoned without assistance. No account was taken of their interests, nor even of their lives....

Admiral, your conduct towards us gives me the right to tell you this: you were very lucky to find bishops, missionaries and Christians in Tonkin to blame for the weaknesses of a failed expedition. Silence and caution would have better become you.

Admiral, you have said (to M. Dumoulin in M. Dupuis' presence) that I pushed M. Garnier into taking Hanoi, and that you even understood this from my letters.

I have kept a note of what I wrote to you, and I defy you to prove your assertion without placing a false interpretation upon my letters, which I reject in advance as never entering my thoughts. Your accusation, insulting to me, is all the more false in that, thanks to me, the seizure of the citadel of Hanoi by M. Garnier was delayed by five days. In the first interview I had with him, M. Garnier told me that the mandarins were deceiving him, that it was impossible for him to stay in such a predicament, and that in three days he was going to take the citadel. Fearful of such an initiative, I pointed out to him the misfortunes which could follow such an act and told him that a revolution would certainly break out in the province. I begged him to consider the interests of the population, of the Annamese government and of France herself, and to continue to follow the peaceable course of diplomacy to obtain what he wanted: the opening of the Hanoi river to trade. M. Garnier accepted my reasoning, and if he later resorted to force it was because of the difficulties made for him by the mandarins, especially by Marshal Nguyen Tri Phuong. M. Garnier warned me secretly of the probable attack on the citadel but did not ask me for any more advice, and it was no longer in my power to stop him. I had, moreover begged him on several occasions not to ask me about things which could have been detrimental to the Annamite government or which could have been damaging to anyone at all. What I have just asserted was said before witnesses..... Do you remember that, in (your)...letter of instructions, while commanding M. Garnier to give back the citadel you still recommended him to find a descendant of the Lê dynasty? I have no doubt at all that this was in order to place him on the throne in case the Annamese government refused to sign the treaty which you were so anxious to conclude. Have you not also written in this sense to the Court of Hue?

How dare you accuse me of wanting to overthrow the reigning dynasty

and of favouring the return of the Lê! I protest against this calumny too. Although the Annamese government has given us so many reasons for resentment by ceaselessly harassing us and our Christians, I would never condone such an act.... My conscience has always abjured it. Perhaps you do not know, Admiral, of the reply I made before witnesses to M. Garnier after his arrival at Hanoi. He had obtained information on the Lê dynasty and on the aspirations of the Tonkinese from an Annamese who had asserted as an actual fact that the inhabitants were begging for the restoration of their ancient monarchs. When (Garnier) asked me for my opinion I told him frankly that we missionaries were not concerned with political afairs, that he should not take much notice of the opinion contained in the Annamese's reply, a reply made without serious thought and above all without real knowledge. I added that this family was dethroned so long ago I thought it would be difficult to find a descendent capable of governing or of obtaining popular consent. I know that M. Garnier wrote to you from the beginning that it would be necessary to abandon the idea of restoring this family, and if I remember aright, he added: 'This is also Mgr Puginier's opinion'....
(A.S.M.E. vol. 816, (Lettres de Mgr Puginier). No. 23)

80. Jean **Dupuis'** description of the treatment of the Lê faction after the withdrawal of the French expedition from Tonkin in 1874.

Finally the Lê (faction) made a great effort and arrived to lay siege to Haiduong. The possession of this place on the Thai Binh (river), not far from the sea, would have given them a considerable advantage. It would have secured for them free navigation of the river and, in case of retreat, an impregnable post. In their attack on this place they used ten thousand men and thirty armed war junks captured from the Annamese.
Their ranks increased every day and there is no doubt that if they had once secured control of this citadel the whole Tonkinese population would have risen in rebellion.
The siege lasted a month and Haiduong was close to being taken when the town's mandarin resorted to Commander Dujardin. The latter, in virtue of the signed but still unratified treaty of 15 March, immediately issued a proclamation ordering the Lê to retire and evacuate the Thai Binh in four days, with a guarantee that the Annamese would not pursue them.
This proclamation could not have frightened the Lê much. They actually continued to think of the French as covert friends and whenever one of our vessels arrived in the vicinity their leaders never failed to go aboard and offer presents.

On 1 August the situation grew tense. The Lê had merely held on to Haiduong more tightly. They could have taken it at any moment. M. Dujardin then went to the scene and persuaded the Lê to withdraw their forces and evacuate several captured towns. In return the Annamese began persecuting all those who had sided with the rebels. The commander reprimanded the mandarins for this, but soon afterwards he followed their example and sent the French gunboats against the Lê.

In so acting, M.Dujardin had to submit to the consequences of the step he had taken. The Annamese reasoned: 'You have overturned the country; your presence has encouraged the Lê uprising; we have given you a treaty, now help us pacify the country'.

So in the month of September, three gunboats - the Scorpion, the Aspic, and the Espingole commanded by M. Dujardin and manned with 100 troops, accompanied by twenty Annamese war junks, started hunting down the Lê troops... (Jean Dupuis, Le Tonkin de 1872 à 1886. Histoire et politique. Paris, Challamel, 1910. pp. 314-16)

81.   M. **Lasserre** to J.**Dupuis**, (No date, probably late 1874.)

My dear Dupuis,

I promised to keep you in touch with events in Tonkin and you will also want to know what has happened to the supporters of the Lê after we abandoned them, and especially after we paid them in cannon shells for the services they rendered to the French cause.

My last letter left them at their second engagement with the French troops, after which they had to seek refuge in the Cat Ba hills.

Recently there was a curious occurrence.

Mgr Colomer, (the Spanish bishop who directs the Dominican college close to Haiduong), touched with compassion for the fate of these unfortunates, sought out M. Dujardin and asked him to put a stop to the massacre....

The bishop assured the commander that he would try to obtain the submission of the Lê, on condition however, that they were taken under his protection to save them from the hatred of the mandarins....

In return for the undertaking which duty had inspired him to make, the bishop asked for a promise that the Lê would be respected by the mandarins and placed under the protection of the French flag. He added that it would be better still to send most of these people to Saigon upon their submission.

Commander Dujardin promised Mgr Colomer to take all the Lê under his protection, to prevent the mandarins from taking reprisals, and to write to Saigon if the Lê laid down their arms and made a sincere submission.

All this happened at Haiphong.

While Mgr Colomer returned to his Mission and sent an Annamese priest to the Lê to convey this idea for a peace, the mandarins found means of suggesting to Commander Dujardin that the bishop's proposals were dangerous, that these people were rebels and that it was preferable to exterminate them all, for at Saigon they would cause serious trouble with the governor of the colony, etc. They persuaded the commander to support them with two gunboats, the _Aspic_ and the _Espingole_ while they set off in their junks under the protection of the French flag to attack the Lê.

You can imagine the deplorable outcome of Mgr Colomer's initiative and the awkward consequences it would have for him.

The Lê believed in the good faith of the promises they had been given. They made ready to descend to the riverside and when they saw the smoke of the steamers, they believed that these had come to escort them to Haiphong. Then cannonfire showed them the true horror of the situation. Happily for them, their positions protected them somewhat from French fire and they were able to withdraw without excessive losses to the hills where the timid Annamese soldiers did not dare to follow and attack them. So the expedition returned empty-handed.

Meantime the (Annamese) missionary felt the anger of the Lê, incensed by this betrayel, and returned to his Mission after many difficulties, to report their reply to Mgr Colomer for transmission to Commander Dujardin. The Lê replied that they would in no way submit and that they preferred to die rather than put faith again in any treacherous French promises; and that only one man, M. Dupuis, could, if he came to find them, make them change their minds.

That, my dear Sir, is the fact which I agreed to communicate to you. (Jean Dupuis, _Le Tonkin de 1872 à 1886. Histoire et politique._ Paris, Challamel, 1910. pp. 317-19)

Dupré fails to obtain a protectorate.

Treaty negotiations with the Vietnamese ambassadors in Saigon finally resumed on 9 March 1874. The resultant agreement favoured the development of French commercial and missionary interests in Tonkin, but fell short of Dupré's requirements in one vital respect: it did not reserve exclusive access to Tonkin for the French.

The admiral's essential purpose had been to prevent any other foreign power from making use of the Song Coi route into South-West China. To achieve this the new treaty needed to contain a formula establishing exclusive French protectoral control over Vietnam in terms acknowledged by international law. Dupré had anticipated difficulty in finding an appropriate formula acceptable to the Vietnamese. When he briefed Lt Philastre on 6 December 1873 before the latter's abortive treaty mission to Hue, the admiral had instructed the French envoy to find a suitable term for 'protectorate' which would not offend Vietnamese susceptibilities **(Doc. 68).** French withdrawal from Tonkin had weakened the French bargaining position, forcing Dupré to abandon his demand for a formal protectorate. He tried nonetheless to obtain for France some of the attributes of protectoral authority. Threatening a naval bombardment of Hue, the admiral forced the Vietnamese to sign a treaty on 15 March 1874 containing clauses which gave France control of Vietnam's external defence and obliged the Vietnamese to 'conform' their foreign policy to that of France. But these provisions did not extinguish Vietnam's existing commercial treaties with other powers. Nor were other powers restrained from further dealings with the Vietnamese by the new treaty if they chose to defy its implications. Since the term 'protectorate' was not incorporated in the agreement, the French remained vulnerable to foreign commercial preemption in Tonkin. Fundamentally, Dupré's policy had failed.

There were lesser compensations for the French, though. French diplomatic and commercial privileges in Tonkin were considerably enlarged **(Doc. 84).** Dupré had been able to withold the offer to give back the three western provinces of Cochinchina which the French cabinet had authorised him to make. And most striking of all, an unusually detailed clause enshrining broad new privileges for missionaries was incorporated into the agreement of 15 March.

Mgr Colombert, Vicar Apostolic of West Cochinchina, drafts the clause on toleration.

This article, clause 9, was drafted almost word for word by Mgr Colombert, Bishop of West Cochinchina, at Dupré's invitation **(Docs 82-84)**. Amplifying the article on religion proposed by Admiral de la Grandière in the negotiations of 1868 **(Doc. 20** supra**)**, it gave legal foundation to an exceptionally wide range of new rights and exemptions. The mission received virtually unfettered sanction to purchase, inherit and dispose of property. Vietnamese Christians were to be protected from administrative harassment, and were even allowed to compete for office within the mandarinate without being forced to observe rituals incompatible with their beliefs. Injurious references to Christianity were to be removed from the imperial Decalogue, the huan dich thap dieu. Finally, the dignity of native clergy was to be protected by exemption from physical punishment for criminal acts. The clause met virtually all the French Catholic mission's longstanding grievances. It now gave a foundation of legal privilege to the greater proportion of vicariates controlled by the Société des Missions Etrangères in Annam and Tonkin. It also protected the vicariates of the Spanish Dominican mission in upper and estuarial Tonkin. In some respects all these vicariates now enjoyed wider freedoms than vicariates under direct French political authority in the South.

In presenting the Franco-Vietnamese treaty for ratification, the French government - a cabinet dominated by the monarchist-clerical Right - covered its embarassment over the Garnier affair by stressing the advantages of clause 9. The report of the treaty commission prompted a parliamentary debate in which the Radical Republican opposition to imperialist expansion and to the missionary role in Vietnam was heard for the first time. Speeches in the debate echoed the acrimonious polemics which had broken out in France in the wake of the Garnier affair. By now the reputation of the mission of West Tonkin for aggressive political interference was plainly established in some sectors of French public opinion.

Further reading

L. de Reinach, **Recueil de traités conclus par la France en Extrême-Orient (1648-1902).** (2 vols. Paris, 1902).
J. Dupuis, **Le Tonkin de 1872 à 1886. Histoire et politique.** (Paris, Challamel, 1910.)
L.E. Louvet, **Vie de Mgr Puginier, Evêque de Mauricastre, Vicaire Apostolique du Tonkin Occidental.** (Hanoi, 1894).

82. Mgr **Colombert**, Bishop of Samostate, Vicar Apostolic of West Cochinchina, to Rear-Admiral **Dupré**, Governor of Cochinchina. Saigon, 23 December 1873.

Since you have kindly permitted it, I take the liberty of conveying to you the articles I have drawn up for the paragraph concerning religion in the Hue treaty.... These articles are, at first sight, very long and detailed for a treaty. It is difficult to abridge them, for experience has clearly shown that it is not enough to establish general principles in dealing with Annam: one has to specify particular applications, otherwise the principles will be evaded.... I am heartily thankful, Governor, that you are in such an advantageous position to negotiate and that circumstances have given you a good understanding of the religious question.... The whole future of our Annamese missions depends upon these treaty clauses. We will only have as much liberty as you can procure for us. You can see as I do, Governor, that the security and gratitude of the bishops and missionaries through whom French influence has been introduced into Indochina, and justice and equity established among these people by our country's authority, and 500,000 Christians snatched from the oppression they have suffered for forty years, and the name of France blessed throughout Annam, are considerations which impress every generous heart. I have added... a literal translation of the Pekin treaty (Chinese text)....

'His Majesty the King of Annam, recognising from the example of civilised nations that the Catholic religion teaches men to do good, revokes all the prohibitions hitherto enacted in his kingdom against the said religion, and accords to all his subjects the right to embrace and practise it freely. The Christians of the kingdom of Annam can meet together and worship in church in unlimited numbers. They will no longer be obliged, on any pretext, to perform acts contrary to their religion, nor to submit to special censuses. They will be admitted to public examinations and to all the offices of the kingdom without being obliged as a result to perform any ceremony prohibited by their religion. His Majesty will have the census of Christians compiled during the last fifteen years destroyed. He will have them put back to the same state as they were in before that period. His Majesty will renew his wise prohibition against using, in public language or writings, terms insulting to the Catholic religion. To the same effect he will correct some of the articles of the (huan dich) thap dieu. The goods taken from Christians during the persecution will be restored to them through the mediation of the French Consul at Hue. Bishops and missionaries can preach Catholic doctrine anywhere. They may enter the kingdom and move around freely, after receipt of a passport issued by the governor of Saigon and endorsed by the government at Hue. They will no longer be subjected to special surveillance, and the village where they live and stay temporarily will no longer be obliged to declare their presence or arrival or departure to the mandarins Annamese priests will excercise their sacred duties as freely as the missionaries. If their conduct merits reprobation they can only be judged by a tribunal in which the bishop will be represented. They will not be liable for punishment by whipping with sticks or canes, such punishment, if properly merited, being commuted to an equivalent (penalty). The bishops, missionaries and Annamese priests will have the right to buy plots of land and houses, to build churches, hospitals, schools and orphanages and all other edifices destined for the service of Catholic worship. The preceding provisions apply to the Spanish as much as to the French. A royal edict, to be published after exchange of ratifications, will proclaim in every commune of the kingdom the freedoms accorded to Christians by this treaty'. (A.O.M. Aix. Indochine Amiraux 11,688/27 and 28.)

83. Mgr **Colombert**, Bishop of Samostate, Vicar Apostolic of West Cochinchina, to Rear-Admiral **Dupré**, Governor of Cochinchina, Saigon, 26 December 1873.

As drawn up, the article concerning religion seems really very acceptable. I have made use of the freedom which you have given me to present my observations. In presenting them to you I associate myself with your enterprise and with your lofty purpose of assuring justice, liberty and the common good. (A.O.M. Aix. Indochine, Amiraux 11,688/28.

84. **The Franco-Vietnamese treaty of 15 March 1874.**

Art. 1. There will be perpetual peace, friendship and alliance between France and the Kingdom of Annam.

Art. 2. His Excellency the President of the French Republic recognising the sovereignty of the King of Annam and his entire independence in relation to all foreign powers whatsoever, promises him help and assistance and undertakes to give him freely, and upon request, the necessary support to maintain order and tranquillity in his dominions, so as to defend him against all attack and extinguish the piracy which is desolating a part of the kingdom's coasts.

Art. 3. In return for protection, His Majesty the King of Annam undertakes to conform his external policy to that of France and to change nothing in his present diplomatic relations. This political undertaking does not extend to treaties of commerce. But in no case may the King of Annam make with any nation at all a commercial treaty incompatible with that concluded between France and the Kingdom of Annam, and without having previously informed the French government.

(Gift of five steamships, cannons, rifles and cartridges.)

Art. 4. (The French to supply, on payment, instructors for retraining the Annamese army and navy, together with engineers, financial and customs advisers.)

Art. 5. His Majesty the King of Annam acknowledges the full and complete sovereignty of France over all the territory currently occupied by her and enclosed within the following frontiers: to the East, the China Sea and the kingdom of Annam (Binh Thuan province); to the West, the Gulf of Siam; to the South, the China Sea; to the North the kingdom of Cambodia and the kingdom of Annam (Binh Thuan province).

(Preservation of the Pham and Ho tombs in Cochinchina).

Arts 6 and **7.** (Payment to France of remaining war indemnities owed by Annam no longer required. Vietnamese to pay remainder of the Spanish indemnity through French mediation).

Art. 8. His Excellency the President of the French Republic and His Majesty the King grant a general, full and complete amnesty, with the restoration of all sequestered property, to those of their respective subjects who, until the conclusion of the treaty and before it, have compromised themselves in the service of the other Contracting Party.

Art. 9. His Majesty the King of Annam, recognising that the Catholic religion teaches men to do good, revokes and annuls all prohibitions issued against this religion and gives all his subjects permission to embrace it and practise it freely. In consequence, the Christians of the kingdom of Annam can meet together and worship in church in unlimited numbers. They will not be obliged, on any pretext, to perform acts contrary to their religion, nor to submit to special censuses. They will be admitted to all the public examinations and to public employment without being obliged as a result to perform any act prohibited by religion.

His Majesty agrees that the census registers for Christians compiled during the last fifteen years shall be destroyed, and that in regard to censuses and registers Christians will be treated exactly like his other subjects. He also undertakes to renew his wise prohibition against the employment of terms injurious to religion in speech or writing and to have corrected those articles in the (huan dich) thap dieu in which such terms are employed.

The bishops and missionaries may freely enter the kingdom and travel round their dioceses with a passport issued by the Governor of Cochinchina and endorsed by the Minister of Rites or by the governor of the province. They may preach the Catholic doctrine in all places. They will not be subjected to any special surveillance and the villages will no longer be made to report either their arrival or their presence or their departure to the mandarins. Annamese priests, like the missionaries, shall excercise their ministry freely. If their conduct is reprehensible, and if, according to the law the transgression committed by them is punishable by beating with stick or cane, this penalty will be commuted for an equivalent punishment. The bishops, missionaries and priests will have the right to buy or let land and houses, to build churches, hospitals, schools, orphanages and any other edifices intended to serve the purposes of worship. The goods taken from Christians on account of their religion and which are still sequestrated, will be restored to them. All the preceding provisions without exception apply to the Spanish missionaries as well as to the French.

A royal edict, published immediately after the exchange of ratifications, will proclaim in every commune the freedom accorded by His Majesty to all Christians in His kingdom.

Art. 10. (Provision for a non-denominational Annamese college at Saigon).

Arts 11 and **12.** (Opening of the ports of Thi Nai, Ninh Hai (Haiphong), Hanoi and the Song Coi from the Nhi Ha river to Yunnan and establishing freedom of commerce to French and foreign nationals).

Art. 13. (French consuls to be appointed in these ports with garrisons of under 100 men.)

Art. 14. (Annamese to enjoy trade and consular rights in France).

Arts 15–19. (Matters concerning establishments and jurisdiction).

Art. 20. (A French Resident to be appointed at Hue).

Art. 21. (The Spanish government to be invited to assent to this treaty as a replacement for that of 1862. If the Spanish withold assent, their rights of 1862 remain in force, and the French will discharge remainder of Annamese indemnity to Spain.)

Art. 22. (Arrangements for ratification.)

Signed: Rear-Admiral **Dupré**.
Le Thuan and **Nguyen Van Tuong**.

(F. Romanet du Caillaud, <u>Histoire de l'intervention française au Tong-King de 1872 à 1874.</u> (Paris, 1880) pp. 437-9.)

85. Treaty commission report to the Chamber of Deputies recommending ratification of the treaty of 15 March 1874. <u>Rapporteur</u>: Admiral **C.L.J. Jaurès**

(pp. 1-2)...The treaty of 1862 remained very incomplete in its provisions in favour of christianisation. Article 2 was confined to establishing for the French and Spanish the right to practise their religion in the Empire of Annam and, for the Annamese, the right to embrace Christianity. Article 9 of the treaty of 15 March 1874 stipulates more effective guarantees.... No treaty with the nations of the Far East has supported the practice of Christianity with such extensive guarantees.... It assures to our Annamese co-religionists a treatment identical to that which the laws of the country assure for the other subjects of His Majesty the King of Annam and it confers on missionaries a measure of liberty which they do not enjoy at all in Japan, and which in China is subject to many conditions and reservations....

(p. 8)...The second important point of the treaty is that which gives the Christian religion serious guarantees for its free excercise and development.

On this land, watered with the blood of so many martyrs, where there are now eight bishops, about four hundred missionaries and more than five hundred thousand Christians, it will now be permitted to our co-religionists to profess their faith without having to be afraid of fearsome tortures. The good sense of our bishops and missionaries is a sure guarantee that they, for their part, will take care to ensure that the Christian population shows itself most submissive and respectful towards the authority of the sovereign of Annam.... (Journal Officiel Français, 4 August 1874 p. 5550 ff.)

86. Speeches in the Chamber of Deputies' debate on the ratification of the Franco-Annamese treaty of 15 March 1874.

Georges Périn (Radical) ... I do not think we should ratify a treaty which exposes France to engaging in a series of struggles and distant wars with the Empire of Annam. I do not think we should ratify a treaty which will oblige France to undertake veritable wars of religion...(protests)...to assure our missions an absolute and unlimited freedom to proselytise. (Interruptions on the Right.).

I understand, gentlemen, your desire to assure them this liberty to proselytise. I would not myself oppose it at all if they were able to practice it without our intervention; but I do not think that France should draw her sword for it, and that is what the treaty obliges us to do....

... What I want to discuss for a moment is... article 9, because of the exorbitant power and independence it confers upon the missionaries.

Please note carefully, that by this article 9 you give missionaries entering the kingdom of Hue (sic) and Tonkin a position which prevents the Emperor Tu Duc from having any power at all over them in whatever they do.... I know that Admiral Jaurès in his report shows his conviction that the missionaries will not abuse the independence assured to them by the treaty: 'The good sense of our bishops and missionaries,' says (the report), 'is a sure guarantee that they... will take care to ensure that the Christian population shows itself most submissive and respectful towards the authority of the sovereign of Annam.' Alright, but for that to be so, the missionaries have to give up involvement in politics. I think, for my part, that they will never give it up, and I derive this impression from their own writings.

A reading of the Annales de la propagation de la foi will leave you with little doubt on this point. Listen, moreover, to what the ambassadors from Hue replied to Captain, now Vice-Admiral, Jauréguiberry when the latter was trying to negotiate with them. M. Jauréguiberry was ordered to demand full religious liberty for the Catholic missions. To that Tu Duc's ambassadors replied: 'There are perpetual conspiracies for the overthrow of the dynasty concealed under the cloak of religion; and we do not understand why you wish to make the Cochinchina authorities protect religious propaganda alien to our country'.

.... When one makes a treaty one should presume that it will be adhered to or else one would never make it. That seems perfectly reasonable. Unfortunately the missionaries themselves do not believe that this treaty can be executed. I find proof of this in a letter from Father Tessier, a missionary sent to Saigon last March by M. Gauthier, Bishop of South Tonkin, to petition the governor on behalf of his flock, in peril following the Garnier expedition. Here is what Father Tessier wrote. You will find this letter in the Annales de la Foi for 15 May: 'Satan has never deployed his rage so savagely against the Christians of Annam. Tu Duc has never persecuted religion so cleverly nor so cruelly. He puts the scholars forward so as not to compromise himself in France's eyes. Publicly he calls for concord, whereas secretly he pushes the scholars into organising a general massacre of Christians. With one hand he signs a treaty with France promising full and entire liberty, and with the other he cuts the throats of those of his subjects who have espoused Christianity.'

It seems to me that under these conditions, if you wish to execute article 2 of the treaty (promising to pacify disorder), you will have to draw your sword frequently and make some murderous expeditions.... I say that you will be obliged to resort to force to have the treaty executed. That, moreover, is the opinion of the missionaries themselves.... So you will be resorting to the gun to execute this treaty, and thereby undertaking a veritable war of religion. (Denials from several benches.)

Admiral Jaurès, (Spokesman for the treaty commission). ...As for the missionaries: M. Périn has rendered them homage for their courage, but I think he has exaggerated their ambition and their involvement in politics.

You, like me, have seen how they came aboard our ships asking to be set ashore in almost deserted spots from which to enter and hide away in the country..., how they were almost always obliged to take refuge in forests, risking death from poverty and deprivation, facing daily the prospect of being pursued, tracked down and decapitated, or sawn in half between two planks. Is this what you call conspiracy and involvement in politics? No, these admirable men know of nothing but preaching the gospel and advancing towards martyrdom!.... So they are not conspirators or revolutionaries, they have respect for sovereign authority and they will show all the more respect for it now that, thanks to this treaty, the sovereign is going to give them the freedom to practice their religion. I am afraid of taking up the time of this assembly unnecessarily or I would read out the treaty prepared in 1857: its content is exactly the same as that of article 9: freedom for the Annamese to become Christians and to practice our religion. Now, for that to happen it is necessary to say that they can build churches, that missionaries are permitted to travel the country. This is all there is in Article 9. Consequently there is no danger that this article might cause problems and differences between us and the empire of Annam. It is evident, moreover, that your future representative at the Court of Hue will strive from the outset to make the king of Cochinchina understand that we are not asking for the protection of the Christian religion in order to foment difficulties, but on the contrary, to resolve them....

Finally, gentlemen, one point which M. Périn has not discussed and which is certainly important is that by this treaty you open some new and very important outlets for European trade. It is not only France's interests which are at stake, but the interests of civilised Europe. (Hear, Hear!)

You know how vainly you have searched up the Cambodia (Mekong) river for a navigable route into southern China, and here is a treaty which gives you free access to a magnificent river (the Song Coi) by which you can reach the territory of Yunnan, so rich in minerals of every kind, iron, copper, tin, coal etc., etc. You are opening this route and improving access to these riches for the whole of Europe, so by it you are carrying out the work of civilisation and progress! (Numerous and repeated signs of approval.)

It seems to be feared that this treaty will incite disapproval and cause us complications. No, gentlemen, on the contrary, Europe will consider that you only had in mind the general interests of civilisation and humanity, and that the treaty which I hope you will ratify, is as favourable to European interests as much as to French. (Hear, hear! Applause.)   (Journal Officiel Français, 5 August 1874 pp. 5577-80.)

III C   THE AFTERMATH OF THE GARNIER AFFAIR AND THE OPERATION OF
THE TREATY OF 1874.

Anti-Christian massacres and popular insurrection in South Tonkin and
North Annam, 1874.

As Franco-Vietnamese diplomatic dealings continued through the winter of
1873-4, popular reaction to the Garnier expedition, organised by the
scholar elite, proliferated rapidly, with the massacre, looting and
burning of Christian villages in Tonkin. In February and March, 1874
the efforts of the Vietnamese court to moderate reprisals against
Christians provoked a movement of anti-governmental insurgency which
resulted in the seizure of provincial administrative centres in northern
Annam. This was the first popular challenge to imperial authority to
result directly from French intervention. Spilling over from Tonkin
into Nghe An, Bo Chinh (Quang Binh province) and Ha Tinh in northern
Annam, these mixed anti-Christian and anti-governmental disturbances
reached as far south as Quang Nam. Two memoranda (**Docs 87, 88**) written
internally for the French colonial undersecretariat in 1874, paint a
vivid picture of the social and political conflict. The anti-Christian
massacres may have begun spontaneously and coincidentally; but the
rapidity with which widely separated Christian communes and mission
stations were destroyed across the region suggests the development of a
measure of coordination between localities.

Seeking to restrain scholar-led attacks on Christians, Tu Duc had
issued a proclamation justifying his continued cooperation with the
French in terms of military realism:

Do you really wish to confront such a power with a pack of
cowardly soldiers? It would be like mounting an elephant's head
or caressing a tiger's tail. How would we differ from a swarm
of flies dancing over the grass; or from a host of locusts
kicking a carriage? With what you presently have, do you really
expect to dissolve the enemies' rifles into air or chase his
battleships into hell? (I)

In their responses, scholars implied criticism of the emperor's
pusillanimity. Some begged Tu Duc for sanction to offer resistance:

Our troops await only an order to recover the lost territory.
All subjects of the kingdom with an ounce of intelligence or a
stitch of strength swear to Heaven and Earth to wash out the

175

stains.... Who dares to pretend that our troops are inadequate or that they are cowardly. On the contrary, their columns are as long as our rivers and their courage as high as our mountains....! (2)

Other petitions threatened defiance of imperial restraint **(Docs 89, 90).** Indignation at French intervention was not confined to scholar elements: evidence from some French sources suggests that sympathy was being shown for the scholars' movement by part of the mandarinate and even by some detachments of the imperial forces **(Docs 88, 92).**

Repression.

In his response to these manifestations, Tu Duc showed as much concern to reassert his own authority as to stifle the scholars' provocation of the French. He ordered units of the Tonkin army to suppress social disorder in both Tonkin and northern Annam, and even resorted to recruiting Christians to help repress political dissent in Nghe An **(Doc. 93).** The decisive role in the suppression of the scholar-led nghia quan ('righteous armies' or partisan groups) appears to have been played by Prince Ton That Thuyet, the military mandarin commanding the imperial forces at Son Tay. A decade later, as Regent in 1885, Thuyet was to split the Vietnamese court by leading the Can Vuong movement of resistance against the French. Even at this early date his compliance with the Emperor Tu Duc's policy of appeasing the French seems to have been uncertain. After some hesitation Thuyet finally pronounced against the scholar forces in Nghe An, and his declaration seems to have been responsible for procuring their rapid demoralisation and collapse **(Doc. 88).**

The missions and the operation of the 1874 treaty.

The operation of the religious clause of the new treaty led to some transitory difficulties in relations between the Vietnamese and French authorities.

Vietnamese officials evidently hoped to prevent the details of a diplomatic agreement so damaging to imperial authority from becoming popular knowledge. French officials protested strongly at Vietnamese reluctance to publish the terms of the clause on religious toleration, as the treaty prescribed **(Doc. 96).** Even after publication, the Vietnamese authorities were still slow to eliminate disparaging references to Christianity from the huan dich thap dieu, or imperial Decalogue, in fulfilment of clause 9. Vietnamese officials also tried to thwart another of the treaty's politically unpalatable provisions: the acceptance of Christians as examination candidates for entry to the mandarinate. The implications of allowing pro-French Christian candidates into the official hierarchy were far-reaching, and covert evasion of this provision was perhaps predictable. French consular officials noticed that examination procedures had suddenly been modified to facilitate identification - and, presumably, discrimination against - Christian candidates. Through steady diplomatic pressure the French forced the Vietnamese to give effect to these aspects of the treaty. By the end of the decade French authorities were generally satisfied that their complaints on the operation of clause 9 were being met, though relations with Hue remained abrasive on other points. Even missionaries conceded that clause 9 was being generally observed **(Doc. 105)**, that Christian communes seemed to be suffering little administrative harassment, and that freedom of movement had been restored.

Missionary disputes with Vietnamese authorities.

For their own part, French Catholic missionaries seemed intent on exploiting the advantages of the mission's improved political position. They strained the patience of both French and Vietnamese authorities by a tendency to press for further concessions beyond the terms of the treaty.

In southern Annam missionaries succeeded in persuading Vietnamese authorities to allow Christian communes to become tax-exempt 'corporations'. The captain of the Duchaffaut testified to the socially disruptive effects of this measure and deplored it **(Doc. 104)**. Meantime, Bishop Puginier in West Tonkin demanded permission from the imperial court to allow missionaries and bishops to deal direct with senior provincial officials in all disputes affecting Christians. He argued a special need to protect Christian communes from petty harassment by Vietnamese minor officials - the administrative level with which they were always in closest contact. Puginier was well aware that the privilege of direct mediation with the highest levels of officialdom would vastly increase the social authority of the missionary, and thus his power to attract new converts. The Vietnamese court **(Doc. 99)** and the French authorities in Cochinchina were equally outraged at Puginier's presumption. From Saigon, Admiral Lafont - an exceptionally pro-clerical governor anxious to uphold French treaty rights - supported Vietnamese insistence on traditional procedure for referring problems affecting Christians systematically up the ladder of hierarchy ·**(Doc. 102)**. For his part, Lafont insisted on the right of French consuls to handle disputes between missionaries and Vietnamese officials in all cases involving infringement of the new treaty.

The thorniest issue raised by missionaries in the wake of the treaty of 1874 was the question of indemnities **(Docs 94, 97)**. Clause 9 merely authorised the restitution of Christian property which had been officially confiscated. It did not provide for indemnification in cases of massacre and destruction. After the recent scholar-led massacres in Annam and Tonkin, Tu Duc had adopted a policy of conciliation. Even though he blamed Christians for inciting much of the destruction from which they had suffered **(Doc. 95)**, he had authorised compensation. But the bishops continued to advance enormous claims, probably hoping for French official support. Indemnity demands put forward by Mgr Gauthier were particularly large. Gauthier's vicariate of South Tonkin covered the ravaged provinces of Nghe An and Ha Tinh, and the bishop appeared to want total restitution. The French chargé d'affaires at Hue, Captain Philastre, warned that civil war might ensue if those non-Christian communities which were responsible for the destruction were forced to meet Christian claims in full. Philastre, who was personally hostile to the missionary presence, concluded that the indemnities already advanced - some 550,000 ligatures - were adequate **(Doc. 97)**.

From the way in which these disputes arose and were settled in the later 1870s, it seems that French and Vietnamese officialdom had come into transitory alignment on issues affecting the interests of Christians and the pacification of social disorder. French colonial officials were as anxious as the Vietnamese authorities for social restabilisation in the wake of recent religious and political upheavals. Despite the shortcomings of the new treaty, French officials did not seem to want to make use of the grievances of the Catholic missions to increase French political leverage and influence in Annam and Tonkin, even though the opportunity for this plainly existed. French consular and colonial authorities agreed to support the traditional procedures of Vietnamese administration and the authority of the monarchy. They wanted the treaty to operate effectively in its own terms until policy changes from France determined otherwise.

Overall, the Catholic missions in Annam and Tonkin were to emerge from this period of stress considerably strengthened. They were protected by substantial new treaty rights, and as a result missionary social influence had also increased. Attributing the subsequent growth in conversions to the effectiveness of protection offered by the new treaty, Puginier reported that adult baptisms in his own vicariate of West Tonkin 'strengthened and grew progressively', increasing by 21,000 between 1877 and 1883 (See infra **Doc. 191**).

(1). Truong Buu Lam, Patterns of Vietnamese response to foreign intervention: 1858-1900. (Yale U.P. 1967.) pp. 106-7

(2) Ibid. p. 107

Further reading

Truong Buu Lam, **Patterns of Vietnamese resistance to foreign intervention, 1858-1900.** (Yale U.P., New Haven, 1967).
J. Dupuis, **Le Tonkin de 1872 à 1886. Histoire et politique.** (Paris, Challamel, 1910.)
L.E. Louvet, **Vie de Mgr Puginier, Evêque de Mauricastre, Vicaire Apostolique du Tonkin Occidental.** (Hanoi, 1894).
P. Philastre, **Le code annamite.** (2 vols. Paris, 1876).
Ministère des Affaires Etrangères. **Documents diplomatiques. Affaire du Tonkin,** 1ère partie, 1874 - déc. 1882. (Livre Jaune).
N.D. Lê, **Les Missions-Etrangères et la pénétration française au Viet-Nam.** (Paris, Mouton, 1975).

Documents

87.   Memorandum for the colonial undersecretariat. Undated, probably 1875-1877. 'Note on the persecution of Christians following events in Tonkin.'

.... The hatred of the scholars, encouraged by the tacit connivance of the mandarins, found pretext in the edict of Tu Duc published on 2 December 1873 in Nghe An, to start an unprecedented persecution. The killing and burning followed immediately upon the seizure of Nam Dinh by the French on 9 December 1873.   In the provinces of Nam Dinh, Ninh Binh and Hanoi they became very violent when it was learned that the French were probably going to abandon Tonkin.   On 19 January eighty Christian villages were burned and several hundred inhabitants and native priests massacred.   The inaction of M. Philastre, who put no pressure on the mandarins of these three provinces, gave the greatest freedom to the bands raised by the scholars.   All the same he was forced to send thirty French soldiers to protect So Kieu (Ke-So), Mgr Puginier's residence, a town in which the Mission's big seminary, college and press were situated. From the end of January, from fear of the French, the disorders ceased in these three provinces. Thirty thousand Christians were at that moment absolutely without provisions.

Provinces of Nghe An and Bo Chinh (Quang Binh). In these two provinces, by contrast, the massacres only began later, in the month of February. Bands raised by the scholars Cuu and Mai, previously condemned to death for burning twenty Christian villages in 1868, profited from the disarray of the Annamese administration to join the rebels and massacre Christians. The localities of Tanh Huyen, Nam Duong, Hoi Yen, Dong Thanh, Quynh Luu, Van Tac, and Mi Du were burned and sacked, about 3000 Christians were killed and 115 villages burned. At about the middle of March the Christians began to resist. Xa Doai, residence of Mgr Gauthier, where 12,000 Christians had taken refuge, repelled the assault of the scholars' troops and inflicted considerable losses on them. The mandarins, vanquished on all sides by the rebels, received orders from Hue to ally themselves to (the Christians), and in June 1874, thanks to their help, succeeded in suppressing the insurrection. After that they took as little account as possible of (Christian) help, but all the same the persecutions ceased.

Provinces east of the Song Coi. The persecution which followed our abandonment of Tonkin did not rage in the apostolic vicariates belonging to the Spanish Dominicans. The missionaries (here) kept their relative freedom and were the object of marks of benevolence. The bishop, Mgr Colomer, received from Tu Duc some gifts of land for constructing churches, and medals of gold and silver as thanks for the useful help he gave in keeping order in the provinces east of the Song Coi. (A.N.S.O.M. Paris. Indochine, (A.F.) 28 bis/A 90 (4))

88. **Memorandum written for the colonial undersecretariat.** Undated, probably 1875 or 1876. 'Revolt in Southern Tonkin in 1874'.

When representations were made to the government of Tu Duc the latter took steps immediately after the signature of the treaty of Saigon on 15 March 1874 to halt the massacre of the Christians and repress the excesses of the scholars. He sent troops to disperse the bands of arsonists and ordered their principal leaders to be executed. Opinions hostile to the king were immediately manifested and since the mandarins were covertly favouring the malcontents, an insurrection began on 25 February (sic) 1874 which soon engulfed the whole of Nghe An province. On 31 May the rebels took the citadel of Ha Tinh, capital of the province of the same name which is an enclave in Nghe An, without encountering resistance. A few days later the five <u>phu</u> of Nghe An were in the hands of the insurgents and 20,000 of them laid siege to Vinh or Nghe An Phu, the capital of the province. The scholars with their bands made common cause with the new troops of rebels, but while the latter attacked the king's forces openly, the scholars tended to deal more with the Christians, and the persecutions which had slackened off somewhat then became more violent than ever. Tu Duc had sent 4000 men against the rebels but this small army was inadequate and the revolt came nearer (to Hue). One force of rebels cross the Deo ong gia pass which separates Tonkin from Cochinchina (<u>recte</u> Annam) and defeated the king's men near Bo Chinh. Ha Tinh, the last town occupied by the rebels was captured in the month of June. Meanwhile Prince T(h)uyet, the commander at Son Tay raised a body of troops and marched on Nghe An.

Since he was, it is said, an aspirant to Tu Duc's throne, it was hard to know whether he would side with the rebels or with the king and mandarins. In the hope of seeing him declare for them, the rebel scholars continued their campaign despite the loss of their fortresses. Entering Nghe An, T(h)uyet decided that he should have nothing to do with the rebels and declared himself against them. The insurrection immediately collapsed and reprisals began. Nearly 2000 rebels were decapitated and the rest had their thumbs cut off. As for the Christians, the mandarins, emboldened by Tuyet's presence and no longer needing them, demobilised them without paying anything in return for their services and without giving them justice against their exploiters.

They even aggravated their already sad predicament by new regulations from that time on.... **(**A.N.S.O.M. Paris. Indochine, (A.F.) 28 bis/A 90 (4) **)**

89. Part of a petition received by the Emperor and distributed to all mandarins commenting on the proposed treaty terms. (1874)

...If one follows the precepts of true reason it is impossible for a true religion and a false religion to exist side by side. Also the scholars and loyal people habitually make this oath: 'Better to be in disgrace with the Court than to suffer the shame of living with the followers of a perverse religion.'

Thus to the south from Quang Nam and to the north from Nghe An, as soon as a priest appears the people rush him under...

The Emperor **Tu Duc**'s marginal comment on the above:
This petition from the mandarins contains some truth, but the right

moment has not yet arrived. Let them be told to keep their advice secret.

27th year of Tu Duc, 10th day of the first moon (27 February 1874).
(J. Dupuis, Le Tonkin de 1872 à 1886. Histoire et politique. Paris, Challamel, 1910. pp. 281-2)

90. Petition by the scholars to the Emperor (Feb.-March 1874).

We look furtively upon the wise and knowledgeable face of Your Majesty, we who are small and despicable, and we ask if we may propose a way of driving off these Europeans. We raise our eyes to you. May Your Majesty deign to hear us and allow us, humble as we are, to show our fidelity to you. We are the scholars and leaders of the people, and we are permitted to think that from all time, following the precepts of reason, the true way has been followed and the false way abandoned, and the heart of the people is always ready to fight for our country. If we do not raise our voices to ask if we can fight the guilty, how can we call ourselves courageous?

If we do not try to unmask their double-dealing promptly, if we do not hurry to heal this sore, we will be bound to shed tears later, for it will be impossible to apply a remedy. If we do not act promptly to lance this swelling with a thorn now, later on it will be necessary to use a hatchet. If it is required that we wait to test the faith of this peace, the French will gain time to find themselves an impenetrable position and will become even more redoubtable.

It would be best to arm ourselves with courage and begin by beating them, cutting off their wings and lopping off their branches. Only then will we be strong enough to wipe out all trace of the French.

We prostrate ourselves at your feet, most resplendent and merciful Majesty, who possesses the power of former kings, who is learned in scholarship and strong in arms, who possesses great wealth and many soldiers, who distributes his plenty and who guilefully treats these European savages with honour. They, in their stupidity, presume upon it like the evil, useless race they are. They have a frightening ferocity and pride. It is not only the Court which hates them: the people too are indignant.

Work in the fields has been abandoned and we have already found 70,000 of the best soldiers and 2000 able commanders. Our arms are sound and we have the usual signals. We wish to parade the heads of these people on pikes and cut their bodies into pieces; but we are afraid because we have not yet received the royal edict. So it is with full hearts and faces aflame that we make our supplication to the capital and dare to ask permission to act only for the best so that we can burn their books and their houses and stop them living among us in this kingdom, behead their priests and catechists and destroy entirely this race of European barbarians. As for mere Christians who refuse to apostatise, and their leaders who have joined with the French to make rebellion, we will kill them all without letting a single one escape. Only in this way can the people in its weakness hope to prove to the court a small measure of its devotion, and only thus can the royal tombs obtain a long repose.

We, the many scholars and leaders of the people, vile and small, who live in a corner of the kingdom of Annam, who are rustic and crude, feeble and infirm, who have made arms from our ploughshares and harrows, we are afraid that our troops are not well drilled. Cultivators have become generals and we fear that this might discredit the military calling, but Heaven and Earth will not pardon rebels. Let anyone kill them who can. Everyone knows good from evil. Whoever wishes to do good without doing it does not merit the name of hero.

That is why we dare to bare our whole heart to Your Majesty and beg him to hear us. If He deigns to consider, we beg him to hear our words and let the water be drawn, the fires be lit, so that these beings who are not part of the human race can be utterly destroyed and ploughed under. If we are fortunate and the sea becomes calm again and the waters quiet, the kingdom will have no more to fear, neither hunger nor thirst. We send up our suppliant cry to Your Majesty on high. Here below we consult the provincial mandarins so that we can agree together in order that our petition can be sent promptly to the Council, to let it know that the people see this affair as an important matter. We beg the Court to make a firm decision and grant our wish, so that we may avoid resisting the orders of Your Majesty. (J. Dupuis, Le Tonkin de 1872 à 1886. Histoire et politique. Paris, Challamel, 1910. pp. 277-82)

91. Paul **Rheinart,** Resident at Hanoi, to Rear-Admiral **Krantz,** Governor of Cochinchina. Hanoi, 29 March 1874.

It is most regrettable that the Christians should have formed a kind of political party, so that when they feel supported they show no more regard for the feelings of the scholars than the latter show for theirs. Persecutions are often mere reprisals. Nothing similar is occurring among the Spanish missionaries where there is less political involvement. (A.O.M. Aix. Indochine, Amiraux, 13,505)

92. Fr **Galibert** to Mgr **Charbonnier**, Bishop of Domitiopolis, Vicar Apostolic of East Cochinchina. Tra Kieu (Quang Nam), 21 June 1874.

Mgr Sohier wrote on the twelfth of this month to tell me that the scholars had arrived at Song Giang where they interrupted all communication with the north. I am assured by more recent news that the scholars have crossed the river, so their ravages have reached Mgr Sohier's mission (Hue and North Cochinchina). The court has, on two or three occasions, sent troops to defeat the scholars; but the soldiers arrive at the site of the carnage and do nothing, or rather they make common cause with the scholars. These facts are reported by eye witnesses and can, I think, be given credence. Now here is what is happening in Quang Nam. Latterly at Ha Tinh the Ong Doc Hoc (he is the mandarin appointed by the king to the capital of the province to teach Chinese character script) sent round a letter for all the scholars to sign. This letter contained no less than a formal promise to massacre all the Christians. More than thirty signatures had already been collected before an adversary of the Ong Doc Hoc got possession of the letter and sent it to the mandarins, accusing the Ong Doc Hoc of having committed a culpable act which merited punishment. The mandarins made haste, not to punish the Ong Doc Hoc, but to silence his denouncer. What happened in secret after that I do not know, but what is plainly apparent is that everyone is talking of the massacre of the Christians as a certainty which will happen soon. For few months certain <u>Ba Ho</u>[1] have been having lances forged and I am even assured that all the arms in the <u>phu-yen</u> have been put at the disposal of the scholars. All in all I am convinced that our last hour is approaching. (A.S.M.E. Vol.750, (Cochinchine Orientale, 1845-1880). No. 260)

(1). Notables (lit. 'Richest of a hundred families.').

93. Paul **Rheinart**, Chargé d'Affaires at Hue, to Commandant **Rivière**. Hue, 2 February 1883. (Private.)

The Christians of Nghe An, whom I mentioned to you in my last letter, are in a far different situation from those in Tonkin. They never provoked anyone and never took sides, but were very badly treated by the scholars' party which is particularly hostile to them and is very active in this province. These Christians were absolutely neutral in 1873 during the Garnier business, but the scholars took up arms against them in the aftermath of this affair - and because of it. There were more than 2,000 people killed - men women and children (even more, 2,200) - and hundreds of houses burned and pillaged. It was a real disaster. The scholars, highly excited at the time (in 1874), finding their government too soft on Christians, rose against it and took possession of the citadel at Ha Tinh. I have precise knowledge of the business - I was in Tonkin at the time - and in 1875 and 1876 I had to follow the matter up, and it was not settled until 1877. Passing through there on board the Decrès and taking a rest for the day, I saw an Annamese steamer conveying reinforcements there against the scholars - they asked for help from the Christians to recapture Ha Tinh.

In 1876 there were again fears that the scholars might take to arms: the Christians of this region have never done anything and only asked to live in peace; but they were made to pay cruelly for what we were doing in our own interests, and were forced to suffer for the capture of Hanoi, and I think it is only right that we should take care of these poor devils as far as circumstances permit. A boat appearing from time to time and docking there if time allows would be enough to restore confidence, give the scholars pause for thought and remind them that they will have to pay for their misdeeds if they try to start a new massacre.... (A. Masson, Correspondance politique du Commandant Rivière au Tonkin, Avril 1882 - Mai 1883. Paris, 1933. p. 184)

94. M. **Turc,** Consul at Haiphong, to Rear-Admiral **Duperré,** Governor of Cochinchina. Haiphong, 1 April 1876.

In Nghe An province, southern Tonkin... the Christians, prompted by the events of 1874, demand the indemnities due to them and punishment of the guilty. On the other hand the scholars, who are very numerous and influential, resist. And the Annamese government, which in principle supports the claims of the former, declares itself almost incapable of managing the latter and of forcing them to obey.... (A.O.M. Aix. Indochine, Amiraux 13,130)

95. The Emperor **Tu Duc.** Royal edict on the treatment of Christians. Hue, 28 October 1875.

And you Catholics, even if you have your own religion, is your nature any different from that of others? If you do not practice the Rites you cannot become complete men. The loyalty binding sovereign and subjects, fathers and children, is a reality. How can you bear to abandon father and mother and, even more, myself who tolerates you, guides you, nourishes you and looks upon you with the same humane feelings as upon all my people? You have recently been allowed to compete by examination for entry into public office according to ability. In this I have shown you my greatest benevolence. Have you taken account of that? For you still dare to violate the Rites. Are not examinations and public office of great importance after all? Is it not you who disqualify yourselves from them? Whose fault is that? Yet you continually complained and behaved with such pride and disdain that lawbreakers were recently driven to burn your villages and caused me worry as to how you could be rescued. The resultant public expense and private loss has been considerable. You had not shown yourselves worthy of my favours, but once peace was restored I conferred favours on you nonetheless. I exempted you from personal tax and field taxes, and I distributed alms. Both you, and those who attacked you were in the wrong. So who should make restitution? Once the will of the sovereign was made known it merely remained for you to follow it. If you cannot keep to yourselves, if you look for issues to quarrel and fight over, it is you who are to blame. You disregard my benefactions, I who have nurtured you. Know from these lengthy admonitions that, whatever problems occur, you are simply part of the general population. How can one protect and come to the assistance of all of you? My essential desire is to lose not a single one of my subjects. That is why I give moral guidance to all without distinction. If you do not behave yourselves, will the French Resident not tire of you? In the same way that a girl who has lost her chastity is abandoned and despised, are not the unpatriotic and the disloyal rejected for employment by outsiders? Necessarily so. Do your daily work to earn your living like all peaceable people, but avoid wrongdoing. When the mandarins condemn you for your crimes will the Resident come to your rescue? No, he will simply condemn you just as forcefully. France and Annam are now like two brothers sharing the same house, each going about his own business. A man ought to be selected as Resident who is used to respecting the Rites and Justice, for this guarantees his friendly feeling towards us. He would be known as a Foreign Servant, showing as much respect to the king of a friendly country as to his own. But what use are such titles if he has no comprehension of the Rites? Understanding the Rites implies taking account of the individual's obligation to look after the business of his sovereign. Moreover, a Resident is nominated to look after the affairs of two nations, and not to investigate the business of ordinary people, good or bad.... (A.O.M. Aix. Indochine, Amiraux 12,774. Enclosed in M. Rheinart, Chargé d'Affaires at Hue, to Rear-Admiral Duperré, Governor of Cochinchina, 9 October 1875.)

96.   Paul **Rheinart**,   Resident   in Annam, to Rear-Admiral **Duperré,** Governor of Cochinchina. Hue, 30 October 1875.

The edict has appeared at last.... They wanted to amend the words 'have corrected the articles of the thap dieu', and put that the thap dieu would no longer need to be compulsorily recited.   I categorically refused since I wanted complete reparation in the form of a public retraction for the insults inserted in the thap dieu.   The edict contains absolutely nothing but the text of article 9, without commentary, details or explanations.   It is enough for the moment....
(A.O.M. Aix. Indochine, Amiraux 12,776)

97.   Captain **Philastre,** Chargé d'affaires at Hue, to Rear-Admiral **Lafont,** Governor of Cochinchina. Hue, 7 March 1877.

In the dossier sent by M. Turc I have seen the claims made by the Christians, who refer to lands abandoned by pagans and ask for the concession or use of them as reparations.   The minister asserts that the measure was then sanctioned, but only in opposition to the general opinion of the governing Annamese, and merely as a last resort to appease Christian complaints promptly.   He claims to have made observations on this point to my predecessor.... And so it was that, having no means of dealing briskly and effectively with Christian claims, they sanctioned the measures proposed by the latter for the concession and use of vacant land.   It is a detestable expedient, but it was the only one which could silence the Christian clamour rapidly, and it is certainly one more reason for the animosity between these two factions of the population.   As for the question of indemnities, the minister argues that the claims repeatedly presented by Mgr Gauthier (Bishop of Emmaus, Vicar Apostolic of South Tonkin) amount to nearly 3,000,000 frs.   He says that the total reimbursement made in land, pagodas, houses and silver amounts to 550,000 ligatures, but that claims keep arriving and that Christians are demanding total indemnification for the losses they have sustained. Well now, he asserts that only the villages which are guilty should pay reparations, and that all that can be done on this score has been done: to go further would be moving towards civil war.   If they had simply seized the goods of individual culprits, the compensation would have amounted to very little. For this reason, all the villages most involved had to be penalised..... He adds, moreover, that the sum already paid is enormous for the area; and that even if it does not match the full figure for damages, its sheer size is causing discontent among all who are not Christians, even among

187

those who have made no contribution.... (A.O.M. Aix. Indochine, Amiraux 10,451)

98. M. **Turc**, Consul at Haiphong, to Rear-Admiral **Duperré**, Governor of Cochinchina. Haiphong, 1 April 1876.

To sum up, from the dealings I have had on various issues with the (Spanish) Vicar Apostolic of East Tonkin, I have gained the impression that Mgr Colomer is a moderate, trustworthy and sensible man. More moderate and sensible than a number of his colleagues from the Missions Etrangères. I feel certain that whatever position we are forced by political events to adopt in this country, the behaviour of the Spanish missionaries will give us nothing to complain of. Pending fuller information, I consider them sensitive enough to avoid mixing spiritual matters too much with temporal, and to render always unto Caesar what is Caesar's. I willingly admit that their cautious attitude can be partly attributed to patriotic sentiment, and we cannot blame them for that; but whatever the reason, the outcome will always be better for us than the kind of trouble produced by exaggerated claims and by an inability to distinguish spiritual from temporal matters. (A.O.M. Aix. Indochine, Amiraux 13,140)

99. Edict of the Emperor **Tu Duc** against interference by missionaries and bishops in the trials of Christians. Decree of Bo-Ho (Ministry of Finance), 25th day, 9th month, 29th year of the reign of Tu Duc (1876)

By Royal Sanction.

Until now the mandarins have not followed true reason in allowing bishops and missionaries to interfere in the trials of Christians. Bishops and missionaries, forgetful of their responsibilities, have welcomed the false reports of Christians and have used their own credit to support them before the mandarins.... These abuses must cease. So anyone, pagan (<u>recte</u> 'honest subject') or Christian, who has complaints to make, must follow procedure and present them first to the mayor, then to the chief of the canton, then to the sub-prefect, and finally to the prefect. And if the matter has still not been sufficiently clarified it can go before the great mandarins and finally to the Tam Phap (High Court of Justice). In acting otherwise they will become liable to the punishments decreed by law. Missionaries may not take up the cause of

Christians nor intercede with the mandarins on their behalf without incurring the punishment of the law. (A.O.M. Aix. Indochine, Amiraux, 10,443 (5).)

100. M. **Turc**, Consul at Haiphong, to Rear-Admiral **Lafont**, Governor of Cochinchina. Haiphong, 10 November 1877.

Doubtless the measure of which Mgr Puginier complains, which consists of preventing the missionaries and even the bishops from intervening with the great mandarins, in no way exceeds the rights of the court of Hue. But such direct approaches by the bishops which are displeasing (to the court) were not made with any other purpose in mind than to avoid recourse to the consuls as much as possible. (Consular) intervention would irritate (the court) much more.

If bishops can no longer refer directly to the higher authorities when they feel they need to make complaints, the latter should not be surprised to see (the French authorities) coming to their assistance, investigating their grievances, asking for explanations and, to put it briefly, departing from the attitude of reserve which we have decided to adopt up to now.... (A.O.M. Aix. Amiraux, 13,164)

101. Rear-Admiral **Duperré**, Governor of Cochinchina: Notes on the organisation of worship. (1876-1877)

... The Annamese, although hostile towards the missions after persecuting them for so long, had nonetheless, in our provinces, accepted almost completely the supervision of Christians by their spiritual fathers. So, since Christians were accustomed to referring complaints against officials or requests for favour to the missionaries, the missionary thought of himself as virtually an official representative of the Christian population in his locality, and now tends to substitute himself little by little for our own agents. Time and time again I have urged our officials and the bishop to end this this abuse and I think it important to stamp out the notion of a parallel private government operating alongside the general administration. Moreover the missionaries, no longer able to excercise their power openly, tend to form their Christians into agglomerations, claiming autonomy for them so as to have the mayors and notables under their thumb.... (A.O.M. Aix. Indochine, Amiraux, 10,273)

102. Rear-Admiral **Lafont,** Governor of Cochinchina, to Admiral **Pothuau,** Minister for the Navy and Colonies. Saigon, 26 January 1878.

Among other matters which force themselves on the attention of the Governor of Cochinchina (is) the need to keep the various interested parties strictly to the terms of the treaty of 15 March 1874.... More than any other of its clauses, those relating to the free excercise of the Christian religion over the whole extent of the kingdom of Annam give rise to difficulties and disputes. The Annamese authorities are all too inclined to infringe them and I have already had to contest their claims several times and ask the court at Hue to retract certain prohibitive measures which are in complete opposition to the terms of the treaty. I am pleased to acknowledge that up to now the Annamese government has always accepted my observations and has put things right promptly. But if on the one hand I have to make the government and its representatives show scrupulous respect for the undertakings made in regard to missionaries and Christians, I consider it my equally strict duty to keep the latter, too, within the limits of the rights conferred upon them by treaty, which they are just as inclined to exceed. Among the various missions which are so devotedly and unselfishly pursuing the work of civilisation in Annam there is a marked inclination to want to assemble the Christians scattered through the country into separate centres in which missionaries themselves would not only be responsible for spiritual affairs but also for material interests. They spare no pains to achieve this, as it would assure for them a powerful means of proselytising among a population which is somewhat indifferent to religious matters and at the mercy of the whims of the mandarinate. I cannot therefore be surprised at the approach made to me on this subject by His Grace, Mgr Puginier, Vicar Apostolic of West Tonkin. In a long memorandum listing a number of charges against provincial governors this prelate requests nothing less than that I intervene with the Annamese government to obtain the right for bishops and missionaries to present the claims of their flock directly to the authorities of the country and even to the court of Hue itself, and also (that they be allowed) to remind them when appropriate to observe the treaties. I was unable to gratify such a request, nor would I encourage tendencies which I should repress vigorously if they occurred in any part of Annam under our own authority. So I replied to Mgr Puginier that though I was resolved to use all means compatible with the ministry's orders to defend the privileges given to the missionaries and Christians, I could go no further; and above all that I would certainly not ask for them to be given an exceptional position which would have the immediate effect of removing them from the direct authority of the country's administrators and natural judges. I added that the Governor of Cochinchina seemed to me to be the sole authority to signify breaches of treaty to Hue....(A.N.S.O.M. Paris. Indochine, (A.F.)12/ A30(14).)

103. M. **de Kergaradec,** French Consul at Hanoi, to Rear-Admiral **Lafont,** Governor of Cochinchina. Hanoi, 1 May 1879.

The only matter of any importance still pending concerns a breach of Article 9 of the treaty of peace (1874) by an official from Ninh Binh province. In a prefecture called Yen Khanh, Christians in dispute with other inhabitants were treated by the prefect (Pham Dinh Phung) in a way which amounts to virtual persecution. This official reproached them in open court for having embraced the Christian religion, summoned them to abandon it, and had catechists who were accused of preaching arrested and beaten. Matters were taken to such extremes that a Christian died from the beating he had received. As soon as I was informed of these matters, I wrote to the Tong doc, Tran (Tran Dinh Tuc), the Governor-General of Hanoi and Ninh Binh, telling him that even though we were not supposed to interfere in quarrels between Christians and the (Emperor's) other subjects, any more than with judgements handed down by the country's magistrates, it was nonetheless our duty to ensure respect for the treaty article which prescribes freedom to preach the Catholic religion, and which establishes full equality of rights for Christians.... At the same time I asked the captain of the gunboat Coutelas to go to Ninh Binh and ask the senior administrator of the province to use his authority and hurry to put a stop to this kind of thing. To be fair to the Governor of Ninh Binh, he ordered an immediate release of the imprisoned Christians and reprimanded his subordinate.

Unbelievable as they may seem, the acts of which the prefect of Yen Khanh is accused do not seem to have been exaggerated. The Governor of Ninh Binh and Governor-General Tran himself both tried to excuse him by saying that he was a young scholar newly promoted to his post. But they also promised that these matters - which, moreover, they do not deny - will not recur. To me that did not seem sufficient. So I felt I had to ask for action to be taken by the competant senior authority and notified to me. If the prefect is guilty he should obviously be severely punished. It is often rather difficult to make out the truth in matters affecting Christians which are referred to us, and we are all too often obliged to ignore the complaints made by missionaries for fear of seeming to interfere in the internal administration of the country. All the more reason then, not to ignore acts like those of which the prefect of Yen Khanh is guilty. They are obviously a grave infraction of the treaty and we should make an example of him.... We should also make use of this opportunity to show the mission that, even if we often have to ignore their claims so as to keep within the limits of our treaty rights, we are still determined to protect Christians energetically against any act of persecution.... (Ministère des Affaires Etrangères. Documents Diplomatiques. Affaire du Tonkin. 1ière partie, 1874-Décembre, 1882. p. 112. No. 5)

104. The captain of the Duchaffaut to Rear-Admiral **Lafont**, Governor of Cochinchina. Saigon, 8 June 1878.

I feel I should add that if, in Khanh Hoa (in the vicariate of East Cochinchina), the hostility against Christians is so vigorous, it probably derives - quite apart from the general feeling among officials, scholars or notables - from a particular cause which explains the phenomenon up to a point. This is that in this province permission was given by the court of Hue at Father Geffroy's prompting for any Annamese converting to Christianity not only to become part of a separate body, even if inscribed (on a village tax register), but also to become exempt from all tax, corvée or military duty on payment of a commutation of twenty ligatures. He was thus freed from the village to which he no longer contributed. However, the village itself was certainly not exempted from a commensurate portion of its (tax, corvée and military) obligations. This has caused growing discontent among the notables of the village precisely because the privileges which were conferred (on Christian converts) prompted all manner of cupidity, and particularly so among the poor who were the hardest hit by (customary) exactions. Exemption from military service is, moreover, a powerful attraction: many soldiers ask to become Christians to benefit from their corporate privileges; and Mgr Charbonnier, in order to avoid violent wrangling, has had to forbid conversion prior to military discharge. Twenty ligatures normally represents more than all forms of annual charge on an inhabitant, and so in most of the other provinces the exchange would not be accepted. But Khanh Hoa is a poor and partly depopulated territory where the registers have remained unaltered following the Annamese custom: so the charges are exceptionally heavy, especially among villages - the majority indeed - which possess very little communal land; and here it is advantageous to enter a Christian corporation. In sum, for the two and a half years in which Christian corporations have been established, there has been a revival in conversions which has upset the interests as much as the feelings of the mandarins and

notables.   Unable to hope for a withdrawal of these privileges by the
court of Hue, which is avid for hard cash, they try to disillusion new
Christian converts by innumerable harassments while carefully avoiding
the appearance of religious persecution.... (A.O.M. Aix. Indochine,
Amiraux 13, 084)

105.   Mgr **Colombert**, Bishop of Samostate, Vicar Apostolic of West
Cochinchina, to the **Superior** of the S.M.E. in Paris. Saigon, 26
January 1883.

...1° I think it helpful to tell you that a communication from Fr
Lesserteur to the Société de Géographie about French policy in Tonkin
has had a bad reception here and has given rise to the accusation that
missionaries lack patriotism.   It may also, perhaps, provoke the French
Minister at Hue to protest.   Certainly the missions have had no
complaint to make against Annam since 1874.   The treaty has been
properly observed and there is enough religious freedom.   Have our
trading and political interests anything to complain of in relation to
the fulfilment of the treaty? This is not clear and, for my part, I
don't know.   Anyway that is none of our business.   In my opinion we
must avoid getting mixed up in these political questions at all costs
and simply wait.   Taking one side or the other is rash and dangerous.
Annam could react with vengeful desperation by flinging in France's face
the heads of any missionaries it has in her power. On the other hand,
sooner or later France will occupy Tonkin: it is a pressing necessity.
So it would be foolhardy to come out against **(**Tonkin's**)** future
overlords. It is best to wait on events, which are in the hands of
providence and, if misfortunes occur they will be the easier to suffer
for not having been provoked.... (A.S.M.E.   Vol.756, (Cochinchine
Occidentale, 1867-1889). No. 698)

IV

THE TONKIN WAR AND ITS AFTERMATH, 1883-1886.

IV A   THE FRENCH MISSION AND THE WAR IN TONKIN, 1883-1885.

The Garnier affair had exposed a serious weakness in cabinet control over the Navy's colonial administration. This realisation prompted closer supervision of the Cochinchina colony's management of relations with Hue during the following five years. In the later 1870s it was still imperative to avoid provoking other European powers with an interest in the Tonkin issue. France was still without allies on the continent. The British had protested formally over the terms of the treaty of 15 March 1874, forcing the Quai to minimise further the quasi-protectoral character of the agreement. A German war scare in 1875 also made local German interest in the Tonkin question a delicate issue. On the insistance of the Duc Decazes at the Quai d'Orsay, naval ministers monitored closely all tendencies to political reinvolvement in Tonkin. A succession of safer appointments to the governorship were made; and Admirals Krantz (1874-5), Duperré (1875-7) and Lafont (1877-9) all remained obedient to their instructions.

A new crisis in Tonkin, 1878.

Central government restraints were certainly needed. From 1875 the colonial administration at Saigon chafed at the shortcomings of Admiral Dupré's treaty, and of the commercial agreement of August 1874 which had followed it. Even if clause 9 of the Dupré treaty operated to French satisfaction, other provisions of the two agreements did not. In Tonkin the French were finding their treaty privileges inoperative in the face of increasing disorders on the upper Song Coi. In principle the treaty opened the Song Coi river to trade, gave the French two garissoned consulates in Tonkin, and allowed them to share in the management of the local customs service. But owing to persistant banditry in upper Tonkin, trade with Yunnan was minimal. Moreover Vietnamese customs officials were reported to be uncooperative. The terms of the 1874 treaties were too limited for the French to resolve these issues locally. In consequence the anticipated commercial benefit of these recent agreements continued to elude them. In 1878 the situation became critical. The British were reported to be opening up a route into Yunnan from Lower Burma through Bhamo. At the same time a further convulsion in the Yunnan rebellion had provoked the descent of waves of Chinese Ho rebels into North-western Tonkin. Here they joined the marauding, nomadic forces of the Black and Yellow Flags. As a result, the Song Coi had become completely blocked to river traffic moving towards Yunnan. The French could not intervene in upper Tonkin unless the Vietnamese themselves activated the defense clause of the 1874 treaty. Instead, Emperor Tu Duc chose to invoke his rights as a tributary of China and appealed to Peking for support in quelling the Tonkin disorders. To the French this move further emphasised the political shortcomings of the 1874 treaty as a quasi-protectoral arrangement. The crisis provoked a broad reassessment of French policy towards Vietnam.

The triumph of Republicanism and French gravitation towards a policy of colonial expansion, 1879-1883.

By now, in 1878, continental and domestic political developments were combining to generate a new, expansionary impetus in French colonial policy. On the continent France's diplomatic rehabilitation as a major power was first signified at the Congress of Berlin. In the wake of the Russo-Turkish war of 1877-8 France had accepted an invitation to associate with Britain, Germany and Austria in persuading Russia to revise the Treaty of San Stefano. Part of the reward for French cooperation in helping to restabilise the Balkans had been an agreement by Britain and Germany to give France a free hand to pursue the development of her interests in Tunis. In the following year Bismarck, making light of German commercial interest in Vietnam, urged the French to consolidate their position in Tonkin.

These international configurations were accompanied by domestic political changes which brought in republican cabinets keen to reactivate policies of colonial expansion. Although France had been a Republic in name since 1873, French parliaments had been dominated for the subsequent five years by the monarchist parties of the Right. These had been - and were to remain - committed to a quietist policy in continental and colonial affairs. The elections of 1877 however, saw a shift in the popular mandate towards the groups of the republican Centre. Unlike the monarchist Right, the 'opportunists' of the republican Centre pursued an external policy of national resurgence. The safest outlet for this lay in the extension of France's colonial domain. By 1879 the combination of international encouragement with republican electoral success had set the course for a series of tentative expansionary moves in the Middle East, North and West Africa, Oceania and Southeast Asia. After Tunis, Tonkin surfaced as the issue of prime concern to the makers of colonial policy.

French efforts to secure a protectoral treaty from Vietnam by diplomatic pressure, 1879-1882.

From 1879 to 1882 successive republican cabinets, still uneasy at the possibility of British, Chinese and by now even Spanish intervention in Tonkin, sought to convert Admiral Dupré's ill-defined treaty of 1874 into a full and unambiguous protectorate capable of excluding all other foreign involvement from Vietnam. However, the means chosen for obtaining a protectorate were mainly confined to the sphere of diplomacy. The political fragmentation of the republican Centre hampered pursuit of more forceful methods of intervention. Cabinet coalitions collapsed with frequency; and parliamentary support for all military initiatives remained capricious and uncertain. Only grudging assent had been given to settling the Tunis issue by force. When the Tunis expedition ran into pacification difficulties in September 1881, the scandal provoked the fall of Jules Ferry's first cabinet in November. This in turn quashed current proposals for a largescale military adventure in Tonkin. So French action was confined to making a succession of diplomatic overtures to the Emperor Tu Duc between 1878 and November 1881, demanding a revision of the 1874 agreement and requesting his acceptance of a full French protectorate. Tu Duc's repeated refusals meant that the French could do nothing to influence the situation in Tonkin beyond funding minor operations in the Song Coi delta to protect commercial traffic from the depredations of the Black Flags. A small force under Commander Henri Rivière was deployed to undertake a series of delta clearances manoeuvres. Sanctioned by the Dupré treaty, it was merely a form of police operation in which the means of action available to the French were extremely limited. Christian communities in Tonkin could be of little practical use in this situation, and Rivière was particularly careful to limit his association with them. In essence he considered the mission to be a source of political weakness **(Doc. 106)**.

The French consider partitioning Tonkin with China: November 1882 - January 1883.

So long as the French restricted their intervention in Tonkin to such relatively innocuous policing measures the Vietnamese could afford to disregard their continuing diplomatic overtures for a full protectorate. But when in April 1882 Commander Rivière overstepped his orders and, like Garnier, occupied Hanoi, the court at Hue was galvanised into renewing the search for political support further afield. After a fumbled approach to Spain, Tu Duc once more appealed to China. As a result, the Tonkin issue developed a wider political dimension. Invoking China's obligations as suzerain of Vietnam, the Emperor Tu Duc succeeded in prompting Peking to make a series of ambiguous military gestures: a small Chinese fleet was despatched to the gulf of Tonkin, and Chinese armies from the border provinces of Yunnan and Kwangsi, already present at Son Tay and Bac Ninh in upper Tonkin, were expanded in presumed preparation for wider deployment. The French responded weakly to these ominous moves. The Duclerc cabinet of July 1882 – January 1883, even more uncertainly supported in the Chambers than its predecessors, attempted to secure Chinese neutrality by negotiating terms for a political partition of Tonkin between France and China. An agreement cast in these terms – the Li-Bourée treaty – was even drafted and initialled.

The groups of the republican Centre unite behind Ferry and press for a forward policy in Tonkin: April – May 1883.

However by now – at the beginning of 1883 – the complexion of French parliamentary politics changed abruptly once again. Since late 1881 the two main groups of the republican Centre had pursued divergent policies on the Tonkin issue. Moderate republicans supporting Jules Ferry had considered it too risky to undertake a Tonkin expedition so soon after the Tunis embroglio, for which Ferry was still being stigmatised. Léon Gambetta's Union Républicaine on the other hand, had been proposing a major military expedition to Tonkin since December 1881. Gambetta had even begun making arrangements for an expedition during his short-lived ministry of December 1881 – January 1882. After Gambetta's fall from office however, his party had been too weak on its own to secure parliamentary support for a powerful initiative in Tonkin. But when in December 1882 Léon Gambetta died, the leaderless Gambettists rallied in support of Ferry's party, and an alliance of the republican Centre was formed under Ferry's leadership. In combination the groups of the republican Centre were to underpin Ferry's exceptionally long-lived second ministry of April 1883 – March 1885. With the Gambettists pressing for an adventurous colonial policy, the new alignment now opened the way for a more aggressive approach to the Tonkin question. Parliamentary prevarication on Tonkin was thereby overcome and the Li-Bourée partition treaty with China abandoned. Buoyed up by a public outcry at the recent death of Commander Rivière during a minor skirmish near Son Tay, Ferry obtained parliamentary assent in May 1883 for a substantial naval and military expedition to eradicate Chinese and Vietnamese deployments along the upper Song Coi. It was now decided to forego diplomacy and impose a new protectoral treaty upon Hue by force.

Jules Ferry's objectives: May 1883.

Ferry's aims were relatively limited at the outset of the Tonkin war.
In essence he needed the new protectoral treaty to exclude the
interference of other foreign powers from Tonkin. He had not been
prepared to share control of Tonkin with the Chinese, partly because the
Chinese were vulnerable to pressure from the British, and partly because
upper Tonkin (which would have gone to the Chinese) was thought to
contain valuable mineral deposits. But to reduce the potential costs of
French domination in Tonkin he intended to avoid creating a wholly
French apparatus of colonial government akin to Cochinchina. He planned
to retain the traditional structure of Vietnamese local administration
in Tonkin, merely substituting French supervision for the authority of
the imperial court. Meantime he saw no profit in assuming direct
control of Annam. Here, he was prepared to leave the traditional
imperial system of government intact and substantially autonomous.

The Tonkin expedition and the collapse of Vietnamese resistance: June – December 1883.

The new naval and military expedition was despatched in June. It was
sufficiently strong to force the prompt capitulation of the imperial
court at Hue by bombarding the Thuan An forts at the mouth of the
Perfume river in August 1883. But French forces were not proficient
enough to procure the immediate collapse of Vietnamese, still less
Chinese, deployments in Tonkin. Despite the formal submission of the
Vietnamese court and even the surrender of its administration at Hanoi,
the Vietnamese commander-in-chief in Tonkin, Prince Hoang Ke Vien, held
out at Son Tay with the assistance of Chinese imperial troops and Luu
Vinh Phuoc's Black Flag irregulars for several months until forced to
fall back and abandon his stronghold in December 1883. Thereafter, with
his forces thinly disseminated, Prince Vien's efforts to combine the
Vietnamese army's operations with those of the Chinese were beset with
difficulties.

The Franco-Chinese war in Tonkin, 1883-1885.

The Chinese forces entrenched in upper Tonkin were a more intractable
proposition for the French, who proved incapable of provoking more than
tactical withdrawals. After the French capture of Son Tay the Chinese
committed further forces from across the border to the conflict in the
guerilla country of upland Tonkin, where French detachments remained ill

suited for effective manoeuvre. Only with the arrival of troop reinforcements in the spring of 1884 were the French able to take major Chinese strongholds - particularly Bac Ninh and Hung Hoa - successes which were striking enough to procure a temporary cessation of hostilities and a resort to negotiation. In May 1884 the Chinese accepted an agreement acknowledging the French protectorate over Vietnam; but the success of the negotiation was due mainly to Chinese misunderstanding of the implications of the new agreement, which they wrongly believed to have left intact their traditional claim to suzerainty over Vietnam. Alerted to their error by French insistence on melting down the Chinese seals of delegated sovereignty at Hue, the Chinese resumed the offensive until, with their success on land declining after Admiral Courbet's naval bombardment of Foochow, they finally accepted terms for a withdrawal from Tonkin in April 1885.

The imposition of the French protectorate: from the Harmand convention (25 August 1883) to the Patenôtre treaty (6 June 1884).

The Tonkin war was, for most of its duration, a Franco-Chinese conflict, for the Vietnamese were virtually overwhelmed in the first months of hostilities. From the outset the capital at Hue proved incapable of resisting an early attack by a French naval and infantry force equipped to overcome the logistical problems which had once deterred Rigault de Genouilly. The Vietnamese had little option but to accept a protectoral treaty while awaiting the outcome of the struggle in the far North.

On 25 August 1883, shortly after the capitulation of the Thuan An forts guarding the approach to Hue, all Vietnam north of French Cochinchina became, in formal terms, a French protectorate. Under the conditions of the convention devised by the French Commissioner-General, Jules Harmand, Annam and Tonkin were accorded different administrative treatment, as Ferry had wished. While Tonkin was subjected to direct French administrative supervision, Annam was to be left substantially autonomous. But Harmand, on his own initiative, devalued the concession of autonomy to Annam by a redefinition of frontiers. He truncated two major Annamese provinces - Binh Thuan in the south and Thanh Hoa in the north - and reassigned them to French Cochinchina and to French-controlled Tonkin respectively. Urging the Quai d'Orsay to ratify this agreement **(Doc. 108),** Harmand reasoned that, among other considerations, the existence of large Christian communities in some of the reassigned northern provinces would increase the ease of governing an enlarged Tonkin. The French cabinet however, was still anxious to limit French political responsibilities. Ferry considered the Harmand convention to be provocative. It would reduce the economic viability of an autonomous Annam and arouse serious political opposition in the longer term. Mindful of the difficulties of pacification in Tunisia which had precipitated the collapse of his first ministry in 1881, he well understood the need to avert a post-conquest rebellion by the Vietnamese. So he shelved the Harmand convention and ordered the pursuit of new arrangements with Hue. The resultant Patenôtre treaty of 6 June 1884 matched Ferry's objectives more closely. It confirmed the imposition of a limited form of French administrative control over Tonkin; but for Annam it prescribed a larger measure of autonomy within its existing frontiers, restricting French commercial and settler privileges and limiting in principle their rights of movement into the interior. Ironically, by specifically reaffirming clause 9 of Dupré's treaty of 1874, the Patenôtre treaty left French and Spanish missionaries with wider privileges of movement, property-holding and settlement than those now accorded to secular French nationals in Annam **(Doc. 109)**.

The crisis of the Nguyen monarchy: the Regency and its secret preparations for resistance, 1883–1885.

At Hue, formal acceptance of these agreements by the Co-mat Vien **(Privy Council)** did not diminish the Vietnamese court's determination to promote eventual resistance. However, the court's powers of action were hampered by factionalism following the death of Emperor Tu Duc in July 1883. The situation of confusion at Hue resolved itself only slowly over the following months. The leaders of the dominant alignment, the Regents Ton That Thuyet and Nguyen Van Tuong, though both anxious to organise resistance to the French, were locked in a bitter rivalry for power with other court mandarins. In the course of this struggle they eliminated two of Tu Duc's successors – the emperors Duc Duc and Hiep Hoa – during the latter part of 1883. With the enthronement of the sixteen year old Emperor Kien Phuoc in December 1883 the authority of the two regents was consolidated. The Regent Ton That Thuyet, who was also Minister for War, then used his ascendency to begin secret preparations to create a large resistance base North-West of Hue at Tan So, beyond Cam Lo **(Doc. 110)**. This was a project which he pursued steadily during the following eighteen months with the intention of moving the court into the hills and raising a popular royalist resistance against French domination – the strategy which ultimately came to fruition after July 1885 in the Can Vuong (Support the Emperor) movement.

The role of Christians in the Tonkin war.

As on previous occasions, French military moves against the Vietnamese were met by spontaneous attacks on Christian communes in several localities. In West Tonkin the death of Commander Rivière on 15 May 1883 was followed a day later by the decapitation of a Father Béchet along with a number of catechists at Ke Han. The bombardment of the Thuan An forts in August 1883 resulted in immediate reprisals against Christian communes situated along the route between Tourane and Hue. The French seizure of Son Tay from Prince Viem on 14-15 December 1883 was accompanied by the destruction of approximately a hundred Christian communes in the provinces of Son Tay and Nam Dinh. Missionaries claimed that secret orders were then sent from Hue for a general massacre of Christians, resulting in the destruction of a number of parishes in Thanh Hoa. Reprisals against Christians were not confined to Vietnam, since the French were also engaged in a war with China. Reports of Christian massacres arrived not only from the border provinces of Ssetchuan, Yunnan, Kwangsi and Kweichow, but from as far afield as Canton and even, if missionary accounts are to be believed, from Manchuria.[1]

From a Vietnamese point of view, the massacre of Christians was not merely an expression of political frustration. It served a practical purpose in striking at a significant dimension of French military effort. For the French, after initial hesitations **(Doc. 106)**, were making considerable use of Vietnamese Christians as auxiliaries in the war. Christian Vietnamese were employed as coolies, interpreters and miliciens; and Vietnamese Christians also financed and organised private forces such as the armée Joseph, a body of about 7,000 irregulars, raised for use against the Black Flags. Above all, as Bishop Puginier pointed out, Christians were useful in gathering field intelligence on Vietnamese resistance preparations and on Chinese force deployments (see infra **Doc. 116).** A later anti-Christian decree of Thuyet, issued in 1885, confirms that it was the intelligence-gathering function of the Christian communes that was particularly feared (see infra **Doc. 113).** Consequently, with the ending of the Franco-Chinese war in April 1885, when the Hue court's secret preparations for rousing popular resistance came to fruition, the call for a wholesale massacre of Christians was to mark a vital element in the Vietnamese strategy of insurgency.

(1). A.Launay, Histoire générale de la Société des Missions Etrangères. (3 vols, Paris, Téqui 1894), pp. 519-23.

Further reading

C.Forniau, 'La genèse et l'évolution de l'affaire du Tonkin', **Revue Historique**, No. 500 Oct.-Déc. 1971, pp. 377-409.

Ministère des Affaires Etrangères, **Documents diplomatiques. Affaire du Tonkin.** (3 vols. Paris, 1885).

J.P.T. Bury, **Gambetta's Final Years: 'The Era of Difficulties', 1877-1882.** (London, Longman, 1982).

J.P.T.Bury, 'Gambetta and overseas problems', **The English Historical Review**, April 1967.

C.R. Ageron, 'Gambetta et la reprise de l'expansion coloniale', **Revue française d'Histoire d'Outre-mer**, LIX No. 215 (1972), No.2.

T.F. Power, **Jules Ferry and the Renaissance of French Imperialism.** (New York, 1944).

P. Robiquet, **Discours et opinions de Jules Ferry.** (3 vols. Paris, 1897).

Un diplomate (A. Billot), **L'affaire du Tonkin.** (Paris, 1886).

J. Ferry, **Tonkin et la mère-patrie. Témoignages et documents.** (Paris, 1890).

K. Munholland, 'Admiral Jauréguiberry and the French scramble for Tonkin, 1879-1883', **French Historical Studies**, XI, Spring 1977.

J. McManners, **Church and State in France, 1870-1914.** (London, S.P.C.K., 1972).

J. Gadille, 'La politique de défense républicaine à l'égard de l'Eglise de France (1876-1883)', **Bulletin de la Société d'Histoire Moderne**, No.1, 1967.

E.M.Acomb, **The French Laic Laws 1879-1889.** (New York, 1941).

A.Launay, **La Société des Missions Etrangères pendant la guerre du Tonkin.** (Paris, 1886).

Nguyen The-Anh, 'The Vietnamese monarchy under French colonial rule, 1884-1945'. **Modern Asian Studies**, 19, 1, (1985) pp. 147-162.

Nguyen The-Anh, **The Withering Days of the Nguyen Dynasty.** (Singapore, Institute of Southeast Asian Studies, Research Notes and Discussions, No.7, 1978).

Documents

106. Commandant **Rivière**, Commander of the French naval expedition in Tonkin, to Governor **Le Myre de Vilers**. Hanoi, 14 November 1882.

Mgr Puginier has it from a good source that the Council at Hue has decided to make war on us. Their move against us would begin, or has even begun, with an insurrection in Cambodia and in Cochinchina, which cholera will have delayed. Nothing much is expected of this insurrection, but it would cut us off in Tonkin where we would be attacked in the wake of a persecution or massacre of the Christians....

I am asking Gadaud to be exceptionally cautious and not to anchor at Ninh Binh or at Nam Dinh. In moving along the river and the arroyos to reconnoitre he is to anchor only in isolated spots. I am also advising

him not to establish his final anchorage at Ke So or Phat Diem (mission
stations) unless occasion demands it. They seem tempted to welcome us
too warmly there.   I never advised Mgr Puginier to compromise himself
for us, first because it would cause us difficulties; and then, for his
own sake, because the Government of the Republic would not fail to let
him down.   Despite that, he seem to have a inclination to do so, and I
do not want to associate myself with this tendency.   One of the
greatest embarrassments that the Annamese could have caused us - or
might still do - is the persecution of Christians. We cannot protect
them but we will cut a sorry figure in not protecting them. So it is
best that they compromise themselves as little as possible for us....
(André Masson, Correspondance politique du Commandant Rivière au Tonkin,
Avril 1882 - Mai 1883. Paris, 1933. p. 158)

107.   Mgr **Colombert,** Bishop of Samostate, Vicar Apostolic of West
Cochinchina,   to   the **Directors** of the S.M.E.   Saigon, 15 July
1883.

Why have they added to, or rather set in charge (of the Tonkin
expedition) Citizen Harmand, a junior doctor and convinced Darwinist who
claims that man is descended from the Ape ?   This nomination has caused
general surprise here, and nobody believes he can keep in step with the
two other (commanders) **for long.   All the same he believes that after**
the experience of Le Myre de Vilers and Rivière, the anticlerical
policies they espoused should be abandoned and the Christians relied
upon.   This means exploiting them for the time being, offering them a
few sops, and when they cease to be useful, throwing them overboard as
happened in Cochinchina.... (A.S.M.E. Vol.756, (Cochinchine Occidentale,
1867-1889). No. 704.)

108.   Civil Commissioner - General **Jules Harmand,** to **P.A. Challemel-
Lacour,** Foreign Minister. Hue, 26 August 1883.

I have given... the great province of Binh Thuan to Cochinchina. I
have a right to feel proud of this because it was absolutely my own idea
for which I sought advice from nobody.... Cochinchina will have a more
distinctive frontier, with the sea roads which she lacked. She will
extend into the territorial belt of Annam proper, able to threaten to
drive a wedge in from there, and able, too, to keep a close eye on the
probable outcome while preparing herself for the future conditions of
her existence.... By extending the zone of more direct French

protectoral administration from Tonkin down to the mountain chain which once served as the old frontier of independent Tonkin (with Annam) I have endowed France with three great provinces as rich and well populated as the Red river delta (Song Coi). Here we will find concentrated more than 100,000 Christians who will be a source of immediate and exceedingly valuable support.... Finally I have obtained a frontier of exceptionally useful military solidity which will allow us, if and when we want, to separate Annam completely from Tonkin, enabling us to reduce all Annam to total starvation if she turns against us, without going to all the expense of a maritime blocade and surveillance....(Quoted in Un diplomate (A. Billot), L'affaire du Tonkin, (Paris, 1886), p. 178.)

109. **The Patenôtre treaty** between France and Annam. Hue, 6 June 1884.

... **Article 13.** Throughout the whole of Tonkin and in the open ports of Annam, French citizens or protégés may travel freely, carry on trade, acquire and dispose of land and premises. His Majesty the King of Annam expressly confirms the guarantees stipulated by the treaty of 15 March 1874 in favour of missionaries and Christians. (Un diplomate (A. Billot), L'Affaire du Tonkin. (Paris, 1886). p. 420)

110. Mgr **Puginier,** Bishop of Mauricastre, Vicar Apostolic of West Tonkin, to General **Brière de l'Isle,** Commander-in-Chief of the Tonkin expedition. Hanoi, 6 November 1884.

(The court) knows that the Protectorate is a step towards (French) annexation, and it understands that any effort to mount a resistance at Hue is impossible. Hence the plan to establish a new capital at Cam Lo, a point on the frontier of Laos. In order to avoid the complete loss of an ascendancy which is receding from the (coastal) plain it is trying to consolidate control over a part of the mountain region where the attacking French will find great difficulty in pursuing it. It will dig in there, obtain supplies of munitions, and secure the services of Chinese irregulars. It will become the cause both of continual anxiety for the French whom it will harass, and of pillage and destruction for the Annamese populations whom it will use every means to provoke into revolt. (A.S.M.E. Vol.816, (Lettres de Mgr Puginier.) No.34)

IV B   THE CAN VUONG MOVEMENT AND THE POSTWAR MASSACRE OF CHRISTIANS.

The withdrawal of the Chinese armies from Tonkin in April 1885 was a devastating blow to Vietnamese hopes of eventual liberation. Until now, Vietnamese capitulation to the French had been merely formal and provisional. But China's abandonment of Vietnam induced a proportion of the mandarinate to accept capitulation as final. However, in Annam part of the court still meditated the possibility of resistance, and the issue remained in the balance for two months after the cessation of hostilities. It was the French themselves who drove the court to the point of decision, and provoked the onset of the long prepared Can Vuong (Support the Emperor) insurrection.

At the beginning of July 1885 the French Commander-in-Chief, General Roussel de Courcy occupied Hue citadel and, in contravention of the Patenôtre treaty of 1884, issued demands for the dissolution of the Co-Mat Vien, the dispersal of the royal army and the dismissal of its commander, the regent Ton That Thuyet. These actions made it appear that General de Courcy wished to turn indirect tutelage over Annam into a form of direct rule. This brought home to the court the reality of its subjugation. Courcy's dictates appear to have prompted a split in the Co-mat Vien between the regents of the new emperor Ham Nghi - Nguyen Van Tuong and Ton That Thuyet - over the question of capitulation. Faced by Courcy's challenge, Nguyen Van Tuong opted to accede to de Courcy's demands, while Ton That Thuyet activated his scheme for mobilising resistance and persuaded the new emperor, Ham Nghi and a proportion of the court to join him. The uprising marks the moment at which the court, having ignored spontaneous popular pressures to mobilise against the French for over two decades, finally assumed the leadership of popular opposition to French rule.

As a signal of rebellion Thuyet attempted to ambush General de Courcy and the French garrison at Hue on 4 and 5 July 1885. The coup failed, but Thuyet succeeded in escaping from the capital with the young monarch, the dowager empress, the treasury and a number of court mandarins. The French military command, forewarned by Bishop Puginier of Thuyet's resistance preparations (see supra **Doc. 110),** anticipated the flight to Tan So by occupying the nearby town of Cam Lo. Leaving behind the dowager empress and part of the court on the route to Tan So, Thuyet and the emperor Ham Nghi were forced to gravitate through a succession of more northerly bases deeper in the hills. On the way, Regent Thuyet began issuing edicts of general insurrection (see **Doc. 116** for Bishop Puginier's translation of one of these). He called for the massacre of collaborating mandarins, the destruction of commercial districts surrounding major towns, and above all for the wholesale extinction of Christian villages.

The Can Vuong movement and the Christians communes.

The Can Vuong insurgents perceived Christians to be a major threat to the effectiveness of their uprising. They knew that during the war in Tonkin French forces had been able to rely on the Christian communes for extensive information on the movement of Chinese and Vietnamese guerilla bands through the countryside. As in the past, but for increasingly urgent strategic reasons, Christian villages were marked down by the Can Vuong for systematic destruction. Thuyet's edicts appealing for the massacre of Christians were to be especially effective in the six provinces of East Cochinchina (Qui Nhon) south of Hue. Here, eight French missionaries and an estimated 25,000 Vietnamese Christians were killed. North of the capital his edicts also met with a strong response: ten Vietnamese priests and approximately 10,000 Vietnamese Christians were reported killed. Large numbers of Christian refugees fled to Hue and Qui Nhon from where a few thousand were taken south on board vessels sent from Saigon by Bishop Colombert.

French pacification and Christian self-help, 1885-1886.

After reconstructing the Co-mat Vien and placing Regent Nguyen Van Thuong in charge of a new puppet emperor, Dong Khanh, the French organised pursuit of Thuyet and the deposed emperor Ham Nghi. The pursuit formed part of a broader drive to repress the growing Can Vuong movement as it spread through northern Annam into southern Tonkin. But French military units operated slowly, inflexibly and with only poor knowledge of the country. Intent on tracking insurgents, they were slow to provide Christian villages with defence against communal reprisals. French missionaries, devastated by the massacre of Christian villages, were virulent in their criticism of the military tactics of French repression. Indignant at the tardiness of French efforts to protect the missions and intensely suspicious of the sincerity of collaborating mandarins (Doc. 114), they demanded the right to arm Christian villages for their own protection. When these appeals were denied, they resorted to self-help. Though Bishop Colombert, from the safety of Saigon, expressed doubts as to the wisdom of involving the mission in arming the Christian communes (Doc. 115), priests in vicariates affected by the massacres showed less compunction. In southern Annam missionaries such as Fr Guerlach and Fr Maillard either formed their own militias or guided French troops in actions against those non-Christian communes which had participated in the massacres. Spontaneous excesses were also committed by Vietnamese Christians intent on revenge. The more spectacular episodes of social warfare mainly affected the vicariate of North Cochinchina (Qui Nhon), where the most brutal and widespread massacres of Christians had previously occurred. Christian reprisals generated extensive recrimination from French officials, and conferred a long-lived notoriety upon the local missionaries which French anticlericals intent on discrediting the mission were to exploit a decade later.

Missionary views on French pacification policies.

Besides complaining at being left defenceless, missionaries were openly critical of the political aspects of French pacification strategy. In the debate which developed in 1885-6 between the French civil and military administrations over whether to invite more administrative collaboration from the Vietnamese elites, or dispense with indigenous intermediaries and rely on military coercion, missionaries threw their weight onto the side of direct, repressive rule. Bishop Puginier in particular sought to persuade French military and civil officials to share his mistrust of the whole Vietnamese elite, from the mandarinate down to the local scholar notables. Missionaries bitterly castigated some French commanders for being the dupes of collaborating Vietnamese officials **(Doc. 114)** and warned repeatedly of the dangers of trusting the scholar class. It is not easy to evaluate the influence of missionary opinion upon the early stages of French pacification strategy. In later years missionaries were accused by anticlerical critics - Governor-General de Lanessan among them - of having dominated French official thinking on pacification. But this may have been an exaggeration. The French army in Tonkin had long been suspicious of the Vietnamese elites, and the campaigning experience of French forces in Tonkin more probably accounts for the preference of the military for direct rule.

The military and missionary case for mistrusting the collaboration of mandarins, scholars and village notables began to lose ground with the arrival, early in 1886, of Paul Bert as the first civil Resident-General of Annam-Tonkin. Under Bert the process of eliciting largescale administrative collaboration from the Vietnamese elites began its uneasy course. For reasons of economy as much as of principle, Bert proclaimed a new political strategy for winning over the mandarinate, the scholars and even what he called the 'Tiers Etat' - the Vietnamese commercial class, such as it was - to acceptance of French domination. He aimed to increase Vietnamese involvement in administration under the direction of French residents. He also created a consultative council of Vietnamese notables. He hoped moreover to rely upon a Vietnamese militia rather than on French troops to maintain internal order, and tried to confine the role of the French military to external defence.

Bert's policy for managing the interests of missionaries and their Christian communes formed an important part of his strategy of political conciliation. Christians, who formed a significant element of the new militia, were still exceptionally useful to the French as auxiliaries in the work of pacification. But they were socially despised and politically detested by the non-Christian Vietnamese. Bert needed to retain Christian support by means which did not further alienate the wider non-Christian community. Though virulently anticlerical in domestic politics - as Ferry's Education minister he had recently laicized much of the French educational system - Bert tried to steer a median course in dealing with the Christian community in Annam-Tonkin. Officially he proclaimed a policy of neutrality in religious matters, as Republican othodoxy required **(Doc. 118)**. Officially too, he insisted upon the strict observance of the treaties in disputes affecting the rights of missionaries and Christians. His administrative directives also enjoined a balanced approach to intercommunal conflicts **(Doc. 122)**. Informally, however, he offered the missions considerable moral support, as Bishop Colombert's letters indicate **(Doc. 117)**. And when confronted by the problem of sectarian disorders following the recent massacres in Annam and southern Tonkin, he helped to secure subsidies for the missions towards the relief of hardship, and countermanded the directives of subordinates who had tried to prevent missionaries obtaining arms for the defence of Christian communes. But when missionaries began urging Bert to exact compensation from those non-Christian villages responsible for recent massacres, he rejected their appeals. The levying of indemnities under Tu Duc in the 1870s had intensified social grievances in the past, and Bert seemed determined to to break the cycle of retribution and counter-reprisal which was being perpetuated by enforced compensations.

Bert's policy towards the missions represents the first stage in the formation of an administrative policy of official neutrality in religious matters in Annam and Tonkin. Given the utility of the missionary establishment to the new French administration one might have expected a more overt promotion of missionary interests. But the French protectoral administration in Annam-Tonkin now occupied much the same arbitrational role in relation to the Christian and non-Christian Vietnamese communities as the French colonial government of Cochinchina. To maintain social order it had to mediate between a collaborating, but recently subjugated Vietnamese elite which detested and felt threatened by Christians as a class; and a growing Christian minority which, though aligned to France politically, retained a capacity for promoting social tensions which threatened to alienate further the non-Christian majority. So long as pacification remained a problem the French administration could afford to antagonise neither community. Hence the policy of religious neutrality proclaimed by Republicans in France aptly suited the new French administration's political predicament in Annam-Tonkin.

Further reading

C. Forniau, 'Les traditions de la lutte nationale au Vietnam. L'insurrection des lettrés (1885-1895)', in J.Chesneaux, G.Boudarel et D.Hémery, **Tradition et révolution au Vietnam**. (Paris, Anthropos, 1971), pp. 89-107.

D. Marr, **Vietnamese Anticolonialism, 1885–1925.** (London, U. of California Press, 1971).

Le Général X, **L'Annam du 5 Juillet 1885 au 4 Avril 1886.** (Paris, 1901).

R. Bourotte, 'L'aventure du roi Ham Nghi', **Bulletin des Amis du Vieux Hué**, XVI, 3, July-Sept. 1929.

J. Kim Munholland, '"Collaboration strategy" and the French pacification of Tonkin, 1885-1897'. **The Historical Journal**, 24, 3 (1981) pp. 629-650.

J. Chailley-Bert, **Paul Bert au Tonkin.** (Paris, G.Charpentier, 1887).

P. Vial, **Nos premières années au Tonkin.** (Paris, Voiron, 1889).

Documents

111. Mgr **Puginier,** Bishop of West Tonkin, to General **Roussel de Courcy,** Commander-in-Chief of the French forces in Tonkin. Ke So, 7 July 1885.

... I know for certain that for some time the government at Hue has been sending secret letters to the Tonkin mandarins through large numbers of lesser mandarins and trusted soldiers called <u>thi-ve</u>. Some of these have confided to friends that the Annamese government has decided not to put up with the current situation any longer, and that the letters that are being transmitted order the mandarins to quit their posts at a prescribed moment.

I am equally sure that secret letters have been sent by the court to influential individuals urging them to make common cause with the Annamese government. Before the official document is handed over they are asked to sign their agreement to the plan outlined in the letter.... (J.Dupuis, Le Tonkin de 1872 à 1886. (Paris, 1910) pp. 544-545)

112. Mgr **Puginier**, Bishop of Mauricastre, Vicar Apostolic of West Tonkin, to General **Roussel de Courcy**, Commander-in-Chief of the French forces in Tonkin. Hanoi, 17 July 1885.

... The attack made on your troops (at Hue) was not planned by the Second Regent, Ton That Thuyet, alone: he has neither sufficient influence nor authority for such a serious and compromising act. The coup was agreed by both Regents and accepted by the whole court. The Annamese counted on success, or at least hoped to inflict serious damage on you. When on the morning of the attack they saw that they had been routed, they took flight. That is when the first Regent, Nguyen Van Tuong, seeing that the manoeuvre had failed, chose in his politically devious way to break with the First Regent in the hope of tricking you into thinking that he had had no part in the plot....

You know enough of the First Regent, General, not to be fooled by his deceitful assurances of innocence and goodwill. He is an enemy of France, the greatest, most dangerous and most irreconcilebale of all in Annam....

Both Regents are equally hostile to you. The Second, Ton That Thuyet, is the impassioned one, but he is far from being as dangerous as Nguyen Van Tuong. The latter is politically cunning, full of trickery and unscrupulous as to the means employed provided they attain his goals. These two men hate each other, but while they were both influential they acknowledged a mutual interest in cooperating to fight the French. Beyond this common end they kept a wary and mistrustful eye on each other. The First Regent has for long been frustrated by the rivalry of the other, and wanted to be rid of him. But it was not easy. He is taking advantage of the recent turn of events to heap all the blame on him so as to get ahead and wield effective power in the name of the king, as he has always wanted.... (J.Dupuis, Le Tonkin de 1872 à 1886. (Paris, 1910) pp. 546-547)

113. **Royal decree** ordering the massacre of Christians. (Undated. Probably issued after July 1885).

The Minister for War, obeying the order of the King (sic) has had drawn up the secret edict which follows:

'Since food and drink are provided by Heaven, so it is Heaven which has set the boundaries of kingdoms. From the year Dinh Ti (1857) when the European barbarians came to ravage this country, the Cochinchinese fought them vigorously and paid heavily with their lives for their faith to the King. Seeing which, the King, who is the father and mother of his people, no longer knowing how to show his compassion for his subjects, had to make peace and reserve for the future his search for a ruse by which his vengeance could be fulfilled. In latter years these barbarians have committed atrocities without number and the King, touched by compassion, has frequently poured forth tears of blood, knowing not what measures to resort to. But these barbarians are not appeased. Masters of one place they want to become masters of another. So can the King's subjects still remain inactive? Whoever can take part in devising a stratagem or in resorting to force should show his fidelity to the King. Let the door not be opened to rebels. Let us not suckle a tiger which will strike fear into us later.

It seems that the devotees of this perverse Christian religion have secretly joined the French cause and hope to profit from the disorder. Also, although there is a royal edict which, in order to stifle suspicion, treats Christians like pagans (recte 'honest men'), nonetheless those who enjoy the King's blessings should show their gratitude by destroying them as one cuts grass, and as one pulls up roots, and as one cuts off feathers and wings. When peace has been won back the King will reward merit and will not forget his promises, and then his devoted subjects will be recognised. If the Sun loses a corner in the East, should it not rightly recover it in the West?

The above words are a secret royal edict addressed to the scholars and to the notables of Tonkin whether on land or sea.' (Exact translation. + P. Puginier, Ev. Vic. Ap.)
(A.S.M.E. Vol.816, (Lettres de Mgr. Puginier.) No. 21)

114. Fr **Geffroy**, missionary at Qui Nhon, to the **Superior** of the S.M.E. Qui Nhon, 28 September 1885.

The letter that I wrote you on 8 August has no doubt reached you already. Since then our disasters - already so great - have merely got worse and God only knows when we will see the end of it all. Since then, too, the policy of the Annamese about which I notified you has become clearer and more obvious, and the uniformity of its implementation in the six provinces of our mission is firm evidence that it is simply a fulfilment of commands from higher up....

Unfortunately, while the harassed French were tiring themselves out in this foolish campaign (of pursuit after Thuyet and Emperor Ham Nghi) the Annamese took all the time they needed to carry out their long prepared plan for executing all the Christians in the south, that is to say, in our poor mission. What is happening now in the missions of Hue and southern Tonkin we still do not really know; but, from the way in which the French are proceeding in repressing this revolt and punishing so many crimes here, it is to be feared that the extermination of Christians is taking place all over Annam and in Tonkin.

A despatch from General de Courcy has no doubt already informed you of the capture of Binh Dinh citadel at the end of August. They should have sent this expedition a month earlier and then we would only have had to lament the loss of Quang Ngai, that is, the death of three missionaries and 600 christians. But they always come to rescue us after time has run out.

General de Courcy was certainly not short of information even well before the Quang Ngai attack, and these facts do not come merely from missionaries who, naturally, are always misinformed - but from a good number of creditable individuals.

Eventually the expedition got under way and won an easy victory, which was doubtless needed in France to calm public opinion. That was practically the only gain, because there is no let-up in the search for and massacre of Christians who have fled for safety to the mountains in Binh Dinh and the other provinces....

So much for high-level French policy! The mandarins, the irreconcileable enemies of France who have just massacred so many thousands of her faithful allies, are listened to and treated with great politeness and respect; whereas Christians, who have never parted company with the French cause, who have fought and spilt their blood for her or because of her, are treated as a merely negligeable quantity and left at the mercy of their enemies, despite all the treaties by which she was bound to protect them. Not only that: not only have they been abandoned to the fury of their enemies, who have exterminated them till no trace was left, but the French are now trying to pour shame on them and use every means of blackening their memory. O! If the Christians had wronged the pagans 10 or 100 or 1,000 times less we should have seen how prompt and severe their punishment would have been. At the first news brought by the pagans of their danger at the hands of Christians, (the French) would have rushed to their rescue and made the Christians pay dearly for their presumption....

The Christians of Annam are the only natural allies of the French; time and time again they have proved their attachment, and never during all the revolts that there have been in Cochinchina has a single Christian ever been found among the rebels. So why treat them with such disdain and show favour only to dubious allies who so quickly turn into notorious enemies? What nation other than France has behaved like this in a country she is trying to subdue?

Setting generalities aside, I have some detailed news which will interest you more. So let us review all the provinces of the mission starting with the north.

Quang Nam. In this province Fr Bruyère and Fr Maillard are still keeping well, but they have to put up a strong fight against the rebels. Some days ago it was rumoured that the citadel of Quang Nam had been seized by the scholars. It was an official rumour designed to mislead public opinion. The regular government declared itself incapable of putting down the revolt here like everywhere else, and disclaimed all responsibility. In reality it was the mandarins who, after making full preparations, had themselves besieged and allowed themselves to be captured after a token siege, all the better to hide what they were up to and avoid being accused of giving a free hand to the scholars to massacre the Christians. So this news signified that the massacres and burnings were beginning. Actually three or four days later Fr Maillard informed us by letter that he could not go to the rescue of Fr Bruyère who was cut off in his mission of Tra Kieu. He himself had his hands full defending his own and had already had to beat off several attacks. In one fortunate sortie made against the rebels he wrested three cannon and some munitions from them and killed twenty-three of their men. What a life! Our poor colleagues! Finally in the last few days we heard that an expeditionary column leaving for Tourane had managed to relieve Fr Bruyère. That was our last news. What has happened to the district managed by the native priest Can Du in the south of the province? What has happened to the secondary missions in the three districts of Quang Nam? Is the citadel occupied by the French? We just do not know.

Quang Ngai. In this province which, less than three months ago was so flourishing, where our work was developing so well under the direction of Frs Garin, Poirier and Guégan, there is not a single Christian left today out of the 7,000 there before. However they are not all dead. Two thirds of them from the native priest Can Kham's district to the north escaped after defending themselves heroically for over a month. The Christians hid under cover of the mountains where it was difficult to cut through. They had to beat off eighteen attacks in which they killed 150 to 200 of the enemy, one of them a high mandarin and several other leaders. They also captured several cannon and some important documents. The leading mandarins prepared a formidable expedition against them and would probably have crushed them when Fr Maillard arrived to save them. Our colleague, knowing that they were still holding out, armed his Christians and ferried them to the rescue on board the Chasseur. Captain La Gorrée commanding this sloop was under orders not to allow a single sailor to land, but he did at least fire shells to cover Fr Maillard's management of the Christians' retreat. He then took about 1,000 of them on board and conveyed them to the French post at Tourane....

General de Courcy made fair promises. From Tonkin he should have sent arms to the Christians who could have been put under the orders of the Resident to pursue and punish wrongdoers. Since then, no arms have appeared and M. Navelle has received no written instructions about them.

General Prud'homme's opinion was that neither Christians nor pagans should be allowed to carry arms. If you are attacked, he said, call us and we will defend you. Alas! We have seen what French protection is worth: if it arrives at all it is always too late. (A.S.M.E. Vol.751, (Cochinchine Orientale, 1881-1900). No.62)

115.   Mgr **Colombert**, Bishop of Samostate, Vicar Apostolic of West Cochinchina, to Fr **Lemonnier**, Procurator-General at Hong Kong. Saigon, 12 April 1886.

Today I telegraphed the word 'Nothing' to you. It means that there are difficulties about sending the arms to Qui Nhon either direct or via Saigon. Resorting to arms does not appeal to me. It is not justified by the Bible. It is too human a measure. It is also a dangerous measure. The mandarins are accusing the Christians of rebellion before the French authorities who are predisposed to believe them. To put arms into the hands of Christians is to furnish the mandarins with a positive argument. So, arming Christians does not seem to me prudent unless the French authorities consent to it. But do we have their consent? On the contrary, we do not.

The present attitude of the Resident at Qui Nhon (M. Hamelin) is a serious impediment to despatching (arms). This Resident proclaims himself a friend of the pagans. He wants to place the Christians under the control of pagans who have just cut the throats of 40,000 of them. Can a Frenchman be so stupid? That, however, is the Resident of France at Qui Nhon and we must take practical account of him. I am supported in my views by M. Lagorrée (sic), Commander of the Chasseur, an excellent man, very well disposed to us, who when asked for advice on this question replied that it would not be prudent to annoy the Resident and the Customs by sending arms to Qui Nhon.

We should wait before sending them off. Paul Bert (Resident-General of Annam-Tonkin) has shown his distaste for the nomination of Hamelin (as Resident) whom he did not know. If he can have him packed off, his successor might perhaps be more amenable.

Anyhow, if we send arms to Qui Nhon sooner or later, I ask that <u>they should not be sent via Saigon.</u> Since the entry of arms into the colony is forbidden, they would require formalities and approaches to the authorities who, far from keeping it all quiet, would publicise the fact and comment on it.

(A.S.M.E. Vol.759, (Cochinchine Occidentale, 1881-1898). No 212.)

116.   Mgr **Puginier**, Bishop of Mauricastre, Vicar Apostolic of West Tonkin. 'Notes towards a study of one of the phases of the Tonkin question: The Insurrection.' Hanoi, 13 September 1886.

You do not seem to suspect that the mandarins may regain by political stealth what they have lost by fighting. Weak and without serious means of defence of its own, the Annamese government has been able to fight for twenty-eight years against France, which has sometimes deployed considerable forces in fighting it. (The Annamese government) has suffered much, it is true; but it is not beaten, and it has always been able, through astute, devious, dishonourable but clever means to keep itself going. This is what the mandarins themselves are like in general. The greater part of them have sworn to hate France until their dying day because they know that the establishment of her influence means the ruin of their dominance, their prestige, their authority and their incomes....

Among the authors of the insurrection are also the scholars whom France, I know for certain, will always have as enemies both as a class and as individuals. The party which wants to fight to the end knows them well, has always made use of them, and is still making use of them today as its agents. The scholars render the greatest services to the resistance and are completely dedicated to it. It is the scholars who, by slow, secret but effective work and by covert and daily activities work upon a population which cannot escape from their influence. This resistance party is capable of anything, even of making its submission if need be, when its resources are exhausted. More important, it is capable of doing so without being reduced to this extremity and, if it needs to, it would make magnificent promises for the future; but that would all be an act of hypocrisy with the aim of gaining our confidence to work more effectively at undermining French influence and continue working for revolution in the shadows.... But never, never will this change of heart be sincere: I regard it as impossible, seeing that its views and interests are diametrically opposed to those of the protectorate...

What is the aim of those who are fomenting the insurrection?

Their aim is nothing less than the extinction of French influence. To attain it more effectively, the enemy first revolutionises the country to make it hostile to the French. It then endeavours to harass the French troops by fighting in a way that is feeble and devious, but which will seem dogged, in the hope of demoralising and tiring them. After having organised insurrection, the enemy massacres the Christians and loots and burns their villages. One would be completely mistaken to think that the first and main motive for these incredibly cruel excesses is religious hatred. It is true that the scholars say so sometimes; but this is solely said to mislead and because, counting on the neutrality of the French authorities, they can more easily continue their work. No! This religious hatred is only a secondary and remote motive for the atrocities committed against Christians. The main aim of these exterminations is to deprive France of a source of immense support in the country. They know that the more Christians there are in the kingdom, the more friends France has, though they cannot characterise them as enemies of their own government. The number of Christians frightens them; and the services rendered by Christians and missionaries, the information they provide and the practical things they can tell the French, these are what worry them inordinately.

The rebels know that they cannot hope to fight with any advantage against the French until after the priests and Christians have been exterminated....

What methods are the authors of the insurrection using to attain their ends?

It is certain that in principle the population of Tonkin was not hostile to France. One could even say that, tired of the exactions and the regime of oppression excercised by the mandarins they were fairly ready to accept another, more benevolent protectoral authority. In sum, they merely asked to be left in peace to cultivate their fields and indulge in commerce. Moreover, among influential Tonkinese some remembered that barely a hundred years ago their country formed an undependent kingdom. In these conditions it was not easy for the fallen party of Ham Nghi and the Regent Thuyet, in itself little recognised, to raise the whole country suddenly against a victorious France which already occupied the important points of Tonkin and disposed of considerable forces. The enemy understood this very well. So it used all its forces to revolutionise Annam first, because French forces were less imposing there.

It advanced rapidly but carefully, and seeing that it was not capable of embracing the whole country in one movement it waited until the insurrection had taken serious hold in the southern provinces before progressively extending its action to those of the north.

The enemy party, which had in its service the scholars and those mandarins who were hostile to the French cause, was careful to use them to spread hatred for the measures taken by the French authorities: population censuses, taxes, coolie duty, boat requisitions, cattle supply etc. Pages could be written on each of these items. Nothing was neglected, they turned everything to use, they exaggerated or falsified everything; they put an odious interpretation on actions which were good in themselves; they pressured the population in a frightening way, even more than under the Annamese regime, and represented it all as coming from the French.

They have been consistently making the French odious to the population for three years now. But they really started working on opinion to spread hatred for France by means of all these exaggerations and calumnies after the scholars began preparing the uprisings.

Once this preparatory work was done, the hostile mandarins and the scholars - for they always acted together - made ready for revolt. They chose audacious and discontented men and gave them the title of mandarins with ranks more or less equivalent to their personal value and the number of men they could raise for the moment of action. At first there were only the skeletons of bands, and individuals staying quiet in their villages. When everything was ready they gathered their men together and raised the standard of revolt. Normally the signal was given by meals and a sacrifice.

Then the third phase began. The enemy did their work fast for fear of being caught by surprise and eliminated. Lacking means of subsistance they levied rice and money from the villages, and realising their weakness they forced the population to come and join their side on threat of being held to ransom or pillaged. Some communes - the most intensively worked upon - joined the insurrection voluntarily. Others did so only with difficulty and because they were forced to it; but once compromised and committed to the wrong path they became as hostile as the rest.

Once this third period began one could regard the whole country as inimical to us. That was when the fate of the Christians became critical....

I enclose herewith the translation of a document which the enemy is circulating secretly around the country through the medium of the scholars. It shows clearly the purpose they are following as well as the measures which they have already used and which they intend to use henceforward because they have proved successful:

We cannot fight against the French, so we have to know how to bend to their pressure. When we see them arrive somewhere we should hide our arms and then go to meet them, compliment them and provide them with coolies. When the French see this they will not think of burning villages any more. When we see mandarins passing with large forces we should do the same and then the French can do nothing to us.

We should take steps to massacre all the phu huyen so that no one is left to provide the French with coolies. That done, we should try to burn all the mercantile districts around the provincial citadels so that only four or five mandarins are left with the French in these citadels. The latter will then tire of their predicament and leave the territory. That has already been done from Nghe An to the other side of Annam and we already see signs that our purpose is achieved. If all influential men from every province agree with our opinion, the French will undoubtedly be unable to stay in this country and will have to go home....

All the Christians from Nghe An and from the rest of Annam have already been massacred and if any are left they can only be few. In the province of Thanh Hoa all the Catholic villages in the sub-prefecture of Ha Trung and in those of Ngoc Son and Nong Cong have already been razed. We will take care to do the same in the few phu huyen of the upper part of the province.

For Ninh Binh and the rest of Tonkin we have already taken all steps to put the same plan into effect....

If the French have been able to come here, if they have been able to know all the roads, all the rivers and to become familiar with all that is happening in the kingdom, it is solely thanks to the Christians and to their bishops and their priests.

Consequently if we do not massacre all the Christians we cannot hope to reach our goal without difficulty. Although China came to our aid it was still difficult, because whenever we made the smallest move the Christians went to warn the French, and before we had even completed our preparations the latter came to destroy us. That is what has happened every time up to now. There are some among us who are silly enough to think that the French have no confidence in the Christians;

but that is quite erroneous.   There is complete unity of heart and mind among all of them without exception.

That is why we ask everyone to bend resolutely to the task of completing the extermination of the Christians, and follow the example of the scholars of Nghe An, Ha Tinh and other provinces of the south.   If this end is achieved we can affirm that the French will be doomed to complete paralysis, just as crabs with broken claws are totally unable to drag themselves along.

Seventh lunar month, Commander in Chief of the left wing, Great Generalissimo of the attack upon the French (Ton That Thuyet)....

Here are some explanations of the principal points raised above.

The rebel scholars in the service of Ham Nghi and Thuyet have, until now, put into complete effect the plan for 'bending' before the French. Every time that the presence of an enemy band is proclaimed in this or that place, as soon as the French troops arrive to fight them they find that the rebels have 'hidden their arms', and have intermingled with the population, or, if need be, have taken off by cart. The village inhabitants 'present themselves' to offer the greetings normal for the country, sometime offering a few trivial presents, fruit etc. in token of respect for its mission. They swear that no bands of rebels have been seen there, and they furnish guides for the rest of the route and coolies for carrying the baggage. We have often been caught out by these ruses and false demonstrations. Those who denounced the presence of (rebel) bands have been suspected of wanting to wear our troops out and have paid dearly for their loyalty....

By whom have the plots against the French been revealed up to now? By the missionaries and the Christians.... Where has the most important information come from at moments when it was necessary to take action, fight the enemy, attack the citadels occupied by the Chinese? From the missionaries and the Christians. The rebels know this and that is why they are desperate to dispose of the missionaries and the Christians at all costs by a general massacre. In effect, without the missionaries and Christians the French would find themselves surrounded by enemies. They would not be able to trust anybody; they would only receive false information maliciously offered to undermine their situation. They would be reduced to being incapable of acting and would be exposed to real disasters. In a word their position would no longer be tenable. They would be forced to quit the country when their interests and even their existence would be gravely compromised. The plan of the rebel scholars is relatively profound, well conceived and clever. It is to be hoped that they will not be able to achieve it completely....

It is incontestable that Tonkin has been quietly and completely worked over by the scholars...belonging to the party of Ham Nghi and Thuyet.... The whole country is ready for a general insurrection: one sees it in the attitude and language of the population, which has visibly changed, especially in the last month. This change is becoming general and is growing stronger daily: all the letters I am receiving from different parts of the mission notify me of it....(A.O.M. Aix. Indochine, Amiraux, 11,782)

117. Mgr **Colombert**, Bishop of Samostate, Vicar Apostolic of West Cochinchina, to Father **Lemonnier**, Procurator-General at Hong Kong. Saigon, 25 March 1886.

I think it may interest you to hear of Paul Bert's attitude. It is clear that he wished to cut off his anticlerical tail in coming to the East....

Immediately on disembarking M. Vial came to tell me that P.B. was well disposed to us and wanted to see me. The governor (of Cochinchina), apprised of this, invited me to a big gala dinner given the day after his arrival. After dinner, P.B.'s son-in-law presented himself and said his father-in-law wanted to speak to me. The governor presented me, and from the top to the centre of the great room we spoke with gusto for a good half hour, the whole of Saigon stupefied to see such a pair. Several people came up to be presented; he shook their hands and continued his conversation with me. He told me some interesting things and I had some of my own to tell him. This new attitude was wholly voluntary on his part, it was perfectly understood and generally approved by the Saigon community. He asked me for a meeting at my place for the following morning. He arrived on time and the tête-à-tête lasted an hour and three quarters. I had prepared my brief and told him everything I wanted to. Vial told me to be perfectly frank with him. At his request I summed up our conversation and sent him an unsigned note with all the verbs in the infinitive.

I was astounded by the accuracy of his observations on the situation and about personalities. He is studying the position closely and is gathering honey from every bloom, even from (publications like) Les Missions Catholiques and Les Annales Dominicaines. He has the same opinions as we have on certain personages who have left Annam. As far as the Christians are concerned he repeated twice that they were massacred for France, that it is a great crime, that we have a considerable moral debt to them. I strengthened this impression for him in item 8 of my note, of which I enclose a copy. He had ill-founded prejudices against Mgr Caspar and Fr Maillard. I hope I have shown him the plain absurdity of this. I was especially concerned about the case of Fr Maillard.

There it is. I am going to put Mgr van Camelbecke, Mgr Caspar and Mgr Puginier in the picture.

What can one hope for from all this? I am not basking in any illusions. If he cuts his tail off it is from tactical motives: it will grow again as soon as it can. However, so long as he proffers his hand we cannot turn our backs on him. Since we are in a position to tell him the truth we have a duty to do so, since he is the authority of the moment. At least we will not have to regret missing our chance. If he is as fair minded as he is intelligent he will do us less damage than the infamous de Courcy and will prevent the Oriental from suffering complete disaster.

..... Item No.8 of my note to P.B.
No doubts to be cast on the fidelity of the Christians to the French cause.... Nobody is asking for them to be favoured unduly, but it is fair to treat them as friends, to procure their safe return to their villages and to indemnify them at least partially since they have lost everything in our cause. Those who seized their lands to return them. Those who pillaged and burned their houses to be obliged to reconstruct them. The villages which participated in the confiscations to be made materially responsible. That is what was done at Nghe An following the massacres of 1874, when the government of Saigon raised its hand to procure justice and justice was done: the mandarins gave in, as they always will when faced with a just and firm attitude. (A.S.M.E. Vol 756, (Cochinchine Occidentale, 1867-1889). No. 727)

118. **Paul Bert,** Resident-General of Annam-Tonkin, to an unnamed correspondent. Hanoi, 29 June 1886.

... Every religion is a great school of morality vitiated by the delegation of divine power to men: it is always the priest and never religion itself that stands indicted.

But leaving aside such philosophical reflections and attending to political facts, particularly in relation to the present day religious question in Annam, I am glad to see that we view matters from the same perspective. However, I feel I should explain my thinking more precisely.

There was a time when France considered herself the protector of Christians in the sense that, convinced of the superiority of their religion over that of others, she promoted its development with all the means which a great nation has at its disposal. As 'the eldest daughter of the Church' she helped her mother to conquer the world, placing her guns and her moral authority at the service of the Catholic faith and its priests, so that her acts were the same as those of the God of the Christians. Gesta Dei per francos.

This antiquated conception was overthrown by the revolution of 1789. France no longer needs to consider herself as having the right to evangelise. She no longer acknowledges a state religion, and the Catholic religion is simply subsidised in common with the Protestant, Jewish and Muslim faiths. So she no longer has to bother with promoting the Christian religion abroad, any more than she would promote Islam.

But she does acknowledge a higher duty. She has become the guardian and protector of freedom of conscience. She cannot allow in her own territories or in others over which she has some authority or influence, the persecution or punishment of any man for following his own religion. So she no longer intervenes to claim privilege but to demand equality and justice.

These are our modern principles: they shape all French legislation. I know that in practice and until recently we have had to apply them a lot, especially in your territories, so that Christians have been able to imagine that they enjoy a privileged situation and special rights under a guarantee of French protection, with the result that (Annamese) non-Christians have tended to fear encroachment upon the rights of constituted authority.

But all that has well and truly changed, and for good. The coming of the Republic in France has resulted in the proper application of the principles of the revolution of 1789. Both I myself and the government which I represent are fully resolved to follow them. I will not cease insisting to the Annamese authorities that Christians have the same rights as other subjects of the king; but neither will I cease telling Christians that they may only claim their rights on condition that they show obedience to all the country's laws and to the mandarins authorised to apply them. But if they want special legislative treatment, if they refuse to pay taxes to the authorities, if they want to form small states within the State, I will stop defending them. I am ready to do anything in the name of Equality, but I will do nothing in the name of Privilege.

(Quoted in J. Chailley, Paul Bert au Tonkin, (Paris, G. Charpentier, 1887) p. 325)

119.   **J.L. de Lanessan,** commissioned by the Quai d'Orsay to report on the <u>mise en valeur</u> of the French colonies, 1886-9.

Missionaries and the protectoral policy in Indochina.

In Tonkin and Annam - territories whose political, administrative and social independence (<u>sic</u>) we have guaranteed by treaty, and where the native authorities and populations had a right to rely upon the honest operation of a protectorate - a brutal, maladroit and expensive policy of annexation and conquest has been applied by incompetent or badly directed agents. Urged on by missionaries whose sole preoccupation is to overthrow all obstacles to religious proselytism, our agents are alienating themselves by thousands of vexations from the scholars and mandarins, in other words from the most intelligent, the best educated and richest elements of the nation. These elements are, it is true, the most faithful to the traditions of the Annamese people and possess the highest degree of national feeling, but they are also the elements which would best serve our interests if we could attain our ends by honourable dealing.

This policy of hostility towards the Annamese government and the national elite, this policy of conquest and annexation is not only unworthy of a people which prides itself on being the most ardent proponent of the ideas of liberty, but also has the serious inconvenience of forcing us to deploy men and money out of all proportion to the advantages which the country can offer to our commerce and industry. (J.L. de Lanessan, <u>L'Indochine Française</u>. (Paris, 1889), p. 755)

120.   **J.L. de Lanessan,** Governor-General of Indochina (1891-4).

Bishop Puginier on the scholar elite.

It seemed very clear that the hostility of (Bishop Puginier) towards the scholars was above all inspired by his Catholicism. So I remarked to him that the scholars must know how the missionaries felt about them: they might think that the French officials felt the same way since they shared the same religion, and that in consequence the scholars must have developed real apprehensions about their own future as a class. It required no more than this to turn them into enemies of France. I added that (the scholars) would probably have a different attitude if we treated them properly, as they had a right to expect, by showing regard for their religion, customs and administrative traditions etc. In a word, instead of taking the unrealisitic and dangerous course of threatening to suppress them, we should treat them well and reassure them about their future.

Nothing that I said had any effect. I met with an intractable response and both the conversation and the dinner ended with this final reply: 'They must be suppressed.'

Now, in Annam as in China the scholars represent the governing class of the population. They are very attached to the laws, customs and religion of their own society because of their education and because of their elite status within this society. So naturally they become annoyed when foreigners incessantly attack everything which they themselves revere and which forms the basis of their own authority. Consequently it is not from among them that missionaries might hope for religious conversions. In fact during the two centuries and more that the Catholic missions have been operating in China and the Indochinese peninsula they have probably not converted more than ten scholars in all. The entire educated and governing class of the population has evaded their proselytism. And it could hardly be otherwise, for in making themselves Catholics this element would lose all moral authority and would be despised by the majority of society....(J.L. de Lanessan, Les missions et leur protectorat. (Paris, Alcan, 1907), pp. 40-1)

121. M. **Hector**, Resident-Superior in Annam, to **Paul Bert**, Resident-General of Annam-Tonkin. Hue, 18 August 1886.

In the enclosed dossier you will find proof of the arrest by Catholics of a mayor. A Catholic woman was murdered by rebels. The bishop says simply that he sent armed men only to bring back her corpse. However, these men brought back the mayor at the same time and made him sign this unheard-of declaration aknowledging responsibility for her murder. One does not have to have known the Annamese for more than a week to be certain that this declaration is apocryphal or extracted under duress. The dossier also contains the claims of the head of a canton, of several sub-chiefs and of the notables of a village in Ha Tinh against the Catholics who have made arbitrary arrests, and have installed their own customs posts. I was notified of this latter fact last year by all officers crossing Ha Tinh. I drew the attention of the Resident to the question but M. Idatte has not yet looked into it.

What is important to note about all these claims is (that)...the Catholics think of themselves not as the subjects of the king of Annam but as subjects of their missionaries who make them obey or disobey the mandarins at their pleasure....(A.O.M. Aix. Indochine, Amiraux, 10,508.)

122. **Paul Bert,** Resident-General of Annam-Tonkin. Circular to all Residents and Vice-Residents. Hanoi, 30 August 1886.

... The treaty of 6 June, 1884 confirms the terms (of article 9 of the treaty of 1874) and in consequence we are bound to enforce it. The missionaries were our precursors in Indochina and, in times of trouble, were the first victims of insurrectional movements. They used to help us with their information and advice. Moreover the Christian population was frequently maltreated and persecuted, not only for religious reasons, but as friends of the French. We must not forget our debts of gratitude.

You will not, however, lose sight of the fact that the guarantees stipulated in the treaty of 15 March 1874 do not give Christians a privileged position nor exempt them from the obligations which bind all subjects of the empire both to the king (sic) of Annam and to the Protectorate.

You will give them your full support if they are prevented from following their religious duties or if their property or persons are threatened.

On the other hand you will require them, in normal conditions, to obey the law and pay their taxes, supply men for the provincial militias and carry out the orders of the mandarins.

In times of unrest it is logical that they should prepare for their own defence and you must take care to ensure their security: a few weapons may be given to their villages, and also to loyal villages which are not Christian. But you must take care to prevent a return to practices which have had results as deplorable for Christians themselves as for our own influence; and you must never authorise them to take the offensive or resort to reprisals. If they do not obey this rule you may summon the missionaries responsible and reprimand them severely or tell them that no one has the right to make their own justice; and if necessary you should notify their bishop. Finally, if the circumstances are exceptionally grave and those responsible remain deaf to your representations, you must subject them to French justice if they are Europeans, or to Annamese justice if they are natives. But you must never use such extreme measures without prior reference to me.

I want you, gentlemen, to convey these observations to the mandarins and to the missionaries....

(J. Chailley, Paul Bert au Tonkin, (Paris, G. Charpentier, 1887) p.341)

V

THE FRENCH MISSIONS AND THE CONSOLIDATION OF THE FRENCH IMPERIAL FRONTIER IN SOUTHEAST ASIA, 1881-1904.

V A FRENCH FRONTIER PROBLEMS IN THE MEKONG VALLEY, 1881-1885.

As the French extended political dominion northward from Cochinchina and Cambodia to Annam-Tonkin, they became increasingly aware of the vulnerability of their possessions to pressure from British interests proliferating across mainland Southeast Asia. To the west, the British had buttressed the Indian empire by the aquisition of most of Lower Burma between 1824 and 1852; and they had also begun reinforcing their settlements at the Straits from the mid 1870s by installing residents among of the Malay sultanates. By the early 1880s two independent kingdoms - Upper Burma and Siam - still separated British territories from France's new acquisitions, but the British were assumed to excercise informal sway over both these asiatic monarchies. Britain's informal predominance over Upper Burma and Siam had sinister implications for French trade and security interests. For the outer fringes of these kingdoms converged with the undemarcated hinterlands of Vietnam and Cambodia in the Mekong valley. The threat of British encroachment into the Mekong region presented the French with a complex of frontier problems which took more than a decade to resolve.

In considering the prospect of British advance towards the middle and upper Mekong, the French faced two issues of particular importance. First, British political preeminance in Upper Burma and Siam threatened to open access for British commerce to trade routes into the reputedly valuable markets of South-West China. One prospective route kept to Burmese territory for its whole course into China, but geographical difficulties greatly reduced its utility: it ran up the Irrawaddy past Bhamo to Tali-fu. The other, a potential rail route enthusiastically advocated by the British chambers of commerce, passed through the Lao states of northern Siam across the upper Mekong into Yunnan. This was the route of greatest concern to the French. If the British succeeded in entering the South-West China market by an easy rail route, the monopoly of access which the French themselves hoped to establish through control of Tonkin would be broken.

Second, Britain's informal ascendancy over Upper Burma and Siam confronted the French with a problem of frontier security in the vicinity of the Mekong river. It seemed vital to prevent the British from exploiting the suzerain rights of Upper Burma and Siam in the

Mekong valley to gain access by proxy to territory on the river. As a medium of communication the Mekong offered France the prospect of linking up her inland territories from Cochinchina to Yunnan. Moreover, the river basin contained several potential invasion routes leading to Hue, Phnom Penh and Saigon. Ultimately the French hoped to incorporate the river itself into a clearly defined eastern frontier. But this was a problematical aspiration, for the French protectorates of Vietnam and Cambodia could claim historic suzerainty over very few of the petty Lao principalities in local possession of the Mekong valley. Owing to their lack of prescriptive rights, the French were forced to move obliquely and with caution in pursuing solutions to the Mekong problem.

Even before obtaining full political control over Annam and Tonkin the French had begun to devise strategies for indirectly countering the threat of British advance. As early as 1881 they started to compete informally with the British for a measure of leverage over the courts of Bangkok and Mandalay. French prospects of succeeding seemed poor. France lacked any obvious source of commercial or political influence in either kingdom, where the only major French interests to have been locally established were the missions of the Société des Missions Etrangères. Inevitably, as the French developed policies to meet the complex of difficulties presented by British regional preeminence, the role of these Catholic missions fell into the general ambit of their calculations.

French policy in Siam, 1883–1885.

In Siam the French consul appointed in 1881 - Jules Harmand - at first attempted a commercial strategy to entrench French interests more firmly. He hoped to vamp up France's indirect political influence in central Siam by inducing French banks, shipping lines and canal building companies to develop a footing in the kingdom. But French investors responded sluggishly to his appeals. More significantly, the Siamese government, alert to the political dangers of allowing French investment to percolate freely, declined to issue development concessions.

Consul Harmand would have liked to turn the presence of the French Catholic mission to political account, for it represented the most extensive French interest so far established in Siam. The apostolic vicariate of Siam, first founded in the mid seventeenth century, was much the largest foreign mission of any currently established in the kingdom. In a population roughly estimated at 7 million, its 27 missionaries ministered to 13,150 converts, most of them concentrated in approximately 30 chrétientés.[1] In the 1850s and 1860s the mission's French bishop, Pallegoix, had earned considerable influence at the Bangkok court. He had acted as Siam's diplomatic emissary to France before the establishment of a French legation, and developed a close friendship with King Mongkut, whom he tutored in Latin, French and Mathematics, and for whom he also acted on occasion as interpreter. Since the death of Pallegoix, and particularly of King Mongkut in 1868, the mission had lost any serious political influence, and by the 1880s, under Bishop Vey, it maintained virtually no privileged contact with the new monarch, King Chulalongkorn, or his court. Nonetheless, as a major French presence in terms of personnel and moral influence, the mission might have served in some capacity as a political agency for French political aims.

Superficially, the general objectives of the mission and of the French consulate coincided. While Consul Harmand urgently wanted some means of strengthening French informal influence among Siam's Lao vassal states in the Mekong valley, the mission was anxious to expand its own proselytising endeavours among the Lao principalities of northern and eastern Siam. Missionary access to the Lao states had, in principle, been granted by a Siamese royal edict of September 1878, and the mission was keen to take full advantage of the privilege. The mature Buddhist culture of Siam proper had always been found impermeable to large-scale conversion, but the mission had high hopes of making progress among the more eclectic Lao.

However, the mission and the French consulate were unable to cooperate in pursuing their respective aims. The main problem was that the antagonisms generated by missionaries among some of the Lao chiefs obstructed the political objectives of the Siamese government in the region, and this in turn threatened to sour relations between the Siamese government and the French consulate.

Constitutionally, the Lao states were still vassal territory lying beyond the reach of direct administration from Bangkok. The Siamese, threatened by the growth of western imperialism in Southeast Asia since the 1860s, had adopted a policy of eroding Lao autonomy in order to draw these outlying regions into closer political dependence upon Bangkok. Ultimately this policy of centralisation was intended to lead to direct Siamese administration of the Lao regions. Meantime the Lao offered intermittent resistance, and Siamese progress was slow and uneasy. Siamese authorisation of missionary work in the Lao states was itself an expression of centralisation, but missionary proselytism tended to exacerbate Lao resistance to Siamese interference. Occasionally, therefore, the Siamese hesitated to issue passports to missionaries wishing to enter Lao territory.

This situation gave the mission motive for complaint, and the bishop pressed strongly for French consular mediation. Consul Harmand, however, treated missionary denunciations of the Siamese with extreme caution **(Doc. 123)**. This was partly because the sheer quantity of missionary grievances against the Siamese, and the abrasive tone of their complaints were creating fruitless diplomatic tension **(Doc. 124)**. But it was also due, in part, to the fact that they intended to direct the main thrust of their proselytism into the politically sensitive middle reaches of the Mekong valley where the consulate expected to the future Franco-Siamese frontier to run. Consul Harmand's unfortunate experience of missionary collaboration during the later stages of the Garnier expedition in 1874 (see supra **Doc. 73**) may have left him mistrustful of missionaries as a class, for he decided to treat them as an unreliable instrument for the development of French political leverage in Siam **(Doc. 125)**. Instead, he relied on a secular agent to develop a local influence for France on the upper Mekong. In this he was particularly unsuccessful: he despatched a Dr Néïs to Luang Prabang, a strategically crucial Lao territory on the upper Mekong, for the purpose of securing a secret pledge of political allegiance from the local Chao m'u'on, King Oun-Kham. Néïs, however, turned back before reaching the capital of Luang Prabang owing to banditry in the territory. Despite this failure, the French consulate continued to avoid using missionaries as potential agents for strengthening France's frontier position in any part of the Mekong valley.

French policy in Upper Burma, 1883-1885.

As the failure of Harmand's attempts to obtain commercial and political leverage in Siam became evident towards the middle of 1883, French policymakers adopted a more daring and wideranging strategy for strengthening the vulnerable frontiers of their possessions in Indochina. Having made no serious headway in Siam, they tried to develop a position of advantage in Upper Burma, whose position as an independent state bordering on India was a source of potential strategic weakness to the British themselves. In terms of relations between the French consulate and the French Catholic mission, the situation which evolved in Upper Burma took precisely the reverse course to that which had developed in Siam. For on the upper Irrawaddy the French consul found a need for assistance from the French mission, but the mission itself chose to hold aloof.

A crisis in Anglo-Burmese diplomatic relations in 1878 had resulted in the withdrawal of the British Resident from Mandalay in 1879 amid succession of acrimonious exchanges over issues of protocol and the interpretation of commercial treaties. This diplomatic breakdown, and the growing hostility of the Burmese monarch, King Theebaw, towards British interests, offered the French an unforseen chance to develop an influence on the upper Irrawaddy in competition with the British. The French hoped that, once established, such a position of advantage could be used to redress the strategic weakness of the French position further south, in Siam **(Docs 127, 128).** As at Bangkok, French success in establishing a footing at Mandalay depended in part on obtaining the active cooperation of the Burmese court, and this became the objective of a series of commercial negotiations authorised by Jules Ferry from 1883. By early 1885, with the signature of a supplementary Franco-Burmese commercial treaty and the despatch of a French consul – Frédéric Haas – to Mandalay, Ferry's policy approached fruition.

As in Siam, French interests in Upper Burma were mainly represented by the presence of a branch of the Société des Missions Etrangères. Though the French Catholic mission was not large (approximately 9 missionaries ministering to 1,800 Catholics),[1] its Bishop possessed canonical authority over a group of French nuns who were noted intimates of the influential Burmese queen, Supayalat. Haas, the new French Consul, was anxious to make some use of Bishop Bourdon's influence to obtain favour at court **(Doc. 131),** but the political outlook of Mgr Bourdon proved the reverse of that of his episcopal counterpart in Siam. Bourdon had little use for the French consulate other than as an instrument for forcing the king of Burma to honour his debts and contracts with French nationals, especially with the Catholic convent at Mandalay, which was owed approximately 35,000 rupees **(Doc. 126).** Although Catholic missionaries needed political help – they were severely restricted in their mobility and freedom to procure conversions – Bishop Bourdon appeared quite uninterested in engaging French diplomatic pressure to promote the work of conversion. Since there was no question of a French seizure of Upper Burma, Bourdon looked essentially to British annexation to remedy the mission's general problems **(Doc. 129).** Bourdon held British management of Lower Burma in high regard and attributed the deepening economic and political crisis in the kingdom to Burmese maladministration. So while Mgr Vey at Bangkok had been anxious to see the mission's activities promoted through French diplomatic mediation, at Mandalay Mgr Bourdon preferred to distance himself from the machinations of the French consulate **(Doc. 130),** and looked to the British for salvation.

This early phase of French political effort to improve the security of their imperial frontiers in Southeast Asia came to an abrupt end when, in the wake of a further crisis in August 1885 the British finally invaded Upper Burma and annexed it to their Indian empire in January 1886. Henceforward, in defending their trade and security interests, French policymakers were forced to concentrate on Siam, and particularly on the Lao states of the Mekong valley, for the means to resist further threats of British advance. In the new situation the Catholic missions would be able to play a more active political role.

(1). Société des Missions Etrangères. <u>Lettres communes. Tableau général de l'état des missions et des résultats obtenus en 1882.</u>

(2). Société des Missions Etrangères. <u>Lettres communes. Tableau général de l'état des missions et des résultats obtenus en 1885.</u>

Further reading

P.J.N. Tuck, 'Jules Ferry, Upper Burma and Siam: the defence of the French frontier in mainland Southeast Asia, 1883-1885', **The Journal of Imperial and Commonwealth History**, VI, 3, (May 1978).
D. McGilvaray, **A Half Century Among the Lao**. (New York, 1912).
D. Woodman, **The Making of Burma**. (London, Cresset, 1962).

Documents

123. Mgr **Vey**, Bishop of Geraza, Vicar Apostolic of Siam, to the **Directors** of the <u>Société des Missions Etrangères</u>. Bangkok, 27 September 1881.

It is most regrettable that the French government cannot understand how important and useful its moral support would be for missionaries. How little it appreciates the nature of Far Eastern peoples. These oriental populations find it in no way extraordinary that a missionary should intervene directly in the affairs of his Christians. (Oriental) customs, habits and traditions allow a religious leader to take a hand in dealings concerning the members of his flock. The complaints, if complaints there have been on the part of these (oriental) governments, appear to have originated in the criticisms (of missionaries) made by (French) consuls who have only known and invoked French law for a population which knows nothing of this code. Such criticisms which state publicly that the priest should confine himself to Church matters alone, have prompted attempts to deprive him of all influence. In consequence he has lost all prestige, and with it all remaining social respect. Without such prestige the missionary has no further social authority in present circumstances, and his words remain without effect on the poor pagans in whose eyes he has been degraded. (A.S.M.E. Siam. Vol 888, No. 318)

124. **Jules Harmand,** French Consul-General in Siam, to **Charles Le Myre de Vilers,** Governor of Cochinchina. Bangkok, 4 March 1882.

The missionaries, who are by nature much inclined to exaggerate and who will not admit that they or their flock can ever be in the wrong - which is far from true - consider any just or unjust action as a veritable betrayal by the consulate if it does not turn to their greater profit and to the confusion of their adversaries.

The Siamese government is truly tired and annoyed at the mass of complaints made every day by the missionaries either directly to them or through the French consulate. Three quarters of our voluminous correspondance with the (Siamese) ministers is composed of letters and notes relating to their contestations. With Your Excellency's permission I would, within the bounds of justice, like to control this habit. For the irritation caused to the Siamese government by this practice might at any time compromise our political action and change the favourable attitude which it normally tries to show towards France.... (A.O.M. Aix. Indochine, Amiraux 13,656.)

125. Mgr **Vey,** Bishop of Geraza, Vicar Apostolic of Siam, to the **Superior** of the S.M.E. Bangkok, 9 March 1883.

The French consul at Bangkok disapproves of missionary preaching to the Lao. He has witheld a passport which should have been issued under the terms of the treaty. On pretext of the imaginary danger of compromising or committing the honour of France in unforeseen circumstances, he would only issue this passport on terms which would have made our colleague's journey completely useless. (A.S.M.E. Siam. Vol. 888, No. 347)

126. Mgr **Bourdon,** Vicar Apostolic of Upper Burma, to Fr **Péan,** Assistant Superior of the S.M.E. Mandalay, 8 September 1884.

No one here believes that a (French) consul has been nominated for Mandalay.... We need a man with strong influence and a firm hand to make things work a bit better. The King (Theebaw), instead of paying his employees monthly as agreed, is letting his debts mount up. Some people have not been paid for 30 months, and others not for 18 or 20. The Queen (Supayalat) owes the Sister Superior of our convent about 30 - 35,000 rupees, which the Sister in turn owes to various other people. What a fine state of things! (A.S.M.E. Birmanie Septentrionale. Vol 935, No. 314)

127. **François Deloncle,** Rédacteur at the Direction commerciale of the Quai d'Orsay. Evidence to the Panama Commission, 1897.

Jules Ferry's objectives in negotiating a
commercial treaty with Upper Burma in 1884-5.

What was this supplementary (commercial) convention? M. Jules Ferry asked me to negotiate it in such a way that Britain would see in it our desire to obtain something in independent Upper Burma, where she was so jealous of her influence. This would make her more amenable to a trade-off which would enable us, should the occasion arise, to secure advantages in Siam, or at least a means of holding the British in check in the Malay peninsula.... What Ferry wanted was the conclusion of an agreement with Burma which would give (us) the tiller in Siam. (Quoted in L. de Reinach, Le Laos. (2 vols. Paris, 1901). vol.II, Annexe xvi, pp. 88-90).

128. **Lord Dufferin,** Viceroy of India, to **Lord Cross,** Secretary of State for India. Simla, 10 September 1886.

Harmand (now French Consul-General at Calcutta) related to me how, during a personal interview with M. Ferry in Paris, he had tried to dissuade the Minister from an aggressive policy in Upper Burma. He said that M. Ferry had, of course, no intention of annexing Upper Burma to French dominions, but that his plan was to establish large French commercial interests in Mandalay and to secure the political ascendancy of France in the upper valley of the Irrawaddy, with a view to acquiring a situation which would enable (France) to put pressure on England, and thus obtain whatever advantages such a condition of things might procure. (Public Record Office, London. FO 422/13, Foreign Office Confidential Print Series. <u>Correspondance respecting British influence and policy in the Malay Peninsula, 1886.</u> No.28)

129. Mgr **Bourdon,** Vicar Apostolic of Upper Burma, to Fr **Péan,** Assistant Superior of the S.M.E. Mandalay, 26 March 1885.

Ah! If the English weren't so <u>estioupides,</u> my God. They are off 'fighting for the King of Prussia' against the Mahdi who is thrashing them, but don't want to see that everyone here is holding out their arms appealing for their intervention. It is said they have a lot of common sense: they must have a lot, because they are not using any...
(A.S.M.E. Vol. 935, Birmanie Septentrionale, No.324)

130. Mgr **Bourdon,** Vicar Apostolic of Upper Burma, to Fr **Péan,** Assistant Superior of the S.M.E. Mandalay, 13 July 1885.

With a (French) consul, difficulties have arisen. Tomorrow is the 14th - an odious day, a date of blood. That baleful day is the feast day of republican France. I want to stay away (from the consulate), but they press me so insistently that I have had to give in. Moreover, they threaten to give me the cross (of the Légion d'Honneur), as if I do not have enough crosses to bear. Perhaps it is a joke, or a polite gesture. But whatever it is I want nothing from the Republic... and I profoundly despise all these rascals. (A.S.M.E. Birmanie Septentrionale. Vol. 935, No. 332)

131. **Frédéric Haas,** French Consul in Upper Burma, to **Charles de Freycinet,** Minister for Foreign Affairs. Mandalay, 18 July 1885.

This Roman Catholic prelate (Mgr Bourdon, Vicar Apostolic of Upper Burma), despite the anti-liberal influence of the hierarchy to which he belongs, is nonetheless French at heart and in his ideas. Without asking him for what he cannot give, we will always find him a devoted patriot and a generous heart, and all the French here testify to this.
 Your Excellency will no doubt consider that it was important to rally round the French flag all the support which we have a right to count on for the promotion of our moral authority and for the completion of our work... (M.R.E. <u>Correspondance politique des Consuls, Angleterre,</u> Vol.

132.   Mgr **Simon**, Vicar Apostolic of Upper Burma. Annual report, 1889.

(Before 1886) the intransigence of the Burmese government, all too strongly supported by the animosity of the provincial governors, prevented any movement of conversions among the pagans. Permission to establish ourselves anywhere was always and invariably refused. Year after year we sowed only the seed of our tears and fruitless labours on soil that was truly the dry and trackless waste of which the Bible speaks...

As soon as King Theebaw (deposed in November 1885) departed we set to work. Thanks to the new religious situation accorded to us under the liberal régime of the British, we have already been able to explore fresh pastures. The word of God has been spread to places where we had never before set foot....

How times have changed! Viewed as a caste apart until now, with no right to regard or consideration from anyone, we were forced to stay in the shadows for fear of upsetting national sensitivities. Today we are free to come out into the open and practise our great and beautiful ceremonies openly, and we are greeted with religious respect everywhere....

(However) I witness with a heavy heart the ever-growing invasion of Protestant competitors. They fell voraciously upon our unhappy city as soon as the conquest took place.... (From A. Launay, Atlas des missions de la Société des Missions Etrangères. (Lille, 1890). No. 26, Birmanie Septentrionale.)

French attempts to create a counterpoise in Upper Burma to offset their position of weakness in Siam finally collapsed when the British annexed Upper Burma to the Indian empire in January 1886. With the British now able to pursue Burmese claims to suzerainty over Lao (Shan) territories on the upper Mekong, and with British influence still preeminent in Siam, French security in the Mekong valley seemed critically imperilled.

In other circumstances French policymakers might now have considered resorting to force and seizing control of Siamese territories on the middle Mekong. But political changes which had taken place in France in 1885 hampered French policymakers from considering such a course for the time being. The fall of the Ferry cabinet in March 1885 symptomatised a widespread reaction against colonial adventures, and this revulsion was confirmed by the success of anti-colonial groups - Radicals and Monarchists - in the autumn elections of that year. During the life of the ensuing legislature and for part of the next, French cabinets were forced to tread warily in dealing with all colonial issues. In regard to the Mekong valley they sought to improve French frontier security by a variety of novel - but essentially peaceable - improvisations. In these constrained conditions, the missions were at last able to play some part in furthering French expansionary designs.

French policymaking for the Mekong valley after 1885 was not a unified or consistant process. The French foreign ministry - the Quai d'Orsay - based its policy on the assumption that frontiers would eventually have to be established by diplomatic agreement with the British and Siamese. France's negotiating case would rest on what information could be found by explorers and local officials to support Vietnamese and Cambodian claims to at least the East bank of the Mekong river. But the policy of the Quai d'Orsay lagged behind the aspirations of other bodies and agencies with influence on the outcome. Since the Siamese were already advancing frontier posts along the East bank of the Mekong and since the British, too, were known to be preparing to explore Burmese links with the Lao states on the upper Mekong, local French agencies such as the military authorities at Hanoi, the Lt Governor of Cochinchina, and the Government-General of the newly formed federation of Indochina, pressed the Quai d'Orsay to establish a preemptive French presence at all major strategic points in the region. This objective was supported in France by the embryonic leadership of what was soon to become a powerful parliamentary pressure group, the Parti Colonial, which nursed an even wider ambition of seeing Siam as a whole eventually annexed. In 1889, under pressure from such influences, the Quai d'Orsay adopted a strategy of covert preemption for the East bank of the Mekong. The task of coordinating exploration, collecting legal and historical information, and establishing a network of trading comptoirs across the region was given to Auguste Pavie, a French consular agent based upon Luang Prabang on the upper Mekong. Pavie later acknowledged the importance of the assistance and local knowledge of missionaries in helping him to direct his exploration and research, and it is evident that missionaries were anxious to cooperate with the colonial authorities now more than at any other time. The team of Mekong explorers directed by Pavie received local assistance from mission stations situated mainly along the middle reaches of the river, while from Tonkin Bishop Puginier, expressing the French community's general fears of a British forward movement on the upper Mekong, transmitted a digest of information drawn from missionary sources on the nature of Vietnamese claims to that part of the region. Puginier prefaced this with an appeal for the prompt annexation of the upper Mekong. **(Doc.133)**

The Mayrena affair, 1888–1890.

Further south, missionaries became directly and heavily embroiled in a confused adventure which symptomatised the colonial administration's difficulties in advancing French control into the wilder parts of the East bank. Here, in the territories of the unsubdued Bahnar and Sedang tribes of the mountain hinterlands behind Qui Nhon - an unhealthy, dangerous and economically unevaluated region, where formal French administration had never penetrated, and where even traditional Vietnamese administration had hesitated to advance - missionaries alone of all French interests, had established a presence. In 1852 the vicariate of East Cochinchina had installed a mission station at Kon Trang which succeeded in christianising a portion of the Bahnar, Sedang and Jarais tribes. The colonial authorities had taken no particular interest in the area, but since Siam's claims of historic suzerainty on the East bank extended to this territory, it figured as part of the overall strategic problem currently faced by the French. When, in 1888, Governor-General Constans received an offer from a private explorer, Marie-David de Mayrena, to investigate the Sedang/Bahnar country and draw it into political dependency upon the French colony, the suggestion was accepted and Mayrena received formal sanction for his mission.

Mayrena was a confidence trickster with a vivid criminal past who owed his current credibility to the patronage of a gullible Mayor of Saigon. His exploration among the Sedang escalated into a bizarre and embarrassing adventure which compromised both local French missionaries and the colonial government. By exaggerating the degree of official support which he enjoyed, Mayrena obtained missionary help to persuade the Sedang population to elect him 'King of the Sedangs', with all the conventional trimmings: a written constitution, a flag, a titular aristocracy, an official religion (Catholicism), a budget and a post office. When the French authorities witheld acknowledgement of his new Sedang monarchy, Mayrena threatened to transfer Sedang allegiance to Britain or Germany and sought contact with the Siamese authorities. On being warned by the French Resident-Superior against having further dealings with Mayrena, the vicariate of East Cochinchina hastily dissociated itself from the Sedang venture, and it finally collapsed with Mayrena's death in 1890. The Mayrena affair, constantly recalled in the French colonial press, provided material for the virulent anticlerical polemics which developed in Indochina later in the 1890s and did immense damage to missionary credit in the colony. At the conclusion of this incident many colonial officials were left believing that the mission had been treasonably seeking to establish an independent missionary state like that of the Jesuits in Paraguay **(Docs 134-7).** But despite the scandal, the French authorities, still unwilling to establish formal administration in such an unpromising region, decided to entrust Catholic missionaries with responsibility for reporting regularly on the condition of the territory. Even after its annexation in 1893, official aversion to entering the dangerous Sedang/Bahnar region remained so strong that the same missionaries who had been involved in the Mayrena affair were assigned formal administrative responsibility for the whole area until the early 1900s **(Doc. 138).**

The Siam crisis of 1893.

France's general frontier crisis in the Mekong valley was largely resolved by the Franco-Siamese conflict of 1893.

With the revival in 1890-2 of parliamentary support in France for colonial expansion, the Quai d'Orsay decided by March 1893 to abandon preparations for a negotiated settlement at Bangkok. Troops were despatched from Cochinchina and Annam to seize the East bank of the middle Mekong. But the Siamese offered dogged resistance, and the French were finally forced to undertake a gunboat action at Bangkok. Since there was also a British gunboat presence in the gulf of Siam, the French move threatened to spark off a major international crisis.

At the height of this embroglio the French cabinet, under pressure from the Parti Colonial, discussed the possibility of annexing the kingdom of Siam in its entirety, a course which the French Bishop of Bangkok, among other interested figures, vigorously pressed French officials to pursue. Although Mgr Vey made allusion to the material advantages of Siam's annexation in his official correspondance (Doc. 140), he appears from his private letters to have been moved essentially by sectarian considerations. Mindful of the situation in Upper Burma, where British annexation had encouraged the arrival of protestant missions (see supra Doc. 132), Bishop Vey wanted to keep British colonial rule at bay in Siam to prevent the small, local Protestant missions benefiting from British financial and political patronage (Doc. 139).

But in the general context of this crisis Bishop Vey's opinion counted for little. Even the clamour of the powerful colonial interest in France was not influential enough to sway the French cabinet to annex Siam. For in order to limit the diplomatic repercussions of the crisis, the Quai d'Orsay was forced to bow to British pressure and leave the bulk of Siam independent. The British then gave grudging assent to the French seizure of the East bank of the middle Mekong, and when the French issued a ultimatum to back their territorial demands, Siamese resistance collapsed.

So the Siam crisis subsided in a Franco-Siamese treaty negotiation to confirm France's territorial gains and indemnify the French for their costs. During negotiations for the new agreement Bishop Vey pressed strongly for the extraction of further treaty rights and privileges for the mission (Doc. 141). Despite the current strength of the French bargaining position, the Quai d'Orsay rejected the Bishop's demand. For by prior agreement with Britain the new Franco-Siamese treaty could only embody the terms of the recent French ultimatum, and this had made no mention of missionary grievances.

The Catholic mission as a source of French political influence in Siam, 1894-1904.

The French had now obtained the middle Mekong for part of their western frontier. The remainder - the upper Mekong - was assigned to them three years later under the terms of a general diplomatic agreement with Britain. But the resolution of the problem of establishing a frontier line in the Mekong valley merely raised French appetite for promoting French influence in Siam, and a new phase of Anglo-French rivalry for leverage over Bangkok began. It was to persist until the Entente Cordiale of 1904.

The Quai d'Orsay and its agents remained anxious to promote local French interests of whatever kind in competition with the British.

Since French trade and investment in Asia continued to bypass the Siam market, the French consulate began to make more systematic use of its other local sources of influence. It adopted the policy of claiming legal and diplomatic responsibility for as large a segment of Siam's immigrant ethnic and minority religious groups as it could legitimately enrol on the French consular registers. In the context of this new strategy, Consul-General Pavie recommended that all asiatic Catholics in Siam should be placed under French diplomatic protection. The French authorities expected to capitalise politically not simply from the existing size but from the further expansion of the Catholic mission. Hence when the Siam treaty indemnity of three million frs was finally distributed by a French parliamentary commission in 1894, the vicariate of Siam received a notably large sum - 250,000 frs - to promote the extension of its proselytism.

Thereafter, until the Entente Cordiale brought this phase of British and French rivalry to an end, the French Catholic mission was regularly acknowledged by the Quai d'Orsay to be an exceptionally useful part of the small network of local French interests. Without becoming the object of any further consular stratagems, the Catholic mission continued to receive intermittant but fairly generous French subsidies for its hospital and medical work in order to boost the general moral influence of France in Siam.

Further reading

P.J.N.Tuck, 'Jules Ferry, Upper Burma and Siam: the defence of the
    French frontier in mainland Southeast Asia, 1883-1885', **The Journal
    of Imperial and Commonwealth History,** VI, 3, (May 1978).
P.J.N.Tuck, 'Auguste Pavie and the exploration of the Mekong valley,
    1886-1895'. **Terrae Incognitae** 14, (1982), pp. 41-60.
C. Jeshurun, **The Contest for Siam, 1889-1902. A Study in Diplomatic
    Rivalry.** (Kuala Lumpur, 1977).
J. Marquet, **Un aventurier au XIXe siècle: Marie ler, Roi des Sédangs
    (1888-1890).** (Hue, 1927).
M. Ner, 'Compte-rendu des ouvrages de J. Marquet et de Maurice Soulié',
    Bulletin de l'Ecole Française de l'Extrême-Orient, XXVII (1927)
    pp. 308-350.
P. Dourisboure, **Les sauvages Bah-Nars.**12th edn. (Paris, Téqui, 1922).
C.M. Andrew and A.S.Kanya-Forstner, 'The French "Colonial Party": its
    composition, aims and influence, 1885-1914'. **Historical Journal** 14,
    (1971) pp. 99-128.
D. Woodman, **The Making of Burma.** (London, Cresset, 1962).
C.M. Andrew, **Théophile Delcassé and the Making of the Entente Cordiale.**
    (London, 1968).

133. Mgr **Puginier**, Bishop of Mauricastre, Vicar Apostolic of West Tonkin, to Etienne **Spuller**, Minister for Foreign Affairs. Hanoi, 7 September 1889.

You will be aware, Minister, of Britain's pressure on the court of Siam to proclaim exaggerated rights (of suzerainty) with a view to pushing back the Tonkinese frontier as far to the East as possible. This is done to diminish the possessions of Annam and increase those of Siamese Laos proportionately. This question of greater territory or less in regions which are a long way off, unhealthy and underpopulated might seem at first sight insignificant. But one can see that (this region) could become for Britain the route of penetration into China, linking it with Burma through Siamese Laos. That is the real political and practical purpose which they are pursuing in putting the court of Bangkok under pressure.

Sooner or later the importance of this question will be recognised, but it would be regrettable if it were noted too late. Let France preserve intact all the territory which her efforts have merited: she has Right on her side. (A.N.S.O.M. Paris. Asie Orientale (A.F.) 62/(2))

134. Governor-General **Richaud** to **Emile Jamais**, Undersecretary for the Colonies. Hanoi, 14 December 1888.

At the beginning of 1888 (Marie David) de Mayrena had the idea of trying to explore the mineral rich territories to the west of Binh Dinh on the frontiers of Annam and Siam. These are inhabited by the Mois, the Giarais, the Bahnars, the Sedangs etc. ... He addressed himself to the Government-General for the necessary assistance, claiming that he wanted to reach these regions before a Prussian expedition with the same objective.... In the course of April 1888 I learned by telegram from (M. Hector) the Resident-Superior at Hue, that he was making treaties with the Mois which he was sending to Paris and Saigon. I immediately notified M. Hector that M. de Mayrena had no official mission and authorised him to disavow all the latter's acts... Since then the newspapers both in France and in Indochina have taken up the question and we heard a short while later that M. de Mayrena had gathered all the peoples of this territory into a sort of confederation, had given them a constitution, had had himself proclaimed king of the Sedangs and, asserting the complete independence of these peoples, was proposing that he should become a vassal of France. Moreover he was claiming that the country was very rich and that the rivers were rolling with gold nuggets which the natives were using primitive methods of separating from the sand.

The role of the Mission in these circumstances was very regrettable. Independent tribes cannot be admitted to exist in the whole of this region where Annam is in direct neighbourhood with territory dependent on Siam, even if we have not yet undertaken a regular delimitation. M. de Mayrena's efforts to have himself acknowledged as king of these territories would not in itself be a serious matter. What is gravely important is the fact that the Mission should have chosen to side with a person who is claiming to detach from a country placed under our protectorate a region which is dependent on it.... (A.N.S.O.M. Paris, Indochine (A.F.) 19/A30(77))

135.   M. **Paul Rheinart**, Resident-Superior of Annam, to Mgr **van Camelbeke**, Bishop of Hierocésarée, Vicar Apostolic of East Cochinchina. Hue, 27 November 1888.

The political map of Indochina contains no 'blanks', any more than the religious map drawn up by the Société des Missions Etrangères. The country is divided into states which are regularly constituted and <u>recognised</u>, leaving no room for independent tribes, just as it has been divided into apostolic vicariates directly contiguous to eachother, so that no region is left beyond the limits of potential missionary activity. The rights of the vicariates are in no sense diminished by their current incapacity to excercise their respective roles there, any more than the rights of the native states over those regions are limited by not being excercised everywhere.

Your Grace should entertain no delusions as to the existence of independent tribes in your apostolic vicariate. In this whole region, Annam is in direct neighbourhood with territories dependent on Siam. At an appropriate moment we will have these rights acknowledged and resort to a regular delimitation... What is really serious is that the Mission has taken the side of a person who claims to have detached a region dependent upon a country under our Protectorate. Moreover, this person has given us to understand very clearly that he is going to transfer the country to foreign domination if we do not treat with him, yet the Mission has not seen fit to dissociate itself from him.

... I know how patriotic all our missionaries are, my Lord Bishop... I am too well aware that none of them has forgotten his Mother Country.... (A.O.M. Aix. Indochine, Amiraux, 11,894.)

136. Fr **Guerlach** to M. **de Cuers de Cogolin,** editor of Le Courrier d'Haiphong. Haiphong, 30 December 1888.

...Everyone knows that reports from Qui Nhon presented the conduct of the missionaries in a poor light and necessitated my going to Hanoi. What should one think of the suspicions expressed against the patriotism and honour of the missionaries? What should one think of the explorer Mayrena? What reliance can be placed on a man who characterised himself as the virtual representative of the missions?

In my letter of 13 November (1888)... I explained how, as a French missionary, I made every effort to help a French explorer sent to our mountains by the French government. To the ample proof of the official mission conferred on M. de Mayrena, I can add a letter written by M. Lemire, the French Resident at Qui Nhon, a letter which asked the explorer to 'go and take action'. In this context no doubts could persist. M. de Mayrena spoke the truth in presenting himself as a government envoy, but he deceived us as to the character of his mission.

I learned that the kingdom of Annam, and in consequence the French protectorate, claimed possession of the Mois country up to the Siamese frontier. So the French government could not expect to have this country taken by an explorer. M. de Mayrena's mission consisted of reconnoitering the route from Annam to the Mekong and studying the territory. I have heard it said that M. de Mayrena was sent to the Mois to be got rid of because he was becoming an embarrassment at Saigon, something we did not then know. On his arrival the explorer made himself at home and spontaneously took it upon himself to organise the different villages into a kingdom which would then be turned over to France....

Fr Irigoyen and myself accompanied M. de Mayrena as guides and interpreters, and we signed, as eye-witnesses, the varous treaties concluded between the explorer and the savages. We ourselves concluded with M. de Mayrena in his capacity as king of the Sedangs, a defensive alliance against the Jarai, just as we concluded one with the natives, the only difference being that in the first instance we signed a piece of paper, and in the second we slaughtered a bull according to the custom of the country.

M. de Mayrena wanted to make use of this agreement against the Jarai as a weapon against France, saying that we were ready to take up arms at the first signal from him. M. Lemire believed in his threats and, without investigating further, accused us of being hostile to our country and of favouring a man who was threatening to give himself to England or even to Prussia (sic)....

I can quite see how the facts outlined in the official reports upset the higher authorities and provoked the action taken at Qui Nhon and elsewhere. Such facts seemed increasingly serious as M. de Mayrena's words and actions became stranger and more compromising. This man boasted on the steamer of having been consecrated King by the Bishop of Qui Nhon (East Cochinchina), whereas he reproached His Grace and the missionaries for not calling him Sire and Majesty.... This man also said that the mission had signed a letter of credit for 20,000 piastres because he had left a trunkful of gold with us, and that is how he duped an unfortunate Chinese from whom he ordered 10,000 uniforms for his royal guard.... (Quoted in Jean Marquet, Marie I, Roi des Sedangs, (Hue, 1927) p. 65)

137. M. **Guiomar**, Vice-Resident at Qui Nhon, to M. **Hector**, Resident-General of Annam. Qui Nhon, 6 May 1889.

...The missionaries consider the country which they occupy as their property and they never willingly encourage any European at all to settle there.

Far from contradicting this, the Mayrena story confirms my assertion. We saw all the missionaries and the bishop himself initially support Mayrena not only with their influence but even with their financial credit, then reject him no less energetically. If one wants to know the reason for such a brutal change of behaviour one should not even consider the possibility that they might have wished to oblige the French government which had disowned Mayrena. It stems from the fact that, after first dreaming of founding a free state like that of the Jesuits in Paraguay and thinking that they had found in Mayrena a pliable instrument who would be entirely at their disposal, they soon discovered their mistake and found that he had an appetite for independence. So they preferred to abandon their projects rather than find themselves subordinated to a master. This business has nothing to do with Patriotism. I consider it certain, from what I have seen and heard, that the missionaries never considered Mayrena to have been an envoy of the French government. In the interests of their work and in order to justify their subsequent conduct, they repeatedly avowed that their patriotic impulses had been abused. That is a somewhat inaccurate assertion. I need no more proof than the nervousness which they showed when confonted by Mayrena's threats. I think it obvious that if he carries them out we are in for some curious and certainly unexpected revelations. Frs Vialleton, Guerlach and Irigoyen, who have been seriously compromised by this adventure, repeated to me on many occasions that that they hoped that nobody would attach any credit to the stories which might be made of it. What need for such nervousness if their conduct had not been ambiguous?

.... Until today the fathers have had complete freedom of action in these regions, together with a certain authority which they owe to their European origin and above all to their knowledge of the language. For these reasons...and notably to eliminate the memory of their active participation in the Mayrena enterprise and because in reality my presence could help them, they were eager on this occasion to assist my excursion, even accompanying me despite the rigours of the journey. Will one still find them so helpful when they see that we are slowly but progressively extending our control over territories which they regard as theirs, and where we will be bound in the nature of things to excercise a certain amount of restraint over their activities? I am afraid we will not, and I fear we will soon be confronted by a latent hostility which will be all the more dangerous because we cannot combat it openly.... So we find ourselves at an impasse: either we let the missionaries do more or less as they like and confine ourselves to giving them general instructions which they may follow if it is in their interests to do so or if they feel like it; or else we have to do without their cooperation altogether.

If I may express an opinion, I would say that if our occupation of the Bahnar and Sedang country is not to be even a remote step towards the occupation of the left bank of the Mekong, then it would be burdensome and even useless to proceed with it, for this region produces only what is strictly necessary to feed itself. To uphold our influence it would be sufficient for a simple annual visit to be made to the principle villages, which, moreover, one could leave the missionaries to make: they will be all the more helpful to us for being given more independence.... (A.O.M. Aix. Indochine, Amiraux, 11,896.)

138.　M. **Tournier**, Commandant-Superior of Lower Laos, to Fr **Vialleton**, Superior of the mission to the Bahnars. 7 March 1898.

...For the regions over which our influence has definitely extended, as for those which in twenty-five years of persevering effort you have made civilised, the question is completely settled. All the tribes, all the villages subject to your spiritual authority are substantively attached to the administration of Lower Laos.

So it remains to make practical arrangements for attaching them to this administration....

...Up to now your Mission has held all forms of authority, religious, civil, military and judicial. Let us see which of these can be left to you for the greater benefit of the territory.

First, my firm conviction is that in the present condition of the country the administration cannot be better represented than by yourself. I would go further and say that thanks to the brilliant results obtained so far I would consider it an error to remove it from you. There is no one better than you and your devoted collaborators, no one else who has such profound knowledge of the country and its inhabitants and could succeed in completing a work of penetration which has been so favourably started. So I am leaving the direction of this territory to you, while officially attaching the territory of Kon Tum along with the others which have not yet been entered and where your influence will eventually come to extend, to the government commissioner of Attopeu.... (J.B. Guerlach, 'L'oeuvre néfaste.' Réplique de Père J.B. Guerlach, Missionaire Apostolique, au F. Camille Pâris, Colon en Annam. (Saigon, 1907) p. 110.)

139.   Mgr **Vey**, Bishop of Geraza, Vicar Apostolic of Siam, to Fr **Péan**, Assistant Superior of the S.M.E. Bangkok, 10 April 1893.

I have a fear which may, unfortunately, be well founded, that while the French are bickering with the Siamese over the valley of Laos, the rich (Menam) valley of Siam will finish by falling into the hands of England.

The latter will not fail to take advantage of everything to obtain this fine pear which could well fall into her mouth in a few years as Siamese bitterness towards France grows because of frontier and contiguity difficulties. I have this fear not because I am afraid of British administration as a government, but because from the day we fall under their authority we will, without a doubt, be inundated with religious preachers gorged with money and political influence, who would prevent Siam coming to us.... (A.S.M.E. Siam, Vol.896.)

140.   Mgr **Vey**, Bishop of Geraza, Vicar Apostolic of Siam, to Consul-General **Auguste Pavie**, French Minister in Siam. Bangkok, 21 June 1893.

At the first sign of difficulty or danger (the Siamese) will turn to England. England will hasten to accord them a Protectorate. The longer the present crisis lasts, the less likely it is that this protectorate will be imposed; but the crisis will end and once arrangements are made with France her rival will regain her full freedom of action.

The English are greedy to acquire Siam, the exhaustion of the soil of many provinces of India is pushing them to it, and they understand the full value of the delta land of the Menam. Even if the Siamese government is not, as has just been said, disposed to appeal for British protection, the danger is not entirely absent for all that. With their 20,000 protégés or subjects spread out across the whole of Siam through the immigrant Burmese element, British influence is infiltrating and propagating itself more and more. All who shelter beneath her flag will now become the objects of her attentive solicitude, the British sphere of action will grow, one day the pear will be ripe, the British will pick it and France will have contributed to ripening it faster.... If France profits from circumstances which are so favourable to her at the moment and takes the whole of Indo-China she will have done a service to humanity and will no longer have to regret the loss of her Indian empire so much.... (M.R.E., C.P.C Siam vol. 16.)

141. **Charles Le Myre de Vilers,** French Plenipotentiary to Siam, to **Jules Develle,** Minister for Foreign Affairs. Bangkok, 21 August, 1893. Tel. No. 11.

...It will also be necessary to make provision for (treaty) dispositions to protect the interests of missionaries and Christians. You have the Bishop's proposals. I am not sufficiently experienced in these matters to draft a text, and I beg you to transmit me one. (A.N.S.O.M. Paris. Papiers d'Agent. Le Myre de Vilers, APC 7, Carton 5.)

142. **Jules Develle,** Minister for Foreign Affairs, to **Charles Le Myre de Vilers,** French Plenipotentiary to Siam. Paris, 29 August, 1893. Tel. No. 10.

As far as missionaries and Christians are concerned the bishop's proposals are unclear and seem exaggerated, so I leave it to you to make requests which you consider just and profitable to missionaries and Christians as well as to the development of French influence without risk of exciting the Siamese government's suspicions...
(A.N.S.O.M. Paris. Papiers d'Agent. Le Myre de Vilers, APC 7. Carton 5.)

VI

THE MISSION UNDER POLITICAL ATTACK IN FRENCH INDOCHINA, 1891-1914.

VI A   THE GROWTH OF ANTI-CLERICALISM IN FRENCH INDOCHINA, 1891-1899.

As Governor-General from 1891-4, Jean de Lanessan seemed bound to clash with the French Catholic mission in Indochina. Unlike his predecessors he was a Radical in politics. He was also a freemason - an honorary member of the Fraternité Tonkinoise lodge. A committed anti-clerical, he was later to write a devastating indictment of the Quai d'Orsay's 'protectorat des missions' - its tradition of protecting Catholic missionary interests abroad. Even before his appointment as Governor-General in 1891, Lanessan had publicly condemned missionary influence upon the pacification policies of Paul Bert and his successors. He believed, without serious justification, that missionary hostility towards the Vietnamese mandarinate had been the main obstacle to the political reconciliation of Vietnamese elites to French rule.

On arrival in office Lanessan took a stage further Bert's attempt to accelerate pacification by political conciliation. The essence of Lanessan's strategy was to encourage Vietnamese collaboration by reviving and strengthening the administrative authority of the Vietnamese mandarinate. In provincial Tonkin, Vietnamese officials were allowed greater freedom from supervision by French Residents and given more initiative in the management of local administration. The prestige of the Kinh Luoc, the Vietnamese Imperial Commissioner in Tonkin, was also strengthened.(1) These and other mollifying tactics - such as the Governor-General's subsidies for Buddhist worship and attendance at official Buddhist ceremonies - were anathema to Bishop Puginier, who excoriated Lanessan's policy from the pulpit of Hanoi cathedral.(2)

However, contrary to expectations, Lanessan's period of office resulted in little detriment to the mission **(Doc. 143).** This was partly because it coincided with a movement of reconciliation in metropolitan France between political Republicanism and a portion of the hierarchy of the Catholic Church. The <u>Ralliement</u> of a proportion of Catholics to Republicanism suited the interests of a papacy intent on diverting the republican movement from further anti-clerical enactments, and especially from its general aim of separating the Churches from the State. The <u>Ralliement</u> also met the tactical needs of moderate republican groups who, confronted by the rising popularity of Radicals and Socialists at the polls, chose to turn to the clerical elements of the Right for intermittent parliamentary support in the years between

1892 and 1899.

The pro-clerical inclination of the republican Centre in the 1890s forced Lanessan to deal cautiously with missionaries in Indochina - indeed he intervened occasionally on their behalf. This was fortunate for the missions, since Lanessan's period of office coincided with the beginnings of a local anti-missionary press campaign which, during the following decade, was to develop into a substantial movement of pressure for the wholesale expropriation of both French and Spanish missions in Indochina.

The missions and freemasonry in French Indochina.

The main source of organised criticism of the missions was the network of masonic lodges which now covered Tonkin and Annam as well as Cochinchina. In French political tradition, freemasonry was closely associated with Republicanism. By the 1890s the masonic movement had come to be dominated by Radical Republicanism in particular, and manifested a strongly anti-clerical animus. As in France, freemasons in Indochina were well represented in the printing and publishing trades as well as in local journalism. The editors of Le Courrier d'Haiphong, L'Indépendance Tonkinoise and Le Mékong - de Cuers de Cogolin, Alfred Levasseur and Ulysse Leriche - were leading figures in the Hanoi, Haiphong and Saigon lodges, as were the Saigon printers Rey and Curiol, and F.H. Schneider of Hanoi. These newspapers regularly encouraged a variety of contributors to voice antagonism to the missions in articles to which missionaries were sometimes allowed a reply. The leading anti-clerical polemicist to emerge in Indochina in the 1890s was Camille Pâris, a postal official turned planter in Annam, whose enterprise had been adversely affected by competition from the mission's local agricultural estates **(Doc. 148)**. His vituperative indictments were all the more effective for being entertainingly written. From the missionary clergy Pâris' boutades brought forth explosive ripostes in the truculent rhetorical style favoured by the L'Univers, the principal French Catholic newspaper, and La Croix, the main organ of the Assumptionist press in France **(Docs 146-7)**.

Despite the rhetorical artifice and random abusiveness of contributions by both sides, fundamental issues of belief and commitment were engaged. Missionaries were worried at the likely impact of anti-clerical accusations upon their proslytism and upon the commitment of their Vietnamese converts. Pâris and his associates were, for their part, intent on establishing their case that the Catholic missions were a socially retrograde institution, subversive as much of French colonialism as of Republicanism itself.

These press polemics placed Lanessan in an awkward position. With the onset of the Ralliement in France, domestic political pressure forced him to pacify a dispute in which his sympathies were plainly on the side of the mission's critics. In persuading Puginier's successor at Hanoi, Bishop Gendreau, to keep out of press controversy, Lanessan played down the significance of press attacks and contacted newspaper editors to urge restraint (**Doc. 144**). In this he was relatively successful. He secured the regard and cooperation of the mission, without losing credit with the Indochina lodges. Recalled in disgrace in 1894 after disclosing confidential correspondance without authorisation, Lanessan's dismissal was deplored in an indignant letter to the Grand Orient by the Haiphong lodge, the Etoile du Tonkin, and attributed to 'Jesuit skulduggery'.[3] When, after Lanessan's departure, Camille Pâris revived his accusations in the Cochinchina press, Bishop Depierre at Saigon felt sufficiently confident of official support to take the drastic step of an appeal for redress to the judiciary, though without recorded result (**Doc. 146**).

These polemics of the 1890s were merely a foretaste of the onslaught upon the missions that was to develop in the early 1900s. With the seismic shift in the alignment of French Republicanism towards the Radical left after 1899, anti-clericals in Indochina were to feel encouraged to develop a still more vigorous campaign of denunciation. The Catholic missionary role was to fall under more systematic and hostile public scrutiny than ever before, and a broad attack on the legal and property-holding status of the Catholic Church in Indochina ensued.

(1). Jean de Lanessan, La colonisation française en Indochine. (Paris, F. Alcan, 1895) pp. 31-32.

(2). Jean de Lanessan, Les missions et leur protectorat. (Paris, 1907) p. 69

(3). Bibliothèque Nationale. Rés. FM² 142. Indoch. Haiphong, L.'. Etoile du Tonkin, 1895.

Further reading

In addition to the works of Lanessan cited above:

J. McManners, **Church and State in France, 1870-1914.** (London, S.P.C.K., 1972)

D. Ligou, **Frédéric Desmons et la Franc-maçonnerie sous la Troisième République.** (Paris, Gedalge, 1966).

A. Sedgwick, **The Ralliement in French Politics, 1890-1898.** (Cambridge, Mass. 1965).

J. Kayser, **Les grandes batailles du Radicalisme, 1820-1901.** (Paris, 1962)

Documents

143. Mgr **Colombert**, Bishop of Samostate, Vicar Apostolic of West Cochinchina, to the **Directors** of the S.M.E. Saigon, 27 January 1893.

At the risk of scandalising you I must tell you that I am not displeased with (the new Governor-General, Jean de Lanessan). He has been very courteous, and has granted all my requests. This is from political not from religious motives; but what he has done is done and remains done. If his motives are not good he will not earn grace by his actions. That is his business. But good relations have brought us some peace, and that is something.... (A.S.M.E. Vol.757, (Cochinchine Occidentale, 1890-1919). No.22)

144. Governor-General **de Lanessan** to Mgr **Gendreau**, Bishop of Chrysopolis, Vicar Apostolic of West Tonkin. Hanoi, 18 July 1893. Personal and confidential.

I greatly regret that you were unable to see me at Hanoi during the fête nationale because I wanted to speak to you about the polemic started by Le Courrier d'Haiphong on the subject of the missions....

For two years I have done everything possible to suppress them and I have succeeded more than once despite the strength of feeling - whether sincere or self-interested - of some of these people. But I have only succeeded with the greatest difficulty. Moreover I was very upset when I saw that you yourself had entered the fray. Direct intervention by you or your missionaries in these press polemics can actually make them more bitter by endowing them with an importance which they would lack if their authors were left to their own devices.

The local press is starved of material: it agitates in a vacuum and the public has given it little credence for some time now. This will no longer be the case if one could believe it was having some effect upon those who are the targets of its attacks, especially once such people get carried away and resort to journalism themselves in their own defence. It is quite obvious that the newspaper will then have earned a special importance and will stimulate the curiosity of even the most indifferent public.

I beg you, Your Grace, to weigh these reflections carefully. They are inspired by my keen desire to see all Frenchmen live in harmony with each other - despite the efforts of those who wish to spread discord - and for us all to forget what may divide us, remember our common fatherland and unite to promote the progress of the civilisation which France has taken as her task to introduce into this country....
(A.S.M.E. Vol.705, (Tonkin Occidental, 1888-1905). pp. 574-575.)

145.   Mgr **Gendreau,** Bishop of Chrysopolis, Vicar Apostolic of West Tonkin, to Governor-General **de Lanessan.** Hanoi, 23 July 1893.

... Taken by themselves press opinions of whatever kind leave us indifferent.... And if I chose to break my silence it was for the following reasons:

1° In my opinion the accusations made against us (usury, hoarding, bribery etc.) exceeded the right to criticise and were of a kind which dishonoured and vilified our ministry.

2° I knew that a great number of Europeans were upset and even dumbfounded by these attacks, composed as they are with such self-assurance. Our silence astonished the public which considered it virtually an implicit admission of guilt.

3° These accusations had reached the ears of the Annamese and were being translated and commented upon to many native officials.

4° The anonymous and generalised character of these assertions, in which no one was named nor any precise facts adduced, made it impossible in my opinion, to resort to law against the authors.

The situation was such that I employed the only means I could to defend our honour and prevent public opinion being led astray...
(A.S.M.E. Vol.705, (Tonkin Occidental, 1888-1905). pp. 578-579.)

146.   Mgr **Depierre,** Bishop of Benda, Vicar Apostolic of West Cochinchina, to **M.Assaud,** Procurator-General and head of the Justice Department at Saigon. Saigon, 12 June 1897.

For the last month Le Mékong has been pouring torrents of calumny...upon the mission.   In its number for 22 May the paper in question asserts that one of the ten nursing sisters of Haiphong has abandoned the veil to take up a life of prostitution.   This assertion is absolutely false, defamatory and outrageous in its expression to those ten nuns and to religion.   In the following number for 24 May the same newspaper states that a missionary from one of the ten posts in the west of Cochinchina has had obscene songs sung in his church at midnight mass. He is also described as profaning the sacred precincts and as a 'rutting sectarian'. In the number for 10 June Le Mékong, in an article penned by a former postal official from Tourane, M. Pâris,... accuses the missionaries of the Binh Dinh mission of having massacred natives, and pillaged, and stolen and burned down houses in 1886; of having intercepted letters and postal packages from the nuns of Tourane, and of having dishonoured and violated one of them. These statements are absolute lies. They are defamatory and in the highest degree outrageous. For a month Messrs Leriche and Pâris have indulged in the falsification of history, have blackened and denigrated missionaries and their work, have described the Christian communes as hotbeds of opposition to the French administration etc. and all this with the calculated, premeditated intention of damaging an honourable class of citizens in the eyes - I won't say of our compatriots, for the authors of these slanders are too well known in our colony - but in the minds of the natives, who are literally scandalised by all this impudence and villany.... (A.S.M.E. Vol.759, (Cochinchine Occidentale, 1881-1898). No. 452)

147.   Mgr **Depierre**, Bishop of Benda, Vicar Apostolic of West Cochinchina, to **Ulysse Leriche**, editor of Le Mékong. Saigon, 25 May 1897.

...I have the right and duty to object to your impudent and lying assertions, and to protest before the whole country at such unjustified attacks. You lie like a lackey when you say that our Christian communes are 'veritable hotbeds of opposition to French domination.' You lie like a clown when you assert that 'the pernicious influence of the Catholic missions hampered France's relations with Annam and held back our establishment in the country by a century.' You are the most miserable of all liers when you accuse the missions of offending the moral and religious beliefs of the Annamese people. If there is anything to scandalise the Annamese people in Cochinchina it is certainly your own venality and disreputable behaviour. Don't force respectable people to expose all your misdeeds and avoid you like a mangy dog or a putrid corpse. When you insinuate mistakenly that the missionaries 'have souls as black as their cassocks' you judge them by your own black conscience, if one can believe that you retain any glimmer of honesty or justice at all. How dare you of all people, Ulysse Leriche, give us lessons in patriotism, morality and devotion to worthy causes! Your audacity reveals the crassest ignorance, a complete absence of conscience and utter impudence. I hope that one day the government of Cochinchina will put a stop to all your shameful and notorious machinations.... They disgust anyone with a fraction of moral sensibility and shame our country in native eyes.... **(A.S.M.E. Vol.759, (Cochinchine Occidentale, 1881-1898). No. 451)**

148. 'Protée' **(C.Pâris),** Du rôle néfaste joué par les missions en Annam. (Pamphlet written in 1889 and published by the lodge La Fraternité Tonkinoise, Hanoi, 18 October 1897.)

M. de Mayrena had no inkling of the Sedangs. No serious studies had revealed them to him. He did not have the reputation in Cochinchina of being a hardworking man or an explorer passionately seeking discoveries useful to humanity. He was pursuing a social position and he jumped up the ladder in a single bound. The missionaries constructed the ladder for him. They could not excercise any temporal power officially. They needed a puppet for a king, whom they could make talk and act by pulling strings. They offered M. de Mayrena all the honours of royalty, and proposed to meet all the expense of it themselves; and they advised him, if he accepted, to take with him, as attributes of his sovereignty merely a few arms and a box of conjuring tricks with which to undermine the influence of the sorcerers who are all powerful in mountain country. M. de Mayrena does not speak of this in his letter to Le Courrier d'Haiphong: King Marie Ist must not appear to have conjured up his crown. In fact, however, (one evening) at Qui Nhon he gave us a performance in the Residency after having delivered a lecture inspired by Fr Guerlach on the ways and means by which he was going to found a kingdom among the Mois.

So it was that the kingdom of the Sedangs became new geography: a state governed by a conjuror who had as his ministers the apostolic missionaries Guerlach, Vialleton and Irigoyen.

This story of kingdom-building missionaries would be farcical if it did not contain a warning to us of grave complications for the future.

A Christian kingdom was founded between our two great Indochinese colonies (sic) (Cochinchina and Annam). It was an enclave thrust into our peninsula by the missions, and it it is from there that ant-like formations of intolerant Catholic savages will emerge, who will glory in the massacre of Buddhists. For it is there that these fanatical missions are preparing their revenge against the scholars for 1885. So that instead of enrolling the 10,000 men whom Mayrena offered us, we will one day perhaps be obliged to defend ourselves against them, for they will have arrived without our summoning them....

VI B THE TRIUMPH OF RADICAL REPUBLICANISM, AND THE LEGISLATIVE ONSLAUGHT ON CLERICAL INTERESTS.

In France the _Ralliement_ ended in 1899. The union between the conservative _Ralliés_ and republican groups of the Centre was discredited by the suspicion that conservative army chicanery had influenced the verdict in the Dreyfus trial; and with the relative success of Radical and Radical-Socialist groups in the election of that year, the way was open to new political formations on the Left towards which the Centre groups themselves now turned. The creation of a new _Bloc des Gauches_ of Centre Republicans, Radicals, Radical-Socialists and Socialists made pursuit of anti-clerical measures in France inevitable, for anti-clericalism represented the only common ground uniting all these Centre and Left groups. The first enactments were, however, relatively mild, for the _Bloc_ was still dominated by the Centre republican Union Démocratique from 1899-1901, rather than by the Radicals and Radical-Socialists. The latter did not come into their own until after the elections of 1902, when with Radical deputies returned in still larger numbers, the _Bloc_ itself tilted further to the Left. So it was to be the Chamber of 1902-1906 - particularly the cabinet of Emile Combes (1902-4) - which supplied the impetus for fierce new enactments against the clergy, and gave a savage twist to the operation of the mildly anti-clerical measures already passed by its predecessor.

The Law relating to the Contract of Associations, 1 July 1901.

When first passed by parliament, the Law of 1 July 1901 had merely been intended by its sponsor, Waldeck-Rousseau, to define the terms on which those religious orders which were not yet officially authorised could apply for authorisation and continue to operate in France **(Doc. 149)**. A 'Concordat for Religious Orders' was the benign soubriquet commonly given to it. The law had been intended for selective, not draconian, application; it was expected to affect a few unauthorised congregations only; and it was not aimed at missionary orders in the colonies at all (see _infra_, **Doc. 185**).

However, after the elections of 1902 when the Radical and intensely anti-clerical Emile Combes succeeded Waldeck-Rousseau as Prime Minister, the Law of 1 July 1901 came to be used as a weapon for the general destruction of all unauthorised religious congregations. Moreover, the new government's intention was to have this and other anticlerical measures uniformly applied to the colonial system as well as to metropolitan France. Of the 3,216 religious orders of all kinds operating in France and in the colonies, only five male and 909 female orders had been authorised by previous governments, and were in principle safe from attack. Apart from three further exceptions sanctioned by Combes himself, the remainder were dissolved and a massive exodus began.

The Société des Missions Etrangères however, escaped outright destruction. It had been one of the handful of male congregations already authorised, and was, in principle exempt from complete legal liquidation. But the conditions of authorisation for religious congregations had been redefined under the new law to give the executive considerable powers of intervention and dispossession. Hence the terms of the law of 1 July 1901 relating to property came to be of great significance to the Société des Missions Etrangères in Indochina. If the new law were applied there, the S.M.E.'s establishments could be threatened with restrictions which would cripple its proselytising role.

Two provisions of this law, if enforced in a hostile or destructive spirit, were of particular significance: Chapter I, article 6, section 3 limited a religious order's powers of property ownership to properties 'strictly needed for the accomplishment of its defined purpose' **(Doc. 149)**. In the case of missions this could be interpreted to include only churches, convents, presbyteries and mission stations. Landed estates, vital for the support of the Christian communes and therefore fundamental to the the mission's proselytising strategy, would be awkward to justify to a hostile administration, and on a narrow interpretation, might be held to fall outside the terms of the clause. The obvious means of evading the force of this clause was for the mission to hold land through proxies. Tenure by proxy was already common practice in the Indochina missions as a means of evading the taxe d'accroissement, a fiscal regulation against mortmain. Substantial properties were already held in the names of individual missionaries, or in the personal names of the Bishops, or by Christian notables on behalf of the mission. But the terms of the new law - Chapter III, article 17 - blocked this loophole. Taken together these two provisions of the Law of 1901 would give the Indochina administration broad new powers of despoliation. In effect, the economic foundation of the whole mission in the colony was threatened.

The new law was not, however, scheduled for instant application to the colonies. The cabinet was aware that the variations in political and administrative arrangements across the colonial system called for the adaptation of the law to fit a variety of local conditions. Hence, along with other anticlerical measures, the Law of 1901 was referred for scrutiny to the Colonial Ministry where it remained under active consideration until the emergence of the Dislère report in 1907 (see infra, section **VI D**).

Meantime the Combes government resorted to several new anticlerical measures, some of which were for immediate application in the colonies. Combes obtained the assent of parliament for the laicisation of all public establishments in 1903 - a measure which mainly affected nursing clergy in state hospitals. The regulation was applied in Indochina without delay, resulting in the eviction of the nursing order of St Paul de Chartres from government hospitals. Government schools in the colony were also forced to dispense with the services of teaching clergy like the Christian Brothers **(Doc. 150)**; and all religious emblems were removed from government buildings.

The law abolishing clerical teaching orders, 7 July 1904.

Following these measures Combes began pursuing his dream of imposing a complete state monopoly over education, again intending his legislation to apply to the French colonial system. He sought the entire destruction of the educational role of those authorised teaching orders that had so far escaped dispersal. They could remain in being, but they could not teach. As far as missionary orders were concerned, strictly speaking these were not teaching orders per se, even though they ran their own educational establishments. Combes wished to include them in the provisions of the new law nonetheless. But here he encountered opposition from among his own supporters within the Union Démocratique. This group, a vital part of the Bloc, favoured the educational role of missionaries in the colonies on the argument that the teaching of French to France's to colonial populations tended to encourage native identification with French imperial rule. Combes was forced to give way on this point, but he demanded that missionary orders should not be allowed to educate their own members in France. Again his plans met with a setback. Opposed once more by the Centre Union Démocratique Combes was unable to prevent the passage of the Leygues amendment, which allowed missionary orders to retain their novitiates in France. The debate on the Leygues amendment was notable for airing the issue of the political value of missionary education, and particularly for evoking a recent celebrated controversy over the misuse by Bishop Mossard at Saigon of official subsidies for the teaching of French **(Doc. 151)**. In its amended form the Law against Teaching Orders was finally passed on 7 July 1904.

The Law of Separation, 9 December 1905.

The final measure enacted by the Bloc in its general onslaught on clerical interests was the Law of 9 December, 1905 separating the

Churches from the State. This measure drastically affected the situation of missionaries filling salaried parochial positions in Concordatory colonies such as Réunion, Guadaloupe and Algeria; but in Indochina the absence of Concordatory arrangements exempted the mission from most of its effects (see _infra_ **Doc. 163).** Even though the Bishop and Curé at Saigon were expelled from their official residences, which the colony owned, and from the cathedral of Saigon - also a government possession - these establishments were leased back to the mission in due course.

All in all, therefore, it was the law of 1901 which represented the greatest threat to the missions in Indochina, and for this reason the question of whether and how this particular measure should be applied was to become the focal issue of debate within the Union.

Further reading

M.O. Partin, **Waldeck-Rousseau, Combes and the Church 1899-1905. The Politics of Anticlericalism.** (Durham, N.C. 1969).
M. Larkin, **Church and State after the Dreyfus Affair: the Separation issue in France.** (London, Macmillan, 1974).
L. Capéran, **L'invasion laïque de l'avènement de Combes au vote de la Séparation.** (Paris, Desclée, 1935).
Adrien Dansette, **Histoire religieuse de la France contemporaine,** vol.II, (Paris, 1948).

Documents

149.   Law of 1 July 1901 relating to the Contract of Association.

Chapter I

(Articles 1-9 define the procedures for forming and maintaining all authorised associations, and penalties for infringement of regulations.)

Article 6. Every regularly declared association may, without any special authorisation, make legal use of, acquire by payment, possess and administer without subsidies from the State, departments or communes:

1º   The   subscriptions   of   its members, or the sums for which these subscriptions may have been commuted, provided that these   sums   do   not exceed 500 frs

2º   The premises set aside for administering the association and for convening its members.

3º   The property   strictly   needed   for   the   accomplishment   of   its defined purpose....

Chapter II

(Articles   10-12   outline   the   legal   rights   of   such   associations, particularly in regard to the acquisition and ownership of property.)

Chapter III

Article 13.   No religious order may be formed without an authorisation given by law which will define the conditions of its operation.

It   may   found no new establishment except by virtue of a decree given by the <u>Conseil d'Etat</u>.

The   dissolution   of   the   religious   order   or   the   closure   of   any establishment may be declared by a decree issued by the Cabinet.

Article 14.   Nobody   is permitted to run, either directly or by proxy, any kind of teaching establishment whatsoever, nor to teach there, if it belongs to an unauthorised religious order.

Those who infringe this regulation will suffer the penalties provided by   paragraph   2   of   Article 8 (fines of up to 5000 frs and imprisonment for up to a year).   The closure of the establishment may, moreover, be declared as part of the sentence pronounced.

Article 15.   Every religious order will keep an account of its receipts and expenses;   it will draw up every year the financial accounts for the previous year, and an inventory of its landed and moveable property.

The full list of its members, mentioning them by surname as well as by the   name   given   to them within the order, their nationality, age, place of birth and date of entry, must be kept at the seat of the order....

Article 16.   Any order formed without authorisation will · be declared illegal.... (Its   members   to be punished under the terms of article 8, paragraph 2 and its founders to suffer twice the prescribed penalty).

Article 17.   All agreements between living persons, or testamentary dispositions either involving payment or by free gift and concluded either directly or by proxy or in any other indirect way, with the object of enabling religious orders that are either legally or illegally founded to avoid the effects of articles 2, 6, 9, 11, 13, 14 and 16, are declared null and void.

The following will be considered to be proxies acting for the profit of religious orders, unless proof is offered to the contrary:

1° Associates to whom sales have been made, or gifts or legacies, unless, in the case of gifts and legacies, the beneficiary is the heir in direct descent from the owner.

2° Any associate, or civil society or commercial grouping wholly or partly composed of members of an order which is proprietor of the entire real estate occupied by the order.

3° The proprietor of any real estate occupied by the order after it has been declared illegal. It may be pronounced illegal at the request of the public ministry or at the request of any interested party.

Article 18. Religious orders in existence at the time of the promulgation of the present law, which have not been previously authorised or recognised, must testify within three months that they have made the necessary effort to comply with its provisions.

Failing this they will be deemed legally dissolved. The same applies to orders which have been denied authorisation.

The liquidation of their property-holdings will take place in due legal form. To arrange this the Court, at the request of the public ministry, will nominate a liquidator who will have all the powers of a sequestrating administrator for the duration of the liquidation.

(Legal arrangements for the dispersal of property of the religious orders. Some of it to be applied to providing pensions for needy members of these orders). (Bulletin des Lois, XIIe. série, vol. 63, 2e. semestre de 1901. No. 2295, pp. 1273-1278.)

150. **Gaston Doumergue**, Minister for the Colonies, to Governor-General **Beau**. Paris, 12 December 1903.

You will have noted that the Senate, when discussing the bill on secondary education, removed the right to teach from all religious orders whether authorised or not. You will also have seen that the government has anounced its intention of tabling a bill debarring religious orders from other types of teaching. The bill will be tabled before the end of the month. There is no doubt that Parliament will sanction this measure and will prevent members of any religious order from teaching.... Its purpose is not to limit freedom of conscience or worship any more than to limit the work of purely religious proselytism which any order of missionaries may pursue. It aims to separate two sorts of activity which should remain even more distinct in Indochina than elsewhere, namely evangelisation and teaching. It is imperative to avoid allowing the teaching we give to seem in native eyes to be solely intended to favour religious propaganda....

The position which the missions in Indochina could acquire as a result of the freedom and privileges conferred on them up to now could cause serious political difficulties for us in that country, possibly quite soon. Already the situation of the missions in Indochina is all too strong. It would be wise to take the matter in hand and put a stop to the growth of a power which, I have noticed from many small indications, is already beginning to want us to take account of it, and which undoubtedly thinks a lot more about its own interests than about those for which we are responsible... (A.O.M. Aix. Indochine, G.G. 7719)

151. Speeches in the parliamentary debate on the **Leygues amendment.** 21 March 1904.

M. Georges Leygues. Teaching by religious orders is suppressed in France; but it is suppressed in France alone. Why have we made this concession, of whose importance everyone is aware? Because it is felt that we cannot let the echos of our political disputes travel beyond our frontiers, and because we have to safeguard important interests in the outside world which would be compromised if we broke up the immense network of schools, orphanages, charitable works of all kinds which the French missions have founded.... The missions constitute one of our most valuable means of influence and propaganda outside France. We cannot abandon them.... We possess (in the East) excellent schools attended by more than 100,000 pupils. Hemmed in on all sides by German, English and American Protestant organisations, and by Austrian and Italian missions, we cannot lose the ground we have gained from them, for at the present time French schools alone account for more pupils than all the schools of other foreign missons combined.... We also possess lay schools, which I prefer, but they are too few in number. We should maintain and encourage the excellent teachers who manage them.... But what hope is there that we will ever have enough resources in money and personnel to establish as many as our country's interests require? So let us accept all the support we are offered: Catholic, Protestant, Jewish establishments, what does it matter? As long as they are French they have a right to our sympathy and encouragement....

M. Gaston Doumergue, Minister for the Colonies. We understand that those who defend the existence of the novitiates in France, as well as the missions abroad, are moved by the consideration that teaching the national language promotes the influence of our country. We have heard reference to schools in the Levant in which missionaries teach French and where it is said that thanks to them one can hear all the natives of the country speaking our language. What may be true in parts of the Levant, the Near East and the Far East does not hold true for our French colonies. There the missionaries have a single boast : that they do not teach French. (<u>Applause on the Far Left and the Left</u>).

The Marquis de La Ferronays. So what do they teach? This is plainly slanderous, because it is quite the opposite of what happens!

M. Doumergue. I would not make such an assertion without offering immediate and incontestable proof. I have in my hands the minutes of the Colonial Council of Cochinchina for its regular session of 1902. In Cochinchina the mission is strong: it has been receiving from the colony important subsidies for a long time, and I believe it has also received some from the Society for the Promotion of the French Language. Thanks to these subsidies the mission has developed to the point of acquiring very extensive property in the territory. (<u>Exclamations from the Far Left</u>). (The mission) wrote on 13 October 1902:

'To the President and Colonial Councillors:
Complaints have been made against the Saigon mission for not teaching French to the children who frequent its schools in the interior, in conformity with the requirements of the administration and the Colonial Council, and for not having thereby supplied the service for which these subsidies have been given to the mission.

I consider that the teaching of French to young children of whom many leave school at twelve years old, and who have no other prospect than to be tied to the soil constitutes a dangerous...' (<u>Applause from the Left and the Far Left</u>)... 'and useless accomplishment for most of them....'

M. Lamendin. That is what I call a <u>coup de grâce</u>.

M. Georges Leygues. Which missionary order is this?

M. Doumergue.

'So I have the honour to inform you that if this teaching is insisted upon for all our schools in the interior, I cannot undertake responsibility for it. In consequence I renounce the benefit of the subsidy normally accorded to the mission under the heading: Subsidy for the mission's schools in the colony and allocated for the teaching of French.... Signed, MOSSARD. Bishop and Vicar Apostolic.' (<u>Renewed applause on the Far Left and Left</u>)....

This letter, as you may imagine, caused a considerable stir in the Colonial Council and in the whole colony. But, gentlemen, it was not an isolated act. It occurred after this bishop, Mgr Mossard, had published a pamphlet in which he said the following: 'The Annamese who know French are, with few exceptions, those who like the French least, who respect them the least and who, at heart, are the most hostile to them...', (<u>Various movements</u>) ...'Surely to increase the numbers of the socially rootless,' the bishop added...

M. Jaurès: That's it! Very good!

M. Doumergue:'...constitutes a danger for public security in Indochina and a serious danger for French influence.' (<u>Exclamations on the Far Left</u>)...........

M. Doumergue..... If we wish to draw the natives to us, there is only one way to do it, and that is to teach them our language, to teach them French. In this way, gentlemen, we can bring them over to our side, and prevent them from communicating in a regular and dangerous way with their powerful neighbours. For my part, I feel that the teaching of French in our colonies is, to a supreme degree a national task, a political task. I believe that this task can only be undertaken by our lay schools, and by our lay teachers.... (<u>Journal Officiel</u>, Vol. 70. Chambre de Députés, 21 March 1904, pp. 832-838.)

VI C FREEMASONS AND THE POLEMIC AGAINST THE MISSIONS IN INDOCHINA, 1905–1907.

Among French colonists in Indochina support for Radicalism was manifested in the early 1900s by a growing number of newly formed and interrelated political groups, of which the most prominent were the Ligue des Droits de l'Homme, the Comité Radicale du Tonkin, and from 1910 the Comité Républicaine Radicale et Radicale-Socialiste. Membership of these groups often coincided with membership of the local masonic lodges of the Grand Orient. The triumph of Radicalism in France, marked by the recent plethora of domestic anticlerical legislation, encouraged these groups to press for the application of the same enactments against missionaries in Indochina. Their pressure was spasmodic and uncoordinated, and it took different forms: polemical books and articles in the press; anti-missionary petitions circulated to senior officials and to the network of lodges in France; electioneering for the Cochinchina seat on behalf of parliamentary candidates pledged to pursue anticlerical policies in the Chamber of Deputies; the lobbying of other deputies in France, notably Pressensé, the president of the Ligue des Droits de l'Homme; and the application of direct pressure on the colonial ministry itself.

The masonic lodges of the Grand Orient - particularly the Fervents du Progrès and the Réveil de l'Orient of Saigon and the Libre Pensée d'Annam of Tourane - provided perhaps the most vigorous and consistent pressure. In 1905 the lodges sponsored the publication of a notoriously combative work, Les missionaires d'Asie. Leur oeuvre néfaste **(Docs 152,153)**. Written by Camille Pâris and his associate, A. Barsanti, this pamphlet amplified longstanding accusations which had appeared in Le Mékong and Le Courrier d'Haiphong since the early 1890s. With their political position so precarious, missionary bishops hesitated to defend themselves as aggressively as in the past against Pâris' accusations for fear of provoking the authorities. But Fr Guerlach, whose activities in the wake of the massacres of 1885 and in the Mayrena affair figured prominently in Pâris' book, offered a spirited defence on his own behalf in newspaper articles and in a book, L'oeuvre néfaste. Réplique du Père Guerlach **(Docs 154, 155)**. This merely provoked ripostes and further indictments. When Pâris finally accused the missions of trafficking in slaves **(Doc. 156)** he was taken to court by Guerlach's bishop, Mgr Grangeon; but the mission's case failed on a technicality. This celebrated Pâris-Guerlach controversy epitomised some of the main issues raised in the anticlerical campaign against missionaries, and provided anecdotal material which came to be used by anticlerical controversialists in France. Such was the heat aroused by the Pâris-Guerlach duel that when Pâris himself was killed on a tour of the wild Bahnar region in 1908, the masonic press accused missionaries of having had him murdered.

Pâris' opposition to the missions was regarded as scurrilous even by some Radicals in the colony. But the essence of his case was more soberly deployed by Jean de Lanessan in a devastating polemic - Les missions et leur Protectorat, published in 1907. Lanessan, by now editor of the influential Parisian Radical paper Le Siècle, drew on his experiences as a former Governor-General to offer the most powerful articulation of the Radical case against missions to emerge in this period. Lanessan developed a counter-myth to match the political case normally advanced by missionaries in their own defence. Traditionally the missions had relied upon pragmatic rather than spiritual arguments to justify their demands for administrative consideration. Missionaries maintained that their proselytism served a patriotic cause. They argued that in converting a large Vietnamese minority they had created a socially orderly collaborating class, rescued from paganism and civilised by exposure to Christian morality. In particular they emphasised that Vietnamese Christians were hostile to politically unreconciled traditional Vietnamese hierarchies; and that they were also indifferent to the appeal of modern Vietnamese nationalism. Lanessan however, reversed the terms of the argument. He maintained that the missions' aggressive Christianising tactics were a regular cause of social disorder within families and communes, and that this in itself led to the breakdown of a system of traditional morality that was in no way inferior to that of Christianity. He contended that the Christian minority was not so much loyal to France as economically subjugated to the mission; and that French missionaries were themselves hostile to French rule because its administrative restrictions and fiscal burdens reduced the effectiveness of their proselytism **(Doc. 157)**. Finally, he asserted that however patriotic the Christian minority might be, missionary activity was an assault upon the traditional values of Vietnamese culture and that this prevented the majority of the population - particularly the mandarin and scholar elite - from becoming reconciled to French rule. He suggested that the repression of the missions would win the French popularity among the bulk of the population.

Freemasons added further elements to this body of argument, maintaining that the fruits of the missions' profiteering from agriculture and banking in Indochina were swelling the 'Black Treasury' of the Vatican, enabling the Pope to subsidise the subversion of Republicanism in France itself **(Docs. 158, 159)**. Radical-Socialists in particular took the line that as an obscurantist, socially repressive influence, missions were obstructing the intellectual and social emancipation of Vietnam and hampering its educational and material progress.

In 1905-7 when the various domestic anticlerical enactments first came to be considered by the administration for application in Indochina, lobbying by the masonic lodges and other groups became particularly intense. Since their pressure failed at first to bend an authoritarian administration to their viewpoint they adopted subtler and more circuitous methods later in the decade.

Further reading

J.L. de Lanessan, **Les missions et leur protectorat.**(Paris, 1906).
M. Larkin, **Church and State after the Dreyfus Affair: the Separation issue in France.** (London, Macmillan, 1974).
J-A. Faucher et A.Ricker, **Histoire de la franc-maçonnerie en France.** (Paris, Nouvelles éditions latines, 1967).
M.J. Headings, **French Freemasonry under the Third Republic.** (Baltimore, Johns Hopkins Press, 1949).
H. Coston, **Un état dans l'Etat: la franc-maçonnerie. La République du Grand-Orient.** (Paris, La librairie française, 1976).

Documents

152. **Camille Pâris** and **A. Barsanti,** Missionaires d'Asie. Oeuvre néfaste des congrégations.(Paris, 1905)

PREFACE

We have just published a topical book. The religious orders which France has thrown out, are invading Asia and discrediting the French name. People under the protection of the French flag who are subject to them are cursing them. They accept our traders and industrialists willingly, but they do not want our missionaries. It is time to show them that we do not wish to impose upon them by force the religious communities whom we are expelling. We ask that the government abandon its protectorate over Christians in Asia and that it apply the law concerning religious orders (sic) to Indochina.

Our book exposes the immorality and arrogance of the missionaries. We think that its natural place is in the libraries of Free Thought, and especially in those of the masonic lodges, which are in the vanguard of the movement for emancipating the human races. We hope that you will give it a fraternal welcome....

153. **Camille Pâris'** indictments against the Mission in Indochina.

p.70
The Residents, apart from a few royalist clericals with rigid principles, inevitably become the adversaries of the Missions as soon as they come to administer a province.

p.88
In Annam the European population consists of 159 officials, 80 'colons' and 119 missionaries. The latter have had themselves registered as planters in order to win election to the Chamber of Agriculture and Commerce where they form the majority. One can see on page 795 of the gazeteer for 1900, eighteen missionaries including the bishop, whose name appears without his title, mentioned as planters in the province of Binh Dinh alone; whereas there are only three planters there, Citizens Montpezat, Rideau and myself. In such conditions Free Thought becomes a dangerous creed to follow....

p.92
The Law on Religious Orders (sic), by sparing them (here), has considerably increased their numbers and power. Every mailboat from France brings new groups of missionaries to Indochina and China. As a result of an overgenerous tolerance, laicization has come to a halt, lay education is given insufficient credit and lacks premises and teachers. The missions are accumulating landed property and constructing comfortable schools wherever French families are established, and thus achieve their ideal: to keep the Annamese in ignorance and the French in a state of error in order to put off indefinitely any moral juncture of the two peoples, which can only occur in the absence of religion....
(C. Pâris et A. Barsanti, Missionaires d'Asie. Leur oeuvre néfaste. (Paris,1905)

154. Preface to Fr **Guerlach's** reply to Pâris and Barsanti.

I am informed that the masonic lodges have organised a press campaign against the missionaries in order to stir up public opinion with their calumnies and prepare it for the persecution decreed by the Grand Orient. Like a submissive slave you obey the order of the day, and show a noble pride which will have its reward. Who knows? The cross of the

LEGION OF HONOUR may be your payment for this 'exceptional service'....But you may be rejoicing too soon. I have heard certain freemasons say that you have been clumsy, and have forced the pace too hard, and that this has spoiled the effect of your pamphlet.... (J.B. Guerlach, 'L'oeuvre néfaste'. Réplique du Père J.B. Guerlach, Missionnaire Apostolique, au F∴ Camille Pâris, Colon en Annam. (Saigon, 1907).)

155. Fr **J.B. Guerlach** on Missionaries and French officials. (1907)

Enemies of the colony's settlers the missionaries are supposedly hostile to its administrators....
   The truth of the matter is this:
1° A few sectarian administrators are, from partisan prejudice, opposed to the work of missionaries and become, for that reason alone, enemies of the missionaries. These gentlemen belong to the same (masonic) affiliation as you.
2° Certain administrators are inimical towards certain missionaries, and their animosity could have been prompted either by personal friction or by particular administrative misdemeanors committed by these missionaries....
3° I think I can affirm that the generality of French administrators and officials live on good terms with the missionaries. If a misunderstanding occurs a clear and frank explanation is enough to clear it up, restore harmony and rekindle mutual regard.... (J.B. Guerlach, 'L'oeuvre néfaste.' Réplique du Père J.B. Guerlach, Missionnaire Apostolique, au F∴ Camille Pâris, Colon en Annam. (Saigon, 1907). pp. 52-5.)

156. **Camille Pâris:** 'Slavery for Jesus'. 14 March 1907.

All these (twenty Annamese child slaves) came from a school for preparing slaves called the Sainte Enfance de Go Thi, situated in the outskirts of Qui Nhon.... (They were formed into a convoy for despatch to the mountain territory of the Djarais). There they were chain-ganged to till the rice fields for their (missionary) masters, and when their tired, suffering little bodies, undermined by malaria, finally found repose in death, Fr Salomé, director of the Sainte Enfance at Go Thi and procurator of this charnel house, would send others.
   It was with the survivors of this shameful human traffic that for thirty years the Catholic mission at Tra Ngao, with its headquarters at

Kontum, has become populated by 2,000 agrarian serfs kept by eighteen French priests.

Hence the mission at Kontum holds enslaved about 2,000 individuals stolen by its agents or bought from the savages with whom they have regular slave trading arrangements: these are used to aggrandise its estates. And the government has never intervened to stop this criminal 'charity'. And our compatriots in France, who can become indignant over an ordinary citizen whipping his houseboy, remain impassive at these deliberate crimes because the perpetrators are priests.... A sensible, energetic, freethinking and wise official devoted to the great task of organising a savage territory and liberating its inhabitants, should reside at Kontum in the centre of this (missionary) lair and take in hand the direct administration of its Catholic agglomerations in the name of a liberating Republic, and in the name of human rights, which are much more sacred than those of Christianity....

(Camille Pâris, 'Les négriers de Jésus,' Le Courrier d'Haiphong, 14 March 1907.

157. J.L. de Lanessan, Governor-General of Indochina (1891-4).

Missionary preference for Annamese rule.

The reasons why the missionaries in Tonkin cared little whether France took possession of the country or not can easily be guessed. While the mission was faced with Annamese authorities alone it could, by invoking the name of France, obtain for its Christians privileges which France herself would not have given them as mistress of Indochina. Before our arrival in Tonkin the missions were almost entirely closed to the Annamese authorities. They paid hardly any taxes and were exempt from native justice there. After French occupation, things changed. Our egalitarian principles allow us to make no distinction between native Christians and Buddhists: all are equally obliged to pay taxes and answer to justice. Missionaries were formerly sovereign within the confines of their establishments: today they are merely citizens like all the rest and their Christians cannot escape our administrative supervision. This is why the missionaries and their Christians offer real but tacit opposition to French domination....

(J.L. de Lanessan, Les missions et leur protectorat. (Paris, Alcan, 1907). p. 52)

158. M. **Loye,** Venerable of the Réveil d'Orient lodge of Saigon to the Grand Master of the Grand Orient. Saigon, 26 May 1907.

The mission is working for the conquest of the municipality and has its spies everywhere. The results of the Saigon municipal elections will be the same as for the next legislative elections, and we might have reason to be apprehensive. The mission is very rich, and we are only rich ourselves in Republican energy and goodwill. But that is not enough. Come to our assistance.

(Enclosure.)
Minutes of the solemn meeting of the Réveil d'Orient masonic lodge of Saigon on 4 May 1907.

Motions carried:
   That it is painful to have to refer again after so much vocal and vociferous warning not only to the uselessness and danger of the presence of the men in black in this country, but also to the current peril of not applying the (anticlerical) laws which control them in France.
   That it is nonetheless necessary and urgent to say and to repeat that the mission in Cochinchina possesses the best ricefields and the most fertile land, and holds immense quantities of these; and that the enormous sums brought in by the land, for which their labour costs are minimal, go to swell the Black Treasury of the Vatican to nourish the army of enemies of our beloved Republic and of Progress....
   That... the government of the colony of Cochinchina be invited to remove from the bishop and the curé of Saigon, as well as from all other curés and missions of the interior who are in the same situation, the episcopal seat and curacies which they are presently enjoying, and remit them to the colony or to the communes for whatever use seems appropriate.... (Bibliothèque Nationale, Paris. Fonds Maçonnique. Fonds du Grand Orient, Rés. FM²142. 'Saigon: Réveil d'Orient'.)

159. Extracts from the discourse presented by B(rother)∴ **Serres,** Venerable of the Grand Orient lodge La Libre Pensée d'Annam at Tourane, 12 October 1907.

But, you may say, how could the missions have acquired the property and (capital) reserves which seem to go to support the church in France and the officials of the Vatican?
   How? Very simple. With few exceptions every missionary is involved

in agriculture and lending money to natives. You know how high interest rates are in our territories. So to create an impenetrable muddle, each priest arriving in the colony adopts a native name and all his commercial dealings are made in this name or in the name of one of his faithful flock. The native priest, on taking orders, sells all his possessions and gives the money to the mission. Every new convert goes to the mission to obtain assistance. Needless to say he pays a hundred times over for this in <u>corvées</u> or river porterage. Unknown to the administration the mission levies a tithe on all lands given to Christians as compensation after each of our struggles with the Annamese empire, and one hardly needs add that most of these lands belong to it even though, officially, they belong to X or Z. As for the favoured situation enjoyed by most of them as regards the payment of land and other taxes, it is beyond belief.

How can one combat this?

Let us declare first of all that it is not the Catholic religion as such which we are trying to expell from this country, so much priests in particular who are using their ill-gotten gains against France and against the Republic. We think it indispensible to ask the home government:

1/. To promulgate (here) the law of 1 July, 1901 relative to the Contract of Association, with the reservation that its application in regard to clauses I and II be limited solely to European associations.

2/. To promulgate in the colony the law of 7 July,1904 or at least a decree suppressing teaching by religious orders. As for the disposal of property, we will be discussing this below.

3/. To abrogate promptly clause II of the law of 7 July 1904 (the Leygues amendment) relating to the suppression of teaching by religious orders. This article has the effect of authorising teaching orders to recruit members intended for French schools abroad and in colonies and protectorates. It is a gratuitous insult to our lay teaching personnel.

4/. Indochina has never been subjected to the Concordat. There are no vicars or parishes here, only Christian communes served by French missionaries or Annamese priests. Moreover since Cambodia, Annam and Tonkin have kept their administrative autonomy by treaty agreement, the promulgation of the law of 9 December 1905 concerning the Separation of Church and State does not bind these (missionary) landlords. Hence the promulgation of articles I, II, and III of this law is pointless. But a decree applying to Indochina the principle of the prescriptions contained in articles IV, V, and VI insofar as these are compatible with our rather special administrative organisation seems to us to be indispensable. Royal ordinances in Annam and Cambodia concerning police supervision of worship and of associations for the exercise of Catholic worship would prevent native priests from occupying a privileged position. It is indispensable, in my opinion, to ask for all this from now on.

But in a country where the mission has been able to gather round itself so very many interests, and where it has acquired an influence which it would be childish to deny, is it possible to apply our laws? Should we not be afraid, as a certain clerical newspaper has remarked, of rousing a serious movement of resistance against France?

To that I reply No, so long as the French governement has the firm intention of imposing respect for the law everywhere, by force if necessary. Do not be dismayed by my use of this last phrase. You know the missionaries, you have seen them inciting our protégés to revolt, spreading disunity and hatred among the Europeans and natives because the political solution adopted at Hue by the French government was detrimental to their interests. Believe me, they will deploy against us all, against dutiful officials, against France herself, some of the sad rabble which constitutes the greater part of their clientele. But if the unfortunate natives see that we are determined to act, order will return.

Can we leave out of account the immense majority of those who only see the missionary as someone who has exploited and maltreated them for years, a sworn enemy of their beliefs which he ridicules on every occasion? Do you think the mandarin will oppose his expulsion?

In a country whose inhabitants are as devoted to the land as the Annamese, the question of devolving (church) property should interest us. It would be a mistake to forget it. The many lawsuits which have arisen over contested ownership of land, the hostility of a certain part of the Catholic population, the credulity of the Annamese mind which in many cases does not comprehend the purposes we are pursuing, should prompt us to ask the government to adopt a special system which, while bringing us closer to that of France, takes account both of the difficulties which the government has to avoid and of the impact which any important administrative measure has upon the mind of our protégés....

...As far as freedom to teach is concerned, the Spanish clergy has never taught its catechists a word of Castilian. So the Spanish government has long realised that its influence is non-existent here and, if it objects to French and Annamese government suppression of teaching by the religious orders in this country, it will only offer arguments based on sentiment.

Mindful of the _de facto_ position which the Spanish mission has created for itself, I observed a few moments ago that it would be politic in devolving mission property in Indochina to provide a special regime which, while similar to that in France, would take account of the various contingencies which have to be noted in Indochina, especially in Annam and Tonkin. It is the French government's responsibility to find the means of dealing with Spanish susceptibilities in seeking a basis for agreement with the Madrid cabinet, but it is important to stress the fact that the Spanish missions had shown as little respect as the French for the terms of the treaty of 1874....

The missions have caused the natives to become disaffected towards us, their self-interested advice has led us to make many mistakes. At present the Government has to reckon on dealing with a State within the State, a power that is highly organised and hopes to remain at all costs in control of the destinies of the officials and senior Annamese mandarins in order to keep its capital and influence intact, and, in pursuing its ends, is fully ready to ally with the worst enemies of France, and to preach revolt against our policies.

We do not ask in the least for special legislation, simply that the laws of France, with a few changes of detail, be applied to Indochina.

I propose that we send the Grand Orient a motion which consists of the proposals already made in my discourse. This motion will be addressed to all our lodges in Indochina and to our lodges in France. It will make an urgent appeal to their Masonic loyalty to recommend action to the Grand Orient, asking for their intercession with our F(raternal) members of parliament to hasten the moment when the reign of the conquistadors and little inquisitors such as still exists in Annam and Tonkin may be finally extinguished. If our own peasants hailed the night of 4 August (1789) with a great cry of joy, believe me that the nha-que of Annam will burn a host of incense sticks on their ancestral altars to celebrate the departure of these voracious landlords....(M.R.E, Papers of Governor-General Paul Beau, Carton 6.)

VI D THE DEBATE WITHIN THE INDOCHINA ADMINISTRATION ON THE APPLICATION OF THE LAWS OF 1901, 1904 AND 1905 AGAINST THE MISSION, (1905-1907).

The question of whether to apply the laws of 1 July 1901, 7 July 1904 and 9 December 1905 to the French colonial system was referred in 1905 to a colonial ministry commission presided over by Paul Dislère. The Dislère commission consulted the Indochina administration on two separate occasions: once in 1905 to ascertain views on the application of the laws of 1901 and 1904; and then again in 1906 to ask for reactions to the Law of Separation of 1905.

On both occasions the question of application was treated by Indochina officials in subtantially the same way. Their replies sought to answer two questions: what degree and form of control, if any, should be applied to missionary activities? And in what ways would metropolitan legislation, if applied, need to be adapted to local circumstances? The current practice of shuffling senior officials frequently between the major territories of the Indochina Union as intérimaires to replace colleagues on leave resulted in an unusually wide canvass of official opinion. Views were received on substantially the same questions twice over from a succession of different administrators. The relatively uniform reaction received from all parts of the federation is therefore noteworthy, and a sample of these views is reproduced below.

It is plain that officials considered the entire future of the mission to be at stake. For a hostile adaptation of these measures would have undermined the mission's main strategy for obtaining conversions, based as it was primarily on the acquisition and distribution of land to Christian communes. In general, officials offered consistently strong political arguments for opposing any form of dispossession or dispersal of mission property under the terms of Chapters I and III of the Law of 1 July 1901. Over Indochina as a whole the Christian population was by now approaching 800,000, and the total landed property of the mission, though unassessed, was assumed to be very large. In Hanoi alone the mission was reported to own over seven million francs worth of land and housing. Cambodia and Laos were only sparsely Christianised, and there the issue seemed a secondary matter; but for Annam, Tonkin and Cochinchina most officials argued that a draconian application resulting in dispersals of mission property would cause a scramble for land leading to widespread social disorder, particularly in the densely populated, landhungry, and more heavily christianised North. It was suggested in some quarters that an attack on mission property would provoke missionaries to foment political dissidence among the Christian Vietnamese; and this prospect was all the more unwelcome in that the

Russo-Japanese war, currently turning in favour of Japan, was already expected to have some political repercussion among the Vietnamese population (**Docs 162, 164-5**).

The second standard objection offered by most officials concerned the effects of dispossession upon the educational, hospital and orphanage work not only of the missions - Spanish Dominican as well as French - but also of other religious orders operating under the aegis of the Société des Missions Etrangères, particularly the nuns of St Paul de Chartres and the Christian Brothers. From Tonkin it was reported that the religious orders built and ran their educational and medical establishments 'ten times' more cheaply than the administration could; and from Tonkin and Cochinchina it was observed that the effects of buying out or substituting for the religious orders in these spheres would be 'disastrous' for the local budgets for these territories (**Docs 160-2**).

The effects of recent measures for 'laicising' public services in 1903 supported these assertions. The eviction of the Pauline sisters from the major government hospitals of the federation had left a medical service - which contained only 200 doctors - critically short of skilled nursing auxiliaries. A masonic petition ludicrously proposed the wholesale recruitment of 'respectable laundresses' as substitutes for nursing nuns, but the suggestion was not taken up. In the leprosaria and in subsidised native hospitals of the provinces the Pauline nursing sisters were quietly retained for fear of letting these medical facilities collapse. Most senior officials seemed to agree by 1905 that the 'laicisation' of medical and educational services was an expensive ideological indulgence. In 1907 Governor-General Beau, himself a mason, proposed a compromise set of measures based on the Law of 1901 which met some metropolitan demands but was calculated to cause least upheaval locally. Following the opinion of Acting Governor-General Broni (**Doc. 166**), Beau intended that selective application of some parts of the Law of 1901 should be used to freeze the mission's ability to acquire further property. But he opposed any policy of wholesale dispersal (**Doc. 167**).

The Quai d'Orsay opposes the application of the Law of 1901 to Annam and Tonkin.

Beau expected his proposals to apply to the whole of the Indochina Union. However it became evident by 1907 that opposition from the French foreign ministry would make it impossible to apply the Law of 1901 to Annam and Tonkin. These parts of the Union of Indochina were protectorates in which French rule was regulated by the treaties of 1874 and 1884. Here, the privileges enjoyed by French missionaries had been specifically extended to the Spanish Dominican missions of East Tonkin. The application of the Law of 1901 in Annam and Tonkin would have required the Spanish government's assent to the revision of the protectoral treaties, and the Quai d'Orsay declined to make the necessary overture to Spain, on the grounds that such an approach would cause annoyance **(Doc. 169)**. The French Foreign Ministry's opposition almost certainly concealed deeper calculations. The Quai was conventionally allowed considerable autonomy in the formation of foreign policy, whatever cabinet was in power. Traditionally the Quai had always championed missionary interests in the Levant and Asia from a belief that missionaries were a useful instrument of French political influence abroad. In spite of the rupture with the Papacy following the passage of the the Separation law of 1905, the Quai had continued, covertly, to support the <u>pacte confessionelle</u> in foreign affairs in the hope of improving relations with the Vatican: its <u>protectorat des missions</u> was at stake. Plainly the prospect of applying the Law of 1901 to Annam and Tonkin was an issue which had far-reaching diplomatic implications.

The Quai's opposition to the application of the Law of 1901 to Annam and Tonkin was not challenged. When in July 1907 the Dislère commission reported the Quai's refusal to negotiate with the Spanish, the scope of the Law's prospective application to Indochina was narrowed. The commission finally proposed the immediate application of part III of the law - the portion affecting religious orders - only to Cochinchina and Cambodia **(Doc. 169)**.

Further reading

J.L. de Lanessan, **Les missions et leur protectorat.** (Paris, 1907).
M. Larkin, **Church and State after the Dreyfus Affair: the Separation issue in France.** (London, Macmillan, 1974).

(On the Quai d'Orsay's continuing support for missions elsewhere:

W.I. Shorrock, 'Anticlericalism and French policy in the Ottoman Empire, 1900-1914', **European Studies Review** 4, 1 (1974), pp. 33-55.

160.   M. Fourès, Resident-Superior of Tonkin, to Governor-General **Beau**. Hanoi, 13 March 1905.

One has to imagine a situation in which the Missions, which hold influence over more than a million Catholic natives, might refuse to submit to this law (of 1901) Would that not create a movement hostile to our administration?

The Catholics constitute a rich and intelligent part of the population. Grouped mostly in the best provinces of the delta they enjoy a standard of living which gives them - not legally but in practice - a relatively privileged position. Since they have great confidence in their missionaries, is it not to be feared that the latter, if dispossessed and obliged to leave the country, might make unwise remarks and incite defiance and hatred for our administration among the Catholic population?

What motive, moreover, might foreigners like the Spanish have for refraining from a campaign directed against our domination? We could not legitimately invoke the principle of patriotism. Should we not also be apprehensive of the covert influence of Catholic mandarins ....?

The Annamese peasant, Christian or Buddhist, attached as he is to his plots of riceland, would often resort to unjust acts. A bitter and persistent struggle would spread from commune to commune, from hamlet to hamlet, from family to family. The thought of securing well cultivated and high yielding fields cheaply or even free of charge could break up the family itself.

So all in all it seems that the promulgation of the law of 1 July (1901) would result either in temporary, violent upheavals, or in a profounder disruption welling up from the most intimate concerns of the native peasant, and could, as a consequence, overturn the two fundamental institutions of the Annamese people: the commune and the family....

In regard to medical facilities the regular orders have given unquestionably good service. Even now, in most of the provinces, the native hospitals employ the nuns of St Paul de Chartres, and it would be difficult to find lay nurses to undertake such distasteful work for the same conditions of pay. As for education, the religious orders have for long possessed the best run - one might even say the only - teaching institutions... To buy back their establishments or construct similar ones and provide substitutes for their hospital and teaching services.... would have disastrous financial consequences for the local budget. The Administration could not do it in the same conditions as the religious orders and would burden its resources to an enormous extent.... The missionaries build and develop in an exceptionally economical way: they are their own architects; they rely on the prestige of their ministry among their catechumens to obtain labour and materials virtually free of charge or at least for never more than cost price. Their teachers are paid little and serve as supervisors, bursars, nurses and administrators.... It is no exaggeration to say that (substituting) for the missions could cost the administration ten times as much.

Where could one find the resources? From the local budget! ...It can stand no further appeals for expenditure... The financial consequences of such a step would be disastrous....(A.N.S.O.M. Paris. Indochine, (A.F.) 29/A90(15))

161. **M. Moulié,** Acting Resident-Superior of Annam, to Governor-General **Beau.** Hue, 18 March 1905.

In Annam the priests of the Catholic missions are not organised into communities; they are spread out in the districts as free priests. The mission properly speaking gives them an annual allocation of 600 frs and they are free to administer the districts and the parishes which they establish there as they like. They generally acquire land through proxies and sometimes they use the Annamese name which each missionary takes. Hence their landholdings are regulated by Annamese law. I think that in Annam the mission itself, as a body or association, possesses little or nothing.

Hence the law of 1901 would have no useful effect at present on the possessions of the association. As individuals the missionaries would promptly secularise themselves, continue to preach the Catholic religion as before and expand their landed patrimony in their own names....

Events taking place in Manchuria show us that the yellow peril is becoming more and more menacing and it is important to meet all new intrigues by developing as much as possible every French interest without concerning ourselves as to its source, whether commercial, agricultural or religious. (A.O.M. Aix. Indochine, G.G. 15,795)

162. Acting Governor-General **Broni** to **E. Clémentel**, Minister for the Colonies. Hanoi, 19 September 1905.

The influence which the missionaries have established over the increasingly numerous native Catholic population is undeniable, especially in Cochinchina, Annam and Tonkin where they are surrounded by entire villages and disseminated through the richest centres. A movement of hostile opinion would perhaps develop if the religious orders were no longer authorised. At a time when we are trying to gain the confidence and the attachment of our subjects and protégés in anticipation of external difficulties, one might ask what effect (the law of 1901) would have on the state of mind of an appreciable proportion of the people. We might feebly hope that French missionaries would not try to arouse an insidious agitation on the issue of their expulsion; but the Spanish are unlikely to show similar restraint. Moreover, I fear that without any control or supervision from European clergy... the very numerous and growing body of Annamese priests, if returned to private life or only authorised to excercise their ministry in purely parochial conditions, would be naturally inclined to use their prestige with their co-religionists to start a secret opposition to French administration.

The non-Catholic natives themselves, given the credulous and impressionable nature of the Annamese race, might also be disturbed and made anxious by the formalities involved in the sale of property which would follow the dispersal of the religious orders. Would not the system of landed property which, in Annamese territory, is of primordial interest and is the basis of social and economic life, go through a troublesome crisis? Would not the present rivalries between hamlets and families of different religions, which sometimes degenerate into bloody conflict, find new scope to proliferate as a consequence of the strict application of the law of 1 July 1901?

In right and equity its application should result in a juster shareout of the burdens imposed by the state on landed property. But in practical effect, will it not aggravate the hostility existing between the two parts of the population? And is the French administration yet capable of keeping order and ignoring the discontent of a whole caste which will still stay on in the colony, or, if it emigrates, might stay close to its frontiers?

...One wonders how the local budgets will be able henceforth to bear the running costs of the public services required to replace clerical education and hospital work. To enable the growth of expenditure in these categories to be appreciated, I give below a table of the credits allocated for hospital work and public education from the years

1902-1904 and those anticipated for 1906, which do not include those increasing costs which figure in the provincial budgets.

| | Cochinchina | | Tonkin | |
	Assistance	Education	Assistance	Education
1902 -	176,216$	462,900$	32,160$	109,224$
1904 -	196,470$	528,328$	81,310$	139,116$
1906 -	158,909$	444,174$	207,772$	231,844$

| | Annam | | Cambodia | |
	Assistance	Education	Assistance	Education
1902 -	35,316$	15,600$	39,254$	20,941$
1904 -	58,535$	20,360$	59,509$	65,265$
1906 -	93,875$	33,357$	125,766$	102,017$

...I think I may be short of the mark when I say that (the immediate promulgation of the laws of 1901 and 1904) would at least double the estimates for 1906. (A.N.S.O.M. Paris. Indochine (A.F.) 29/A90(15))

163. Governor-General **Beau** to E. **Clémentel**, Minister for the Colonies. Telegram. Saigon, 26 January 1906.

The separation of the Churches from the State already exists in practice, so no part of the new law (of 1905) is, in present conditions, applicable to Indochina. (A.N.S.O.M. Paris. Indochine, (A.F.) 29/A90(15))

164. **M. Levecque,** Acting Resident-Superior of Annam, to Governor-General **Beau.** Hue, 31 August 1906.

If the treaties should be modified, all measures taken to enforce the devolution of mission property... would instantly alienate the Catholic Annamese population - and possibly part of the Buddhist population too - if these modifications cause changes in the excercise of personal property rights. For they would not in the least understand what we are trying to do.

It would clearly be impolitic at the present time to touch the moveable and landed property of the Missions Etrangères or of the missionaries, but we can always take appropriate measures to combat scholar class, the ruling class of Annam, would certainly take pleasure in seeing the Catholic religion subjected to common law.... (A.N.S.O.M. Paris. Indochine, (A.F.) 29/A90(15))

165. **M. Groleau,** Acting Resident-Superior of Tonkin, to Governor-General **Beau.** Hanoi, 20 October 1906.

As for the property owned by the Catholic missions the tax officials are obliged to rely upon declarations which are made by the interested parties themselves, and it is virtually certain that these declarations do not always conform to reality. Aside from certain landed properties which are no less part of the Mission's holdings for being held in the names of native priests, there are others whose nominal proprietors, all natives, are probably only proxies. It is also worth noting that in recent times purchases of land have been made in the names of Vicars Apostolic or their ecclesiastical subordinates and not, as in the past, in the name of the Catholic mission.

This state of things is all the more regrettable because, in the present condition of legislation the administration has no means of remedying it.

This country is going through a moral crisis at the moment, if I may so put it. France's role of protection and civilisation is being constantly undermined and there are visible symptoms of this: the attitude of the native population is still unsettled after the agitation set off by the Russo-Japanese war; and the malaise resulting from the flooding of the last harvests is only just passing off. The masses are wavering. Would it really be appropriate in such a situation to carry out a measure which is not very obviously useful in itself, in order to disturb and upset a small and inoffensive number of obscure missionaries in their rather useful work, at the risk of provoking a profound and durable reaction from nearly a million native Catholics?

...However, I am far from recommending the maintenance of the status quo.... It is plain that the missionaries have enjoyed up to now a freedom of action which is absolutely incompatible with the protectoral administration's undeniable rights of control and surveillance. I am not referring to the excercise of their worship, in which we are not involved, but to their public activities: the acquisition of land, the foundation of pious establishments, the organisation and reorganisation of religious districts, the creation of schools and seminaries.... This absolute liberty of acquisition enables the Catholic missions to amass a ceaselessly growing patrimony, to perpetuate it, to immobilise it, to give it an independent existence as a possession held in mortmain which exempts property from the fundamental economic law by which it should be divided and recirculated to improve its utility.

It is not necessary to resort to inquisitional measures: the missions have done nothing to deserve that. All that is needed is for the Protectorate to be kept informed of the changes being made by the missionaries to the economic and social life of the natives, so to speak. Lands are being acquired, schools built, seminaries founded, chapels erected, ceremonies celebrated in villages here and there as often as not without the provincial authorities knowing anything about it, or only hearing indirectly. It is essential that the administration resumes its prerogative of control and police in these matters. A ruling made locally in the form of a decree would suffice without the need for a general sanction.... (A.N.S.O.M. Paris. Indochine, (A.F.) 29/A90(15))

166.   Acting Governor-General **Broni** to **M. Milliès-Lacroix**, Minister for the Colonies. Hanoi, 12 December 1906.

If one wants to change the relationship between the Churches and the State in the colony.... there is scope for applying certain provisions of the Law of 1 July 1901 on the Contract of Association which enables us to submit the acquisition of land by associations to the rules of public law, which have been completed and clarified by the above-mentioned legislation.

It emerges from all the reports of the heads of the local administrations that no difficulties to speak of would result in relations between ministers of the different religions and the government; but that in the long run the progressive extension of the patrimony of religious congregations could result in certain inconveniences from a political and economic point of view... (A.N.S.O.M. Paris. Indochine (A.F.) 29/A90 (15))

167.   Governor-General **Beau** to **M. Milliès-Lacroix**, Minister for the Colonies. Hanoi, 22 April 1907.

The religious orders which supply the service of Catholic worship in Indochina are in a truly privileged situation. The Law of 2 January 1817 has never been promulgated in the colony, so their acquisitions, whether by purchase or through gifts, are not subjected to any (concordatory) controls. In France the authorised religious orders have never enjoyed such liberal treatment in this respect.

However, the same economic and social considerations apply in Indochina which have prompted all governments in France, whether monarchist or republican, to restrict the right of acquisition by moral bodies.

As M. Broni remarks, it is not a question of reverting to the past and removing the rights conferred by favourable treaty arrangements or by the absence of sufficiently precise internal legislation. Although certain elements of the press are already seeking to spread confusion on this matter with the evident aim of stirring up an agitation in the colony, the measures which seem to require adoption will only hold good for the future.

They would consist of submitting the existing religious orders in Indochina to regulations similar to those which are contained in articles 6 and 11 of the Law of 1 July 1901, according to which even an association enjoying rights as a legal entity may not possess or acquire more real estate than is necessary for the purpose for which it exists, or receive gifts and legacies without authorisation.... One might note that for (the Spanish missionaries) as much as for French missionaries the new legislation would not have the result of removing certain rights from them, but simply of fixing the conditions on which these can be excercised.... (A.O.M. Paris. Indochine,(A.F.) 29/A90 (15))

168.   Mgr **Mossard**, Bishop of Médéa, Vicar Apostolic of West Cochinchina. Report... for 1905-6. Saigon, 15 October 1906.

Left to its own devices, the Indochina government would, I think, leave religious matters as they are. Informed of the growing antagonism of the pagan population towards France, knowing a little of the supposedly secret activity of foreign agents who are preparing the way for their respective governments with a view to future complications, our governors are not going to squander lightly and completely the only goodwill remaining to them here - that of the Christians whose long history keeps them attached to the French cause.

But above the Indochina government is that of France whose sole preoccupation for some years seems to have been to ruin Religion. Will it be restrained by the political danger? There is no reason to think so. So we should be ready to see the laws applied which will restrict religious development here.... It is said that the implementation of the decree might give rise to a movement of sedition whose importance cannot be calculated; and that the (Indochina) government knows this and will not dare to apply such a law, which was, incidentally, made especially for France.... But it will probably not flinch from implementing it.... (A.S.M.E. Vol. 757, (Cochinchine Orientale, 1890-1920.))

169. **A. Lebrun,** Minister for the Colonies, to Governor-General **A. Sarraut.** Paris, 24 October 1911.

The Minister for Foreign Affairs, when consulted (in 1907) as to the implications of the Annamese treaty of 15 March 1874, made it known that the formal stipulations of this treaty - to which Spain has adhered - do not permit us to apply the Law of 1901 to the Spanish congregations established in Annam-Tonkin without a revision of this diplomatic instrument, and that it is advisable to avoid any measure which could give offence to the Spanish government.

In consequence, the (Dislère) commission set up in 1905 merely drafted a decree making Part III (Religious Orders) of the Law of 1901 applicable to Cochinchina and Cambodia. (A.O.M. Aix. Indochine, G.G. 15,805)

The transitory threat from Japan.

The question of applying the enactment of 1901 was being considered by
the Indochina administration not merely in terms of its local political
impact, but within a broader configuration of internal and regional
crises linked to the activities of Japan. Japan's military and naval
success in the Russo-Japanese war of 1904-5 underlined the extreme
vulnerability of the Indochina Union to external attack. At the same
time, Japan's defeat of Russia provided inspiration for indigenous
nationalist movements opposing European systems of rule through most of
Asia, including Vietnam **(Doc. 170)**. The internal and external security
problems of Indochina had not seemed closely related; but in 1905-6 the
French discovered that Japan had begun giving direct support to groups
of exiled Vietnamese nationalists, offering them hospitality and
protection at Tokyo. This protection was, moreover, proving significant
for the survival and growth of the nationalist movement.

The formation of the Vietnamese nationalist movement.

Since Vietnamese nationalists were currently preparing an insurrection
against French rule, the period between 1905 and early 1909 was to
become an acutely uncomfortable episode of crisis for the French.

   In 1904 the formation of the Vietnamese nationalist Modernisation
Society (the Duy Tan Hoi) by the scholar-patriot Phan Boi Chau and
Prince Cuong De, a scion of the imperial dynasty, had signalled the
resumption of organised political resistance to French colonial
domination. In adopting an insurrectional strategy, the new movement
presented the most serious political challenge to French rule since the
extinction of the Can Vuong.

   The Duy Tan Hoi departed from the traditionalism of the Can Vuong, and
proclaimed a programme of reform which sought political independence for
Vietnam under a monarchical constitution. The group had been small,
vulnerable, unpublicised and critically short of funds until the
Japanese gave its leaders hospitality and a refuge in 1905.   From the
safety of Tokyo, and with the help of contributions raised both locally
and in Vietnam by Duy Tan Hoi members, Phan Boi Chau and Cuong De were
able to promote the rapid growth of the movement. From Tokyo they
issued a quantity of nationalist tracts, manifestos and histories for
circulation in Vietnam, and arranged for the education of some two
hundred young Vietnamese in Japanese academies. In order to raise more

funds and develop plans for a largescale popular insurrection, Phan Boi Chau had formed a new organisation, the Viet-Nam Cong Hien Hoi (Viet-Nam Public Offering Society) in 1907. An army of irregulars under a guerilla chief in Tonkin, De Tham, then pledged its support for the rising; and the insurrection was planned to begin on 27 June 1908 as a mutiny of the Vietnamese troops of the Hanoi garisson. However the Hanoi mutiny, which was to begin with the poisoning of the French garisson officers, was betrayed by a Christian participant to his confessor and suppressed. De Tham's troops consequently failed to move, and the general uprising was stifled at birth. For the French, this revolutionary project in the North seemed all the more threatening in that it coincided with a severe economic depression in central Vietnam. Here, in March-April 1908, the spontaneous outbreak of tax riots and demonstrations against mandarin oppression had spread from Quang Nam province through Nghe An, Ha Tinh and Thanh Hoa, encouraged by a separate group of nationalists led by Phan Chu Trinh, who followed an anti-Japanese, republican programme. Though the French were confronted by a coincidence of separate manifestations rather than by a coordinated revolt, their political confidence was severely shaken by the two crises.

The administration then retaliated with a mixture of diplomatic and police initiatives which reflected a renewed obsession with internal security. An agreement with Tokyo, which secured the expulsion of all Vietnamese nationalists from Japan, was signed in July 1908; and in Indochina a thoroughgoing campaign of repression resulted in the execution or imprisonment of those nationalists who could be identified and seized. The itinerant fundraisers of the Viet-Nam Cong Hien Hoi were pursued with particularly bitter persistence in order to starve the nascent nationalist movement of resources.

The Governor-Generalship of Antony Klobukowski, 1908–1910.

Since the onset of the anti-clerical campaign at the turn of the century, the political activities of the mission had fallen under official suspicion. Missionaries had long been suspected of pursuing influence over the Vietnamese emperor at Hue by seeking conversion of members of the royal family and high officials; and by 1907 the French administration knew for certain that in 1889 a catechist had secretly obtained the baptism of the emperor Thanh Thai during an illness before his elevation to the throne. Though Thanh Thai had long since shrugged off any spiritual allegiance to the mission, he had occasionally allowed Vietnamese Catholics to reach positions of influence at court, as in 1906, when a former catechist, Nguyen Huu Bai, was appointed imperial

Minister of Works. When Thanh Thai was deposed by the Resident-Superior Sarrien of Annam in 1907 on the grounds of insanity, the pro-missionary Avenir du Tonkin infuriated Governor-General Beau by directing a barrage of criticism against Sarrien. The mission subsequently acted as a channel for transmitting finance for Thanh Thai's ensuing press campaign in France. By the time that Governor-General Klobukowski arrived to take up office in 1908, the administration was actively searching for further signs of missionary political agitation: missionary participation in press controversy, and missionary attitudes towards the involvement of converts in Vietnamese nationalism became the issues of principle concern.

Recently initiated as a freemason, Governor-General Klobukowski was also, incongruously, a Catholic. Tepid in all his ideological loyalties, he was a pragmatist temporising for political survival. A son-in-law of Paul Bert, he repeatedly proclaimed his religious neutrality in language of which Bert would have approved: he left France proclaiming to the Mission Laïque that 'clericalism is not for export'; and on arrival in Tonkin, he told Bishop Gendreau that 'Anti-clericalism is not for export'. Klobukowski's attitude to the missions remained in the balance during the early period of his governor-generalship. Essentially he wanted to pacify religious wrangling, but his temporising conformism could well have led him to respond to Radical pressures and turn against the colony's clerical establishment.

In Indochina recent press controversies, including that between Pâris and Fr Guerlach, had been followed by the mission's purchase of shares in the influential Hanoi newspaper the Avenir du Tonkin. This move had strengthened the impression that the mission was gearing itself up for a press war against Radical influences **(Doc. 172)**. At a briefing in Paris before taking up his appointment, Klobukowski was warned to expect a campaign of political criticism from the pro-missionary press **(Docs 171-2)**, and he arrived at Saigon convinced of missionary sedition. Determined to suppress it, he uttered a prompt and particularly strong warning to the bishop of Saigon, Mgr Mossard, to refrain from involvement in political controversy **(Doc. 173)**.

Within a year of Klobukowski's arrival the administration's worst fears as to the mission's subversive tendencies seemed to be confirmed with the discovery by the Resident of Vinh that three Vietnamese priests of the vicariate of South Tonkin had been had been deeply implicated in fundraising for the exiled nationalist Viet-Nam Cong Hien Hoi **(Doc. 175)**. Investigation of the case had cast considerable suspicion on the political loyalties the local bishop, Mgr Pineau: the three Vietnamese priests implicated had occupied important positions in

Pineau's household, and it seemed inconceivable that the elderly prelate could have been ignorant of their political activities. The significance of the case was variously interpreted. Some officials minimised the affair in view of its apparently exceptional character. For others, Radical opinion seemed triumphantly vindicated: here was evidence that the political loyalty of Vietnamese Christians to France was in doubt, and that missionaries were far from being the patriotic force they claimed to be (**Doc. 177**). Klobukowski, however, had been impressed by the fact that a group of French missionaries in Mgr Pineau's vicariate had been helpful in gathering evidence of the conspiracy for the provincial authorities. This was the aspect of the affair which he stressed in his telegram to Paris (see **Doc. 177**). The Directors of the Société des Missions Etrangères cooperated anxiously to smooth over the incident. Denounced by a group of his own missionaries, Mgr Pineau was abruptly retired and his vicariate temporarily transferred to a bishop in whom the French administration had particular confidence, Mgr Gendreau, bishop of West Tonkin (**Docs 174–6**).

So the mission ended by earning considerable political credit with the French authorities for their handling of the Pineau case (**Docs 175–6**). By using the opportunity to stress their anxiety to act as a force for the social control of the large and growing Vietnamese minority, French missionaries, particularly Bishop Gendreau, lent weight to the arguments urged by some officials on their behalf for leaving the mission's legal and propertyholding status undisturbed. The mission further capitalised on the fact that the Pineau affair turned out not to have been an exceptional case of Christian involvement in the nationalist movement. Over the following five years evidence continued to accumulate that fundraising by other Vietnamese Christians, some of them ex-catechists – was continuing. The administration deduced from the size of the donations being collected without signs of pressure or resistance from the Christian community, that Christian sympathy for the nationalist cause was widespread – at least in the perenially disturbed provinces of northern Annam. The inference drawn by Resident-Superior Groleau of Annam was that more reliance should be placed on the French clergy to recall Christians into alignment with the aims of French rule (**Doc. 178**).

By the time Klobukowski left Indochina in 1910 he had become convinced of the need to handle the religious question with particular circumspection. The authorities in Annam advised playing down the issue of Vietnamese Catholic involvement in nationalism in order to muffle the local repercussions of recent incidents; and Klobukowski himself minimised the issue in reports to the Ministry, possibly to avoid giving Radical opinion food for polemic. Meantime, in one of his final recommendations, he mounted a subtle and covert defence of the mission's interests in the property question. He put up a series of somewhat transparent objections to the application of the Law of 1901 to Cochinchina and Cambodia, and recommended that the whole issue should be kept in abeyance **(Doc. 181).** If Klobukowski finally came down on the side of the missions in the controversy over the application of the Law of 1901, this seems to have been because threat to French security from Vietnamese nationalism had considerably enhanced the value of missionary collaboration.

Further reading

W.J. Duiker, **The Rise of Nationalism in Vietnam, 1900–1941.** (Cornell U.P. 1976).

D.G. Marr, **Vietnamese Anticolonialism, 1885–1925.** (London, U.of California Press, 1971).

Nguyen The-Anh, 'L'élite intellectuelle vietnamienne et le fait colonial dans les premières années du XXe siècle', **Revue française d'Histoire d'Outre-mer,** LXXII (1985) No.268, pp. 291-307.

R.B. Smith, 'The development of opposition to French rule in Southern Vietnam, 1880–1940', **Past and Present,** 54, Feb. 1972 pp. 95-105.

P. Chack, **Hoang-Tham, pirate.** (Paris, 1933).

Nguyen The-Anh, 'L'abdication de Thanh-Thai', **Bulletin de l'Ecole Française d'Extrême-Orient,** LXIV, pp. 257-264.

Documents

170. Acting Governor-General **Bonhoure** to Governor-General **Klobukowski.** Hanoi, 3 July 1908.

Since Japan's success, the outlook of asiatics has been transformed. A national revival is getting stronger among an Annamese elite and ambitions provoked by the beginnings of ill-directed western education have developed among our former collaborators. Whether scholar-patriots or discontented interpreters, these agitators are hurrying to change the face of things. The population in general has not yet begun to move; but it is being worked upon, and it has to be admitted that our methods, our taxes (much more by their form than by the amounts imposed) give troublemakers some rather good opportunities for mobilising the people... **(A.O.M.** Paris. Papiers d'Agent PA9, Papiers Sarraut. Carton 1.)

171. Report to the Minister for the Colonies of a meeting at the Colonial Ministry between former Governor - General **Beau**, Governor - General **Klobukowski** and M. **Vasselle**, Political Director. Paris. 1 July 1908.

The religious orders have been trying for some time, under cover of the Catholic missions, to gain control of the most important publicity organs of the Protectorates.... The Mission is plainly showing its intention of excercising a political influence over public opinion.... Following recent events the attitude of the Catholic natives has been extremely suspect, and it has been established that they have supported the reformist (nationalist) agitation.... (A.N.S.O.M. Paris. Papiers d'Agent PA9, Papiers Sarraut. Carton 1.)

172. Acting Governor-General **Bonhoure** to Governor-General **Antony Klobukowski**. Saigon, 12 August 1908.

I have to... notify you of an impression which I am receiving more and more clearly, but for which I cannot furnish any proof. I note that it is shared by all sincere Republicans around me.... I have the feeling that the Mission is undertaking a conscious press campaign. (The Mission) has been trying more and more to buy up newspapers and to play an obliquely oppositional role against France. Although I have always been a very resolute Republican and freethinker, I do not feel I am an out and out hammer of the clergy, and I have never followed a militant policy in the colonies where metropolitan controversies do not arouse great passion. But I believe I can observe today in Indochina those clerical forces which have been defeated in Europe trying to create problems for us and relishing our colonial difficulties. If we are to be chased out (of Indochina) the missions would themselves be attacked by the Annamese people, and I doubt whether any Vicar Apostolic here is thinking of becoming a Mgr de Béhaine to a new Gia Long. Nonetheless despite this objection and although Mgr Gendreau at Hanoi has given us some good advice at times (but he is not at the head of it: there are the Fr Artifs and the Fr Lecornus), the anti-French (tendency) of the work seems certain. The pleasure of revenge, the hope that we might ask for their help and that we will cease to apply the registration laws - these perhaps are the motives for it; and they probably think that a reaction will occur in France before catastrophe strikes them in Indochina, a reaction which the missions might benefit from in Indochina as elsewhere..... M. Beau, if I am not mistaken, thought the same before he left. (A.N.S.O.M. Paris. Indochine, (N.F.) 32/(451))

173. Governor-General **Klobukowski** to M. **Milliès-Lacroix,** Minister for the Colonies. Saigon, 7 October 1908.

... I thought it useful to put before you a document which bears out the accuracy of the information conveyed by my predecessors M. Paul Beau and M. Bonhoure about the part being played in politics locally by certain Catholic missionaries.

I may add that on receiving a visit recently from the Bishop of Saigon, Mgr Mossard, I asked this prelate in the presence of M. Bonhoure, if it was true that the Mission was involving itself in politics. I remarked that such an attitude would be plainly contrary to its interests. 'I have no partisan bias, you know,' I told him. 'The Republican government does not follow an anti-religious policy: it respects freedom of thought and conscience, but since it bears full responsibility for our operations in Indochina it will not allow its efforts at harmonising French and native goodwill to be obstructed. So if the missions deploy against us the means of influence which they have acquired in Indochina, we will be forced to take a strong line. For my own part I would be very sorry if things came to such a pass, for in all the different posts I have held I have never found myself in conflict with the missions to whom I have always shown the goodwill which the Republican government and its representatives owe to all French citizens. However, I would not hesitate to notify the Colonial Minister of the serious repercussions which could occur in present circumstances of the Catholic missions constantly and actively interfere in our business as if they wished to wreak in our colonies their revenge for the policy which, it is said, they reproach the French government for instituting in France.'

Bishop Mossard protested vigorously. He assured me of his absolute respect for Authority.

'I assure you,' he said, 'that none of the missionaries directly under my orders, is involved in local politics and that they only have one desire: to serve the influence and interests of France to the best of their ability. If there are any missionaries involved in politics they are not under my authority.'

By these words the bishop plainly meant the Reverend Fr Artif who is, in fact, under the authority of Procurator Robert (Far Eastern Procurator-General of the Missions Etrangères).

I have reason to believe that Bishop Mossard is being sincere. He is much esteemed here and his attitude has never given rise, at least openly, to criticism. He is, moreover, intelligent enough to take account of the considerable difficulties which a tactic of abandoning their hitherto beneficial neutrality would cause for the mission....

Fr **Artif**, Procurator of the S.M.E. at Saigon, to Governor-General
Klobukowski. Saigon, 3 October 1908.

As for the newspapers which the missionaries have helped to found, these
are solely instruments for defence. Once the persistent and perfidious
assault on us stops, the missions will no longer have recourse to the
press.   While the attack lasts the right of self-defence cannot be
denied without turning (the missions) and   their   million   native
Christians into a class of parias.

Moreover a newspaper cannot exist without taking account of politics,
otherwise it will have no readers.   Hence it is necessary that
newspapers interested in the work of the missions should take their part
in the struggles of the day.

In the battle of ideas these organs will always be decidedly in
support of the established order and of any liberal and strong
government. (A.N.S.O.M. Paris. Indochine (N.F.) 32/451)

174.   Fr **A.J. Klingler** and nine missionary co-signatories from the
vicariate of South Tonkin, to the **Directors** of the S.M.E.   Bao
Nham, 17 October 1909.

I am in conscience bound to break silence. The harm that has ensued
(from the Pineau affair) is already immense, and it is impossible to
predict all the further damage not only to our own mission but to all
the Indochina missions that will follow.... It is highly probable that
the person (Mgr Pineau) who, by his silence, his incompetance and, I
might add, his complicity, bears much responsibility for what has
happened, will now try to divert the blame from himself as usual.... I
sincerely hope you will make haste to apply the only possible remedy for
these misfortunes by removing their cause. (A.S.M.E. Vol. 710, (Tonkin
Mériodional, 1881-1920.), No. 229)

175.   M. **Groleau,** Resident-Superior of Annam, to Governor-General
Picquié. Hue, 11 February 1911.

The leaders of the (nationalist) movement... went so far as to enrol in
their party several native priests or catechists of Nghe-Tinh province
by making promises of future support, avowals of friendship and no doubt
offering compromises of a more material kind.   Through (these priests)
the (nationalist) party obtained extensive political influence over the

Catholic portion of the population of this region. This (Catholic) community is one which we least expected to see join up with the representatives of a party which had always been hostile to them, and which was exclusively made up of enemies of its caste and religion, a party which had once been its persecutors and might be so again. Through the medium of these priests they spread effective propaganda against us among the Catholics. Large subscriptions were levied whose purpose was plainly understood by their contributors: they went to swell the resources of the Cuong De party.

Three of these native priests, all of them resident at the seat of the bishopric of South Tonkin, Xa Doai, were arrested on 12 June 1909 by the Resident of Vinh. They were charged with having dealings with our political enemies, particularly Cuong De and Phan Boi Chau, both exiled in Japan, and with their agents.

They were condemned by the regular tribunal of the province to nine years of forced labour and deported to Poulo Condore. This sentence and those handed down to their accomplices served as a grave warning to the Catholic inhabitants who had rallied round the rebel party.... These measures deprived our opponents of a very valuable source of moral and pecuniary support.

The French missionaries and several native priests did not hesitate to provide the Resident of Vinh with all the information they possessed. Their attitude in this affair shows that even if the harm was already widespread, it was not irremediable. It was also shown that the native Catholic population had merely followed their native spiritual leaders in the usual fashion without always understanding exactly where they were being led.

The bishop at Xa Doai (South Tonkin), Mgr <u>Pineau</u>, an aged and timorous prelate whose role in this affair seems always to have been to look for excuses for the faults of his native subordinates, left for France a few months later. His temporary replacement was Mgr Gendreau who for many years has shown proof of enlightened patriotism and absolute loyalty. This has had the effect of restoring among the Catholic population of North Annam the sentiments of loyalty and attachment which it has always shown. These feelings have been manifested on many previous occasions, notably during the events of 1908. It would appear to be sound policy on our part to strive to sustain them.... (A.O.M. Aix. Indochine, G.G. FO3 (57))

176. M. **Labbez**, Resident at Nghe An, to M. **Groleau**, Resident-Superior of Annam. Nghe An, 28 December 1909.

... Mgr Gendreau will demonstrate his patriarchal authority by more firmly patriotic directives than those of his predecessor. He will take a much profounder view of the real interests of the Mission. These are, at the moment, bound up on essential points with those of the Protectoral government. The hierarchy well understands what irreparable damage the Mission would suffer if it ever gave the appearance of association with the enemies of public order and of France. From the government the Mission would no longer be able to expect the benevolent liberality which has allowed it to prosper and develop. The French priests would lose an authority over native Catholics from which some of the latter are trying to shake free. Even from a strictly religious point of view the destruction of their moral ascendency would be harmful. The Catholic community is in total disarray at the moment. The culpable activity of some of its members and the sanctions which this has provoked have created an atmosphere of embarassment and ambiguity between native Catholics on the one hand and French missionaries and the bishopric on the other. The feeling of reciprocal mistrust which has developed can only end by arousing widespread discontent. The government has as strong an interest as the mission in seeing it end. No doubt it will disperse under Mgr Gendreau's influence: he will restore confidence and unity to his flock. The nomination of this prelate... proves that the government can rely on the cooperation of the Mission for its work of defence and sterilisation. (A.O.M. Aix. Indochine, G.G. F03 (56))

177. Reaction in the French Radical press. **La Lanterne,** 3 July 1909.

In the cable addressed to the government by M.Klobukowski, it is said, apparently, that the missionaries gave 'loyal support' in this situation to the local authorities.

We want to believe it, but how can this be when these missionaries have shown us no loyalty for so long? Were they not in a position to cut short the agitations of their disciples from the outset? Could they not have anticipated these agitations? Could they not have used their very natural influence over these native ecclesiastics - who were probably former students of the mission - to set them back on the proper course? And if their persuasion was unavailing, could they not at least have warned the administration in time?

Whatever the attitude of the missionaries has been in the course of this enquiry, we can see yet again what religious proselytism can lead to in our colonies. Here there are missions where the French priests are neighbours to the Spanish; missions which enjoy exorbitant privileges; missions which draw to themselves, on pretext of conversion, the least respectable natives; missions which even seek to set up a native clergy there, whose favourite disciples are in league with insurgents, and who even foment revolt themselves! O! The black cassock is the same everywhere. You can expect intrigue and treason wherever it appears.

178. M. **Groleau,** Resident-Superior of Annam, to Governor-General **Picquié.** Hue, 18 October 1910.

Enquiries already made confirm our information about the attitude of native Christians towards us. Those who are of some account by reason of their wealth, their social position or their education - in a word those who are at all well known - are hostile to us. It is doubtful whether we could overcome this attitude by resorting to force, and whether arrests and sanctions would have any other effect than to transform those we condemn into religious and patriotic martyrs. The French clergy must apply itself to reviving the loyalty of native catholics and put the priests of this race in their proper place: (Vietnamese priests) have become far too independent in Nghe An. This is a long term task which should test the patriotism of the missionaries of the apostolic vicariate of South Tonkin. **(A.O.M. Aix. Indochine, G.G. FO3 (56))**

179. M. **Groleau,** Resident-Superior of Annam, to Governor-General **Picquié.** Hue, 11 February 1911.

The arrest and condemnation of the three native priests of Xa-Doai did not cause much reaction. Moreover it was desirable not to make too much fuss about an unexpected act which seemed to rally to the cause of the rebellion elements which one never expected to see join it. Greater publicity would have stirred up public opinion over this incident, spreading surprise and foreboding. One would, moreover, have risked giving offence and arousing mistrust among the Catholic populations in Vinh province and the surrounding area. These number, for North Annam, more than three hundred thousand adherents. It would have caused great difficulty if we had seemed to be casting vague suspicion on this whole community. It seemed preferable to keep it under close but essentially discreet surveillance....
(A.O.M. Aix. Indochine, G.G. FO3 (57))

180.   M. **Sestier,** Resident-Superior of Annam. Report to the Governor-General for the third quarter of 1911.

(Certain emigrés, the majority of them former seminarists) Gia-Chau, Gia-Khanh,and Chan, have returned to Annam and are finding among their co-religionists enough support to allow them to evade all our investigations.   I think, on this point, I should report the systematic opposition to the administration shown by the Catholic community of Nghe Tinh, opposition which is, in the circumstances, anti-patriotic (sic) to say the least.
  Thanks to their support and information Gia-Chau and Gia-Khanh may be considered our most dangerous enemies, but it is painful to note that their influence would fast evaporate if the mission in Nghe An wanted to give us its full cooperation.... **(A.O.M. Aix. Indochine, G.G. FO3 (57))**

181.   **M. Dalmas,** Director of Personnel, Ministry of the Colonies. Paris, February 1910.

NOTE

M. Klobukowski has... told us that he considers that the moment has not yet come to promulgate the laws of 1901 and 1904 in Indochina.
  He thinks it would be impolitic to make a distinction in this matter between natives and Europeans, and he thinks it would be dangerous to promulgate a measure to give natives an unreserved right to transform their secret societies into legal associations.
  As far as chapter III (of the law of 1901) relating to religious orders is concerned, M. Klobukowski notes that, if the government decides to proceed, it can only be promulgated after the completion of the inventory procedure currently in hand.   This will be a long task because of the absence of a cadastral survey.   He noted moreover that it should be applied to all confessions (Christian, Buddhist etc.) which will not fail to provoke a movement of discontent among the natives. The property used for worship by all confessions is communal property and does not belong to the religious orders, and he is apprehensive of the effects of a measure for which the agreement of the governments of Annam and Cambodia probably cannot be obtained.
  The Governor-General has spoken to the Prime Minister about this matter.   **(A.N.S.O.M. Paris, Indoch. AF Carton 29 A90 (15))**

Radical opinion in the colony was not deterred by the recent internal crisis from pressing its attack on the missions **(Doc. 182)**. Moreover, as a result of an electoral change its pressure could now take more effective political form. The Parliamentary elections of 1910 removed the colony's Centre-Left deputy, François Deloncle, and brought in a Radical-Socialist as Deputy for the Cochinchina seat. Paul Pâris (probably no relation of Camille Pâris), was a mason of the Reveil d'Orient lodge and a fervent anti-clerical. During the election he had accused Deloncle of courting missionary support in previous elections and of opposing the application of the 'lois de laïcité' in the colony. Upon his election Pâris formed the Comité Républicain Radical et Radical-Socialiste de Cochinchine, with the slogan 'défense laïque' as a prominent element in its programme. He had declared in his manifesto that his political strategy for procuring change would be to accumulate parliamentary backing to lobby French colonial ministers on all issues affecting the colony. This approach resulted in a series of insistant reminders to colonial ministers from Radical deputies that the Law of 1901 should be applied promptly in Indochina.

While Pâris and his political associates in France continued to revive inter-departmental debate on this issue, the top echelon of the Indochina administration also displayed greater energy in pressing for the application of the Law of 1901. Acting Governors-General Picquié **(Doc. 183)** and Luce, both enthusiastic masons, appealed in 1910 for the law to be extended to Indochina; and when Albert Sarraut, a leading light of southern Radicalism was appointed Governor-General in July, 1911 the missionary cause on the property question seemed to be finally doomed.

However during the long period of delay from 1911-1914, reactions from the less senior administrators directly responsible for its implementation seem to have been evenly balanced. Some of them appear to have deployed practical objections to combat arguments of principle: the lack of a full cadastral survey, for instance, created problems in locating and registering mission property in Cochinchina and were said to be holding up arrangements for applying the law **(Docs 184-5)**. To judge from his private papers Sarraut himself seems to have taken little interest in this issue, contrary to expectations. Although in mid-1913, under ministerial pressure provoked by Pâris, Sarraut promised to proceed more rapidly with arrangements for carrying the law into effect in Cochinchina and Cambodia, nothing further had been done by

August 1914 when the outbreak of the First World War diverted attention to the national crisis in France.

The onset of the First World War brought the Radical onslaught on the Catholic Church to an abrupt halt both in France and in Indochina. The acrimony and virulence of the debate evaporated in the face of a war crisis in which all political groups rallied to Poincaré's call for an 'Union sacré' - the pooling of all domestic differences in the face of German invasion. By the time the war ended, missionaries and colonial administrators were to find that pre-war assumptions scarcely applied in the new condition of things.

Documents

182.   F. C. 'L'oeuvre des missions Catholiques en Indochine'.

It is a fact well known in Hanoi that the prettiest types have been brought together at the (mission's) sewing school: it is a sort of distribution centre. In a word, the mission sells the more beautiful slant-eyed girls....

Smugglers themselves, the missionaries have opium smugglers released from custody and split the profits with them....

The fruitless campaign of pursuit for De Tham, the reappearance of piracy the conspiracies breaking out everywhere, all are a flagrant consequence of our tolerance of the missions.

...The thinking masses of Indochina have been provoked to defiance of us by the fanaticism and commercialism of Portuguese, Spanish and French missionaries who have trampled their most ancient traditions underfoot.... (L'Acacia, vol. 17, No. 12. December 1911, pp. 776-86.)

183.   Acting Governor-General Picquié to G. Trouillot, Minister for the Colonies. Hanoi, 10 June 1910.

(I wish) to call your attention urgently to the necessity for extending the application of the law of 1901 to the colonies and particularly to Indochina, where the order of the Missions Etrangères already possesses an immense amount of rural property whose acquisition and operation are in no way managed for the purposes of worship but for agricultural and industrial exploitation.... I consider that it would be useful to proceed without delay in this matter in view of the increasing economic power with which the Catholic mission of Tonkin, Annam and Cochinchina are underpinning their moral authority.... (A.N.S.O.M. Paris. Indochine, (A.F.) 29/A90 (16).)

184. **J. Bosc,** Director of Political and Native Affairs: Note for the Governor-General, 21 June 1912.

Moreover it is doubtful whether the Law on Associations (1901) would encounter strong opposition on the part of native catholics. The Annamese population cannot be roused over a matter which will not affect them, and no demonstration will occur unless the mission itself stirs up opinion in native quarters. Such an agitation would impose a grave responsibility upon those who provoke it and the authorities would certainly receive enough warning to stop a movement developing.

In all, from a political point of view it seems that the obstacles to applying the law... of 1901 can be easily overcome.... (A.O.M. Aix. Indochine, G.G. 9,097.)

185. Procurator-General **Simoni:** Note for the Governor-General. Saigon, 4 July 1912.

This law (of 1901) was not declared applicable to the colonies. Senator Decrais, Minister for the Colonies, declared in the Chamber during the course of the parliamentary discussion:

For many reasons of a political or diplomatic nature the government thinks that, in the present state of things, the law should not be applied to our colonies and especially not to our colonies of domination, our recently acquired possessions in Oceania, Asia and Africa.... The law which the Chamber will vote upon is not designed for the colonies; it does not apply to them, and its silence on this point is perfectly clear. Nothing is to change in the regime affecting them....

(A.N.S.O.M. Paris. Papiers d'Agent P.A.9, Sarraut papers. Carton 13.)

186. Mgr **Mossard,** Bishop of Médéa, Vicar Apostolic of West Cochinchina. Concerning the Law on Religious Associations. Saigon, 8 June 1912.

As conceived and drawn up, this law, as everyone knows, is a weapon which they can use to wound or kill at will. Those who are currently asking for it to be applied want it to be the instrument of our extinction. When the decree is applied, these same men will be there to supervise its execution and to ensure that the weapon wounds before killing....

...On the day when the law is applied the work of (winning the loyalty of the Annamese to France through Catholicism) will be halted. The Annamese will not understand any more why the French treat their enemies as friends and their friends as enemies. It could even happen that a new sort of development might begin in the other direction. The Catholic part of the population could return to the exclusionist ideas of its race and follow the anti-foreign movement.... (A.S.M.E. Vol. 757, (Cochinchine Orientale, 1890-1920). No.1)

VII

EPILOGUE

THE GROWTH OF VIETNAMESE NATIONALISM, AND ITS IMPLICATIONS FOR THE MISSION, 1919-1924.

The First World War transformed political attitudes to religious questions in France. The clergy of the the Catholic Church, given ample opportunity to manifest its patriotism in wartime conditions, won political credit with the Centre and Left for its contribution to the conflict. Postwar parliamentary discussion of legislation affecting the Catholic Church led to the revocation or suspension of some of the measures of the early 1900s, particularly those affecting the religious orders. In Indochina, although anticlerical feeling revived periodically in milder form, the general debate on applying the 1901 legislation never resumed. Nor were any further efforts made locally to restrict the acquisition of land and other property by the mission.

On the contrary, as Vietnamese nationalist groups multiplied in the 1920s, the colonial administration showed greater concern than ever before to court the mission politically in the hope of isolating the Catholic Vietnamese community from nationalist influences **(Doc. 189)**. In this connection, a major change in the missionary policy of the Vatican seemed particularly ominous to the French colonial establishment. Prior to the war, the Holy See had tolerated and even supported the political collaboration of missionaries with colonial regimes. But in 1919, through the encyclical Maximum illud, Pope Benedict XV directed missionaries in European colonies to divest themselves of their secular political loyalties. The papal encyclical also encouraged the nationalism of native Christians by proclaiming an imminent transfer of canonical authority from missionary bishops to national clergies in the colonies **(Doc. 187)**. Although the Superior of the Société des Missions Etrangères greeted the papal directive with apparent enthusiasm **(Doc. 188)** the encyclical posed particular difficulties for missionaries in Indochina: the overwhelming majority of them were French, and their political sympathies inevitably conflicted with the burgeoning nationalist loyalties of their own congregations.

Hence the changes in France produced by the war, the spread of Vietnamese nationalism, and the new papal policy came, in combination, to create a new ambiguity in the political role of the Catholic mission in Indochina. To a colonial government preoccupied by the growth of nationalism and no longer embarrassed by the pressures of Radical anti-clericalism, the Catholic mission had gained in significance as a potential auxiliary sustaining the apparatus of French rule. It was needed more than ever as a mechanism for the social isolation and political direction of its own congregations. Yet, paradoxically, with the political loyalty of the French mission now inhibited and uncertain, Catholic missionaries seemed to be losing their political value at the very moment that the French authorities needed them most.

Further reading

Adrien Dansette, **Histoire religieuse de la France contemporaine,** II, (Paris, 1948).

J.R. Clémentin, 'Le comportement politique des institutions catholiques au Vietnam', in J. Chesneaux, G. Boudarel et D. Hémery, **Tradition et révolution au Vietnam.** (Paris, Anthropos, 1971).

P. Grandjean, **Le statut légal des missions catholiques et protestantes en Indochine française.** (Paris, Recueil Sirey, 1939).

Documents

176. Pope **Benedict XV.** Encyclical <u>Maximum illud</u>. Rome, 30 November 1919.

INDIGENOUS CLERGY

The education and organisation of indigenous clergy should be one of the principal concerns of every mission director. The native priest who is attached to his flock by everything - birth, mentality, outlook, ideals - is wonderfully equipped to acquaint souls with the Truth. More than any other, he knows how to open doors into their hearts. That is how he can obtain easy access to many souls which the foreign priest cannot reach.

<u>Education.</u> It should be full, perfect and complete in all the branches which it covers, the same even as that which priests of civilised countries receive.

<u>Utility.</u> (Indigenous clergy) should not merely be destined to serve as helpers in the humbler functions of the ministry any more than foreign missionaries.

<u>Leadership.</u> They, too, should be allowed to take in hand the direction of their flocks one day.

It is regrettable that, despite this wish on the part of Sovereign Pontiffs, countries awakened for centuries to the Catholic faith still

...s lacking a clergy worthy of the name.

MISSIONARY PRIESTS

Remember that you have a kingdom to build, not of men, but of Christ....
(The missionary) represents the interests of Christ and in no way those
of his own nation.... How sad to see missionaries forget the dignity of
their office and preoccupy themselves more with the interests of their
country than those of Heaven, and show unseemly enthusiasm for the
development of the power of their country and its expansion and glory
above everything else!

Such attitudes are like a plague in the Apostleship.

Suppose that the missionary lets himself be partly guided by human
opinion and that instead of behaving always like a true apostle, he
shows an equal concern to serve the interests of his country. All his
actions would immediately be discredited in the eyes of the population,
which will easily come to think that Christianity is only the religion
of a particular foreign power and that to become Christian is apparently
to accept the supervision and dominance of a foreign power and reject
one's own country...

188.   Mgr **de Guébriant**, Superior of the S.M.E. Lecture to the
        Institut Catholique de Paris. Paris, February 1924.

...the French missionary more than any other, because of the tact
characteristic of his race, is not a pioneer for any nationality. He is
a pioneer for God.... So the role of the missionary is not to blaze a
trail for colonial empire builders: the profit which (his country) may
derive from him should be found on a higher plane...esteem, respect,
sympathy, confidence - that is what the French missionary earns for
France, no more and no less. (Direction des Affaires Politiques et
Indigènes. Report: Les Missions Catholiques en Indochine. 1 October,
1924. A.O.M. (Paris). Indochine 198/ NF1475 (1))

189.   **Direction des Affaires Politiques et Indigènes.** Report on the
        missions in Indochina. 1 October 1924.

... Although profoundly obedient and devoted to their pastors, native
Catholics, and particularly Annamese Catholics, would prefer control of
the churches not to be reserved exclusively for European clergy. They
think that Annamese priests could and should be given the highest
positions in the ecclesiastical hierarchy. This aspiration is merely an

expression of the nationalist sentiments beginning ... ...
Catholic community, which until now has remained impervio...
of 'Young Annam'.

Without the knowledge of their bishops, Annamese pries... ...e
transmitted their complaints to the Holy See. H.E. Nguyen Hu... Bai,
(Catholic Minister of the Interior and of Finance for Annam), in the
course of a conversation with the Sovereign Pontiff in May 1922, acted
as their spokesman....

H.E. Bai's intrigues would not be dangerous if they were intended
merely to satisfy his pride, but instead they serve the purposes of the
Prefect of the Sacred Congregation of the Propaganda Fide: van
Rossum. ... Among Catholics (Cardinal van Rossum) is understood to be
hostile to France.

...To flatter the nationalist sentiment of the Indochinese population,
Van Rossum submitted for papal approval a decree giving native clergy
equivalent status to European clergy.... He has (also) ordered the
heads of missions to raise the standard of training in the seminaries so
that the education of native clergy should be in no way inferior to that
of European priests and laymen. He now demands the participation of
native priests in the election of bishops purely in order to facilitate
their own election to the episcopate.

Following his line of thinking, and interpreting the ideas of Rome,
Mgr de Guébriant said at Lyon on 3 May 1922:

'It is time to regard as being imminent, if not immediate, the
changeover which, by progressive stages - sooner in some countries and
later, much later, in others - will result in the substitution of a
normal complement of native - or, if you prefer, national - clergy, for
the missionary establishment....'

....Confronted by the continual development of official education in
Indochina, the Catholic Church has sensed the necessity of conforming to
the needs of the moment in order to keep as strong a hold over native
Catholics as in the past....

Whatever our policy in Indochina may be, it would be reasonable to go
on making use of this docile but powerful force in the best interests of
the colony. While assuring the Catholic church of the liberty which she
enjoys by virtue of the treaties, it seems possible to give her in
Indochina a legal status that would assist her social and evangelical
role without harm to relations between Church and State in France
(provided that the administration retains enough control) to
temper...any possible collaboration between Rome and native Catholic
nationalists.... (A.O.M.(Paris) Indochine 198/NF 1475(1))

CONTEMPORARY PERCEPTIONS OF MISSIONARY PROSELYTISM.

The role of French domination in encouraging conversions.

From the late seventeenth century to the arrival of Admiral Rigault de Genouilly's naval expedition in the mid-nineteenth century the Christian community in Vietnam developed slowly, doubling from approximately 200,000 in 1682 to over 400,000 by 1860. Then in the mere half century of French colonial expansion before 1914 the Christian population, according to missionary statistics, more than doubled again to approximately 870,000 (Spanish vicariates included). Demographic increase played some part in this growth, but missionaries explained their success mainly in terms of rising rates of conversion of adult non-Christians. The precondition for accelerated rates of conversion was the despatch of increasing numbers of missionary personnel to Vietnam by the S.M.E. from the 1840s onwards. The training by these missionaries of still larger numbers of native priests and catechists – the essential medium for contacting potential converts and for running Christian communes – had further exponential effects. There were other important factors involved in procuring conversions, but contemporary perceptions of their significance varied. Administrators and missionaries differed particularly in their assessment of the importance of French political rule as an encouragement to conversion.

In explaining the growth of the missions, French administrators gave the problem little thought and tended to assume a simple identification between expanding French rule and rising conversions (Doc. 190). Missionaries did not deny a general correlation, but some considered that French domination also counteracted the work of the mission in important ways. Bishop Miche for instance complained of the damage done to Christian proselytism by the spread of the colony's 'impious' system of lay education (Doc. 45); and Mgrs Colombert and Depierre considered that disappointing conversion rates in West Cochinchina were in part a consequence of the degraded morality and seductive materialism of the French colonial presence, a refrain commonly heard in this vicariate since Lefevre's time (Docs. 25, 28-29, 192). Bishop Marcou of Maritime Tonkin fully conceded that the prestige conferred on missionaries by French domination had been of general benefit in procuring conversions before the 1900s, but he also suggested that the recent anti-clerical campaign of the Radicals had destroyed this advantage. He could not complain that anti-clerical influences had created formal hindrances to missionary work however. As his own dealings with the administration in

1903-4 over the Quang Hoa case show, senior officials restricted proselytism only in instances where it threatened to cause serious political or social disruption **(Docs. 193-5.** See also **Doc. 196).**

Whatever their reservations as to the broader impact of French colonialism upon christianisation, most missionaries assigned prime emphasis to the importance of local conditions in explaining success or disappointment in the drive for converts. Wide variations in economic conditions, and the diversity of political, cultural and administrative traditions across the region were reflected in contrasting rates of conversion between vicariates. In parts of West Cochinchina for instance, the phenomenon of rural nomadism made it difficult for missionaries to hold on to new converts and retarded the development of Christian communes. In Cambodia, a vicariate of hinduised culture, progress among the Khmer was likewise slow. Here missionaries were operating in a Theravadan Buddhist milieu which offered considerable ideological resistance to Christian proselytism; and so the mission made headway mainly among immigrant communities. Further North on the other hand, the over-populated coastline of the Red river delta in Tonkin, and the perenially impoverished provinces of Nghe An and Thanh Hoa in North Annam provided more promising opportunities for conversion, particularly in times of political disturbance or during periods of famine. Here the vicariates of Central, Maritime and South Tonkin showed intermittantly rapid rates of expansion before 1914.

Proselytism and its political repercussions in the village commune.

The motives of adult non-Christians in accepting conversion were usually material rather than spiritual **(Docs 197-8)**, as missionaries themselves frequently acknowledged. Missionaries therefore depended heavily upon a complex of primarily economic strategies designed to provide refuge for the destitute, the socially marginalised, and those under bureaucratic or political pressure. Where possible the mission tended to segregate converts into self-supporting chrétientés. But many converts remained in their ancestral villages after accepting Christianity. They expected missionaries to support them in family and village quarrels, to mediate effectively with French administration in suits and disputes, and to support Christian factions in competition for resources and social power within the commune. Hence at the village level, christianisation could become a political as much as a social and economic process, as Bishop Mossard conceded in his Annual Report for 1908: 'Almost always the isolated conversion of one individual upsets a whole village; and when there is a wave of conversions affecting a certain number of families, it assumes the importance of a political act.' Some of the social and economic implications of such conversions for the rest of a Vietnamese family or community are instanced by the captain of the Duchaffaut (**Doc. 104**), and by Governor-General de Lanessan, who tended to stress the socially and culturally disruptive consequences of aggressive proselytism (**Doc. 199**).

But conversion to Christianity was not always actively or aggressively procured by missionaries and their catechists. Non-Christian groups already pursuing longstanding social rivalries within their communes sometimes resorted to conversion as a useful political option, with the result that missionaries could find themselves caught up in apparently sectarian disputes which had an essentially non-religious basis. An apt illustration of this is the Moc-Hoa case of 1895-6, examined in R.B. Smith, Vietnam and the West, pp. 61-2: superficially this had appeared to be a Catholic/ Buddhist struggle for administrative control of a commune, but analysis suggests that it may have been a clan quarrel of profounder, and essentially secular, origin. While the full variety of missionary methods of proselytism, and the complexity of their repercussions lie beyond the scope of this survey, the documents which follow illustrate further some of the social and political issues to which the process of conversion could give rise.

Documents

190. **M. Lévecque**, Acting Resident-Superior of Annam, to Governor-General **Beau**. Hue, 31 August 1906.

The Missions Etrangères, though established in Indochina for a long time, only made headway after the start of the French conquest.

The political influence which the missions are supposed to have enjoyed from the beginning of our occupation enabled them to develop and implant themselves in the country. For it was by developing the material riches around them, thanks to the altogether special protection which they enjoyed, that they were able to make their influence grow.

It should be noted that the missions all involve themselves generally in agriculture and native banking. The distribution of rice in times of famine or epidemic is one of their main means of propaganda...(A.N.S.O.M. Paris. Indochine, (A.F.) 29/A90(15))

191. Mgr **Puginier**, Bishop of West Tonkin. 'Notes and information on one view of the situation in Tonkin...1889.'

Twenty years ago, in a few scattered areas, a small wave of conversions to Christianity occurred for the first time and only then did it prove possible to introduce the Catholic religion into villages which had formerly been exclusively pagan. At first the mandarins did not seem to attach any importance to it. The movement of conversions was so restricted that it did not engage their interest. But the notables of the communes were hostile from the start to the introduction of the faith into their villages because it caused them difficulties. So they always opposed it strongly....

Following the events of 1873 we had to pass through a very painful crisis. After the death of M. Garnier, the Annamese ambassador Nguyen Van Tuong, who had accompanied the new representative of France to Tonkin to reclaim the conquered provinces from him, revenged himself on our Christians.... The hurried withdrawal of French troops from their posts in the interior and their redeployment to Haiphong where only a very small contingent was left, occasioned a period of troubles and hesitations in the country. In the middle of such real disasters for us, the movement of conversions ceased altogether for two years.

In August 1875 when we saw a French consul established at Hanoi with a company of marine infantry, those who were not hostile to us felt reassured and tried to rally to us. Already by the beginning of 1876 a proportion of many pagan villages asked to embrace Christianity, and from that time on the movement of conversions strengthened and grew....

The events of 1883 and the following years, which were accompanied by a fulmination across the whole of Tonkin, retarded conversions for a while. Now that people have just begun to feel reassured, the pagan villages are again beginning to ask to embrace Christianity in far greater numbers than before and beg us to send them catechists.... The mission, despite its numerous personnel and the enormous sacrifices which it has imposed on itself for this work, cannot satify all the requests and there are many villages whose instruction we have had to defer by several months for lack of catechists.

This movement of conversions which began twenty years ago, feeble at first but then more pronounced, gave us 58,000 pagan baptisms of which 15,000 were in the first period from 1869 to 1876; 21,000 in the second period from 1877 to 1883; and 21,509 during the third period from 1884 to 15 June 1885. The last three years have given us 43,000 pagan baptisms. In the table for 15 June 1888 to 15 June 1889 alone we have had almost 73,000. In addition about 12,000 people are studying doctrine and prayers at the moment, or else they are awaiting catechists to instruct them. Previously we could not obtain more than a few conversions in the communes where Christians already existed; but for a few years now we have introduced the Catholic religion into 230 pagan villages and it has made very evident progress in them....

These are the circumstances and motives which normally lead to conversions:

The mayors and notables of the communes generally abuse their authority.... They do not distribute the communal fields equitably and they keep a large part for themselves. Tax and <u>corvée</u> duties are allocated unfairly etc. In a word all the advantages are for them and all the burdens are for the people. On top of that, inferiors are oppressed and victimised by appallingly unjust measures. The latter see that in the Catholic villages there is more justice and more protection, and then they agree among themselves and ask to be made Christians. At other times there are rival groups jealous of one another which cannot agree. One of the two turns to religion for help and to escape pressure from its rival. Sometimes it is a weaker hamlet, despised and overwhelmed with charges by scholars and influential notables of a larger hamlet in the same commune.

In a word, it is ordinarily the weak and oppressed who turn Christian to get help against the stronger oppressor.... (M.R.E. Mémoires et documents. Vol.75, Asie-Indochine 40, 1889.)

192. Mgr **Colombert**, Bishop of West Cochinchina. Annual Report. 1 September 1893.

Considering the number of those working for conversions, and the freedom we enjoy, the number of adult baptisms (in West Cochinchina) is disappointing. It is painful to acknowledge that this has been so for many years now. There are several reasons for this. One of them is that those who preached the Gospel had more authority and more success when they did not have to contend with the presence of Europeans in these territories. But since (the conquest) the pagans have been scandalised by the conduct of foreign Christians. They began to doubt the good faith of our evangelists, who had only spoken to them of the virtues of these western Christians.... and made them think 'Since these Christians are living like pagans, why should pagans bother to become Christians?' They would not become better men, and they would gain no temporal advantage either. So why not imitate the Europeans who, for them, have prestige, authority and money, and know how to obtain all the good things of life for themselves. Men of little faith succumb easily whereas, removed from scandalous example, they might have kept to the true path. Our lack of progress among the pagans derives from this.... (A.S.M.E. Vol. 757, (Cochinchine Occidentale, 1890-1919). pp. 2-4)

193. Mgr **Marcou**, Bishop of Maritime Tonkin, to the **Directors**. Phat Diem, 14 September 1902.

... We would have had many more converts if the civil authorities had shown more sympathy to the missionaries and their activities.... At present the best method of apostleship seems to be to multiply our works of charity and corporal assistance as much as possible. Only a few years ago, numerous groups of pagans came to us in the hope of benefitting in some way from our influence, real or supposed, with the French authorities. Henceforth we can hardly count on this attraction, not regularly anyway.... (A.S.M.E. Vol. 712, (Tonkin Maritime, 1902-1919). No. 3)

194. M. **Moulié**, Resident at Thanh Hoa, to M. **Auvergne**, Resident-Superior of Annam. Thanh Hoa, 18 December 1903.

The latest news I have received from the Upper Song Ma shows that the peace which the Muong population of the region has enjoyed these last few years is beginning to be disturbed by the establishment of missions in this region. Numerous complaints reached me a few months ago following the first installation of a French missionary in Ba-Tho's territory - that is, in the <u>chau</u> of Quang Hoa - especially complaints concerning the activity of catechists.

According to the complaints reaching me, the latter are installing themselves at will or on the missionary's orders, usually against the wishes of the chiefs and regular village authorities. Despite the refusal of the inhabitants to receive them, they are behaving like masters of the territory, demanding food for themselves and their followers, requisitioning coolies, demanding that wood and bamboos be cut from the forest without payment, interfering in local affairs, judging disputes, administering indiscriminate canings, continually threatening villagers with intervention by the provincial and residency authorities, and seeking in all sorts of threatening ways to obtain written consents or <u>diem chi</u> sealed contracts for all these (exactions) without the natives really understanding (these documents).

The mandarins of Thanh Hoa and the Muong chiefs of Song Ma declare that these conversion tactics and the behaviour of the catechists are profoundly disturbing the country. They ask for our direct and urgent intervention to put a stop to these activities which can, they say, have the gravest repercussions in the region. The situation has got worse very recently following the arrival of three new missionaries and numerous catechists. Ba-tho's sons arrived two months ago to complain about this situation. When you received them during your visit to

Thanh Hoa they put their grievances to you personally.   Ba-tho himself came down a few days ago to insist on an urgent solution.   They are asking   that   missionaries, and especially catechists, be refused authorisation to settle in the region or to found establishments;   and that if the French government does not want to take such a radical step, that a modus vivendi should be arranged safeguarding everybody's interests. The administration could agree with the Muong chiefs where to site Catholic villages, which would be administered either in the custom of the country through the medium of catholic seigneurial families, or in Annamese fashion by the constitution of communes with all their usual functions.   Anyone wanting to become a Catholic would have to leave his tribe and install himself in the usual way, either in a tribe which accepts him, or in one of the Catholic communes whose creation awaits an administrative decision.

It is certain that the establishment of a mission in the Muong country must be causing profound problems.   The regime to which these peoples have been strongly attached for centuries - a feudal organisation tempered by a sort of patriarchal communism - cannot accomodate the conversion of part of its population to Catholicism.   They are basically indifferent as to whether the inhabitants are Catholic or Buddhist or merely practise ancestor worship, or worship various mountain spirits.   But they cannot lightheartedly accept the effective authority which the missionary and especially his catechists are claiming to excercise in the tribe through the medium of their neophytes.

In principle, land and people belong to the lord of the country. Every family in the population enjoys only the plot of land it cultivates. But in reality a modus vivendi exists which has had the force of law for centuries.   It regulates relations between the families of the chiefs, <u>tho ty</u> or <u>quan lang</u>, and those of the tribe, so that the respective rights of each is acknowledged: this tempers the excessively strict application of the feudal regime....

... Fifteen years ago...I... presented the main chiefs of Cho Bo to the Director of Civil Affairs at Hanoi.   (He)... asked the chiefs gathered in his office if they would like to have individual property rights established through the issue of titles to every family in the tribe. This provoked a lively agitation... and one of them declared very violently that the day the French government did this it would not only have all the <u>tho ty</u> or <u>quan lang</u> chiefs against it, but also all the tribes. The Director... was wise enough to abandon his plan.

The Muong chiefs of Song Ma find themselves threatened today particularly by the form taken by religious proselytism in their country... The creation of Catholic villages is a necessity and so is

the obligation of taking up residence there once the tribe of origin ha[s]
been abandoned by the new convert, who by this means repudiates th[e]
authority of the tho ty or quan lang, abandons all the divers[e]
obligations of the tribe and refuses his share of contributions on th[e]
grounds that they might go towards supporting a cult which he ha[s]
repudiated... and refuses also to fulfil his share of corvées which h[e]
says he owes instead to his new religious masters.... The history of th[e]
last few years has shown what bloody troubles the efforts of the Missio[n]
in Muong country has often caused once the abuses of catechists have
become too extreme. The proposals of the Muong chiefs seem wise...
(They) seem to reconcile the rights of free proselytism with the customs
and social organisation of these regions. (A.O.M. Aix. Indochine,
Gouverneurs-Généraux, 5,935.)

195. Mgr **Marcou**, Bishop of Maritime Tonkin, to the **Directors**. Phat
Diem, 27 March 1904.

For a year in the Chau Hoa (sic) and its neighbouring territories there
has been a fairly important wave of conversions, not only among the
pagans but also among the Christians and catechumens evangelised more
than twenty years ago by our colleagues, but who had abandoned all
religious observances following the troubles which had devastated this
whole region after 1883.

Ba-tho, the chief of Chau Hoa, wanting to halt this movement of
conversions, repeatedly complained to the French and Annamese
authorities, and has even had his complaints conveyed to the
Governor-General of Indochina. He hoped to obtain the expulsion of the
missionaries from the whole of his territory.

To achieve his ends, and unable to find a serious grievance against
the missionaries, he has attacked their catechists. Unfortunately
these have furnished Ba-tho with the pretext he wanted, by involving
themselves in purely civil matters unbeknown to our colleagues. Their
indiscretions, exaggerated by partisan prejudice, have given Ba-tho the
excuse to insinuate to the French Resident of the province that unless
the government intervenes there to stop the excesses of the catechists,
trouble is to be expected in this region.

In accordance with Ba-tho's requests an enquiry was set up and it
emerged that a catechist had had a pagan whipped, had uttered threats
against some former Christians of 1880 who had refused to reconvert, and
had committed a number of other faults of this kind. Although the acts
alleged were not very serious, they could have prompted an
administrative reaction in view of the state of mind of our governors:
(imprisonment of the catechist, official circulars condemning excessive

proselytism by missionaries, the authorities ordered to maintain their neutrality etc.) These measures could have been used against us and might have nullified the efforts of our colleagues.

(Governor-General) Beau with whom I had to settle this matter, showed severe displeasure at the facts revealed by the enquiry and I had to offer some means of satisfying him without compromising the work of conversion among these peoples. For this purpose I gave an undertaking that our colleagues would no longer send Annamese catechists to give religious instruction in places distant from the missionary's residence, as they do now. In return the government promised to allow missionaries the fullest possible freedom for the excercise of their ministry.

This is going to alter our system for evangelising in these regions and will increase the workload of our colleagues. Even if our Annamese catechists treated the local natives harshly, they fulfilled an invaluable service teaching the catechism and prayers... (A.S.M.E. Vol. 712, (Tonkin Maritime, 1902-1919). No.17)

196. Governor-General **Sarraut** to **J. Morel**, Minister for the Colonies. Hanoi, 21 February 1913.

...By a letter of... 12 December 1908... M. Klobukowski requested the French Minister at Bangkok to ask his United States' colleague in Siam to request his nationals to refrain from all religious proselytism in North Laos. The reasons given for this by the Government-General were the following: the religious sensibilities of the higher native authorities and the fears which they had expressed; and the state of feeling in the population of a distant region over which we have very few means of direct action and where, as a result, any cause for agitation should be avoided in order to maintain public order.

The motives given by the Government-General in 1908... have, in my view, lost none of their force.... This ban on proselytism applies, of course, to all concessions, and Catholic as well as Protestant missions have been forbidden to found establishments in this region.

On the other hand Catholic and Protestant missions have been installed in South Laos without causing protests or incidents by their presence.... (A.O.M. Paris. Indochine, (N.F.) 198/1475 (1).)

197. **Petition** from seventeen Catholic inhabitants of the village of **Dong Du'ong**, in the Phu of Ung Hoa, for permission to renounce the Catholic religion and return to Buddhism. Received by the French Resident at Hanoi, 8 April 1899.

We were once Buddhists. In the year 1886 it was said that we were free

to be Buddhists or Catholics. Moreover the native curé told us that if we embraced the Catholic religion we would be exempt from the public taxes and duties which Buddhists are obliged to bear. That is why we were converted to Catholicism....
(A.O.M. Aix. Archives du Résidence Supérieur du Tonkin, F94/56,736.)

198.   J.L. de Lanessan, Governor-General of Indochina (1891-1894).

The economics of missionary proselytism.
When a mission receives a territorial concession on which to set up an establishment, it summons all the poor of the region and promises them lodging, the loan of seed for sowing, the provision of buffalo for cultivation and sustenance from the produce of its land in return for their conversion to Christianity. More discreetly it offers them protection against the local authorities.... (J.L. de Lanessan, Les missions et leur protectorat. (Paris, Alcan, 1907). pp. 42-3)

199.   J.L. de Lanessan, Governor-General of Indochina (1891-1894).

Tactics of missionary proselytism.
Ancestor-worship requires each family to maintain an inalienable financial reserve, managed by the head of the family, from which a revenue is drawn for the purposes of worship. If a member of the family becomes a Christian, the missionaries have no difficulty in persuading him that he should claim his share of this fund; and that he should refuse to participate in the family's rituals, since he no longer professes the family religion....
So one frequently sees native converts claiming their share of such funds. The family resists these claims, quarrels break out, and if some upset occurs discussion turns to violence. Most of the massacres of Christians which occurred in Tonkin and Annam at the time of our invasion of the country resulted from quarrels of this kind, and I had to deal with some myself when I was Governor-General there.
The missionaries naturally suffer from the repercussions. Viewed with antipathy by the scholars whose interests they threaten, they are also detested by every family from which they have detached a member - all the more so if such a family is relatively rich, though this is not often the case. In general Catholic missionaries only recruit from among the lowest classes, and mainly among those who, for various reasons have been rejected by Annamese society. (J.L. de Lanessan, Les missions et leur protectorat. (Paris, Alcan, 1907). pp.42-3)

Appendix ii.

STATISTICAL TABLES.

NOTES

Tables A and B. S.M.E. statistics for growth and fluctuation in the overall size of the Catholic population are unreliable and should be treated as approximations. They were unsystematically compiled and derived variously from paschal communion figures or deduced from baptismal figures. In years when no returns were made by particular vicariates, figures for the last recorded return were merely repeated. Sudden falls in returns for all categories can be accounted for mainly (1) by periodic devastation of vicariates in the 1880s; and (2) by the progressive subdivision of vicariates from the mid 1890s onwards.

Table C. Statistics for children in mission schools seem to have been returned with greater precision and regularity, possibly because they were easier to compile.

Tables D - F. Native priests, and especially native catechists were vital intermediaries between missionaries and the Catholic population, and a vicariate's development was closely related to growth in the scale of its indigenous personnel. While the rise in numbers of French missionaries levelled off in the quinquennium before 1914, the ordination of native priests showed a steady expansion. Figures for catechists however, show more uneven rates of growth in different vicariates, some of which continued to expand while others, like West Cochinchina, remained virtually static.

Spanish vicariates. Figures drawn from the A.P.F. (1857) show that in 1855 the Spanish Dominican vicariate of Central Tonkin recorded a Christian population of 150,500, administered by 1 bishop, 6 missionaries, 37 native priests, and 169 catechists. Figures drawn from J.P. Migne, Dictionnaire des missions catholiques, (Paris, 1864) show that for East Tonkin in 1859 the Spanish Dominican mission recorded a Christian population of 54,179, administered by 2 bishops, 3 missionaries and 25 native priests. However no figure for catechists is given.

By 1907, the Spanish Dominican mission had grown substantially. The combined figures for the Spanish vicariates of Central, East and North Tonkin, and the prefecture of Lang Son are as follows: 304,616 Christians; 61 Spanish Dominican priests; 156 native priests; 579 catechists; 1150 schools; 16,283 pupils in lower schools, and 422 pupils in higher schools. (Drawn from H.A. Krose, Katholische Missionsstatistik (1908) and reproduced in J.R. Mott, Statistical Atlas of Christian missions, (Edinburgh, 1910) p. 97.

315

TABLE A. Catholic population of Indochina in French vicariates, 1874-1913. (Triennial intervals).

	1874	1877	1880	1883	1886	1889	1892
W. Tonkin		155,000	155,000	155,000	180,000	200,000	220,000
S. Tonkin		71,465	73,000	73,483	68,000	75,262	88,227
N. Cochinchina	32,461	34,865	27,058	28,597	18,700	22,202	28,040
E. Cochinchina	41,340	44,555	36,327	37,734	15,000	20,330	32,717
W. Cochinchina			51,043	53,140	55,000	56,000	57,050
Cambodia	9,493	11,327	12,837	15,785	16,445	18,480	21,130

	1895	1898	1901	1904	1907	1910	1913
W. Tonkin	201,732	201,732	214,970	132,230	140,379	141,216	141,216
S. Tonkin	98,234	112,635	120,370	129,544	136,584	142,404	142,404
Upper Tonkin	17,000	18,138	18,460	19,200	21,130	24,160	25,239
Maritime Tonkin				81,836	89,000	96,000	102,000
N. Cochinchina	33,132	61,340	55,665	49,671	57,576	54,275	60,290
E. Cochinchina	45,449	61,924	73,051	81,171	83,100	60,467	60,956
W. Cochinchina	60,200	61,910	64,693	63,485	63,256	69,461	71,418
Cambodia	25,200	28,537	31,516	34,485	40,017	44,847	49,014
Laos			9,877	9,569	11,544	12,137	12,509

Note: The vicariates of Upper and Maritime Tonkin were created in 1894 and 1901 respectively out of the vicariate of West Tonkin. The vicariate of (French) Laos was not formed until 1899.

Source: Statistical tables taken from the Comptes-rendus annuels of the S.M.E.

TABLE B.   Catholic population of Indochina in French vicariates, 1882-1892. (Annual returns).

	1882	1883	1884	1885	1886
W. Tonkin	155,000	155,000	155,000	155,000	c.180,000
S. Tonkin	73,483	73,483	73,483	73,483	c.68,000
N. Cochinchina	27,615	28,597	28,193	c.20,000	18,700
E. Cochinchina	37,734	37,734	41,234	c.17,000	15,000
W. Cochinchina	52,000	53,140	54,850	c.55,000	c.55,000
Cambodia	14,832	15,785	16,280	16,101	16,445

	1887	1888	1889	1890	1891	1892
W. Tonkin	c.180,000	c.200,000	c.200,000	c.215,000	c.220,000	c.220,000
S. Tonkin	68,619	71,846	75,262	78,797	84,052	88,227
N. Cochinchina	18,700	19,932	22,202	24,920	27,014	28,040
E. Cochinchina	17,000	17,773	20,330	25,600	30,311	32,717
W. Cochinchina	c.55,000	c.56,000	c.56,000	c.56,000	57,300	57,050
Cambodia	16,735	17,433	18,480	19,580	20,388	21,130

Source: Statistical tables taken from the Comptes-rendus annuels of the S.M.E.

TABLE C. Numbers of schoolchildren in French mission schools (excluding seminaries) in Indochina, 1874–1913. (Triennial intervals).

	1874	1877	1880	1883	1886	1889	1892
W. Tonkin		5,948	8,273	5,813	5,897	6,455	7,657
S. Tonkin			1,325	838	468	2,448	2,830
N. Cochinchina			636	528	230	988	431
E. Cochinchina	72	489	1,068	1,159	150	540	979
W. Cochinchina	2,450	3,095	6,237	5,242	5,645	7,701	7,298
Cambodia	185	996	828	1,403	1,072	3,293	4,347

	1895	1898	1901	1904	1907	1910	1913
W. Tonkin	6,581	9,316	8,142	10,410	17,605	17,039	23,982
S. Tonkin	3,836	5,245	5,878	5,941	4,875	4,892	4,850
Upper Tonkin	1,109	1,294	1,330	1,419	2,042	3,010	2,270
Maritime Tonkin				8,588	14,406	16,051	16,714
N. Cochinchina	966	1,531	731	582	1,223	2,318	3,296
E. Cochinchina	884	1,325		387	739	652	2,283
W. Cochinchina	11,081	10,885	8,221	8,030	7,495	8,803	10,198
Cambodia	3,969	4,032	4,942	3,996	5,539	5,669	6,851
Laos			770	693	839	1,027	1,706

Note: Upper and Maritime Tonkin were created in 1894 and 1901 respectively out of the vicariate of West Tonkin. The vicariate of (French) Laos was not formed until 1899.

Source: Statistical tables taken from the Comptes-rendus annuels of the S.M.E.

TABLE D. The growth of clergy in the French vicariates of Indochina, 1874-1913. (Triennial intervals).

1. French missionaries.

	1874	1877	1880	1883	1886	1889	1892
W. Tonkin		30	31	36	44	45	53
S. Tonkin		10	18	20	17	25	31
N. Cochinchina		13	13	15	18	21	23
E. Cochinchina	11	16	20	25	19	28	30
W. Cochinchina	38	44	48	48	49	50	52
Cambodia	14	13	19	21	27	28	29

	1895	1898	1901	1904	1907	1910	1913
W. Tonkin	48	59	69	46	47	46	46
S. Tonkin	31	31	32	38	38	37	36
Upper Tonkin	15	20	27	29	28	27	27
Maritime Tonkin				33	37	37	41
N. Cochinchina	30	43	48	47	44	45	43
E. Cochinchina	38	45	51	61	67	65	64
W. Cochinchina	52	58	60	59	61	52	55
Cambodia	30	34	40	44	47	47	45
Laos			22	28	34	33	32

Source: Statistical tables taken from the Comptes-rendus annuels of the S.M.E.

TABLE E. The growth of clergy in the French vicariates of Indochina, 1874-1913. (Triennial intervals).

2. Native priests.

	1874	1877	1880	1883	1886	1889	1892
W. Tonkin		92	88	86	94	95	101
S. Tonkin		54	57	58	53	59	72
N. Cochinchina			43	41	26	26	28
E. Cochinchina	20	21	21	22	12	15	17
W. Cochinchina	22	25	28	35	41	41	44
Cambodia						3	12

	1895	1898	1901	1904	1907	1910	1913
W. Tonkin	98	116	127	85	95	102	107
S. Tonkin	69	66	68	74	80	85	107
Upper Tonkin	12	11	15	19	19	20	21
Maritime Tonkin				53	62	65	69
N. Cochinchina	28	35	36	45	55	63	67
E. Cochinchina	19	27	31	37	38	41	49
W. Cochinchina	51	63	72	76	75	77	78
Cambodia	12	18	25	29	37	38	41
Laos		4	4	4	4	4	5

Source: Statistical tables from the Comptes-rendus annuels of the S.M.E.

320

TABLE F. The growth of clergy in the French vicariates of Indochina, 1874-1913. (Triennial intervals).

3. Native catechists.

	1874	1877	1880	1883	1886	1889	1892
W. Tonkin		320	356	372	350	383	525
S. Tonkin			205	160	182	191	224
N. Cochinchina			47	35	15	16	15
E. Cochinchina	35	95	38	47	17	40	50
W. Cochinchina	25		15	15			62
Cambodia	3	5	12	22	20	50	30

	1895	1898	1901	1904	1907	1910	1913
W. Tonkin	409	547	508	354	342	368	435
S. Tonkin	261	222	260	288	292	290	250
Upper Tonkin	53	56	62	92	103	97	112
Maritime Tonkin				170	185	195	190
N. Cochinchina	15	15	15	15	30	18	
E. Cochinchina	50	72	69	78	76	84	142
W. Cochinchina	48	120	85	37	40	30	29
Cambodia	70	83	82	96	60	71	76
Laos			30	27	31	59	99

Source: Statistical tables from the Comptes-rendus annuels of the S.M.E.

Albrand, F.A., (1804-67). Missionary, b. Hautes Alpes. Ordained 1929. Director of the Collège général at Penang, 1833-9. A Director of the Paris seminary from 1839-43, he became Procurator of the mission at Kweichow. Superior of the S.M.E. from 1855-67. Wrote to the Quai on 8 November 1855 recommending the care of Christians in Siam and Annam to the special attention of the Montigny mission.

Ansart, A.L. (1823-87). Lt, A.D.C. to Admirals Bonard and La Grandière, 1863-4. Captain, August 1864. Military governor, Vinh Long, 1867-8. Fought in the Armée de la Loire, 1870. Retired 1876.

Arbaud, F. d', Brigadier-General, Infanterie de Marine. Interim Governor of Cochinchina, 4 March - 16 December 1872. Retired, 4 September 1873.

Ariès, J.H. d', (1813-78). Rear-Admiral, b. Tarbes. Captain, 1854. Took part in the capture of Saigon in 1859. Commanded the force of occupation, 16 May 1860 - 7 February 1861. Director of the Service of Native Affairs in Lower Cochinchina, 7 February 1861 to 31 May 1862. Military governor of Vinh Long and then My Tho, and commander of the naval division off Cambodia, June 1862 - March 1864. Rear-Admiral, 1872. Commanded the naval division in Oceania.

Artif, J.J.E., (1844-1929). Missionary, b. Angers. Entered S.M.E. 1868. Missionary in Chungking, 1869-84. Returned to convalesce in France, 1884-95. Returned to work at the Nazareth in Hong Kong, 1895-1903. Procurator for the apostolic vicariate of West Cochinchina, Saigon, 1904-1926. Retired 1928.

Aubaret, L.G., (1825-94). Naval officer and diplomat, b. Montpellier of a legal family. Served in the Crimean war, and in the China and Cochinchina campaigns, 1859-63. Aubaret studied Chinese characters, quoc ngu and Vietnamese law and custom. These accomplishments made him useful to Admiral Bonard (qv.) as a political adviser. Captain, 1862. Principal architect of the treaty of Saigon, June 1862. Transferred to the diplomatic service in 1863. With Phan Thanh Gian (qv.) he negotiated the draft treaty of retrocession in 1864. Consul at Bangkok, 1864-7. He negotiated the Franco-Siamese treaty of 1867 which acknowledged Siamese possession of Battambang and Angkor in return for Siamese acceptance of the French protectoral treaty of 1863 with Cambodia. Later served as French consul at Scutari and Smyrna. Though a fervent Catholic, he advised Bonard to follow a laissez-faire policy towards French missionaries within French jurisdiction.

Barou, J.J. (1835-69). Missionary, b. Chalmazelle (Loire). Ordained 1859. Missionary of the S.M.E. at Thu Ngu in West Cochinchina from February 1859. Became emboiled in the revolt which broke out in December 1862 upon Admiral Bonard's retrocession of Vinh Long to Annam. Served in the district of Tran Trieu 1863-6, and at Cho Quan 1866-7, when he retired through illness.

Ba Tuong or **Ton Tho Thuong.** Vietnamese collaborator, Prefect of Saigon. After the 'flight of the mandarins' from the French-occupied eastern provinces of Cochinchina in the early 1860s, the French were without experienced Vietnamese officials through whom to maintain the traditional forms of administration. Ba Tuong, though not a mandarin, was the most experienced of the early collaborators. He had failed his exams for entry into the Vietnamese bureaucracy, but his family had held high office in the mandarinate, and he was familiar with administrative procedures. Ba Tuong escorted Ambassador Phan Thanh Gian's mission of 1863 to Paris for re-negotiation of the treaty of Saigon. Thereafter, as 'Prefect' of Saigon he dealt mainly with native judicial affairs, and with subsequent diplomatic contacts between Saigon and Hue. See J. Davidson, 'Collaborateur versus abstentioniste (Tuong versus Tri): a political polemic in poetic dialogue during the French acquisition of Southern Vietnam,' (B.S.O.A.S., xlix, 2, 1986, pp. 321-363.)

Beau, J.B.P. (1857-1926). Governor-General of Indochina, 1902-1908. A career diplomat with legal training. Attached to the office of the Foreign Minister, 1883. Third Secretary in Rome, 1888-92. Chief of personnel in the Foreign Minister's office from 1892-1901. Appointed Minister to Pekin, March 1901. In July 1902 he was appointed, at Delcassé's instigation, to succeed Paul Doumer as Governor-General of Indochina. As a safe career diplomat Beau was thought unlikely to follow Doumer's dangerous expansionist policies towards Siam and South China. A freemason but not a Radical, Beau tended to temporise on the issue of how to apply anticlerical legislation to Indochina. Retired as Governor-General in February, 1908 and appointed Minister in Brussels.

Bert, Paul. (1838-86). Physiologist, politician and Resident-General of Annam-Tonkin, b. Auxerre. In domestic politics Bert, a republican of the Centre, was an 'opportunist' and supporter of Ferry. As minister for Education in Ferry's first and second cabinets, Bert framed much of the legislation which transformed the primary school system, making it 'free, lay and compulsory'. His repeated and vituperative attacks on clerical influences in education earned him the reputation of being one of the foremost anticlericals of the republican party. As an ardent proponent of French colonial expansion he defended Ferry's Tonkin policy against numerous attacks by Radicals and conservatives in the Chamber of Deputies between 1883 and 1885. Although offered the Ministry of the Colonies by Prime Minister de Freycinet early in 1886, he chose to express his faith in the Tonkin commitment by preferring the post of Resident-General in Annam-Tonkin, at a time when Ferry's acquisition of Tonkin was still the subject of public abuse and parliamentary controversy. As an anticlerical he might have been expected to show hostility towards the Catholic mission in Indochina. But he chose to regard it as a useful political collaborator in the development of French rule. Although he defined a policy of official neutrality in religious matters, he remained accessible to their advice and tended to show them unofficial favour.

Billot, A. Political Director at the Quai d'Orsay from 1882-5. Strongly committed to French military intervention in Tonkin, he played a crucial role during February-March 1883 to secure the incoming Ferry cabinet's rejection of the Li-Bourée treaty. This agreement proposed the partition of Tonkin between France and China, and would have averted the Tonkin war. The fall of Ferry resulted in Billot's resignation from the Direction Politique. His anonymously published book L'affaire du Tonkin, an extremely detailed account of the development of French policy since 1882, was designed to justify the enormous expense of Ferry's Tonkin policy.

Blancsubé, Jules. (1834-88). Colonial lawyer and politician, b. Gap. Formerly a Lazarist seminarist and postulant for the priesthood, he shared a legal practise at Marseilles with Eugène Etienne, a political disciple and intimate of Gambetta, before moving to Cochinchina in 1863. In 1867 Blancsubé set up the first masonic lodge in Saigon, Le Réveil d'Orient, arguing to the Grand Master of the Grand Orient that 'the clerical influence is all powerful here' and should be contested. Though vigorously anticlerical he nonetheless defined himself as a believer and remained on particularly close terms with Frs Le Mée and Noioberne, missionaries at Saigon. Acting Mayor of Saigon from 1874-6, he was elected substantive Mayor from 1879-80. During the 1870s he aroused the disfavour of the naval administration by attacking the arbitrary authority of the Admiral-Governors in his press organ, Le Mékong. He urged the need for for a seat in parliament for the colony and an elected Colonial Council at Saigon sharing wide financial powers with the administration. His friendship with Etienne and Gambetta stood him in good stead, and these changes were made in 1881-2. Blancsubé himself became the colony's first Deputy. Through his newspaper and his clique of supporters on the Colonial Council he dominated the political life of the colony and intimidated its administration until the death of Gambetta at the end of 1882. His influence remained high under Ferry, and he played a significant role in parliamentary debates leading to the formation of the Tonkin expedition in April-May 1883. In 1886-7 he was consulted by the Quai d'Orsay on the future constitutional structure of the Indochina Union.

Bonard, L.A.B. (1805-67). Vice-Admiral and first Governor of Cochinchina, b. Cherbourg, the son of a marine engineer. Served in the Algerian campaign of 1830. Captain, 1842. Repeated tours of duty in Oceania from 1842-47 and from 1849-52. Governor of Guyana, 1854-5. Rear-Admiral, 1855. C.in C. of the Pacific naval division, 1858-61. Requested his posting as Governor of Cochinchina, where he served from 28 November 1861 to May 1863. Vice-Admiral, June 1862. Bonard wanted to construct an economical system of indirect administration, using such elements of the traditional bureaucracy as still remained after the initial conquest. Hostile to the use of Chinese as a language of administration, but forced to tolerate it during his period of office. Keen to see the spread of christianisation, but forced by the financial constraints of his situation to give little direct help to missionaries, other than small tax concessions, petty land grants and funding for a school to train interpreters for administrative use. Bonard was instrumental in having the Vietnamese code of laws translated, despite widespread doubt as to the practicability of administering it in Cochinchina. Bonard's withdrawal in 1863 was intended to be temporary, but ill-health forced him into permanent retirement.

Bonhoure, L.A. (1864-1909), b. Nîmes. Arrived in Annam as a junior residency official in 1891. Deputy Secretary in the Governor-General's office in 1892. Transferred to senior administrative posts in the Ivory Coast in 1896 and in Guyana in 1898. In 1907 he returned to Saigon as Lt Governor of Cochinchina and became interim Governor-General from 18 February 1908. He was present at Hanoi during the abortive insurrection which began with an attempt to poison the Hanoi garisson. After Klobukowski's arrival as Governor-General, Bonhoure returned to Saigon where he committed suicide on 8-9 January 1909.

Bosc, J. Director of political and native affairs in the Government-General (June 1914); Resident-Superior of Laos 9 October 1917-3 May 1918.

Brenier, Baron A.A.F. (1807-85), b. Saint-Marcellin. A career diplomat. Consul-General in Warsaw and Lisbon. From 24 January to 10 April 1851 he was interim Foreign Minister. At the time of his chairmanship of the Cochinchina commission he was Minister to the court of Naples (1855-60). He retired from the diplomatic service in 1860 and was elected to the Senate in 1861. Participated in some of the subsequent parliamentary debates on the Retrocession question in 1864.

Brière de l'Isle, L.A.E., General, b. Martinique 1827 of a norman family. Passed his entire career in the Infanterie de Marine. Took part in the Montevideo expedition (1851-2), the China campaign (1859-60) and the conquest of Cochinchina (1860-2). Transferred into the Inspection des Affaires Indigènes in 1863 as administrator at Tay Ninh. During the Franco-Prussian war he returned to military service as a Colonel and fought at Bazeilles where he was made a prisoner of war. In 1877 he was made military governor of Senegal. In 1884 he was promoted Brigadier-General and given command of the 1st Division of the Tonkin expeditionary corps. Succeeded General Millot as C.in C. on 8 September 1884. Captured Lang Son from Chinese forces on 13 February 1885, and after relieving the siege of Tuyen Quan by Black Flags on 2 March, expelled the latter from their stronghold at Hung Hoa on 11 April. Appointed a Divisional General, he quitted Tonkin on 5 October 1885.

Broni, E.A.M. Director of Civil Affairs for Indochina. Served as interim Governor-General during the absences of Paul Doumer in February-March 1901 and March-July 1902. Interim Resident-Superior in Tonkin 25 October 1902-27 April 1903. As Secretary-General of the Government-General he served again as interim Governor-General from July to December 1905.

Camelbeke, Mgr D.F.X. van (1839-1901). Bishop of Hierocésarée, Vicar Apostolic of East Cochinchina, b. Nantes. Entered the Paris seminary of the S.M.E. in July 1862 and ordained in May 1863. Arrived in East Cochinchina in August 1864, and ministered to Christian communes in Binh Thuan, Khanh Hoa and Phu Yen. Nominated Provicar of the vicariate in 1870. Elected Vicar Apostolic of· East Cochinchina in January 1884. From July to October 1885 his vicariate was devastated and a community of Christians estimated at 41,000 reduced to a reported 15,000. Van Camelbeke fled to Qui Nhon where he remained for two years in a temporary refugee settlement with the remnants of his mission. Returned to the seat of his vicariate at Lang Son in Spring 1887. The mission stations of the vicariate were rapidly re-established, and by 1901 recorded a figure of 71,051 Christian adherents. The bishop's reputation with the French authorities suffered because some of his subordinates, particularly Frs Maillard (qv.) and Guerlach (qv.) were accused of leading Christians in armed reprisals for the destruction of their communes in 1885-6. Van Camelbeke ran into further embarassment with French officaldom by reason of the involvement of Frs Vialleton (qv.) and Guerlach in the Mayrena affair. The problems of the Kontum mission in this vicariate continued to sour relations between the bishop and the authorities for a decade after van Camelbeke's death in 1901.

Caspar, Mgr M.A.L. (1841-1917). Bishop of Canathe, Vicar Apostolic of North Cochinchina, b. Obernai (Strabourg, Lower Rhine). Ordained 1864. Arrived in Cochinchina in March 1865. Opted to retain French nationality after the Prussian seizure of Alsace-Lorraine in 1870. A linguist, he published a Franco-Annamese dictionary in 1877. Shy, scholarly and reclusive, his approach to teaching while a missionary at

Tan Dinh gave rise to complaints. He became Vicar Apostolic nonetheless in 1880, and took up residence at Hue. After the French bombardment of Thuan An, which produced the formal submission of the Vietnamese court in August 1885, Caspar's position at Hue became delicate. All the Christian communes in the vicinity of Thuan An were picketed by Vietnamese troops, some of whom refused to observe the restraints officially imposed on them and began burning mission stations along the route between Tourane and Hue in December 1883. Meantime Caspar was used as an intermediary by the Vietnamese court in dealings with Admiral Courbet in the days leading up to the imposition of the humiliating Harmand Convention of August 1883. News of the fall of Son Tay and of the surrender of the Vietnamese army in December 1883 prompted further massacres in Thanh Hoa. After the Hue coup of 5-6 July 1885 a general pogrom against Christians developed in Quang Tri and part of Quang Binh, covering two thirds of Caspar's vicariate, and over 7000 Christians were killed. When part of the Vietnamese court returned from the flight to Tan So, the Dowager Empress took refuge in Caspar's residence, and the French authorities made him responsible for her custody. According to the bishop's missionary obituarist, Caspar's advice determined General de Courcy's selection of Dong Khanh as Emperor in place of Ham Nghi in August 1885.

Caspar is credited with restoring the finances of the vicariate of North Cochinchina by securing substantial landholdings through gifts and purchases, sufficient to sustain the vicariates seminaries. Caspar encouraged the Pauline sisters to set up an orphanage and a school, and persuaded the Christian Brothers to found two schools, a novitiate, a juvénat and a retreat house, all at Hue. Under his ministry from 1886-1906 fourteen new parishes incorporating more than 200 new Christian communes were founded, and Christian adherents rose from 18,000 to more than 60,000. However, as might be expected with such a sudden expansion, an exceptionally high number of apostacies were indicated in annual reports. Caspar resigned through ill health in 1907.

Chamaison, J. (1812-1880). Missionary of the S.M.E., b. Montauban. Worked in Cochinchina from January 1840 to 1846, when he transferred to the Paris seminary. Resigned in 1859, but returned as a missionary to Japan in 1871. Retired, 1875.

Champeaux, L.E. Palasme de, (1840-89), b. Brest. Entered Navy in 1856 and took part in the China and Cochinchina campaigns. While still an ensign he transferred to the Cochinchina administration in 1867 as a trainee inspector. Inspector of Native Affairs responsible for Saigon in 1880, he was sent as chargé to Hanoi where he remained from 6 October 1880 - 17 August 1881. Consul at Haiphong in 1882. In July-August 1883 he accompanied Dr Harmand to Hue as representative of the governor of Cochinchina for the making of the Harmand convention. French Resident at Hue from 4 September 1883 until February 1884, when he resigned after a dispute with Harmand over his unauthorised dealings with the Kien Phuoc (Viceroy) of Tonkin. Returned to Hue to replace Lemaire as Chargé d'affaires in March 1885, but had no effective authority since full military and diplomatic powers had by now been vested in General de Courcy. Resident-Superior of Cambodia, 14 November 1887 - 10 May 1889. An enthusiastic member of the Etoile du Tonkin masonic lodge, he exhibited some antagonism towards missionaries.

Charbonnier, Mgr E.E., (1821-78). Bishop of Domitiopolis, Vicar Apostolic of East Cochinchina, b. Basses Alpes. Missionary in West

Tonkin from 1848. In 1855 he transferred to Thanh Hóa. Provicar of the West Tonkin vicariate from 1857. During this time he was hunted and in hiding until captured, tortured and condemned to death by Vietnamese authorities in 1861. Released after the signature of the 1862 treaty. Recuperated in France, 1862-4. Appointed to the vicariate of East Cochinchina as Bishop of Domitiopolis and conveyed to Qui Nhon in 1865 by gunboat in order to awe the Vietnamese authorities. His vicariate at this time consisted of 4 missionaries, 22 native priests, 1 seminary with 22 pupils, 8 convents with 300 nuns and a total of 26,000 Christians. All the parishes had been devastated and its churches and presbyteries burned. By the time of his death in 1878 his vicariate had recovered somewhat: it comprised 18 missionaries, 21 native priests and 95 catechists, 177 churches or chapels and a Christian population of 36,000.

Charner, L.V.J. (1797-1869). Admiral of France, b. St.Brieuc. Took part in the Algerian expedition, 1830. Captain, 1841. Commanded the frigate Sirène which conveyed the Lagrené embassy to China in 1844. Rear-Admiral, 1852. Cabinet secretary to the Naval Minister T. Ducos in 1852-3. Served in the Crimean campaign. Vice-Admiral in 1855. Appointed C.in C. of the French forces in the Far East in February, 1860 in succession to Rigault de Genouilly. C.in C. and Minister Plenipotentiary in Cochinchina, February-November 1861. Senator, February 1862. Admiral of France in November, 1864.

Chasseloup-Laubat, Prosper de, (1802-73). Politician and Minister of the Navy under the Second Empire. Conseil d'Etat, 1828. Deputy for Marennes, 1839. Minister of the Navy, April-October 1851. Elected to the Corps Législatif, 1852. Minister for Algeria and the Colonies 24 March 1859 - 24 November 1860. Minister of the Navy and Colonies 24 November 1860 until 20 January 1867. President of the Paris Geographical Society, 1864-73. President of the Conseil d'Etat, 7 July 1869 - 2 January 1870. Deputy for Charente-Inférieure at the Assemblée Nationale from 1871-3.

Cintrat, P. Director of Archives, Quai d'Orsay, and member of the Brenier commission. A career diplomat. Asked to evaluate the Franco-Vietnamese treaty of 1787 in the light of Abbé Huc's proposal of January, 1857 **(Doc. 3)** for a French expedition to Vietnam, Cintrat reported that French treaty rights were too weak to provide legal justification. Asserted that since France had not fulfilled her obligations under the agreement, an attack on Tourane would entail ruinous embarassment. In his opinion the likely cost would far exceed any material advantages, and France had enough interests abroad to occupy her without indulging in a hasardous adventure in the Far East. Cintrat's advice influenced Foreign Minister Walewski to recommend against Huc's proposal at first. Nonetheless Napoleon III insisted on a further investigation of the issues by a full commission.

Clémentel, E. (1864-1936). Lawyer. Deputy for Puy-de-Dôme , 1900-1919. Minister for Colonies in Rouvier's second and third cabinets from 24 January 1905 - 14 March 1906. A member of the Gauche Radicale he pressed for the adoption of policies for eliciting the collaboration of native elites in the colonies.

Colombert, Mgr I. (1838-94), Bishop of Samostate, Vicar Apostolic of West Cochinchina, b. Mayenne. Ordained and despatched to West Cochinchina in 1863. Missionary at Cai Nhum, a district of Vinh Long province. In 1866 he became private secretary to Bishop Colombert at Saigon and Procurator of the vicariate. Became Miche's coadjutor in 1872 and succeeded him as vicar apostolic on 1 December 1873. An able, wryly humourous administrator, Colombert trod far more warily than his brusque and rancorous predecessor in dealings with French authorities. Under his management the vicariate derived considerable advantages from French colonial occupation. He obtained official subsidies for the building of Saigon cathedral in the late 1870s, a confirmation of all the mission's existing property titles, and some increase in the official annual subsidy. Although he was unable to prevent the abolition of the annual aubsidy in 1881-2, he managed to negoatiate the concession of contracts for teaching French in mission schools, which restored official support to virtually the same level. At the same time he worked to maintain the administrative independence of the West Cochinchina vicariate by opposing the imposition of concordatory controls. In consequence, unlike the Churches in France, the vicariate enjoyed official material support without the sacrifice of administrative autonomy.

Colombert was instrumental in drafting clause 9 of the Franco-Vietnamese treaty of 1874. It conferred exemptions and privileges upon the Spanish as well as the French missions in Annam and Tonkin, and came to constitute a major diplomatic obstacle to the imposition of the Associations Law of 1901 upon these parts of Indochina.

Colombert's tact won him the regard of even strongly anticlerical officials, who tended to compare him favourably with his irascible contemporary, Bishop Puginier. After his death on 31 December 1894 the Colonial Council named a road after him in Saigon.

Courcy, P.M. Roussel de, (1827-87). Served in the Crimean, Chinese, Italian and Mexican campaigns, and in the Franco-Prussian war. As a Brigadier-General he was sent to observe Grand Duke Michael's campaign in the Caucasus during the Russo-Turkish war. Appointed C.in C. of the Tonkin expeditionary corps and Resident-General of Annam-Tonkin on 31 May 1885. Following the Hue ambush of 5-6 July 1885 Courcy encountered bitter criticism from missionaries both for the ineffectiveness of his efforts at pursuing Ton That Thuyet and Ham Nghi, and for his refusal to organise adequate protection for Christian villages under threat of massacre. He was replaced on 31 January 1886.

Cua, Paulus, or **Huynh Tinh Cua** (1834-1907), b. Baria. Vietnamese scholar, educated at the seminary at Penang. One of the first seminarists to enter the colonial administration in 1861. Attached to the Translation office of the Direction of the Interior at Saigon. Editor of Gia Dinh Bao, the quoc ngu version of the Journal Officiel. Served on examination commissions for certifying teachers of Vietnamese and Chinese. Translated many Chinese folk tales and plays into demotic Vietnamese. Laboured to provide a body of secular quoc ngu literature and scientific textbooks for the education of Vietnamese in government schools. A collaborator totally committed to French rule. Advised government in 1883-4 on the unification of French and Vietnamese law codes for local use.

Cuong De, Prince. Direct descendant of Gia Long's eldest son Canh, whose children's succession rights had been bypassed. The high point of his career as an early nationalist was his adoption as legitimist pretender to the throne by Phan Boi Chau's revolutionary Duy Tan Hoi movement in 1908. The leading reformist nationist, Phan Chu Trinh, however disparaged the need for a monarchical figurehead. By 1912 Cuong De was being treated even by Phan Boi Chau merely as 'president' of a prospective republic. Cuong De's Restoration society remained an active force in Vietnam until the 1940s.

Deloncle, A.B. François (1856-1922). Diplomat, journalist and politician, b. Cahors. Through family connections secured a succession of posts at the Quai d'Orsay in the early 1880s, culminating in the post of _rédacteur_ at the Direction Commerciale (1883-5). Made a series of subsidised visits to the Far East in pursuit of an ephemeral Kra canal project (Siam). Obtained a political treaty from the King of Burma in 1884, which Jules Ferry declined to ratify. Became Ferry's secretary after 1885, entered parliament in 1889 and developed a reputation as a colonial _enragé_ and leading spokesman for the Parti Colonial. He became belatedly implicated in the Panama scandal and lost his seat in the elections of 1898. Returned to parliament in 1902 when he succeeded Le Myre de Vilers as deputy for Cochinchina. Described himself as a member of the _Bloc des Gauches._ In the elections of 1906 he approached Bishop Mossard for the missionary vote, while covertly sounding out the masonic lodges for support in forming a company to capitalise on the impending territorial dispossession of the missions. He sought to join the Radical-Socialist party in 1910, but, widely mistrusted, he was refused. He lost the Cochinchina seat to Paul Pâris (Radical-Socialist) the same year. He represented the Basses-Alpes from 1912, retiring in 1914.

Depierre, Mgr J.M. (1855-98). Bishop of Benda, Vicar Apostolic of West Cochinchina, b. Savoy. Despatched to Cochinchina, 1879. Taught at the Saigon seminary. Elected Bishop of Benda and Vicar Apostolic, 12 April 1895. Defended the missions against criticism in the local press, particularly against the charge that the West Cochinchina mission had amassed substantial landed assets. In association with Le Myre de Vilers he organised subscriptions for the erection of a statue to Bishop Pigneau de Béhaine in Saigon.

Doumergue, G. Minister for the Colonies, President of the Republic, b. 1863 (Gard). Lawyer. Secured a judicial appointment in the colonial magistracy in Cochinchina in 1890. In 1892 he transferred to Algeria for family reasons. Elected deputy for Nîmes in 1893 as a Radical-Socialist, and continuously re-elected, he became Secretary to the Chamber of Deputies 1895-6. Minister for the Colonies in the Combes cabinet (17 June 1902 - 24 January 1905). He became successively Minister of Commerce (1906-8) and of Education (1908-10). A senator by 1910 he chaired the parliamentary commissions of naval and foreign affairs until asked to form his own cabinet on 9 December 1913. Resigned the premiership on 9 June 1914, but held the Colonial portfolio in successive cabinets until 1917. Became President of the Republic in June 1924.

Duperré, Victor A. Admiral, Baron, Governor of Cochinchina. A Bonapartist in political sympathies and an autocrat in administrative style. Had the reputation of making excessive use of his discretionary powers as governor. Appointed by a cabinet intent on limiting French involvement in Tonkin, Duperré refrained, like his predecessor Krantz, from taking adventurous measures to make the treaties of 1874 workable. Notably active in promoting the construction of Saigon cathedral.

Dupré, M.J. (1813-81). Admiral, Governor of Cochinchina, b. Albi. Family originated in Alsace. Entered the Ecole Navale in 1830. Service on the China station in the early 1840s. Served in the Antilles from

1848-51. Promoted frigate captain in 1854 and fought in the Crimean war. Flag captain, 1858. Worked in the Naval Ministry during the Italian campaign 1859-60, then commanded the East African squadron 1861-3. Governor of Réunion in 1864-7. Served on the China station during the Franco-Prussian war. Governor of Cochinchina from April 1871 until 15 March 1874. After the fiasco of the Garnier expedition Dupré returned to France under a cloud, but successfully defended his conduct in a correspondance with the Naval Minister Admiral Montaignac. Appointed Vice-Admiral in 1875 he became naval governor of Rochefort and then Toulon. Retired, 1879. Offered the naval ministry in 1880 by Jules Ferry, possibly with a view to organising a new French intervention in Tonkin.

Dupuis, J. Entrepreneur. (1828-1912), b. Loire. Son of a muslin manufacturer. Began trading in Ismaelia in 1859 until attracted to Far Eastern commerce by the profitable sale of a cargo on a visit to Hong Kong. He followed the French land expedition in China under General Cousin-Montauban in 1860 and then accompanied the Simon expedition part of the way to the Blue river, basing himsef at Hangkow where he dealt in provisions and munitions for the Chinese forces. Chafed at the length of transit between Hong Kong and Shanghai. In 1868 Francis Garnier arrived at Hangkow with the Mekong expedition and informed him of the trade potentials of South West China, and of the navigational possibilities of the Red River in Tonkin as a short link between the China sea and Yunnan. In February 1871 he journeyed to Yunnan. He reached Manghao, and from there travelled down the Red river into Tonkin as far as the first Vietnamese customs posts without being turned back by Black Flags. His reconnoitre convinced him of the practicability of the river as a trade route. Returning to Manghao he signed provisions contracts with local Chinese military officials in return for promises of Yunnanese tin and copper cargos, and then returned to France in 1872 to obtain the Naval ministry's mediation with the Vietnamese for permission to open the Red River up to trade. The ministry withheld assistance for fear of diplomatic repercussions, but nonetheless commended his venture to the Governor of Saigon, Admiral Dupré. By 9 November 1872 Dupuis had assembled at Haiphong a small flotilla of armed trading vessels with a cargo of guns and munitions. Ignoring official Vietnamese strictures against travelling up river to the capital, Dupuis arrived at Hanoi with his fleet on 22 November, and overcoming further prohibitions set off up river with part of his fleet on 18 January 1873. He crossed into Yunnan and on 4 March 1873 reached Manghao, discharged his cargo and returned to Hanoi with his payment of tin and copper. Here he found that his native assistants had been imprisoned. Dupuis disembarked his small expedition and turned the guns of his ships on the citadel. With a Vietnamese force under Marshal Nguyen Tri Phuong (qv.) assembling on the outskirts of the town, Dupuis unfurled the French flag, thereby forcing the Vietnamese authorities to issue a circumspect protest to Saigon demanding his removal. This request created the opportunity for intervention for which Admiral Dupré had been searching for months.

Following the fiasco of the Garnier expedition and the disavowal of Garnier himself, Dupré detained Dupuis at Saigon for some months to prevent him from causing further embarrassment in France. Ruined by the collapse of his enterprise Dupuis maintained a ten year long campaign for restitution, and though voted a three million fr. indemnity by parliament in 1884, failed to receive more than a small pension from the Colonial ministry. Meantime he engaged in a lively polemic in the press, attacking the conduct of Dupré and Philastre, but defending the mission in West Tonkin, especially the role of Bishop Puginier.

Eveillard, D. (1835-83). Missionary, b. Nantes. Arrived in West Cochinchina in 1861. Taught at the seminary of Saigon. Appointed procurator, he founded the mission press, transferring it to Tan Dinh in 1874. There he published a number of school textbooks and works of devotion.

Ferry, Jules. (1832-93). Lawyer and a leader of of the parliamentary opposition to the Second Empire, b. Alsace. He dominated a sector of the republican Centre, somewhat to the right of Gambetta's Union Républicaine. Gambetta's death in 1882 opened the way to the consolidation of the Centre, and Ferry's second administration (March 1883 - April 1885) was to be the strongest and most long-lived of the cabinets of the early Third Republic. Ferry supplied much of the impetus behind the laicisation of the French educational system, removing Catholic influences from state primary schools. In his colonial policy, however, he encouraged official cooperation with missionary interests. As a result he received vigorous support from some clericals in parliament, such as Mgr Freppel, Bishop of Angers (deputy for Finistère), who broke with his allies on the monarchist right to support the Tonkin venture.

Fleury, E.F. (1815-84). Director at the Ministry of Commerce, member of the Brenier commission, b. Paris. Served with the Spahis in Algeria (1837-45), and then under General Saint-Arnaud in the Kabylie campaign. Lt Col. 1850. Brigadier-General, 1856 and A.D.C. to the Emperor. Director of Foreign Trade at the Ministry of Commerce, and member of Brenier's Cochinchina commission, 1857. During the Italian war in 1859, Napoleon III sent him to offer conditions of peace to the Austrians. Divisional General, 1863. Ambassador to Russia, 1864-5. Senator, March 1865.

Fourès, J.A. (1853-1915). One of the first Indochina administrators to pass his entire career in the Union. Entered the shortlived Collège des Stagiaires at Saigon, 1874. Trainee administrator 1875, serving in Cambodia. Secretary-General of Cambodia and interim Resident-General, 1881-5. Administrator at Soc Trang 1887-8. Secretary to the Direction of the Interior, Cochinchina. Interim, then substantive, Lt Governor of Cochinchina 1892 - August 1895. Secretary-General of Tonkin 1895-9. Resident-Superior Tonkin, June 1897 - June 1907, when he retired. During this period of office he took leave on several occasions, when his position was temporarily filled by J.L.Morel (qv.), E.Broni (qv.), L.Luce (qv.) and E.Groleau (qv.).

Fourichon, M. (1809-84). Admiral. Member of the Brenier commission. b. Dordogne. Entered navy, 1824. Ensign, 1829. Lt 1833. Served in Algeria. Captain, 1843. While commanding the Algérie he conveyed Abbé Huc from Singapore to Suez. Governor of Cayenne, 1852. Rear-Admiral, 1853. Commanded the Pacific Ocean station, then the Mediterranean station. Vice-Admiral, 1859. Minister for the Navy, 1870. Deputy for the Dordogne, February 1871. Senator, 1875. Naval Minister in the Dufaure cabinet, 9 March-16 March 1877.

Galibert, Mgr L.M. (1845-83). Bishop of Eno, Vicar Apostolic of East Cochinchina, b. Tarn. Arrived in East Cochinchina in 1868. Missionary at Tra Kieu (Quang Nam). Superior of the seminary at Nuoc Nhi in 1877. Elected bishop in May 1879. Visited the Bahnars in 1880, fell ill and returned to France in 1881 for treatment. Failed to recover and died in April 1883.

Garnier, Francis. (1839-73). Entered Ecole Navale in 1856. Attached as a Lt to the staff of Admiral Charner in 1860. After a short period of leave in France, returned to Cochinchina in 1863 and became 'prefet' or governor of Cholon, the Chinese town adjacent to Saigon, where local missionaries commended his efforts to suppress opium smoking and gambling. Garnier published his first pamphlets on Cochinchina - opposing Retrocession - in 1864-5. A passionate advocate of French penetration into the South China market, Garnier was among the first to propose a full scale exploration of the Mekong river as a prospective route of access. Attached to Captain Doudart de Lagrée's mission to explore the Mekong, Garnier took charge of publishing its findings after Doudart de Lagrée's death in 1869. The Mekong mission's discovery that the river was unusable as a major trade artery by reason of obstructions at Khone and Kemmerat diverted Garnier's attention to the commercial possibilities of the Red river in Tonkin as an alternative route into South China. Recalled to France during the Franco-Prussian war, Garnier returned to Shanghai in December 1872 to resume his investigation of routes into the South China market. When in 1873 Admiral Dupré began planning a military intervention in Tonkin, his first choice of commander - Captain Senez - fell ill before taking up his appointment. Garnier accepted the appointment largely on his own terms, and claimed to have moderated Dupré's aggressive strategy in discussions prior to his departure.

Garnier's posthumous reputation was somewhat discredited by Dupré, who claimed that his own orders had been exceeded. But by the early 1880s Garnier had become totemised by the colonial movement, particularly after the death of Rivière in parallel circumstances in 1883.

Gauthier, Mgr J.D. (1810-77). Bishop of Emmaus, Vicar Apostolic of South Tonkin. Arrived as a missionary in West Tonkin in 1835. Appointed coadjutor to Mgr Retord as Bishop of Emmaus in 1841, and despatched to the southern portion of the vicariate. In 1846 when the vicariat Apostolic of South Tonkin was created with Gauthier as its first bishop, it comprised 66,350 Christians divided into 345 villages in 19 districts, and administered by 75 catechists, 35 native priests and 4 missionaries. Gauthier spent much of his early career in hiding, even having to quit Tonkin on a gunboat in 1859 during the French campaign in Cochinchina. He returned in 1863 to a devastated mission and began restoring it. The rest of the decade was relatively untroubled for him. In 1867 Tu Duc sent Gauthier to France to obtain the personnel and necessities for founding a college at Hue; but Gauthier returned to find that changed circumstances at court had caused the scheme to be abandoned.

The collapse of the Garnier expedition sparked off a spate of social reprisals agaist Christians which particularly affected the provinces of his vicariate, and Gauthier's pressure for compensation was extreme enough to alienate even some French authorities, such as Philastre, the French chargé at Hue. Governor Duprerré however spoke well of him in 1876-7: '...very old and fanatical, but I have had nothing but good relations with him.'

Geffroy, F.M. Missionary, b. Saint-Brieuc. Worked in East Cochinchina. Emboiled in controversy in 1879 over his inclination to defend Christians too abrasively in quarrels with Vietnamese officials. The French authorities were divided over his case: Consul Verschneider at

Thi Nai defended Geffroy; but Rheinart (qv.) Resident at Hue, who normally showed sympathy towards missionary interests, considered the complaints of Vietnamese mandarins against him to be justified. Governor Le Myre de Vilers adopted Rheinart's viewpoint and demanded Geffroy's transfer to another location within the vicariate on pain of having his passport withdrawn. The 'cas Geffroy' achieved some notoriety in the French administration and provides a further instance of French official reluctance to prevent missionaries from destabilising relations with the Vietnamese court in Annam-Tonkin during the decade between the 1874 treaties and the Tonkin war.

Gendreau, Mgr P. (1850-1935). Bishop of Chrysopolis, Vicar Apostolic of West Tonkin, b. Luçon (Vendée). Despatched to Tonkin, 1873. Military almoner at Haiphong, 1874-84. Collected local testimony for the beatification of the 95 Indochina martyrs. Taught at the seminary of Hoang Nguyen, 1884-92. Appointed coadjutor to Bishop Puginier as Bishop of Chrysopolis in April 1887. Succeeded Puginier as vicar apostolic on 25 April 1892. Encouraged the Christian Brothers to establish themselves in Tonkin. Had a hospital for Vietnamese constructed at Hanoi in 1895, then others at Nam Dinh, Ke So, Ke Vinh and at Vu Ban. Subdivided the vicariate of West Tonkin: created the vicariates of Upper Tonkin and Maritime Tonkin. These were assigned to Mgr Ramond (residing at Hung Hoa) and Mgr Marcou (at Phat Diem) respectively. Founded the leprosarium at Phuc Nhac. Summoned the Redemptorists (1929) and French Dominicans (1930) to West Tonkin.

Just as Bishop Colombert had proved a diplomatic successor to the abrasive Miche, so Gendreau, following Puginier, showed a flair for making himself acceptable to the French authorities, by whom he was highly regarded. Nonetheless Gendreau's letters to Mgr Marcou at Phat Diem show that he took pains to defend the mission against the Associations Law of 1901, by using all legal means to obstruct land registration procedures between 1904 and 1914. Although regarded by the administration as the doyen of the Catholic episcopate in Indochina, Gendreau had no formal authority over his fellow bishops; but he helped to engineer the removal of Mgr Pineau from the vicariate of South Tonkin when the latter's complicity in fundraising for the Duy Tan Hoi was denounced to the directors of the S.M.E. by a group of his own missionaries. The removal of Pineau in 1910 signified an assertion of Gendreau's commitment to French political rule. It helped to convince Governor-General Klobukowski of the need to prevent the application of the Law of 1901 to Annam and Tonkin.

Grandière, P.P. de la (1807-76). Vice-Admiral, Governor of Cochinchina, b. Redon, into a naval family. Captain, 1849. Served in the Sea of Okhotsk during the Crimean war, 1854-5. C.in C. of the naval division off the Syrian coast at the time of the Druze massacres, 1860-62. Rear-Admiral, December 1861. Governor of Cochinchina 1 May 1863 - 5 April 1868. Despite his withdrawal in 1868 he remained titular governor until his resignation in April 1870. Senator, 1870. Naval governor of Toulon, 1870.

Grangeon, Mgr D. (1857-1933). Bishop of Utine and Vicar Apostolic of East Cochinchina, b. Puy de Dôme. Sub-deacon in the Paris seminary of the S.M.E., 1881. Despatched to East Cochinchina, 1883. Witnessed and reported the massacres of 1885-6 in the vicariate. Procurator at Dai An. Elected Bishop of Utine and Vicar Apostolic of East Cochinchina in 1902. Part of his vicariate covered Kontum and the Sedang-Bahnar region, and he became embroiled in the Pâris-Guerlach controversy.

Cooperated closely with Guerlach in devising a strategy for defending the mission in the press and the courts. Grangeon sanctioned Guerlach's polemical endeavours, but constantly urged him to moderation. In 1907 he brought a lawsuit against Pâris, who summoned French officials as defence witnesses. The mission's suit failed on a technicality. Between 1909 and 1914, when the mission at Kontum became embroiled in increasingly bitter controversy with Guénot, the local French délégué, Grangeon was forced once more to prepare a legal defence for one of his missionaries, Father Hutinet, who was finally condemned and fined for violating the délégué's jurisdiction. Hutinet's activities (he attempted to levy a form of taxation on his parishioners) were reported not only to the press but to parliament, through an interpellation by the Radical anticlerical Maurice Violette.

Groleau, J.H.E.   Resident   of   Hai-duong,   1901-11.   Interim Resident-Superior of Tonkin, 30 August 1905 - 10 May 1907; and again from 25 August 1908 - 21 February 1911. Bishop Gendreau of West Tonkin reported that Mme Groleau was a devout Catholic, and that Groleau himself was well disposed to the mission.

Guerlach, J.B.M. (1858-1912). Missionary, b. Metz. Retained French nationality after 1870. Arrived in East Cochinchina in 1879. In 1882, having taught himself Bahnar, he moved to the 'mission des sauvages' at Po'lei Jo'dreh, which he found in decline. Acquired considerable influence among the Sedangs and Bahnars, who were to remain impervious to the Can Vuong rebellion in 1885-6. Led an expedition to defend them against marauding Jarai in 1887. Supported Mayrena in creating a 'kingdom' of the Sedangs in 1888, but disavowed him in 1889 when he realised that Mayrena had no official sanction. As superior of the Bahnar mission he gave considerable help to the explorations of the Mission Pavie in the vicinity. Returned to Tourane to recuperate from illness in 1903, where he gave shelter to the Pauline sisters expelled from the government hospital in conformity with the law of 1903 laicising official establishments. Became embroiled in a press polemic with Camille Pâris in 1906-7, and arranged with Bishop Grangeon to bring a suit for slander, which failed. In 1908 he returned to the Bahnars at Ro Lai, becoming provicar and superior of the mission again after the death of Father Vialleton (qv.) in 1909. Guerlach's letters reveal the development of a bitter and persistant struggle with the anticlerical French délégé at Kontum, Guénot. Guénot considered Guerlach's personal ascendancy over the Bahnars to be an impediment to his own powers of administrative action. He exploited family and village disputes among the Bahnars to procure apostacies and develop an anti-Guerlach faction. Guénot reported some of his difficulties to the press. Through Radical opinion networks this dispute fed into occasional parliamentary discussion of the role of missionaries in the colonies. Guerlach died at Kontum in 1912.

Haas, F. (1843-1912). Consul-General, b. Sirentz (Alsace) Retained French nationality after 1870 and used Alsatian political connections to secure a succession of posts in the French Settlements in India. Counsel to the court of appeal, Pondicherry, 1877. Judge at St Barthélémey (Guadaloupe), 1878. Chef de Service, Mahé (French India), 1879. Director of the Interior of the French Settlements in India, 1881-2. Transferred to the foreign service as Consul at Mandalay, 20 February 1885. At the time of the Tonkin war Haas became obsessed with the need to establish an informal French political and economic ascendancy over Upper Burma in order to perfect French monopoly of access to South-West China. Despite Ferry's fall from power in April 1885 and the promulgation of a policy of inaction at Mandalay by his successor Freycinet, Haas persisted locally in his efforts to boost French influence. Ill health lent a tone of hysteria and confusion to his reports, and by August 1885 officials at the Quai were describing him as 'détraqué', 'un fou lucide', and 'un écervelé'. As the Anglo-Burmese crisis of August-November deepened, Haas' role in pursuing Burmese concessions and contracts seemed increasingly ambiguous and politically sinister to British officials in Simla, Rangoon and Whitehall. The ensuing British annexation is at least partly attributable to Haas' excited machinations. In 1888 Haas inspired leaders of the future Parti Colonial, particularly François Deloncle, to develop, through the Mission Pavie, a new strategy for acquiring political control over eastern Siam and upper Laos. Haas continued to pursue and support schemes for unlocking the imaginary wealth of South-West China until his retirement in 1907.

Harmand, J. (1845-1921). Explorer, ethnologist, diplomat, b. Saumur into a military family. After medical studies he became a doctor in the French naval service in Cochinchina, 1866-8. Served in the Baltic in 1870 and in Kabylie (1871) before returning to Saigon in 1873. Medical officer on the Garnier expedition to Tonkin, where he held the town of Nam Dinh as military governor, 9 December 1873 - 20 January 1874. Pursued ehtnographic and archaeological studies in Lower Laos and Cambodia from 1875-7, exploring part of the Bolovens plateau and the Se Moun valley. Became Vice-President of the Paris Geographical Society in 1878 and Assistant Commissioner for the permanent Colonial expedition in Paris, 1879-81. Nominated by Le Myre de Vilers as Consul at Bangkok in October 1881, Harmand's knowledge of the region secured his promotion as Civil Commissioner-General in Tonkin in June 1883. The Convention of August 1883 which he imposed upon the Vietnamese was rejected by Ferry for its severity. Detested by the naval and military commanders as 'a civilian from nowhere', Harmand found it difficult to secure cooperation. After a jurisdictional dispute over the appointment of General Millot as C.in C., Harmand was withdrawn from Tonkin on 20 February, 1884. From 1885-89 he served as Consul-General in Calcutta, then as Minister in Tokyo from 1894-1905. In 1910 he published an important work of colonial theory, <u>Domination et colonisation</u>.

Hector, S. Administrator, b. Isère, 1846. Lt in the Infanterie de Marine, 1871. Inspector of Native Affairs, 1871-1885. In October 1885 he replaced Champeaux (qv.) as Resident at Hue, where he remained at loggerheads with General Prud'homme. Interim Resident-Superior at Hue 17 May 1886 - 4 May 1889. Resident-Superior at Hue, 10 May 1889 - 27 October 1891. Retired in April 1892.

Hoang Ke Viem or **Huynh Ta Viem,** Prince. Vietnamese general. Brother-in-law of Tu Duc through marriage to a daughter of Emperor Minh Mang. Commander of the Vietnamese troops in Tonkin based on Son Tay, 1872-1883. Engaged forces of Black Flags to resist Garnier in 1873. Used Black Flags again to cut Commandant Rivière's communications with provinces north and west of Hanoi in 1882-3. With his surrender of Son Tay in December 1883, Vietnamese hopes of maintaining resistance to the French seizure of Tonkin were temporarily dashed. Paul Bert hoped to use him to secure the pacification of Quang Binh, North Annam, in 1886.

Huc, R.E. Abbé. Missionary, b. 1814 at Caylus. Entered Lazarist order in 1836. Embarked for Macao, 1839. Made a celebrated journey to Tibet in 1844-6 and published Souvenirs d'un voyage dans la Tartarie, le Tibet et la Chine in 1850. Published several popular works on the missions in Asia, and during the Crimean war joined with others in projecting a new French East India Company to colonise Korea, Madagascar and Tourane, which aroused Napoleon III's interest. Huc's note to the emperor in January 1857, and his subsequent interview with him, sparked off official study of the prospect of military intervention in Vietnam. Huc, who had never visited Vietnam, acted principlally as spokesman for Fr Libois (qv.), procurator of the S.M.E. at Hong Kong, who was also pressing diplomats and naval officers to intercede on the mission's behalf.

Irigoyen, P. (1856-1935). Missionary, b. Bayonne. Arrived East Cochinchina 1883. Worked with Guerlach and Vialleton among the Bahnars from 1884. The mission consisted of 4 villages and 12,000 Christians. Irigoyen was particularly enthusiastic in helping Mayrena found his Sedang 'kingdom', hoping that the arrival of formal administration under a Catholic constitution would promote the authority of the mission. In 1912 he became involved, along with Fr Hutinet, in the Kontum mission's dispute with the French délégué, Guénot, who was actively encouraging apostacy among the Bahnars.

Jauréguiberry, J.B. (1815-87). Vice-Admiral and Naval Minister, b. Bayonne into a Protestant naval family. Captain, 1856. Served in the China and Cochinchina campaigns from 1858-1861, acting as commander at Saigon in 1860-1. Governor of Senegal, October 1861 - May 1863. Rear-Admiral, May 1869 and Vice-Admiral, December 1871. Senator, June 1879. Minister for the Navy from February 1879 to September 1880 in the Waddington and de Freycinet cabinets successively, and again from 31 January 1882 to 30 January 1883 in the cabinets of de Freycinet, Duclerc and Fallières. Strong advocate of intervention in Tonkin from 1879 onwards, but persistantly restrained from pressing his policy by the insecurity of parliamentary support for the cabinets in which he served.

Jaurès, C.L.J. (1823-89). Admiral, politician and diplomat. Fought at Pei Ho in the China campaign, and at Ky Hoa in Cochinchina, 1861. Fought with the Loire army in 1870. Rear-Admiral, 1871. Conservative deputy for Tarn in the National Assembly, 1873. Presented the report of the parliamentary commission on Admiral Dupré's treaty of 1874 with Annam. Vice-Admiral, October 1878. Ambassador in Madrid, 1878 and St Petersburg, 1882. Naval Minister in the Tirard cabinet, 1889. Brother of Vice-Admiral L.J.Jaurès (qv.) and uncle of Jean Jaurès, the socialist leader.

Jaurès, L.J. (1808-70). Naval officer, Member of the Brenier commission. Entered navy, 1827. Captain, 1837. Admiral Laguerre's flag captain, Far East fleet, 1853-5. Member of the Suez commission, and of the Brenier commission, 1857. Rear-Admiral, July 1860. Commander of the China sea squadron, 1862-3. Vice-Admiral, 1864. Not to be confused with Admiral C.L.J Jaurès referred to above.

Kergaradec, A.C.J. de, (1841-94). Naval officer and diplomat, b. Lorient. Entered the navy in 1855. Ensign, 1863. Campaigned in Mexico (1863-4) and Tahiti (1865). Lt 1868. Transferred into the Inspection des affaires indigènes in Cochinchina, 1869-72. Reattached to the staff of the Ministry of Marine in 1874, he became Consul at Hanoi on 16 May 1875, for a few months. Made a reconnaissance of Red River, 1876-7 and

reassigned to Hanoi early in 1879. Consul at Haiphong, 1880-3.
Promoted Captain in April 1883 Transferred to the foreign ministry and
became Consul-General at Bangkok in 1883 (June) - 1891. Consul-General,
Moscow 1891.

Klobukowski, A. Governor-General of Indochina, b. Auxerre (Yonne), 1855.
After a legal training joined the Yonne prefecture. Chief secretary to
the prefectures of Deux-Sèvres (1877), Parthenay (1878), l'Aube (1879),
and Loire (1880). From 1882-5 he was chief secretary to Governor
Thomson of Cochinchina. Chief secretary to Paul Bert, Resident-General
of Annam-Tonkin (1886), then Secretary-General for the Government of
Indochina, 1887-9. Married Paul Bert's daughter. Concul-General at
Yokohama from March 1889, and at Calcutta from February 1896. Minister
Resident at Bangkok from 30 July 1901. Minister plenipotentiary in Lima
from October 1903. Chargé in Cairo from October 1906. Mission to
Ethiopia in April, 1907. Governor-General of Indochina, 24 June 1908 -
January 1910. Ended his career as Ambassador in Brussels.

Krantz, J.K. (1821-1914). Admiral and Naval minister, b. Arches
(Vosges). Entered navy, 1837. Captain, March 1861. Chief secretary to
the Naval minister, February 1871. Rear-Admiral, 1871. C.in C. Far
East fleet, 20 October 1873. Governor of Cochinchina, 15 March - 1
December 1874. Signed the commmercial treaty of 31 August 1874 with
Annam which, in principle, opened Tonkin to foreign trade.
Vice-Admiral, 1877. Minister for the Navy in three cabinets between
1888 and 1889, finally resigning in protest at the reduction of French
forces in Tonkin.

Ky, Petrus Truong Vinh. (1837-98). The most outstanding and competant
of Catholic Vietnamese collaborators with French rule. Son of a
military mandarin and orphaned at the age of nine. Trained in the
Penang seminary of the S.M.E. Ky was an outstanding linguist, fluent in
Chinese, quoc ngu and French. Chose not to become a priest but taught
for the mission and acted as an interpreter for the French in 1860.
Taught at the Collège des Interprètes and at the Collège des Stagiaires.
Edited the Gia-Dinh Bao for a time. In the early 1880s he advised the
French on political affairs, and served as Paul Bert's agent on the
Co-mat or Secret Council at the Hue court in 1886. First Vietnamese to
write a history of Vietnam in French. Ky was highly critical of
Christian reprisals against Vietnamese insurgents in 1873-4, but he
constantly reaffirmed his support for French colonial rule. A prolific
writer and translator of popular Chinese and Vietnamese literature into
quoc ngu.

Labbez, M. Resident at Nghe An, December 1909, became interim
Resident-Superior of Annam, April-May 1913.

Lafont, C.J. (1824-1908). Admiral, last naval governor of Cochinchina.
Served on the China station under Captain Cécille and present at the
bombardment of Tourane in 1847. Fought in the Crimean and China
campaigns. Appointed Captain in 1867, and returned to France to fight
in the Franco-Prussian war. Commanded the East African coastal
squadron. Rear-Admiral August 1875. Naval governor of Cherbourg in
1876. Governor of Cochinchina, 16 October 1877 - 7 July 1879. Sought
to continue the policy of restricting French involvement in Annam-Tonkin
despite the unworkability of the 1874 treaties. Sought to block a
further Vietnamese retrocession mission to Paris, and to prevent the
Vietnamese court from undertaking diplomatic dealings with Pekin.

Considered pro-clerical by missionaries even though he kept Puginier and others strictly to the terms of the treaty of 15 March 1874. Earned the gratitude of Bishop Colombert by confirming missionary property titles in Cochinchina. Nominated an honorary member of the S.M.E. for this.

Lanessan, J.L. de. Governor-General of Indochina, 1891-4. Naval doctor in Cochinchina, 1868-71. Professor in the Paris Faculty of Medicine. A Radical in politics and a committed freemason, and an enthusiast for colonial expansion. A deputy from 1881, he was rapporteur for the Commission for the ratification of the Franco-Burmese treaty of January 1885, which outlined an ambitious scheme for French economic expansion in Southeast Asia. Given a mission by the Quai to report on the 'mise en valeur' of the French colonial system in 1886 he reported unfavourably on the economic potentials of Indochina. In 1891 he was appointed Governor-General after proposing ways and means of resolving both the pacification and budgetary problems of Annam-Tonkin. Pursued a strategy of cheap indirect rule by restoring some of the administrative responsibilities of the traditional mandarinate. Removed from office in 1894 after revealing confidential information to a journalist. Minister for the Navy in the Waldeck-Rousseau cabinet of 1899-1902, he became editor of Le Siècle. In 1906-7 he conducted a strong campaign to have anticlerical laws applied to the colonial system, and argued that the diplomatic tradition of 'protecting' Christians in the Ottoman and Chinese empires should be abandoned.

Lasserre, C. de. Former private secretary to Garnier, Lasserre became Admiral Dupré's secretary in Saigon from where he was able to keep Dupuis informed of events in Tonkin following the signature of the 1874 treaty.

Lebrun, A.F. Minister for the Colonies in the Caillaux and Poincaré cabinets, 27 June 1911 - 12 January 1913 , and 9 December 1913 - 9 June 1914.

Lê Duy Phung. See **Ta Van Phung.**

Lefebvre, Mgr D. (1810-65). Bishop of Isauropolis, Vicar Apostolic of Lower Cochinchina, b. Calvados. Spent much of his missionary career in Cochinchina from 1835 in hiding. Appointed Bishop of Isauropolis and coadjutor of Bishop Cuénot in 1841, he was arrested in 1844 and liberated after French naval intervention. In 1844 the vicariate of West Cochinchina (incorporating Cambodia) was created, and he was made its first Vicar Apostolic. Rearrested and transferred to Hue in 1847, he was again released and expelled, but again returned to Cochinchina clandestinely. After surviving the upheavals of the Cochinchina campaign of 1859-61 he began building up the West Cochinchina mission, with a little financial assistance from the French authorities. He was an acerbic critic of the effects of French occupation, and attributed to it the frustration of his attempts to develop the mission. He resigned through ill health in 1864 and died at Marseilles in 1865.

Lemonnier, E. Missionary. Bursar and teacher at the Penang seminary, 1855. Procurator at Shanghai, 1866-75. Procurator-General at Hong Kong, 1875-91. Retired, 1891. Died, 1899.

Le Myre de Vilers, C.M. (1833-1918). Colonial governor and politician. Son of an army officer of the First Empire. Entered the navy in 1851 and served in the Crimea. Ensign, 1855. Transferred into the Civil administration in 1861. Sub-prefect of Joigny (1863) and Bergerac (1867), he became Prefect of Algiers from November 1869 - September 1870. Both as Prefect of Haute Vienne from May 1873 and as Director of Civil and Financial Affairs in Algeria from 1875-9 he was suspected of Bonapartist sympathies. Appointed first civil governor of Cochinchina on 7 July 1879, he was forced to tread warily in his dealings with the powerful Blancsubé clique at Saigon. The Blancsubé interest dominated the municipality of Saigon and acquired wide powers over the disposal of revenue with the creation of the Colonial Council in 1880. A further ominous circumstance for Le Myre de Vilers was Blancsubé's intimacy with Gambetta's close associate, Eugène Etienne. Etienne, a deputy for Algeria, had developed an antipathy to Le Myre de Vilers from the latter's time there as Director of Civil Affairs.

Le Myre de Vilers showed no overt favour to missionaries, and in his official dealings adopted a severely neutral tone towards them. Bishop Colombert's misgivings about him were not finally resolved until the eve of the governor's departure, when Le Myre de Vilers privately revealed his covert efforts to defend the mission against the establishment of the concordatory arrangements advocated by Blancsubé.

After a period as Resident-General in Madagascar (1886-9), Le Myre de Vilers entered parliament in 1889 as deputy for Cochinchina following Blancsubé's death, and was constantly reelected until 1902. As deputy he vied unsuccessfully with Etienne for leadership of the Groupe Colonial, the parliamentary nucleus of the Parti Colonial, which played a role of considerable significance in the promotion of French colonial expansion from 1892 until 1918. Appointed Minister Plenipotentiary to Bangkok during the Siam crisis in 1893, Le Myre de Vilers hoped to impose a protectoral treaty, but was frustrated by British diplomatic counterpressures. Nonetheless he ensured that French missionaries in Siam should benefit from the crisis, and secured them a sizeable share of the Siam indemnity. In 1894-5 he chaired a committee for raising funds for the erection of a statue in Saigon to Bishop Pigneau de Béhaine.

Lévecque, F.E. Resident and interim Resident-Superior of Annam, 20 April 1906 - 14 August 1908. Governor of the French Settlements in India, 10 June 1909 - 3 June 1910.

Leygues, G. (1857-1933). Politician, b. Lot et Garonne. Lawyer, newspaper proprietor and noted orator. Deputy (Gauche Démocratique) for Lot et Garonne. Minister of Education, 30 May 1894 - 17 January 1895. Minister for the Interior, 17 January - 1 November 1895. As Minister of Education from November 1898 - 7 June 1902, he declined to politicise the national school curriculum as Radical-Socialists were demanding, but reformed it by introducing a larger scientific content. Minister for the Colonies, 4 March - 25 October 1906. In his colonial policy he promoted the ideal of 'association' and repudiated the 'unrealisable' ideal of assimilation. Minister of Marine, 16 November 1917 - 20 January 1920.

Libois, N. (1805-72). Missionary, b. Séez. Left for China in 1837. Sub-Procurator of the S.M.E. at Macao. Procurator at Hong Kong, 1842. Libois was in close contact with French diplomatic and naval personnel in China, especially with the Lagrené mission for which he supplied missionary interpreters. Pressed them vigorously for French intervention in Vietnam from the early 1850s. Used Abbé Huć as his spokesman in France. A major influence in determining French action in 1858-9. Procurator of the S.M.E. in Rome, 1866.

Luce, P.L. Administrator, b. 1856. Artillerie de Marine, 1876. Captain, attached to the military bureau of Governor Thomson of Cochinchina, 1883-4. Attached to Paul Bert's military bureau in 1886. Entered the Indochina administration in 1889 as Vice-Resident. Resident at Vinh, 1891-3. Resident at Thai Nguyen, July 1894. Director of Civil Affairs in Tonkin, 1895. Commandant-Superior of upper Laos, 1897. Served as temporary governor or Resident-Superior of every part of the Indochina Union between 1901 and 1911, when he was made substantive Resident-Superior of Cambodia. Interim Governor-General of Indochina, 17 February 1911 - 1 June 1911. A freemason of the Etoile du Tonkin lodge.

Luro, J.B.E. (1837-77). Naval ensign, 1859. Arrived in Cochinchina, 1864. Lt., 1866. Transferred into the Inspection des affaires indigènes. Along with Aubaret and Philastre one of the most respected French students of Vietnamese law and political culture. Successor to Philastre as head of the department of native justice. Created a training school - the Collège des Stagiaires - for French officials in Saigon in which he lectured on Vietnamese administration. The school lasted only four years. It was restarted in Paris as the Ecole coloniale a decade later. Luro's lectures were published as Le pays d'Annam.

Luu Vinh Phuoc (or, in Chinese, **Liu Yung-fu**). Chinese triad leader and founder of the Black Flags (Co-den). Sought refuge with his followers in Tonkin in 1865 after the defeat of the Taiping rebellion. Developed a force consisting of Vietnamese, Chinese and tribal contingents which came to control the upper reaches of the Red river. Semi-autonomous, but enrolled in the service of the Vietnamese army commanded by Prince Hoang Ke Viem (qv.) in 1872. The Black Flags harassed the Garnier expedition and killed Garnier himself in a skirmish on 21 December 1873. In order to avoid losing their autonomy the Black Flags fought the French in Tonkin from 1882-5 with particular intensity in order to avoid losing their autonomy. Luu Vinh Phuoc was granted a temporary commission as a Chinese general during the Franco-Chinese war. Once his new status as a patriot had become established in Chinese eyes this appointment was confirmed after 1885 by the Empress Dowager. By 1895 he was installed in a new post in Kwangtung province. Those of his Black Flags who had not submitted to the French had dispersed.

Maillard, J.D. (1851-1907) Missionary, b. Doubs. Arrived in East Cochinchina in 1882. Transferred from Vinh Minh to Gia Huu, then in 1884 to Phu Thuong in Quang Nam. Repelled four assaults on his mission between September 1885 and July 1886. Secured French military help in saving the adjacent mission of Tra Kieu from repeated attacks. Maillard formed and armed his own militia and was denounced to the French authorities for his bellicosity, acquiring a certain notoriety among French officials. His exploits provided material for anticlerical press polemics. Interviewed and reprimanded by Paul Bert. After 1886 he investigated tea growing in China, and began successful tea and coffee plantations on land obtained by his mission. For this he was awarded the Mérite agricole and nominated a member of the Chambre d'agriculture et de commerce for Annam. He founded more than twenty new Christian communes, two thirds of them in the district of Le Son. Vigorously attacked in a polemical pamphlet published by Camille Pâris in 1891, he replied in a publication entitled 'Un Camille turbulent et brutal....' (Paris, 1891). A close friend of J.B.Guerlach (qv.)

Miche, Mgr J.C. (1805-73). Bishop of Dansara, Vicar Apostolic of Cambodia, then of West Cochinchina, b. Vosges. Ordained 1830 and arrived in Cochinchina in 1836. Retreated to Bangkok under pressure from Vietnamese authorities, and in 1838 travelled to Battambang, a Khmer province of eastern Siam. In 1840 he re-entered Cochinchina, and was nominated Mgr Cuénot's provicar. In 1842 he was arrested and sent to Phu Yen, where he was imprisoned, tortured and condemned to death. Saved by the naval intervention of Captain Favin-Levêque in 1843, he was conveyed to Singapore but returned to Cochinchina the following year. Appointed Mgr Lefebvre's coadjutor in 1847. In 1848, evading pursuit, he crossed into Cambodia, where the king allowed him to reside at Phnom Penh. On good terms with King An Duong, he was allowed to form Christian communes at Ponhealu. In 1855 Miche travelled to Bangkok and obtained permission from the king of Siam to send missionaries to lower Laos, an undertaking which met with disaster. In 1856 Miche prepared the way for Consul de Montigny to negotiate a treaty with An Duong, but Montigny revealed the project to the Siamese. An Duong, a Siamese vassal, was threatened with reprisal by Bangkok, and his ambassador failed to make his rendez-vous with the Montigny mission. In 1863 however, when Miche again lent his assistance in arranging preliminaries for a French protectoral treaty, the negotiations were kept secret from the Siamese, and the treaty was concluded and ratified. It became the legal basis for the French protectorate. In October 1864 Miche transferred to West Cochinchina as Vicar Apostolic on the retirement of Mgr Lefebvre. He died on 1 December 1873.

Milliès-Lacroix, R. Colonial Minister, b. 1850, Landes. Wholesale draper. Senator for Landes, 1897-1933, as a member of the Gauche Démocratique Radicale et Radicale-Socialiste. Almost completely ignorant of colonial matters, he was made Minister for the Colonies in the first Clémenceau cabinet (25 October 1906), remaining in this post through a succession of governments until 25 July 1909. Clemenceau tended to refer to him as 'le nègre', and Governor-General Beau privately instanced his appointment as a symptom of the mediocrity of the Clemenceau government.

Morel, L.J. (1853-1911). Lt in the 2nd Artillery, 1880. Resigned, 1884. Sub-prefect of Gex, 1886. Chief secretary to Governor-General de Lanessan, 1891-4, then Resident-Mayor of Hanoi. Acting Resident-Superior of Tonkin, March 1899 - July 1900. Resident-Superior of Laos, 10 November 1903. Resident-Superior of Cambodia, 27 September 1904. Director of Customs, 20 April 1905. Resident-Superior of Tonkin, March 1908 - March 1909. Left for France in April 1909, returned 1910 and died 1911.

Mossard, Mgr L.E. (1851-1920). Bishop of Medéa, Vicar Apostolic of West Cochinchina, b. Besançon. Left in 1876 for West Cochinchina. Taught in the seminary at Saigon, 1878-80. Curé at Tan Dinh, 1880-2. Superior of the Ecole Taberd, 1887-1892. Encouraged the Christian Brothers to restaff the school. Missionary at Cholon and Cho Quan from 1892-1898. Curé of Saigon cathedral and prison almoner at Poulo Condore, 1898-9. Elected Bishop of Medéa and Vicar Apostolic of West Cochinchina, 11 February 1899. Took a more evasive, temporising attitude towards the issue of anticlerical legislation than Mgr Gendreau in West Tonkin. When the vicariate was accused by a schools inspector of neglecting the teaching of French for which large contracts had been accepted from the Colonial Council, Mossard admitted the charge and surrendered the contract, but asserted in a letter of self-justification that the spread of French merely caused social dislocation and spread political hostility towards the French. His statement was ridiculed during a parliamentary debate on the Leygues amendment in 1904 by the Colonial Minister, Doumergue. In 1908 Mossard was forced to give an assurance of clerical abstention from public political discussion when the procurator at Saigon, Fr Artif, engaged in a press controversy on the issue of the anticlerical laws. Mossard sought legal advice to defend his vicariate against imminent despoliation in 1910-12, and in 1911 he tried to pacify local anticlericals by agreeing to surrender tax concessions made to the vicariate by Admiral Bonard in 1862.

Moulié, B.P.. Administrateur des services civils, he was interim Resident Superior of Annam from 23 June 1904 - 20 April 1906.

Nguyen Tri Phuong. Grand Marshal. Brother-in-Law of Tu Duc. Defended Tourane in 1858 and commanded the Vietnamese army at Ky Hoa in 1861. Leader of the war party at court, and strongly opposed to the negotiating strategy of Phan Thanh Gian and others whom Tu Duc eventually chose to support. Enjoyed considerable influence at Hue, and in 1872 travelled to Tonkin to help organise resistance to Jean Dupuis' commercial expedition. Garnier's high-handed dealings at Hanoi could not have encountered a more embattled Vietnamese adversary. Garnier's assault on the citadel resulted in the capture of the Marshal, along with the governor of Hanoi and two of Phan Tan Gian's sons. Marshal Nguyen Tri Phuong died within days of the assault of a wound in the thigh.

Nguyen Van Tuong. Regent. Married a niece of Tu Duc. Accompanied Philastre to Tonkin to secure the withdrawal of the Garnier expedition. Taboulet suggests that his reputation at court was enhanced in the later 1870s by his claim that he had obtained French withdrawal by firm negotiation. As chief of the intransigent party after the death of Nguyen Tri Phuong (qv.), Nguyen Van Tuong inspired Tu Duc to authorise resistance to the implementation of the commercial treaty of August 1874.

After the death of Tu Duc, Nguyen Van Tuong became one of three Regents dominating the court at Hue. With the ending of the Tonkin war in 1885 he chose not to accompany the Emperor Ham Nghi and Regent Ton That Thuyet in their flight to the hills, but stayed on at court to serve as an instrument of French control. Missionaries warned the French military administration against being duped by Tuong, whom they accused of organising secret resistance; and within months Tuong was removed from office and exiled to Tahiti. It is not certain whether missionary pressure was decisive in securing Tuong's removal, but the phraseology of part of the official indictment against him (26 October 1885) reflects arguments used by Puginier: 'Nguyen Van Tuong...was also involved in secret intelligence with Ton That Thuyet to initiate attacks on French troops so as to cause misfortunes to the government...' (Nguyen The Anh, The Withering Days of the Nguyen Dynasty. Singapore, 1978. p. 21).

Osouf, P.M. (1829-1906). Missionary. Procurator at Singapore,1856. Procurator-General at Hong Kong, 1866. A Director of the Paris seminary, 1875. Vicar Apostolic of North Japan as Bishop of Arsinoë. · Became heavily involved in diplomatic dealings between the Papacy and Japan over the construction of a new episcopal hierarchy. Archbishop of Japan, 1891.

Page, T.F. (1807-67). Vice-Admiral, b. Vitry-le-François. Son of a hotelier. Served at the seizure of Algiers in 1830. Frigate commander in the Indian Ocean and China sea from 1841-1844. Captain, 1845. C.in C. of the naval station at Réunion in 1848. Government Commisioner in Tahiti, 1852-3. Rear-Admiral, August 1858. In the China campaign, 1858-60, he took the forts at Pei Ho. Served at Ky Hoa and My Tho. Vice-Admiral, August 1861.

Pâris, Camille. (1856-1908). Planter and polemicist, b. Lunéville. Arrived in Indochina as a soldier in the Infanterie de Marine, 1886. Transferred to the Post and Telegraph service. Postmaster at Tourane, 1894. Resigned in 1895 to become a coffee planter in Binh Dinh. Found Cham archaeological remains on his land and received a Ministry subsidy to research for Cham ruins across the whole region. In his précis of the History of Annam he plagiarised the notes of Truong Vinh Ky without acknowledgement. President of the Producers and Exporters Union of Tourane. Vain and truculent but witty and versatile, he used his masonic contacts to publicise his long-running campaign of diatribe against the mission in pamphlets and in the press. He adapted the standard arguments of metropolitan Radicals on the political and economic role of the clergy to colonial circumstances, using local and personal anecdotes. He was killed by tribesmen on an expedition to Mois territory after ignoring missionary warnings to stay away.

Pâris, Paul. Deputy for Cochinchina, b. 1860, Haute Marne. Trained as lawyer. Appointed a clerk in the department of native affairs in Cochinchina in 1882. Attached to the Résidence-Supérieur in Cambodia in Cambodia in 1884, he managed the Résidence temporarily in 1886. Resigned in 1887 and became a barrister in Saigon, while running rubber and rice plantations. Elected to the Colonial Council in 1888. President of the Société des Etudes Indochinoises (1893). President of the Union of European planters in Cochinchina. Vice-President of the Colonial Council, 1898. A freemason, he stood as Radical-Socialist candidate against François Deloncle in the legislative elections of 1910, and won the Cochinchina seat by 1,097 votes to 962 in a constituency of 3,331 voters. In parliament he entered debates on issues affecting pay and conditions for military, naval and colonial personnel, postal communications with Japan, Indochina loans and railway construction programmes in Cochinchina. He pressed the colonial ministry repeatedly from 1910-1913 for the application of the law of 1901 to Indochina. Defeated in the 1914 election by Ernest Outrey, Resident-General of Cambodia, who offered a programme of promises on pay and conditions which appealed to an electorate chiefly dominated by officials.

Pavie, Auguste. (1847-1925). Explorer and diplomat, b. Dinan. Son of a cabinet maker. After a military career in the 62e line and Marine infantry regiments, he entered the Cochinchina telegraph service in 1868. After service in France in the war of 1870 he returned as telegraph clerk to Kampot in Cambodia. He published his spare-time topographical studies of the locality, came to the notice of Governor Le Myre de Vilers, and was recommended for the appointment of Commissioner at Luang Prabang, with the mission of exploring Upper Laos. His success in halting the spread of Siamese political control across the Sib Song Pa Na in 1889 brought him to the attention of the colonial office, which nominated him for a new mission aimed at securing informal control of the whole of the East bank of the Mekong from Siam (1889-91). Though the mission was a qualified failure as a political project, Pavie was appointed Consul-General at Bangkok in 1892. On his missions and at Bangkok he received much assistance from missionaries of the S.M.E., which he acknowledged fulsomely in official reports. Though a laïc, freethinker and mason, Pavie saw missionaries as useful agents of French influence, and gave them much assistance in their educational and hospital projects in Siam. Retired from active diplomacy in 1895 and devoted himself to publishing the results of his explorations.

Péan, A.A. (1838-93). Missionary, b. Mayenne. Worked in Siam from 1862-6. A Director of the Paris seminary from 1867-1893, he taught moral theology there from 1868-91, and was director of novices from 1872-81. Assistant Superior for external matters from 1883 until his death.

Pellerin, Mgr F.M.. (1813-62). Bishop of Biblos, Vicar Apostolic of North Cochinchina, b. Finistère. Arrived in East Cochinchina in 1844. Nominated coadjutor to Mgr Cuénot as Bishop of Biblos in 1846, he was based on Saigon. He became Vicar Apostolic when North Cochinchina was created a separate vicariate in 1850, and transferred to the vicinity of Hue. In hiding or in disguise for much of his ministry, he had escaped on the Capricieuse in 1856, intending to wait in Hong Kong for the persecutions to ease. In the event he decided to return to France in 1857 to put the case for intervention to the French government. After giving evidence to the Brenier commission, he was presented to Napoleon III at Biarritz in June and August 1857, and received a sympathetic reception for his account of the missionary predicament in Vietnam. With the despatch of the French fleet to Tourane, Pellerin became a thorn in the side of the French admiral, Rigault de Genouilly who, in January 1859, rejected the Bishop's insistant proposal for a march on Hue and secured his removal to Hong Kong. Pellerin transferred to the college in Penang where he died without ever returning to his vicariate.

Périn, Georges. (1838-1903). Radical politician, b. Arras. Lawyer. A Radical of the 1860s. Resisted the pragmatic trend in Republicanism exemplified by Gambetta and Ferry. With Clémenceau, he voiced the Radical case against colonial adventures in the 1870s and 1880s in parliament. Elected deputy for Haute Vienne in 1873, Périn attacked Admiral Dupré's treaty of 15 March 1874 and deplored French commitment to the defence of missionary interests in Vietnam. Though keenly supportive of 'scientific' explorations in Africa and Asia - he was himself an enthusiastic traveller - he expressed objection to the 'business imperialism' of missionaries, and to their incitement of colonial expansion. He was the most articulate and noted critic of Ferry's Tonkin policy, even though it was Clémenceau who was to deliver the coup de grâce in the Lang Son debate of 31 March 1885. Failing to secure re-election in 1889, he retired from parliamentary life to travel and write up his voyages.

Pernot, J.C. (1823-1904). Missionary, b. Vesoul. Worked in West Cochinchina from 1852 at Thi Nghe, Dan Nuoc and Cai Nhum. At the outset of the French occupation in 1860 he worked at Saigon, before returning to the Paris seminary as a Director and Procurator for Receipts from 1861. Remained in these posts for 25 years. In June 1877 he became Assistant Superior for Foreign Matters for three years.

Phan Dinh Phung.(1847-96). Can Vuong leader. Highest ranking court official after Ton That Thuyet to take part fully in the Can Vuong movement. b. Dong Thai (Ha Tinh) of a family which had produced twelve generations of mandarins. Passed the regional examinations in 1876 and came top in the metropolitan examinations of 1877. His first position was as district mandarin in Ninh Binh province, where he punished a native Catholic priest accused of terrorising local non-Catholic villagers with implied support from the French. Consul de Kergaradec demanded his punishment and removal (Doc. 103). He was reassigned to court as a member of the censorate (Do-Sat-Vien) where he won Tu Duc's favour by denouncing fellow mandarins for neglecting rifle practice. He won a reputation for high integrity, and his denunciation of the Kinh Luoc of Tonkin after an inspection trip led to the latter's disgrace. As Imperial Censor in 1883 Phan clashed with Ton That Thuyet for opposing the manipulation of imperial succession rights in favour of Hiep Hoa after Tu Duc's death. But he assisted in the preparation of the resistance base at Tan So from 1884-5. During the Can Vuong insurrection Phan retired to his village, formed a militia, and organised arms deployments using the scholar-gentry as his commanders. He attacked two Catholic villages, but escaped the ensuing French reprisals. His brother, however, was captured by the Vietnamese governor of Nghe An, the cashiered former Viceroy of Tonkin, now working as a French collaborator. Phan published his defiance of the governor's threats to execute the brother in a correspondance which was to inspire future nationalists by its expressed rejection of family ties in favour of national loyalties. After the capture of Ham Nghi, Phan maintained his resistance to the French from the hills bordering Ha Tinh, Nghe An and Thanh Hoa, a region of traditional political insurgency which figures repeatedly in the history of Vietnamese dynastic and foreign struggle. The fragmentation and localisation of Can Vuong resistance, and its convergence with other forms of social banditry saw Phan become increasingly isolated as a resistance leader before his death in 1896. Some of his remonstarnces to mandarin collaborators survive and provide valuable insights into the political thought of one of the most highly principled of Can Vuong leaders.

Phan Boi Chau. Scholar-Patriot. Founder of the Duy Tan Hoi. Accepted support from Catholic Vietnamese from as early as 1904. His widely circulated publication Viet Nam Vong Quoc Su (History of the Loss of Vietnam, 1905) proclaimed the acceptability of Vietnamese Catholics as supporters of organised nationalist resistance to the French, and noted their recent loss of favour with the French administration. Founder of the Duy Tan Hoi (Reformation Society), he spent much of his career exiled in China and Thailand. From 1925 he was held under house arrest at Hue.

Phan Chu Trinh. Scholar-Patriot, b.1872 at Tay Loc in Quang Nam. Minor mandarin at Hue until he resigned in 1905. A reformist rather than a revolutionary like Phan Boi Chau, he was also anti-monarchist. Felt that the temporary continuation of a French protectorate was preferable to a return to the traditional imperial system. Enthusiast for using quoc ngu as a language medium. Arrested in 1908 in the wake of tax riots in Annam. Condemned to death but spared after intervention by the Ligue des Droits de l'Homme. Arrested in 1911, he lived in France after his release until 1925.

Phan Thanh Gian (1796-1867). Court mandarin, b. Bao Thanh in Ben Tre province. One of the few mandarins from Lower Cochinchina to reach the highest levels of the mandarinate. Successively Vice-Grand Censor, member of the Co-mat and President of the Tribunal of Rites, he became leader of the peace party at court in 1861-2 during the period leading to the conclusion of the peace treaty of June 1862, which he negotiated with Bonard. Thereafter he pressed for the negotiation of a treaty of retrocession, travelling to Paris to ask for an agreement in 1863-4. Here he secured a treaty drafted by Captain Aubaret (qv.) on behalf of the Quai. This would have entailed French surrender of the three French-occupied provinces of lower Cochichina (except for footholds at Saigon, My Tho and Cap St Jacques) in return for a notional French protectorate extending over the whole of Cochinchina, together with an annual tribute to France in perpetuity. Initially tempted by these terms Napoleon III was eventually dissuaded by press, parliamentary, naval and missionary pressures from ratifying the agreement. Nonetheless the credibility of Phan's appeasement strategy was greatly enhanced at the court of Hue by the near success of his diplomacy, and the Vietnamese were to pursue the chimera of retrocession intermittently until as late as 1878.

In 1864 Phan Thanh Gian was appointed Viceroy of the three western provinces of Cochinchina (Vinh Long, Chau Doc, Ha Tien), which were virtually isolated from the rest of Vietnam by the French zone of occupation. When La Grandière ordered their seizure in 1867, Phan declined to offer resistance. In a final proclamation before committing suicide he asserted: 'By following the will of Heaven in wishing to divert misfortune from falling on the population, I am betraying the Emperor through my surrender....I deserve to die.' He was posthumously stripped of his titles and offices by the court.

Philastre, P.L.F. (1837-1902). Administrator and scholar. Entered the Ecole navale in 1854. Served in the Crimea. Ensign, 1859. Served in the China campaign, then in the Cochinchina expedition. Lt in 1865. One of the first naval officers to enter the newly created Inspection des affaires indigènes. An accomplished scholar and sinologist, he translated the Annamese law code into French in 1874 and wrote on Chinese philosophy and the Chinese classics. Head of the office of native justice, 1868. Served in Paris during the Franco-Prussian war. Served as an advisor on Admiral Dupré's educational commission of 1873. Became embroiled in controversy over his role in securing the withdrawal of the Garnier expedition in 1874. French Resident in Cambodia in 1876. Chargé at Hue from 1877-9. Retired, 1879.

Pineau, Mgr L., Bishop of Calama and Vicar Apostolic of South Tonkin, b. Angers. Arrived as a missionary in the vicariate of South Tonkin in 1866. Created Bishop of Calama and Vicar Apostolic in 1886 during one of the most strained periods of the vicariate's troubled history. Maintained an acrimonious correspondance with the French authorities in the 1880s, generated mainly by the aberrations of some of his clergy. When in 1889 he tried to convey his complaints against French administration to the Paris press and to parliament, his telegrams were stopped on the orders of Resident-Superior Hector. His relations with some of his own missionaries also deteriorated in the 1890s, and in 1905 a large group of them led by Frs Abgraal and Klingler petitioned the Directors of the S.M.E. for his removal. Given Pineau's uneasy relations with both the administration and his own missionaries, it is perhaps unsurprising that he should have given covert encouragement to three of his personal staff to involve themselves in fundraising for the Viet-Nam Cong Hien Hoi. In the wake of the disclosure of these activities in 1909 Fr Klingler again led a group of missionaries in petitioning the S.M.E. for Pineau's removal. Persuaded to resign, he returned to Paris in 1910.

Puginier, Mgr P. (1835-92). Bishop of Mauricastre and Vicar Apostolic of West Tonkin. Along with Mgr Miche, one of the most formidable bishops of the S.M.E. Undaunted by officialdom, he pressed intermittant advice on Deputies, Foreign Ministers and Governors in long, explosive memoranda commenting unfavourably on French policy. Scolded Admiral Dupré like a schoolboy on 10 July 1874 **(Doc. 79)** for scuttling the Garnier expedition. Demanded unprecedented access to the highest levels of the mandarinate in 1877-8 to press the claims of his Christians. Demanded insistantly in August-September 1885 that General de Courcy should imprison Nguyen Van Tuong. Denounced Governor-General de Lanessan from the pulpit in 1891 for encouraging Buddhist worship in Tonkin. The number of adult conversions in his diocese rose spectacularly after 1876: 2385 in 1877; 3720 in 1878; and 5388 in 1879. In 1878 he attempted to extend evangelisation to Upper Laos, but his missionaries were killed and the mission extinguished by Black Flags during the Tonkin war.

Rheinart, P. (1840-1902). Lt in the Marine infantry, entered the Inspection des affaires indigènes in Lower Cochinchina in 1865. One of the earliest French explorers of Laos, he crossed the region with Lt d'Arfeuille in the wake of the Mekong expedition in 1869. Following the conclusion of the Philastre treaty of January 1874 withdrawing Garnier's troops from Tonkin, he was sent to Hanoi as chargé with a garisson of forty men. Transferred as chargé to Hue in 1875, he felt forced to withdraw under pressure of public insults. Resident in Annam-Tonkin from 1882, he broke off relations in May, 1883 following Rivière's death. As Resident at Hue in July 1884 he ordered troops to occupy the citadel after the crowning of Ham Nghi. Resident-General in Tonkin, 8 September 1888 - 4 May 1889. Took a notably sympathetic tone with the Bishop and missionaries of East Cochinchina in the wake of the Mayrena affair.

Rigault de Genouilly, C. (1807-73). Admiral, Naval Minister. Entered navy in 1827. Lt, 1834. Captain on the China station, 1841. Rear-Admiral, 1854, he was present at the siege of Sevastopol. Commanded the China and Cochinchina expeditions, 4 February 1857 - 20 October 1859. Occupied Canton in 1857, but never sanguine about the prospect of easy victory over Hue. Wrote to F. de Lesseps on 24 June 1857 saying that at least 1000 men, two corps of artillery and one of engineers would be needed to capture Hue. Seized Tourane 1 September 1858. Avoided the difficulties of a direct assault on Hue and attacked Saigon instead on 2 February 1859, securing control of the town by 17 February. Senator, 1860. Admiral, 1864. Succeeded Chasseloup-Laubat as minister for the Navy in 1867. C.in C. of the abortive Baltic expedition in 1870.

Rivière, H. (1827-83). Captain, b. Paris of a norman family. Entered navy, 1845. Present at Sevastopol and campaigned in Mexico. Ensign, 1849. Lt, 1856. Captain, 1870. His advancement was slow, but he acquired some prominence in suppressing the Kanak rebellion in New Caledonia in 1878-9. Replaced Captain de Foucault as naval commander at Saigon in November, 1881. In charge of clearing pirates from the Tonkin delta from March 1882, he encountered local Vietnamese administrative obstruction and seized the Hanoi citadel on 25 April 1882 in an operation similar to that of Garnier a decade before. The war party at court proclaimed the need to break off relations with France and offer armed resistance, but Tu Duc declined the advice. Rivière's subsequent offer to return the citadel mollified court hostility. Rivière's force was too small for effective clearance operations, and he interpreted its reinforcement with a detachment of 700 men in December 1882 as a signal to begin clearance in earnest. In March 1883 rumours that the Vietnamese might consign the port and mines of Hongay to the British prompted Rivière to seize Hongay together with the citadel of Nam Dinh, which the Vietnamese were fortifying. During a skirmish on 19 May 1883 Rivière was killed. Ferry's second cabinet had already decided at the end of April, 1883 to demand parliamentary credits for a major expedition to Tonkin. These had been voted on 27 April. News of Rivière's death arrived shortly before the Senate debate in which the vote was ratified, setting off a furore which strengthened the administration's parliamentary support for intervention in Tonkin.

Rodier, Lt Governor, (1854-1913). Entered marine artillery, 1873. Captain, 1886. Attached to the Undersecetariat for Colonies, he was nominated Resident at Hai-duong in 1887. Secretary to Governor-General de Lanessan, 1 March 1893. Acting Resident-Superior of Tonkin from 20 July 1893, he became acting Governor-General from 29 December 1894 - 16 March 1895. Governor of French India, January 1898 - February 1902. Lt Governor of Cochinchina 21 October 1902 - 13 July 1907. Governor of Guyana, 1907-09, and of Réunion 1909-13. From personal dealings, Bishop Mossard considered Rodier to be sympathetic towards missionary interests, and Rodier's official reports seem to support this impression.

Sarraut, A. Governor-General of Indochina. One of the great figures of French twentieth century Radicalism. His family owned the Depêche de Toulouse, the most important radical newspaper of the Midi. The Radicalism of the South tended to be organised through networks of clientage, of which the Sarraut's was one of the most powerful. Elected Radical-Socialist deputy for the Aude in 1902, Sarraut became Undersecretary of State at the ministry of the Interior in the Sarrien and Clemenceau cabinets from 1906-1909. In 1909 he became Undersecretary for War in the Briand government. On 1 July 1911 he was nominated temporary Governor General of Indochina, but did not take up his post until 15 November, remaining in office until 4 January 1914. After further spells of office in Indochina during the war he joined almost every cabinet formed in the 1920s and 1930s. Attempted to define a Radical colonial ideology in his book Servitude et grandeurs coloniales (1931), which expounded the theory of Association.

Serres, G. Secretary to the Resident-Superior of Annam (F. Lévecque), and Vénérable of the Libre Pensée d'Annam masonic lodge. A copy of his lecture on the need to apply anticlerical legislation against the missions ended up in the private papers of Governor-General Beau.

Sestier, H.V. Resident at Thanh Hoa, 1909-1911. Interim Resident-Superior of Annam, 21 February 1911 - 1 January 1912.

Sohier, Mgr J.H. (1818-76). Bishop of Gadara, Vicar Apostolic of North Cochinchina. Arrived in Annam as a missionary in 1842. Consecrated bishop as coadjutor to Mgr Pellerin, Vicar Apostolic of North Cochinchina in 1851. Succeeded Pellerin as Vicar Apostolic on 13 September 1862. When Admiral Bonard and Colonel Palanca arrived in Hue in 1863 for the ratification of the peace treaty of 1862, Sohier profited from their presence to obtain permission from Tu Duc to take up residence at Kim Long in the vicinity of the capital, along with a number of his missionaries. The Vietnamese court tended to make use of the bishops of North Cochinchina as intermediaries with the French. Sohier's successor, Bishop Caspar performed this role in 1883-5. In 1864 Sohier travelled to France on Tu-Duc's behalf to arrange for personnel to establish a school at Hue, but the project ultimately failed to materialise. Following the death of Garnier in Tonkin, Tu Duc sent Sohier on a mission of mediation to Hanoi at the end of December 1873. Sohier exhibited some sympathy for the Vietnamese in their difficulties with the French. Nonetheless in 1874 he advised Dupré on points of detail in the treaty of 15 March 1874. Later, in October 1875, he intervened to ensure publication of the agreement in Annam.

Ta Van Phung or **Lê Duy Phung.** Pretender to the throne of Tonkin. A Christian convert, Ta Van Phung sought French help in 1860 to mount an insurrection in Tonkin. Admiral Charner rejected his overture and in 1861 he made his uprising unassisted. After levying a small force he attacked a Vietnamese fleet and gained a footing in the provinces of eastern Tonkin. His insurrection was sufficiently successful to distract Tu Duc's attention from Cochinchina: it played a significant part in persuading him to conclude the June 1862 treaty with Bonard.

Theurel, Mgr J.S. (1829-68). Bishop of Acanthe, Vicar Apostolic of West Tonkin, b. Haut Saône. Arrived in West Tonkin in 1853. Worked at Ke Vinh with Bishop Retord. Established a printing press for the mission and published several works of piety in quoc ngu. Provicar, 1857. In June 1858 a violent persecution broke out and he was forced into hiding. Despite a summons in 1859 to become a Director of the Paris seminary, he chose to remain in Tonkin. He became coadjutor to Mgr Retord's successor, Mgr Jeantet, and was made Bishop of Acanthe in March 1859. The peace treaty of 1862 provided some relief from persecution. Theurel operated in the open once more. He became vicar apostolic of West Tonkin on the death of Jeantet in 1866. He obtained a royal decree allowing the Christian village of Ke Vinh to purchase back its confiscated lands and re-establish itself. Theurel noted the onset of more popular manifestations against Christians in the wake of the French occupation of East Cochinchina in 1867 shortly before his death on 3 November 1868.

Thinselin, L.J. (1841-95). Missionary, b. Meurthe et Moselle. Arrived West Cochinchina in August 1869. Worked at Thu Thiem; but in July, 1871 Mgr. Miche transferred him to Bai Xan where he remained until 1877, when he became almoner to the military hospital in Saigon.

Thiriet, J. (1839-97). Missionary, b. Meurthe-et-Moselle. Arrived in West Cochinchina in September 1862. Moved from Bai Xan to Tan Dinh and then Xom Chieu. In 1866 he became a teacher in the Saigon seminary, and remained there for 32 years, becoming its superior in 1877. In 1879 he was made provicar.

Ton That Thuyet, Regent (1883-8). Military mandarin responsible for putting down the disorders in Nghe An in 1874. In 1883 he was nominated a Regent of the new Emperor Duc Duc in Tu Duc's will, along with Nguyen Van Tuong (qv.) and Tran Thieu Thanh. Tuong and Thuyet circumvented, displaced, and eventually killed Thanh, and organised the accession of a series of nominal figures to the throne in order to conserve power in their own hands. Thuyet and Tuong were evidently political rivals, though acting concertedly in response to the crisis of French invasion. Thuyet, as Minister for War, took the more active role in organising secret measures for resistance by preparing the base at Tan So ready for the retreat of the court. After the abortive coup of 5-6 July 1885 Thuyet unleashed the Can Vuong insurrection, retreating with the emperor Ham Nghi to the borders of Nghe An and Thanh Hoa. His leadership of the insurrection was however, shortlived. Seeking support from across the border Thuyet left Ham Nghi in the charge of his sons, who were unable to prevent the emperor's capture and exile in November 1888. Thuyet failed to return to continue directing the Can Vuong, but he may have organised a measure of material support from across the border. Thereafter, the movement became increasingly fragmentary. Thuyet survived into the early years of the twentieth century, a politically inactive, somewhat discredited figure exiled in China.

Trouillot, G. (1851-1916). Colonial minister. Jesuit educated lawyer. In 1890 he enrolled as a member of the Union Progressiste and then of the Gauche Radicale. He remained a man of the centre despite participating in several Radical cabinets in the 1900s, believing in the importance of uniting all fractions of Republicanism in defence of the democratic principle. However, he was a fervent laïc, approved of the application of the anticlerical laws, wrote a book on the subject entitled <u>Du contrat d'association</u>, and wrote frequently for <u>Le Siècle</u>. Deputy and later Senator for Jura, he was Colonial minister from 28 June - 26 October 1898, and from 24 July 1909 - 2 November 1910.

Tuong or **Thuong**. See **Nguyen**.

Vey, Mgr J.L. (1840-1909). Bishop of Geraza, Vicar Apostolic of Siam, b. Yssingueux. 'Un brave paysan de l'Auvergne' he arrived in Siam in 1865, when the vicariate contained a Christian population of fewer than 10,000. Said to be mission's best Thai linguist since Bishop Pallegoix. Provicar and superior of the seminary at Bang Xang. Succeeded Mgr Dupont, Bishop of Azoth, in 1875. In 1899 he requested the creation of a new vicariate of Laos, with a Christian population of 11,544, from the eastern portions of the diocese. At the time of his death in 1909 the vicariate recorded a figure of 23,000 Catholics.

Vial, P. (1831-1907). Administrator and marine engineer, b. Voiron (Isère). Arrived in Cochinchina in 1860 as a naval Lt. Director of the Interior, 1 April 1864 - 1871. Set up La Grandière's new educational system for the colony in 1864. In 1886 he arrived in Paul Bert's entourage as Resident-Superior at Hanoi (3 April - 11 November 1886) and acted as Resident-General after Bert's death (11 November 1886 - 29 January 1887). Wrote useful accounts of the establishment of French administration in Cochinchina in the early 1860s and Tonkin in the early 1880s.

Vialleton, J. (1848-1909). Missionary, b. Haute Loire. Arrived in East Cochinchina, 1872. Despatched to work among the Bahnars in 1875 at Kontum. Gained a considerable influence among the Bahnars and Sedangs which he put at the disposal of the adventurer, Mayrena. Compromised the mission by acting as legal witness of Mayrena's royal constitution. In 1890 Vialleton was made Provicar and Superior of the 'Mission des sauvages'. After the French annexation of the East bank of the Mekong, and despite the unfavourable publicity generated by the Mayrena case, Vialleton was given formal administrative responsibility for the Kontum region by the Commandant-Supérieur of lower Laos. In 1901 the French despatched a délégué to Kontum, M. Guénot, a mason and an anticlerical. The disputes that developed between the mission and the délégué fuelled further controversy. (<u>qv</u>. Guerlach) At Vialleton's death, even his will gave rise to official complaint, for treating mission land as personal property to evade tax.

Wibaux, T.L. (1820-1877). Missionary, b. Roubaix. Legal training. Ordained, 1846. Taught rhetoric at a Catholic school in France until the age of forty. Joined S.M.E. in 1857. Arrived in West Cochinchina, 1859. Worked at Tan Dinh, 1861-2. Appointed Provicar in 1863 by Mgr Lefebvre, he was charged with building a seminary for training a new body of native clergy. Used his own money to construct it. Military almoner in France during the Franco-Prussian war, before returning to West Cochinchina in 1871.